SURA'S

The Yoga Vasishta

[Abridged Version]

Abhinanda Pandita's
Laghu-Yoga-Vasishta

**Introduction and Translation
With Synopsis for Second Half of
Nirvana Prakaranam**

By
K.N. Subramanian

SURA BOOKS (Pvt) LTD.

Chennai ● Bangalore ● Kolkata

Price: Rs.250.00

© RESERVED

THE YOGA VASISHTA [ABRIDGED VERSION]

First Edition : July, 2003

Size : ⅛ Crown

Pages : 588

Paper : 13.6 kg Maplitho

Binding : Paperback

Price: Rs.250.00

ISBN: 81-7478-422-5

SURA BOOKS (PVT) LTD.

1620, 'J' Block,
16th Main Road,
Anna Nagar,
Chennai - 600 040.
Phones: 044-26162173, 26161099.

Printed at T. Krishna Press, Chennai - 600 102 and Published by
V.V.K.Subburaj for Sura Books (Pvt) Ltd., 1620, 'J' Block,
16th Main Road, Anna Nagar, Chennai - 600 040. Phones: 26162173,
26161099. Fax: (91) 44-26162173. email: surabooks@eth.net

SADGURU SRI GNANANANDA GIRI

In whom manifest in unison
The majesty of mid-ocean
The firmness of Meru mountain
The nectarine coolness of moon

Swami Sri Gnanananda Giri attained Mahasamadhi
in January 1974 at Sri Gnanananda Thapovanam
Thapovanam: 605 756
Villupuram Dt., Tamil Nadu

Preface

The spiritual seekers of India have derived inspiration and guidance from the spiritual classic Yoga Vasishta of Valmiki through countless centuries. The teachings of Vasishta have percolated to the general people in various garbs-wise sayings, selections, adaptations and quotations. Great traditional scholars like Vidyaranya, Madhusudhana Saraswati and Bhaskararaya and recent thinkers Swami Rama Tirtha, Bhagavan Das, Manilal Dwivedi and Dr. Atreya have been profoundly influenced by the thoughts of Vasishta. Sri Dwivedi rightly says that the idealism of Vasishta alone holds the key to world peace and harmony among people.

Academicians, however, have not paid much attention to the work, possibly because in their view, the repetitions and the contradictions the work abounds in, militate against a coherent philosophy and that the teachings of the Yoga Vasishta unsettle the normal conception of time and space and the accepted chronological order. The transcendental spirit is beyond time and space and if, in the seer's unique unitive spiritual vision, all the notions of time and space disappear as fancies, the fault is not with Vasishta but with the nature of Reality. One other ground for the bias against the Yoga Vasishta is its penchant for repetitions. In Vasishta's method of spiritual instruction, the repetitions, contradictions, similes and stories have a positive purpose and are not a verbal superfluity.

It is Sri Ananda Bodhendra's illuminating commentary, 'Tatparya Prakasika' that discloses to us the method that underlies the mode of teaching in the Yoga Vasishta.

5

Dr. Atreya, the author of 'The Philosophy of the Yoga Vasishta,' a penetrating study, has totally ignored 'Tatparya Prakasika' and that is the reason he complains against the repetitions and contradictions. Vasishta deliberately employs them and in the light of 'Tatparya Prakasika,' everything is in place and the complaint has no grounds.

Abhinanda Pandita's abridged version called 'Laghu Yoga Vasishta, though has not completely brought out the teachings of Vasishta, nevertheless enables seekers to appreciate the unique teachings of the seer, and can inspire further attempt to study and understand the whole work.

That is wisdom after attaining which nothing else remains unknown. Vasishta's Teachings show the path to the attainment of such wisdom. For the seekers of spiritual solace and also for those engaged in the intellectual quest of resolving the mystery of life, Vasishta remains the only perfect guide.

AUTHOR

Introduction

The Importance of The Yoga Vasishta

The Yoga Vasishta embodying the instructions of Sage Vasishta to Sri Ramachandra in the council of Dasaratha was composed by Valmiki at the behest of Brahma himself. As in the case of Purva-Ramayana, this was dictated by Valmiki to his pupil Bharadwaja. This remarkable spiritual classic which, according to the author consists of 32,000 verses, made Sri Rama a perfectly enlightened person, fully competent for the discharge of royal duties. Rama was not the sole beneficiary. All the personages-King Dasaratha, his other sons, ministers and other rishis-became completely enlightened at the end of the discourses, which took place for several days in the royal council.

Sri Vasishta is next only to Brahma in the line of preceptors of the Advaitic tradition commencing from Sri Narayana. Appropriately, his teachings have inspired, guided and moulded countless souls in the quest for and attainment of spiritual wisdom and are bound to fascinate and delight generations of seekers and quench their thirst for supreme spiritual bliss.

The well-known verse[1] associated by tradition with the recitation of Ramayana affirms that the Supreme Person revealed by the Vedas was born as the son of Dasaratha, while the Veda itself issued forth from Valmiki as the Ramayana. It is also well-known that the Veda is divided into Karma-kanda and Jnana-kanda, portions dealing with Karma and Jnana respectively. In the view of the teachers of Vedanta, a person, by adhering to the tenets of Karma-kanda, acquires the mental competence which enables him

7

to pursue the spiritual enquiry, prescribed by the Jnana-kanda and attain realisation. If the Karma-kanda and Jnana-kanda of the Veda are complementary, as means and end, Valmiki's two Ramayanas, the one dealing with the story of Rama called Purva Ramayana and the other recording the teachings of Vasishta to Rama, called Uttara Ramayana or Vasishta Ramayana are also complementary, the former representing upaya, the means, and the latter the upeya, the goal. Only if we interpret it in this way, Ramayana can be considered to represent the complete Veda as affirmed by the traditional verse.

There is reason to believe that the Yoga Vasishta, containing as it does Vasishta's own teachings, was considered as the highest authority in regard to the nature of the Reality and the nature of the world. Ananda Bodhendra, the learned commentator of the Yoga Vasishta, cites a passage[2] from the 15th Chapter of the Aditya Purana in which Shiva says to his son Skanda: "Jnanam (knowledge) is never the characteristic or attribute of Atma (Self). Atma itself is of the nature of Jnana which is all-pervasive, eternal and auspicious. I am the Self of all the beings. The supreme ruler is one only. Shanmukha! All the objects are fictitiously imposed on me. All the world is only Consciousness. Ignorant people see it as world. Wise people see the world as the mere self. This truth, incomprehensible to the ordinary, was taught by Vasishta to Rama in bygone times." It is apparent that Shiva was alluding to the teachings of Vasishta to Rama contained in the Yoga Vasishta, in support of His own instructions to Shanmukha, on the nature of Self.

While commenting on Sri Krishna's observation "Rishibhir bahudha geetam" (Gita, 13-4). Shankara interprets the passage to mean "expounded much by sages like Vasishta." Such an interpretation would be proper, only if

Vasishta's exposition of Brahman as contained in the Yoga-Vasishta, was already well-known. Many minor Upanishads contain several verses from the Yoga Vasishta and utilise the kind of terminology used and ideas explained in it. It should be apparent that the composer of the minor Upanishads had borrowed them from the Yoga Vasishta and not the reverse. Later Vedantic writers, chiefly Vidyaranya (14th Century), Madhusudhana Saraswati (15 Century), Paramasivendra Saraswati, Bhaskararaya (17th Century) have frequently quoted Vasishta in support of their views. Vidyaranya's -"Jivan mukti viveka," describing the ways of a Jivanmukta, the realised soul, is largely based upon the Yoga Vasishta. Further, Vasishta's ideas are traceable in the works "Viveka Chudamani" and "Sarva Vedanta Siddhanta Sara Sangraha" of Adi Shankara and in the works of Sureswara, Sarvajnatman, Prakasananda-all of whom are anterior to Vidyaranya.

Among recent thinkers, Sri Rama Tirtha, who had lectured on Vedanta in America, and Japan was totally captivated by the work Yoga Vasishta and he described it as "one of the greatest books...and the most wonderful ever written under the Sun, which nobody on earth can read without realising God-Consciousness." The noted scholar Bhagavan Das felt that Yoga Vasishta is intended for the people in siddha-avasta, that is, those who have mastered the theory and have become adepts. Seekers and saints have always turned to it for inspiration and guidance. Though academicians in their works on Indian Philosophy have not given much importance to the Yoga Vasishta, this lacuna has been more than rectified by Dr. Atreya's learned work "The Philosophy of the Yoga Vasishta" and modern seekers are increasingly drawn towards Vasishta's philosophy, which is deep, comprehensive, rational and constructive.

"A pupil like Sri Rama, a preceptor like Sri Vasishta, a scripture like Yoga Vasishta, there have never been nor ever will be" so exclaimed Sri Vasudeva Brahmendra Saraswati of Tamilnad, a deep student of the Yoga Vasishta and this verse has been approvingly quoted by Dr. Atreya elsewhere in his writings.

What does Vasishta himself think of his work? Vasishta repeatedly exhorts the listener to study his teachings again and again and affirms that by a mere study of his work, one will become enlightened. Sri Rama is asked by Vasishta at the end of the long discourse, "Rama, your mind has attained realisation. There is nothing more for you to hear. You have accomplished all that has to be accomplished, attained all that has to be attained. Abide in thy own Self. You may yourself tell me after contemplation, how you feel at heart and whether there is anything more for you to know." Sri Rama replies, "Great seer, I feel that I have accomplished all that has to be accomplished. I am supremely blissful. I am exceedingly tranquil. There is no craving in my heart. That which has to be explained has been explained by you; that which has to be known has been known by me. Having fulfilled the purpose, let Saraswati, the Goddess of Speech withdraw into silence."

When the entire assembly rises to pay tribute to Vasishta, Sri Rama exclaims: "The greatest of fortunes, the grandest of visions, the noblest of scriptures, the greatest of literary works, the most beautiful of landscapes, the worthiest of possessions I have now attained." Visvamitra says, "O what a holy deed! After listening to the wisdom from the very mouth of the Seer, we feel as though we have taken bath in a thousand Gangas." Narada states, "What I have not heard in Brahmaloka, nor on the earth before, I have now heard. I have become very holy." Lakshmana exclaims, "You have shown that you are Sun even to the Sun-by extinguishing not only external darkness, but the internal darkness as well."

Available Works on the Subject

According to Valmiki, the work consists of 32,000 verses (BYV 2-17-6) But in the available edition, we find only 27687 verses. It is possible, that from the time it was initially composed, it has undergone changes and the available edition may not contain all the verses composed by Valmiki.

Considering the voluminous nature of the work, one Kashmir Abhinanda Pandita, who is supposed to have lived between 9th and 12th centuries, abridged the work to 5000 slokas and in those days the shorter version must have spread far and wide and contributed to the popularity of the work. Over centuries, many scholars living at different times, have made still smaller abridgements to serve the purpose of their followers. But of all these works, the "Laghu Yoga Vasishta" of Abhinanda Pandita has been the most famous, for obvious reasons, till the present time.

An English translation of the "Laghu Yoga Vasishta" by Sri K. Narayanaswami Iyer was published by the Theosophical Society, Adyar, Chennai. Subsequently, Dr. Atreya's learned thesis was also published by the same institution. There are a number of small publications and abridgements with English translations. In recent years, a number of works have been published on Yoga Vasishta. The English translation of BYV by Sri Mitra and published in 1890 has not done justice to the spiritual ideas of the work and therefore has not received serious attention from the scholars and the seekers. But up to now, the essential teachings of the entire work have not been made accessible to the modern reader, in a coherent form.

The Author and Date of the Composition

Who is the author of this work Yoga Vasishta and when was it composed? All the available manuscripts have ascribed the authorship to Valmiki. But modern scholars have various conflicting opinions on this intricate issue.

But there are traditional scholars who do not agree with their view. In their opinion, in point of style, elegance and abundant use of similes, Yoga Vasishta is very similar to Ramayana and there is no reason to doubt that the work, as we have it today, was composed by any one other than Valmiki. If it is Valmiki, which one, Purva or Uttara Ramayana, was written earlier? It is seen from the Ramayana itself that Valmiki composed the story of Rama when Rama had already become the king and when Lava and Kusha were growing in his Ashram. It was then that he composed and taught it to Lava and Kusha. When Bharadwaja recited the Ramayana before Brahma, the Creator God asked Valmiki to complete the story of Rama by composing the "Maha Ramayana" which would deal with Vasishta's teachings and lead people to liberation. The compassionate seer Valmiki, it appears, set to work on the Yoga Vasishta only thereafter.

There are scholars who opine that the work is posterior to Sri Shankara inasmuch as Sri Shankara has not made any reference to it. Vasishta's ideas are traceable in Shankara's works and Shankara directly quotes Vasishta, at least in two places, that is, in "Sanat Sujatiya Bhashya" and "Svetasvatara Upanishad Bhashya." If Sri Shankara has not frequently quoted Vasishta, there must be appropriate and valid reasons for it but that should not be the ground for asserting that the Yoga Vasishta did not exist in his time.

Unique Features

There are several unique features about Yoga Vasishta

which call for special attention. The view very casually propagated that Vedanta is anti-worldly deserves scarcely any notice in the light of the teachings of Vasishta. When Rama had become extremely despondent and was unwilling to take up royal responsibilities, Vasishta at the request of Visvamitra, through his spiritual counsel, removed the gloom from Rama's mind and infused into him wisdom, vision, courage and competence, and made him an able emperor. Many princes and princesses are seen in the Yoga Vasishta to have acquired spiritual vision which enabled them to discharge their royal duties efficiently. The teachings of Vasishta make one face life, understand it and transcend it, and not run away from it.

The conservative-minded scholars have held that only sanyasis are eligible for Vedantic study and spiritual pursuit. They quote in their favour the scriptural injunction: "Sanyasya sravanam kuryat" (let one renounce, and then commence vedantic study). Sri Shankara has upheld this view in his commentary on the Brahma Sutras, but he also says, whereas sanyasis alone are eligible for pursuing sravanam, all persons, regardless of any distinctions, can aspire for and pursue the means for the attainment of Jnanam. All those who have the requisite qualifications, even if they are women or of the fourth caste, are eligible for the pursuit of spiritual enquiry. Vasishta firmly upholds this view and at the very commencement of the work says, "He who has the conviction, that he is in bondage and seeks release from it, is competent to undertake the study of the work." In the Yoga Vasishta we find royal princesses attaining to exemplary spiritual heights and even asura kings abiding in asamprajnatha samadhi for long periods. Thus, by making his teachings available to all persons irrespective of status, caste and gender, Vasishta has been an universal benefactor, a Guru of the entire world.

One feature that singles out the Yoga Vasishta from other works is the method that the author employs in driving home the spiritual truth. The language, he chooses, is sweet and elegant; the similes, he employs, are apt and captivating; the stories, he narrates, are profound and absorbing. The reliance on quotations from the scripture and the search for pramanas, which one finds in the traditional philosophical works, are surprisingly absent in the Yoga Vasishta.

This discussion about the method of Vasishta's teachings leads us to the consideration of the criticism that has been levelled against him by modern scholars. In their opinion, the Yoga Vasishta, as a work, is not a well arranged one, each idea is not presented exhaustively in its appropriate place, and there is total lack of arrangement as everything is said in every place. There are repetitions of the same ideas and contradictions. It is true that all ideas are stated everywhere and the same truth is repeated again and again. But if we would see the work in the light of the clarifications given in the commentary of Ananda Bodhendra, the repetitions and the contradictions are not what they seem to be.

Yoga Vasishta is not intended to be a philosophical treatise which aims at giving a rational and consistent exposition of the categories of God, soul and world. Vasishta intends to transform a dejected prince, who wants to run away from life, into a wise man of courage, vision and vigour who can mould life in the way he wants. Vasishta is employing a subtle technique while talking to Sri Ramachandra and the rationale behind this technique becomes apparent only at the end of the work. The aim of Vasishta is fully achieved and Rama, having attained complete enlightenment, is ready to shoulder any responsibility. The Yoga Vasishta is not a philosophical thesis that aims at mere mental conviction but is a spiritual vision that ushers in transformation of the individual soul and similes, stories, contradictions, repetitions,are all used to achieve the end-the exalted vision.

As a true Vedantin, Vasishta is absolutely free from narrow beliefs. He does not condemn any school of philosophy. He even approves others standpoints and as emphasised by Dr. Atreya, appeals to reason and does not thrust on us scriptural authorities, though he has himself affirmed that his teaching is derived from the Upanishads. He does not ask the listener to believe something on the basis of mere scriptural authority. This characteristic of his teaching might very much appeal to the modern rationalist.

Another point needs special mention. No philosophical work begins with a disquisition on the primacy of effort, as opposed to fate.Vasishta has purposefully discussed this subject and has exhorted the listener to vanquish fate by superior effort, pursued in the light of scriptural teachings. In his view, what is called fate is only the result of one's own past effort and the present effort directed along the right lines should be strong enough to overpower fate.

The Background of the Work

Valmiki recapitulated the teachings of Vasishta to Rama and Bharadwaja recorded them. Let us now see the circumstances which brought the work to wider circulation.

Sutikshna, the disciple of Agastya, tormented by the doubt whether Karma or Jnana or their combination was the cause of liberation, requested Agastya to clarify the doubt. While affirming that both are required for liberation, Agastya described the conversation on the same subject that took place between Agnivesha and his son Karunya.

Agnivesha asked his son why he was neglecting the

performance of the ordained Karma. Karunya replied that it seemed to him that it was renunciation of Karma that brought about liberation. Agnivesha possibly felt that his son had miscontrued the teaching of the preceptors. He began to tell a long story and asked his son to listen to the story and do what was right in the light of it.

The celestial nymph Suruchi saw a messenger of Indra passing by and asked him the purpose of his mission. The messenger said: "Indra sent me alongwith a vimana to fetch the erstwhile King Arishtanemi, who had performed severe penance. I went with the vehicle and with many nymphs and invited Arishtanemi to Swargaloka (heavens). He asked me about the conditions of life in Swarga and I replied to him that though the denizens of Swarga could have extraordinary pleasures, there was still inequality in the pleasures enjoyed by them, depending upon their merits and that they too were prey to jealousy, envy, etc. Arishtanemi told me that the earthly life was more satisfying to him and sent me back.

I told Indra about Arishtanemi's disinterest in heavenly pleasures. Indra insisted that I should again go to Arishtanemi, take him to the sage Valmiki and request the sage to instruct the king on the means to liberation, as the king was fit to receive spiritual wisdom. I took Arishtanemi to Valmiki and the king requested the sage for instruction on spiritual truths.

Valmiki replied: "O King, I had composed a work on Rama's life and taught the same to my pupil Bharadwaja. He narrated this, somewhere in Meru, to Brahma. The Creator God was delighted to hear it and offered a boon to him. Bharadwaja immediately requested Brahma to give him the wisdom by which the entire humanity would get emancipated from sorrow. Brahma replied to him at once:

16

"Do earnestly request Valmiki to complete this Ramayana commenced by him. By listening to the complete Ramayana, a person will free himself totally from all delusions."

Brahma and Bharadwaja came together to my hermitage. I duly received Brahma and made prostrations to him. He told me: 'The work begun by you should not be left incomplete. I came specifically to tell you this. For the sake of the good of the world, do complete this work. Even as we cross the ocean by boat, the world will save itself from sorrow with the help of this work.' O king Arishtanemi, what I composed following Brahma's advice and taught to Bharadwaja, do thou hear from me. Follow the teaching and you will be an enlightened person."

The Central Teaching of the Yoga Vasishta

Though the work begins with the observation that even as a bird flies with the support of both the wings, a seeker attains liberation through both Karma and Jnana, Vasishta, in the course of the exposition, clarifies that Jnana alone is the means to liberation. But for Vasishta, Karma is neither superfluous nor something that can be casually discarded. In the scheme of sadhana drawn up by him, asubha (impure) vasanas have to be overcome by subha (pure) vasanas and in the achievement of this aim, performance of karma is indispensable. In the case of the person who has attained liberation, he finds himself doing naturally karma that is appropriate to his condition. The hallmark of a liberated person is that he internally renounces everything thoroughly and externally accepts everything that comes in the natural way. The spiritual wisdom that he is equipped with, enables him to shoulder the heaviest responsibility with requisite mental poise. Karma, and for that matter any religious practice like japa, dhyana, pilgrimage or samadhi, has its

2

own utility in the realm of strengthening subha vasanas but the ultimate means of liberation is only Jnana. Worship of God, in final form is also only adoration of the Self and the contemplation of Prana, presented as Kakabusunda's teaching, is only for the purpose of stabilising Jnana. If Bhagavad Gita emphasises the importance of Karma Yoga, if Srimad Bhagavata describes the excellence of Bhakti Yoga, Yoga Vasishta insists on the ultimacy of Jnana in the matter of attaining liberation. But the Jnani of Vasishta is not a recluse taking refuge in false renunciation, but an active person, in the centre of the world, discharging his duties with ease and charm. The main importance of the work Yoga Vasishta does not so much lie in the assertion of Jnana as the means to liberation as in the depiction of an array of effective means that most surely lead one to perfect realisation of Truth.

The Final Teaching

The most interesting and significant feature of Vasishta's teaching still remains to be touched upon. On several occasions during the discourse, Sri Rama raises questions on the fundamental concepts of Avidhya, Jiva, etc. Instead of replying directly to such questions, Vasishta tells that he would deal with these questions when he presents his siddhanta, the final teaching. He justifies this attitude by explaining that the flowers which blossom and the fruits which ripen in the due season alone would be beautiful and delicious. There is a suggestion in these replies that Sri Rama is asking to know what he is not yet ready to understand and accept. In the final portion of the work, where all questions are finally disposed of, the most significant teaching occurs. Is not this teaching to be found in the earlier portion of instructions as well and what is the finality about it, one may justifiably ask.

Through his counselling spread over two thirds of the work, Vasishta prepares the mind of Rama to accept the final truth, that the world does not exist, that the avidhya does not exist and the non-dual blissful Brahman is ever manifest. The beautiful aspect is that at the end, it is the disciple who proclaims so. A distraught Jiva, tossed about like a straw by the rough waves of the ocean of life floats now at the end of the discourse as a happy being on the surging waters of the bliss of the ocean of Truth. "Indeed, nothing is born and nothing is destroyed. The world, is Chit and there is only Brahman," says Sri Rama (BYV - 6-B-204-27). A person who was horrified by the worldly miseries transforms into a new being at the end of this spiritual counselling and he says that the world of sorrow is totally non-existent. This supreme realisation of Rama is the result of the unique mode of instruction Vasishta employs and this spiritual technique is the secret of the Yoga Vasishta. Vasishta interacts with Rama throughout the discourse at two levels. His intellect addresses the intellect of Rama and his spirit communes with Rama's spirit. The reader is told by Vasishta of this technique, only in the final phase of the instruction.

Practical Utility of the Work

Not only men of all religions and all faiths but men of no religion and no faith also would benefit by the teaching of the Yoga Vasishta. Even those who have no quest for liberation would find that the Yoga Vasishta's teachings make one highly refined, noble and detached. Vasishta but holds the mirror to worldly life. His analysis of it does not leave any defect unexposed and any truth unstated. Whoever has achieved anything great in the world, has achieved it only through his superior exertion. Cast away the inauspicious gloom. Visualise the pleasant happenings. Do not say. 'I am dying,' say 'I am reborn,' - exhorts Vasishta. Suferings of life are not to be despised, nor the pleasures of life to be shunned. Life is a creeper that gives two different kinds of fruits-it gives a bitter one to the ignorant and a sweet one to the wise. "The world is all darkness to the blind but is full of light to the one with vision. Live life in such a way that you may avoid all future sorrows"-the sage advises.

Apart from the central teaching of Jnana, Vasishta touches upon a number of subjects that should interest the secular-minded scientist. Contemplation of his teachings would suggest clues which take the unsolved scientific questions nearer the solution. Consciousness has received the attention of the scientists, who have now recognised it as a factor in the universal system. At the other end of the spectrum of thought, stands Vasishta with his bold assertion that Consciousness is everything. If scientific research is not stuck up, the truth as stated by Vasishta is its culmination.

But more than in the field of material science, it is in the field of health science, particularly mental science, one thinks, that Vasishta's teachings have greater relevance in modern times. There is a compulsory need to study them in great detail and evolve a set of techniques to bring relief to the distressed souls, who for want of sympathy and understanding, are driven to psychiatrists and mental clinics. Mind is too subtle an element to be understood by psychoanalytical and allied methods and has layers of residual impressions of countless previous lives not susceptible to redressal, except through special disciplines taught in the work. Yoga Vasishta's analysis of mind in relation to Consciousness opens up methods of counselling and treatment that can provide lasting relief to the distressed mind.

Ananda-Bodhendra Saraswati, The Commentator

Despite the fact that Vasishta uses similes and stories to reinforce the main teachings, it has to be stated that the Yoga Vasishta is not an open book. That is perhaps why, as he himself states elsewhere, even if one does not understand it in the first instance, one should keep on studying it and also read it again and again. He has his own terminology, far different from the one familiarised by the preceptors of the Shankarite tradition. He has his own method, characterised by repetitions. His aim is not to be consistent. He wants the disciple before him to become an enlightened soul and would use similes, stories, persuasive reasoning and even admonition, to achieve this goal.

Many scholars, for the reasons stated above, have found the Yoga Vasishta a difficult and an unprofitable work, more fanciful than factual. But the learned commentator, Ananda Bodhendra has happily rescued this work from this possible trap. His deep insight and subtle clarifications have polished the innumerable diamonds that remain scattered on the bosom of the ocean of the Yoga Vasishta and have brought to light the significant pattern that underlies the whole work.

Ananda Bodhendra Saraswati seems to have been the disciple of Gangadharendra Saraswati of Kashmir who was the author of Swarajaya-Siddhi and a grand-disciple of Sarvagna Saraswati. Out of modesty, he says that what he has done to the teachings is similar to the addition of appropriate quantity of salt to the dishes. It is salt in due proportion, that makes all the dishes delicious.

Scholars like Dr. Atreya blame the commentator for needlessly reading into the Yoga Vasishta the post-Shankarite concepts, but the charge is not valid. The teachings of Shankara are not at variance with those of Yoga

Vasishta. Neither Sri Shankara is anti-rational nor Vasishta anti-Upanishadic. Ananda Bodhendra enables the reader to understand fully the Yoga Vasishta and if we do not avail his help, we miss the gold mine that Yoga Vasishta is. It is relatively easy to go to the foot of the Himalayas or to the fringe of the ocean but it is far difficult to scale the heights of Himalayas or plunge into the depths of the ocean. So it is with the attempt to interpret the Yoga Vasishta. Ananda Bodhendra has admirably accomplished this aim. His benedictory verse tellingly brings out the uniqueness of Vasishta's teaching:

After drinking whose nectarine words, one finds definitely the amrita tasteless,

After ascertaining the meaning of whose utterances, one finds even the desired heaven as prison-house,

After absorbing whose teachings in the mind and getting fully merged in the Self, the world certainly becomes a straw,

To that Guru, Vasishta Muni, I offer obeisance always.

The Laghu Yoga Vasishta

The Brihat Yoga Vasishta, also called as Maharamayana, Uttara-Ramayana, contains, according to the author of the work, 32,000 verses in six sections-Vairagya Prakaranam, Mumukshu Vyavahara Prakaranam, Utpatti Prakaranam, Stithi Prakaranam, Upasama Prakaranam and Nirvana Prakaranam. The Nirvana Prakaranam, which contains two sections accounts for nearly 17,000 verses.

This big work was abridged by a great Kashmiri scholar, Abhinanda Pandita who is believed to have lived between 9th and 12th century. The abridged version, called the Laghu Yoga Vasishta as published by the Nirnaya Sagara Press contains a little more than 5000 verses in six sections. Abhinanda Pandita's was a well-thought out plan and the Laghu Yoga Vasishta became very popular among scholars and became the basic work for further condensation and translation into other dialects.

The NS edition contains a commentary as well. The commentary for the portion upto the end of the Utpatti Prakaranam is called Vasishta Chandrika-composed by Srimad Atmasukha. The commentary for the portion commencing from the Stithi Prakaranam to the end is called Samsara Tarani-written by Sri Mummudi Deva Vidwadacharya. The preface of the NS edition of the Laghu Yoga Vasishta does not throw any light on the two commentators.

Abhinanda Pandita has mostly presented the verses as they are available in the BYV and has himself supplied the connecting lines. The abridged version has all the flavour of the original and yet cannot be said to contain all the important ideas of the BYV. The last section-NP Uttarardha-

which is one fourth of the work, has been completely left out in the abridgement. In fact, this last section of the BYV can be said to contain the final and conclusive views of Vasishta and the reason why the Kashmiri scholar has ignored the entire section is not obvious. A gist of this section which contains 216 sargas, has been provided in the appendix of this work so as to make it complete.

Unfortunately, the NS edition of the work-which is the only available edition-contains wrong readings in many places. However, the NS text has been retained in the present work but the correct readings, as presented in the BYV have been followed in the translation. An edited text with the commentary will fulfill a great need.

List of Abbreviations Used

BYV   - Brihat Yoga Vasishta published by the Nirnaya Sagara Press.

LYV   - Laghu Yoga Vasishta published by the Nirnaya Sagara Press.

TP   - Tatparya Prakasika, a commentary on BYV by Ananda Bodhendra Saraswati.

VC   - Vasishta Chandrika, commentary on LYV by Atmasukha (Upto Utpatti Prakaranam)

ST   - Samsara Tarani, commentary on LYV by Mummudi Deva Vidwacharya (from Stithi Prakaranam to the end)

NS   - Nirnaya Sagara Press

NP   - Nirvana Prakaranam.

Contents

Page

Section-6 - Liberation   563

(Second Half)

The Laghu Yoga Vasishta

Section-1
Dispassion
Chapter-1

The Rise of Dispassion

1. *Obeisance to the luminous all-pervasive Self, which permeates the earth, the space and the heaven and which is manifest both within and without.*

    This verse is in the nature of benediction.

2. *'I am in bondage. Let me attain freedom from it.' - he who has such a conviction and who is neither totally ignorant of nor fully enlightened about the Reality is the person competent for the study of this scriptural work.*

3. Bharadwaja, with due modesty, queried, in soft tone, Valmiki, the all-knowing seer, who was sitting alone:

4. "Great seer, I desire to know how Rama, having attained jivanmukti, conducted himself while facing the ordeals of life. O teacher, tell me about it out of compassion."

31

5. Valmiki replied: "Well, my child, you are a proper person and let me describe the same, after hearing which you will cast away the taint of delusion.

6. *O wise man! The illusory appearance of the world, like the blueness of the sky, must be so forgotten by one that it does not become even an object of recollection.*

7. *If the mind is stripped of the objective content by the realisation that the seen world does not exist, supreme beatitude manifests within.*

    'Drsya-marjanam'-erasing the objective content-is a key concept in Vasishta's spiritual discipline and its significance gets deeper and deeper as the teaching proceeds.

8. Otherwise, for those like you, afflicted by ignorance, who wallow in the mire of the scriptures, there is no redemption even in aeons.

9. The excellent state of the total discarding of the vasanas (tendencies) from the mind is what is called liberation by the wise. The rejection of vasanas is the direct means to bliss.

    Vasanas are tendencies that get lodged in the mind as a result of the deeds in previous lives and prompt the individual to act in similar ways in the present life.

10. *Vasanas are of two kinds: pure and impure. Impure ones lead to succession of birth and death and pure ones destroy rebirth.*

11. The vasanas, which by virtue of ajnana, ignorance, have fully entrenched and which, in turn, further strengthen ahankara, egoity, and which are capable of leading to rebirths are termed as impure by the wise.

12. Those vasanas, which have been deprived of the potency like the burnt seeds to cause rebirth and which after making the aspirant the Knower of the Known (the Truth) exist there, only to sustain the present body, are called as pure ones.

The vasanas of the one who has known the Reality are called Jnathajneya.

13. Those lofty souls who possess pure vasanas, which do not engender the evil of rebirth and who are also called the knowers of the Reality, are spoken of as jivanmuktas-liberated while alive.

14. How the noble-minded Rama attained the state of jivanmukti, let me describe, so that one by knowing it may free oneself from the sorrows of old age, death, etc.

15. After returning from the preceptor's abode (duly completing the studentship), the lotus-eyed Rama spent the time in merry sports freely, without any sense of fear.

16. As the time went on thus, the noble Rama had a strong mental urge to visit the holy and sacred centres dotting the land.

17. Reflecting thus, Rama approached his father, as the hamsa bird the lotus. He offered prostrations at his father's feet, the nails of which shone like the filaments of lotus blossoms.

18 & 19. "Father, my mind is longing to see the holy places, abodes of Gods, woods and worshipping centres. Please allow me to visit them. This request of mine, who has not sought any favour so far, deserves to be fulfilled. There is none in the world who has sought anything from you and who has not been properly rewarded."

3

20.   Thus requested by Rama, Dasartha, after obtaining the consent of Vasishta, readily complied with this only wish which Rama had ever made.

21.   On an auspicious day, Rama with his brothers, left home with the intention to go on a pilgrimage to the holy places.

22, 23 & 24. Beginning with his own Kosala region, he saw, after performing the preliminary rites every morning-snana, dana, japa and dhyana-holy and sacred rivers, woods, centres of worship, wasteland, river banks, sea-shores and mountain ranges. Duly honoured by the celestials and humans, he, after wandering over the entire earth, returned home, just in the manner Siva returned to His abode, fully satisfied with his excursions in all the directions.

25.   Even as Jayanta, the son of Indra, entered the celestial city, Rama entered his city, in the streets of which the citizens had strewn fried rice, flowers, etc., to welcome him.

26.   Since his return, Rama lived in his mansion happily, now and then talking about the customs and manners of the various people living in different regions.

27.   Rising up in the morning, Rama, after performing Sandhya-worship in the due manner, saw his father sitting like Indra, in the council.

28.   He spent the forenoon in the company of Vasishta and other elders listening to stories which contained wisdom.

29.   Permitted by his father, he went in the afternoon alongwith a retinue of army to the forest abounding in boars and bulls, on a hunting expedition.

30.   Returning home later and after performing snana etc.,

and after dining in the company of friends, relatives and well-wishers, he spent away the night.

31. Thus, after returning from the pilgrimage Rama, alongwith his brothers, went through the daily routine and lived in his father's palace.

32. Conducting himself in the way which pleased Dasaratha and delighted the hearts of wise men, the blemishless Rama endeared himself to all and spent the days.

33. But, in course of time, Rama who was yet to complete 16 years of age, began to grow thin like the lake turning dry in the hot summer.

The scheme of sadhana for the attainment of supreme bliss envisaged in the Sruti is this: Performance of duties appropriate to one's varna (class), and ashrama (stage), without any desire for fruit, acquisition of punya (religious merit), the destruction of papa (sin), capacity for mental reflection, understanding the nature of samsara (the worldly life), dispassion, desire for liberation, exploration of means for release, renunciation of karma, approaching the Guru, practice of sravana (Vedantic study), etc., realisation of Brahman, destruction of ajnanam (ignorance) and finally abidance in the Supreme. In order to teach the world this method of sadhana, the author shows that even Rama adhered to this sruti-ordained procedure. Rama is stated to have scrupulously performed karma that leads successively to dispassion, discrimination, realisation and liberation-VC

34. With the passage of time, his face, with lotus-like eyes, became pale as the petal of the lotus, surrounded by the bees, becomes white through sun's hot rays.

35. With palms supporting the forehead, he remained brooding within himself. He was sitting quiet, without doing anything.

36. Getting lost in such contemplation and becoming dejected and despondent, he spoke to none and appeared like a painted picture on the wall.

37. Implored again and again by the attendants, he performed reluctantly the daily routine with anguish and a sad heart.

38. 'My son, what makes you so deeply anxious?' asked Dasaratha again and again, by placing him on his lap.

39. 'Nothing in particular'-replying thus, Rama of lotus-like eyes, would rise up from the lap and keep standing nearby.

40. At this very period, the maharshi known as Visvamitra came to Ayodhya to see the emperor.

41. Seeing the sage in a radiant form, the king led him to a golden seat and profusely offered drink and other articles of worship.

42. When the sage was seated, the king offered him again and again water for washing the feet and made other devout offerings like cow.

43. After worshipping him duly, he held his palms together in a saluting posture and with modesty and joy spoke these words:

44. "By the unexpected visit of thine in such a radiant form, I feel I have been conferred a blessing, like the lotus by sun.

45. That bliss, which is plenary, indestructible, inalienable, has been attained by me now because of you, O seer!

46. Thy arrival is unto me like the attainment of vision by the blind, like the downpour of rain on the parched land and like the drinking of ambrosia by a mortal being.

47. That delight which one gets by travel in space above or when a dead person returns alive, I have attained today by thy arrival, O great seer! I welcome thee.

48. What desire of yours is to be fulfilled? What can I do for thee? You are exceedingly holy. I have been honoured by a lofty soul.

49. That happiness, which arises in one when bathed by the waters of Ganga, is surging in my heart and cools my being, as I gaze at thee.

50. How noble you are, being completely rid of desire, fear, anger, attachment and suffering? Great seer, it is indeed a wonder that thou art here to see me.

51. O great seer, whatever has to be accomplished for you and by whatever means, know that it has been accomplished, because you are worthy of the highest honour."

52. Hearing this wonderful and long speech of the king, the effulgent Visvamitra became delighted. He spoke:

53. "O king, you have spoken in a manner worthy of one who belongs to the great lineage of the world and who has Vasishta as the counsellor.

54. I am pursuing a vow for the sake of attainment of a particular aim, O king! The cruel rakshasas are bent upon throwing obstructions on my pursuit.

55 to 58. It behoves you to protect one who has sought refuge in you.

You have a son who has the valour of a proud tiger.

Rama has the prowess of Indra and is capable of destroying the rakshasas.

O King, give that elder son, whose crest is like that of the crow, who is a dexterous fighter and who is steadfast in adherence to truth.

With my support and by virtue of his own divine valour, he is capable of annihilating the ungrateful rakshasa hordes.

O Ruler, it does not behove you to think of him only as your son and remain attached to him.

59.   There is nothing too great in the world to be given to noble souls. My dear king, let me assure you that with the help of Rama, the rakshasas are as good as killed. Persons like us do not embark on uncertain ventures.

60.   I know the real greatness of Rama of lotus-like eyes. Vasishta of great effulgence and other far-sighted seers know too, who he is.

61.   If thy mind holds dharma in esteem and if you desire renown, then do give me thy son who is dear to you."

62.   After speaking these words which are imbued with dharma, the noble-minded seer Visvamitra became silent.

63.   The king, after hearing the words of Visvamitra, remained benumbed for a while and then in trepidation, said:

64.   "Rama, the lotus-eyed, is not even sixteen summers' old. I do not see in him the strength to fight the rakshasas.

65.   Here is a big division of army with me as its general. Accompanied by it, I shall win the battle against the rakshasas.

66.   Rama is a child and does not know how to assess the strength or the lack of it of the enemy. He has been only to the playground and not to the battle-ground.

67.   O Kausika, I spent nine thousand years without a child. With great difficulty, four sons were obtained by me, through boon.

68.   Of them, the most dear is the lotus-eyed Rama. Separated from him, the other three would even give up their lives.

69.   If that very Rama is to go with you to fight the rakshasas and if I get separated from my son, know for certain that I am dead.

70.   There is one more point. If it is Ravana that is causing obstacle to you, we are not presently strong enough to fight that wicked being.

71.   Times there are, in which certain cosmic elements manifest extraordinary powers and times there are, in which those very powers vanish.

72.   At the present moment, we are not powerful enough to face enemies like Ravana. Such is the decisive cosmic will.

73.   These are difficult times and wise men remain scattered. Even Dasaratha appears, as if he is old and despondent."

      The word Raghava in the verse may also be taken to refer to Rama, instead of Dasaratha.

74.   After listening to these words, uttered with feeling and fear, Kausika angrily replied to the ruler:

75.   "After promising to fulfill my desires, you want to go back on your resolve. A lion you were, and now you have turned into a deer.

76. If you are incapable of keeping your word, O king, let me go back. A descendant of Kakustha you are and yet you choose to go back on your word. Well, be happy with your relations."

77. When the noble-minded Visvamitra was fretting with anger, the entire earth trembled and fear struck the celestials.

78. Finding that Visvamitra, the friend of the universe, was possessed by anger, the wise and courageous Vasishta, of steadfast vows, spoke these words:

79. "If, in spite of the fact that you are Dasaratha and a scion of Ikshvaku family, you do not stand by the word, who else would keep his promise?

80. Because of the law enforced by you and the example set by you, ordinary people do not transgress the bounds. That code you too should not violate.

81. Rama who is protected by the lion among men, Visvamitra, like amrita by Garuda, cannot be vanquished by the rakshasas, regardless of the fact whether he is proficient in the handling of weapons or not."

82. Valmiki said: "When Vasishta spoke thus, the wise king asked the attendants of Rama how and where Rama was.

83. The attendants of Rama said: "Since his return alongwith brahmins from the pilgrimage to the holy centres, the lotus-eyed Rama is cheerless.

84. Only at our repeated request does he attend to his daily chores with a gloomy face.

85. 'Of what use are the fortunes? What if misfortunes befall? Of what use are the mansion and the riches?

All are illusions'-saying thus, he remains in solitude without any activity.

86. O king! He is indifferent to dress, drinks, food, possesssions, etc., and is adhering to severe austerities, as if he is a recluse.

87. He does not want to be praised, does not esteem the kingship. He neither gets elated nor depressed when events of joy or sorrow happen.

88. He mutters within himself that life gets wasted away in futile activities without one striving for emancipation.

89. He gives away everything to persons seeking help with the remark, 'Do you yearn for this wealth that is the cause of all sorrows?'

90. O great king! We know not how we should deal with the prince of such disposition. You are to decide.

91. Is there a supremely wise individual on earth, who can make Rama evince interest in the life's affairs?"

92. Visvamitra said to the attendants: "If that be so, do thou bring here, at once, that great and wise man, even as an elephant is led by other elephants.'

93. *The delusion which afflicts Rama has arisen neither out of distress nor out of attachment. This delusion is only a happy harbinger of wisdom, that one gains only through discrimination and dispassion.*

94. *If this delusion gets wiped away through appropriate counselling, Rama will attain supreme repose, as we have.*

95. He would, then, with all his mind, attend to all the normal and real problems of daily life in entirety."

96. As the seer spoke thus, the lotus-eyed Rama came there to offer prostration at the feet of his father.

97. He offered prostration first to his father, next to the seers Vasishta and Visvamitra -worthy of deep respect, and thereafter to brahmins, relations and other elders.

98. He also conveyed his respect to others through looks or nod of head or words, as expected of kings.

99. Even though the emperor told him, 'Son, sit on my lap,' Rama sat on the seat placed on the floor by the attendants.

100. Dasaratha said: "Son, you are intelligent and have been endowed with all fortunes. Do not allow yourself, dragged by the stupid mind, to fall into anguish.

101. By adhering to the percepts of the elders, brahmins and guru, in the manner you do, a noble state is attained. Such a state is not attained by succumbing to delusion.

102. Son, only so long as delusion does not fully overpower you, the dangers around keep themselves away at a distance."

103. Vasishta said: "O prince of great prowess! You are valorous and have vanquished enemies, the sense-objects, which are difficult for one to destroy.

104. How is it that you, like an unwise man, plunge into the ocean of delusion, with unexpected dangers lurking in it. Only ignorant people fall into gloom.

105. Those afflictions which pierce through your mind-even as rats destroy the hut-wherefrom do they arise? What are they? Why do they arise? How powerful are they?

106. Do thou tell these, O faultless one! You will then attain the blessed state you long for. These afflictions cannot any longer torment you, once you attain that state."

107. Rama, the scion of Raghu's lineage, after hearing the words of the wise preceptor-which contain pregnant sense-discarded the anguish of the heart, just as when the clouds thunder, the peacock discards all sorrows in the faith that its hope will fructify.'

Chapter-2

The Ills of Worldly Life

1.   Valmiki said: "Advised thus by the seer Visvamitra, Rama, after reflecting for a while, spoke beautiful words of deep import.

2.   Sri Rama said: "Divine seer! What you have asked me to say, I shall presently do fully. I am unenlightened and yet who would transgress the words of the wise?

3.   I was born in the mansion of my father, and grew up and acquired learning in natural course.

4.   I was devoted to the performance of ordained duties, O seer, and in that circumstance, I went to pilgrimage to the holy places of the earth girdled by the sea.

5.   At this time, an enquiring disposition, seized me which killed almost all enthusiasm for life.

6.   What is it that is called happiness, in a life in which people are born to die and they die to be born?

7.   All these activities-of living beings and others-are impermanent. Fortunes and acquisitions get sullied by sin and are store houses of dangers.

8.   The living beings are as unconnected with each other as iron balls. The mere imagination of one makes these separate entitites appear related to each other.

9.   What has the kingdom of pleasures to do with me? Who am I? What is this world? If it is unreal, let it be unreal. How has it affected anyone?

Among the body, senses, mind, intellect, chitta, ahankara, ajnana, reflected consciousness (chit-

44

pratibimbha) and consciousness, who am I? Is this world real or illusory? If it is illusory, there is nothing to be obtained from it. - V. C.

10. In the course of such reflection, O seer, a strong dispassion arose in me towards all things. Those who wander in the scorched desert lose interest in life.

11. How does this sorrow come to an end?- this anxiety keeps burning within me, like the fire within the trunk of an old tree.

12. The sorrow of samsara has, as if, converted the heart into a stone. Out of regard for the people around, I do not shed tears and weep.

13. The wealth are grinding stones of mental worries and they do not make me happy. The houses filled with wives and children are but breeding ground of dangers.

14. In this seemingly majestic worldly life, fleeting prosperity surely causes great delusion and gives no true peace.

Next to wealth, Sri Rama criticises prosperity, the cause of wealth.

15. Without going into the merits or otherwise of a person, the cunning prosperity favours the person by the side, as a king does.

16. The milk drunk only increases the poison-content in the snake. The prosperity by promoting acts righteous and otherwise, increases only the evil propensities of the individual.

17. The individual remains happy so long as the icy wind of prosperity does not make him shiver and suffer.

18. Learned, courageous, graceful, efficient and refined persons have been deprived of their grace by prosperity, like the gems of their shine by the dust.

19. Three persons are hard to come across in the earth- the prosperous man who is not despised by the people, a brave person who is unboasting and a rich person with even-minded disposition.

20. Lakshmi is attractive, like the flower-filled creeper that rises up from the pit of mire and is entwined by several snakes; and she is fleeting and mean in nature.

21. Life, like the unsteady tiny drop of water at the far end of the tender leaf of a creeper, deserts the body of a person, at an unexpected time, as if it were an insane person.

Next to prosperity, Sri Rama denounces life itself.

22. Life causes only pain because people get bitten by the poisonous snakes of desires. They do not have strong discriminating sense to save themselves from them.

23. We have limited understanding because of the identification with body. O seer, the life is akin to lightning amidst the clouds of samsara, worldly life, and we do not get excited by it.

24. It is not wise to put trust in life. One can rather bind the air, cut the space or string together the waves.

25. Life is evanescent like the passing summer cloud, the lamp without oil and the falling wavelets. Before one cognises them, they are gone.

26. Men without understanding desire a futile long life only to undergo misery, as the foolish asvatharee desires to bring forth offspring, which only ends her life.

46

Asvatharee is an animal that has sprung from the union of horse and ass and in the process of delivering its issue, the mother dies. The offspring desired by the animal brings about its own end.

27. That alone is life in which one attains the state of bliss-wherein one grieves not.

28. Trees live, birds live, but he alone truly lives whose mind through reflection and realisation becomes, as it were, non-existent.

29. Those men of virtue alone are truly born in this world-those, who are not born again. The rest are decrepit asses.

30. Burdensome is the scripture to the person who has no discriminating sense; burdensome is wisdom to the one who is swayed by attachment; burdensome is mind to the one who is restless; and burdensome is body to the individual who has not realised the Self.

31. Form, life, mind, intellect, ego, deep attachments-all contribute only to the misery of the ignorant man, like burden for the man who carries it.

32. As a wise person removes a wicked person from company immediately, youth takes leave of an unfortunate person in matter of days only.

33. There is nothing like life in the world which is utterly meritless. It is bereft of any abiding good and is vulnerable to instant death.

34. In vain it projects up and in vain it makes itself mighty. We are indeed afraid of this wicked enemy of ahankara, ego, which is totally false in nature.

Verses 34 to 40 are in denunciation of ahankara.

47

35. On account of ahankara, arise dangers; on account of
ahankara, arise numerous afflictions; on account of
ahankara, arise the cravings. There is no greater enemy
than ahankara.

36. I know ahankara as wicked enemy. Hence I eat not,
drink not. How can I enjoy pleasures?

37. Whatever has been enjoyed by me, received by me,
achieved by me, as a result of ahankara is imaginary.
For the reality is not characterised by ahankara.

The acts done with the help of ahankara are as unreal
as deeds in a dream.

38. When the clouds of ahankara are ready to burst into
downpour, the flower-bunches in the kutaja trees of
desires are ready to bloom forth.

Kutaja tree, at the onset of rains, covers itself with a
canopy of flowers.

39. To help me who is miserable to get out of the clutch
of ahankara, O seer, teach me whatever is appropriate.
Let me get out of the grip of deadly ahankara.

40. O noble soul! I do not rely on ahankara which is
inseparably bound up with misery; which is the abode
of all dangers; which is inconsistent; which is devoid
of any virtues. Do thou instruct me in such a manner
that I may release myself from it.

Sri Rama pays for the instruction that will enable him
to cast away the ahankara and abide as mere
witnessing principle of Consciousness.

41. The mind, torn to shreds by maladies, shies away from
all righteous deeds and service of elders and gets tossed
about like the tiny straw caught amidst wind.

42. As though it has purpose, it always leaps from one

thing to another, like the village dog that goes from one extreme corner to another.

43. The mind obtains nothing at any time; even if it obtains enormous wealth, it does not have inner contentment and is like the bamboo basket which cannot contain the water poured into it.

44. The mind is crude and senseless. I am eaten up by such a mind accompanied as it is by the wolf of desire, even as a dead body is eaten up by the dog.

45. I am carried far away by the mind, like the tiny straw by the fierce wind, to be thrown away somewhere or to be borne away by air in space.

46. I remain fettered by the rope of wicked mind, as the bucket in the well is being dragged from patala to the earth and from the earth to the patala.

Patala: the world below the earth.

47. I am as much seized by the wicked mind, as the child by the vetala (demon), which has falsely manifested but which gets destroyed on investigation.

48. O seer! It is more fierce than fire, more dense than mountain and more powerful than thunderbolt.

49. Control of mind is more difficult, O seer, than the drinking of ocean, the uprooting of the Meru mountain and the swallowing of fire.

50. Mind is the cause from which external objects originate. Mind existing, all the worlds exist. If that is attenuated, the world becomes extinct. Therefore, the mind has to be properly disciplined.

Mind is the material cause of the world. If the mind gets annihilated, the world becomes non-existent.

51. Like trees growing in abundance on the mountain

slopes, countless joys and sorrows arise from the mind. If the mind is attenuated through discernment, the sorrows also get effectively dispelled.

52. In the heart, filled with the darkness of desire and pervaded by the space-like soul, rows of owls of vices keep flitting.

Owls are known to fly around during the darkness of night.

Verses 52 to 64 condemn desire, as it is through desire the mind manifests itself.

53. Whenever I resort to practice of some virtue, the desire destroys it, like the rat cutting away the string of veena, the musical instrument.

54. We are incapable of making it to our true abode and, caught in the net of desires, we remain paralysed like the birds trapped.

Our true abode: One's nature as Consciousness.

55. O saviour! I get burnt up by the fire of desire so much, that I feel even amrita cannot quench the heat.

56. Desire is a dark night that can frighten even the brave, can blind even the man with vision and can pierce the heart of even a tranquil-minded person.

57. Desire, like the indisciplined mind of an old harlot, runs after every person, but succeeds not in winning anyone.

58. Even in an impossible situation, desire dares to try, like the aged danseuse attempting to play the tandava dance without a trace of joy.

59. Desire is a restless mokey that leaps to an unattainable object, and even if it is at the moment satisfied longs for something else, and does not remain at one place for any length of time.

60. Of all the evils of samsara, desire is the one that gives the greatest sorrow. Even a person in the inner apartment with women gets involved in a distant disaster by it.

61 & 62. One abandons all sorrows by discarding the thoughts of objects. Discarding of the thoughts of objects is really called the mantra, mystic chant, for the removal of the disease of desire.

Desire is the disease called Vishuchika. Desire for the object arises on account of the thinking that the object is pleasant. By discarding such thinking, the desire is also dropped. Hence, the discarding of thought is called the mantra for the removal of the disease of desire.

63. Disease, begging, women and desire can bring down the stature of even a great person, as the heat of the sun causes the lotus stalk to stoop.

64. Great seer! The sharp edge of the sword, the fire of thunderbolt or the iron balls of fire are not so fierce as the desire lodged in the heart.

65. Desire can cast down in a second to the lowest level, as if he is a straw, even the person great in wisdom and in firmness like Meru.

66. The body composed of fibres of nerves and limbs, which is prone to change and decay and suffering, also manifests in the samsara only to intensify the misery.

Verses 66 to 74 condemn the nature of body.

67. He gets delighted with small things one time and gets displeased with them another time. There is nothing like body which is mean and devoid of merit and is the object of grief.

68. The body is the abode of the ego, who is the house-owner. Let the house perish or survive. What is it to me, o seer?

69. This abode of body-in which senses of cows remain in a herd, the damsel of desire keeps roving and the servant of mind enjoys pleasure-is not pleasing to me.

70. This abode of body-in whose entrance of mouth, remains entrenched the fierce monkey of tongue, such a body consisting of teeth, bones, etc.-is not pleasing to me.

71. Of what avail is prosperity, of what avail kingdom, of what avail body, of what avail desire? In matters of days only, time devours everyone of these.

72. Tell me, what beauty is there in the body, which is full of blood and flesh within and which is perishable by nature?

73. The body becomes old and dies at the due time, whether it is the body of a rich man or a poor man. Death does not recognise any distinction.

74. In the lightning, in the tiny cloud of summer, in the dream city-he who has trust, may as well trust this body.

75. Even if one attains the rare human birth in the vast ocean of samsara, which is full with waves of activities, the state of infancy is fraught with misery.

76. Incapacity, dangers, craving, dumbness, stupidity, desire, casualness, dependence-all these characterise infancy.

77. Mind by nature is fickle; infancy brings in greater fickleness. When these two get combined, is there any limit to unsteadiness?

78. It is from the child's mind, the woman's eyes, the

streaks of lightning, rows of wavelets, mind has learnt fickleness.

79. The child becomes calm with something and becomes angry with something else. The child revels only in the impure dirt, as the dogs in the refuse.

80. How can the child's stupidity, which makes it eat anything that it comes across and which even longs to catch the moon in space, do one good?

81. The child, being afraid of teacher, mother and father and other elder children, ever remains fear-stricken.

82. Childhood which is afflicted with all kinds of desires, like the house of the wicked, O great seer, cannot contribute happiness to anyone.

83. The person with his desires unfulfilled, leaves the childhood and climbs up to youthfulness in hurry, only to fall.

Verses 83 to 89 deal with youthfulness.

84. The ghost of lust lurks in the hole of one's mind and deludes the mind in a hundred ways. The youth gets reduced to helplessness and humiliation.

85. Though the youth is broad-minded, capable and pure, his mind becomes tainted like the waters of the canal during the rainy season.

86. The body is akin to the hot desert, and there arises the mirage of women on it. The deers of young minds run towards them and fall into pits of sense-objects.

87. Whenever the youth grows to the next stage, feverish passions born of lust invade the mind only to lead the person to destruction.

88. They indeed are great men, noble-minded and worthy of regard-they who have easily transcended the

difficult youthful phase without hurting themselves,
O seer.

89. A youth, who is endowed with humility worthy of
wise men, who is kind and virtuous-such an auspicious
being, it is difficult to see, like a forest in space.

90. What is elegant about the woman who is an image of
flesh, whose limbs are activated, as if, by a machine,
and who is an aggregate of nerves, bones, etc?

91. to 93. Those very breasts of the beloved, in which the
necklace of pearls kept gracefully moving like the
stream of Ganga waters on the slopes of Meru, are
eaten with relish, as if they are foodballs, by dogs in
some corner of cremation ground or wilderness.

94. Women are the fierce fire, whose black smoke are their
tresses. They are pleasing to look at but painful for
physical contact. They burn men, as if they are dry
grass.

95. They are attractive to look at from distance and appear
charming, though they are not really so; the women
are good fuel for the fire of suffering raging in the hell.

96. The hunter Kama has, as though, spread a vast net in
the form of women to trap the birds of stupid men.

97. For men who are like fishes in the pond of existence,
wallowing in the mire of mind, women are the meat
attached to the hook tied to the rope of bad tendencies.

98. The women is like a box of jewels of all wicked things
of life. I have no need of woman, who brings with her
a chain of misery.

99. Here is flesh, here is blood, here is bone-in matter of
days only, great seer, the body of woman gets
decomposed.

100. He, in whose look there is woman, has desire for her; how can he, in whose attitude there is no woman, desire for her? If woman is renounced, the world is renounced. Renouncing the world, let the person be happy.

101. The pleasures which are beguiling, which are hard to pass through, which are as fleeting as the wing of the tiny bee, I do not delight-in, for fear of the disease, death and old age they entail. O seer! let me become tranquil and attain through effort the supreme beatitude.

102. Even before one gets satisfied with childhood, boyhood swallows it away and even before he gets fulfilment as a youth, old age takes possession of him. See how inimical the different phases are to each other.

Verses 102 to 112 decry old age.

103. As a woman beaten by co-wife flees home, intelligence leaves the man when he is afflicted with old age in the natural course.

104. Servants, sons, women, relations, well-wishers-all ridicule the old man, as if he is senile.

105. The old age descends on the man who is unseemly, crude, helpless, powerless and virtueless, even as an old avaricious eagle alights on a tree.

106. Desire, which is the cause of helplessness, which brings endless sorrow in the heart and is the sole ally of all the dangers-grows more with age.

107. In the higher world, there is lot of suffering to be undergone by me which cannot be countered. What am I to do?-Such fear afflicts the old man.

108. Craving dominates the mind but one is unable to enjoy all the pleasures. Heart burns on account of

suffering and the energy of the person gets weakened.

109. Old age finds the head with white hair as similar to kushmanda fruit and swallows it away. Time is the ruler of men.

110. O seer! For the king of death, old age is the heralding white fan in the retinue of diseases, mental and physical, that marches ahead of him.

111. In the inner apartment of body, which has been coated with the ointment of decreptitude merrily sport the maidens, incapacity, craving and other dangers.

112. What is there to gain by a life which is fraught with all the hardships on account of old age? Aging has not been conquered by people in the world and in the matter of causing hardship, it outdoes the desires.

113. If, by chance, anyone fancies that there is happiness in life, Time destroys that happiness also, as rat destroys the threads of entire cloth.

114. There is nothing in this world, which the all-devouring Time does not swallow up, as the conflagration does at the time of deluge, the waters of the ocean.

115. Time does not show favour for a second even for a great man. The all-devouring Time dominates over the entire universe.

116. Even as Garuda makes mince-meat of snakes, Time destroys even things attractive, auspicious and as large like Meru.

117. Time is set to devour all these-grass, dust, Indra, Meru, dry leaf, ocean-and assimilate them into itself.

118. Time is, as it were, a fig tree full of fruits in which swarms of insects of cosmic bodies keep revolving in humming tune.

119. Time devours the fruits of cosmic deities, looking ripe like the setting sun, abounding in wild forest of the world.

120. The jewels of wise men of the world remain scattered in the dilapidated hut of the world and they are thrown by Time into the fierce casket of death.

121 to 138. These verses contain description of the Kala and Kala-ratri. The extensive imagery in description is too difficult for translation in readable prose. Time, manifesting as Kala and Kalaratri, is invincible-this is the substance of the verses.

139. The evil of Kala and other things which constitute samsara, being as described above, how can persons like us have longing for it?

140. One's enemies are the senses only; the real has become unreal; manas, mind is inflicting harm on itself and mind itself is mind's enemy.

    The Self, which is of the nature of Consciousness becomes non-self, as it were.

141. The witness of the body gets identified with the body; mind is entirely dominated by ego. The seen entities are devoid of existence and the substrate of things, the Consciousness is not cognised.

142. Mind caught between the real and the unreal gets confounded and perturbed. The disease of desire ravages and a really detached person is hard to come across.

143. If any youth makes effort to seek the truth, the company of the wise is very hard to obtain. There seems to be no way to achieve the aim. Credibility is not to be found.

144. Mind gets confounded. Happiness has fled elsewhere.

We do not notice kindness. Meanness descends on all from somewhere.

145. Wise man becomes cowardly. A person in status falls from it. The company of the wicked is readily available. The company of the wise is rarely obtained.

146. The things of the world are transient; attachment leads to bondage. The cosmic river keeps flowing perennially towards unknown destination.

147. Dhanavas get vanquished. The eternal ones cease to be eternal. The immortals face mortality. How can people like us have trust in life?

    Dhanavas: Asuras

148. Country turns into wilderness. Directions are not recognisable. Mountains get uprooted. How can people like us have trust in life?

149. The celestial world gets eaten up. The earth gets disintegrated. How can people like us have trust in life?

150. Oceans get dried up. Stars get further scattered and lustreless and persons supposed to be immortal die. How can people like us have trust in life?

151. Brahma also seems to pass away. Hari is dragged away and the ever-existent Shiva becomes non-existent. How can people like us have trust in life?

152. Time gets absorbed in something else and the cosmic law is divested of its force. The infinite space gets dissolved finally. How can people like us have trust in life?

153. The worlds are, as it were, derided by the unique reality, indescribable, unthinkable and incomprehensible.

154. 'Today there is festival.' 'This is enjoyable season.' 'We go on a pilgrimage.' 'They are relations.' This is pleasure.' 'That is enjoyment.'-thus in vain, through hundred fancies, the minds of ordinary men of the world get deluded and destroyed.

155. He fancies that the sons, wives, wealth are delightful like the celestial elixir. Everything is considered pleasurable but not so the poisonous swoon into which he finally plunges before departure.

156. After one's enemies have been driven away, after riches have been obtained in plenty, the moment a person desires to enjoy them, death descends on him from nowhere.

157 & 158. In a hundred ways, people imagine feelings of attachment towards one another. Life is a journey, in which people come together, in the form of wife, friend, etc., as a result of maya, the cosmic illusion.

159. If the time of successive kalpas is calculated, Brahma's life-time kalpa is akin to a second, and thus when the time is playing a deceptive game, the sense of duration as short or long is also false.

160. A man given to lust is practising various crafty arts; a good man is hard to come across even in dream; all actions are fraught with pain and bereft of value. I know not how to lead the rest of life.

161. Those days, those great ones, those great fortunes, those deeds all have become objects of memory. We too shall shortly be only objects of such memory.

162. Like the waters getting swallowed by Vadavagni during deluge, Brahma, Vishnu and Rudra and all cosmic entities only rush towards destruction.

Vadavagni: Name of all-consuming fire at deluge.

163. Fortunes occur in a second and dangers befall in a second. The life lasts for a second, o seer! What does last longer than a second?

164. A valorous warrior gets killed by a coward. Hundreds get killed by a single person. Lowly men become lords of estates. The world turns things topsy-turvy.

165. In my heart, which has been burnt thus by the evils of life, desires do not arise, as waters in the mirage.

166. I praise not death. I welcome not life. I remain as before, without any feverishness.

167. O seer! If one does not cure one's mind at this stage with a pure intellect, will there be an occasion at all for curing it?

168. Poison is not poisonous; seeing things as good is poisonous. Poison kills but one body; sense-objects kill successive lives.

169. For an enlightened soul, neither pleasures nor sorrows, nor friends, nor relations, nor life nor death constitute bondage.

170. Life is as precarious as the water-drops in the clouds. Enjoyment is as fleeting as the lightning that courses through the dense clouds. The phase of youth is like a rushing torrent. Considering these all, I have restrained the mind from all pursuits, for the sake of peace.

171. Intellect does not get satisfied with any state. Nor does it get what it wants. Being wedded to the jiva, who is its ruler, she is like the bride in the husband's house.

172. What is that state, which is not unreal, which isnot uncertain, which is not unconditioned and which is

devoid of delusion-attaining which, one remains peaceful and is undisturbed by doubt?

173. O courageous soul! How is it that one soaked in vasanas, tendencies, can remain unburnt in fire like the mercury liquid?

174. One cannot remain in this distressing life without activity, as it is not possible to remain in ocean and be untouched by water.

175. O great seer! Do thou teach me that which will dispel the entire delusion. Wise persons are those who have really transcended sorrow.

176 to 180. O seer! If such a means for transcendence of sorrow does not exist, nor do thou choose to teach me clearly and if I am not able to reach that supreme state by my own effort also-let me, discard ego, eat not, drink not; nor adorn myself. I shall not attend to the routine of bathing, gifting and eating. I shall not take interest in happy or unhappy events. I do not, in this condition, desire anything except renunciation of life. Freed from doubt, jealousy and sense of mine, I shall remain motionless like a picture on a wall."

Valmiki said: Thus spoke Rama, who was exuding coolness and who possessed an awakened mind with a discriminating vision. He became quiet before the wise elders, like the peacock before the cloud as a result of the strain caused by its crowing.

Chapter-3

Detachment

1 & 2. As the lotus-eyed prince Rama spoke these words which are capable of dispelling delusion, all those assembled remained wonderstruck, with their eyes enlarged and hairs protruding as though they were eager to hear.

3 & 4. Rama became silent. As siddhas showered words of praise, flowers forming, as it were, a canopy, fell on the assembly.

5.   As the rain of flowers came to a halt, the persons in the assembly heard the siddhas speak thus:

6.   "We, who have been roaming for aeons among siddhas, have not heard such an exposition which is, as it were, a potent elixir.

These words, which Raghunandana has spoken, are nectarine and bring tranquility and elevated understanding. We have been enlightened by him."

7.   Bharadwaja said: "I am eager to hear the considered opinion of the great seers on the ennobling speech of Rama."

8.   Valmiki said: "All the celestial seers descended on the council in a row.

9.   As the celestial seers descended on the hall, the earthly seers in Dasaratha's assembly rose up to receive them.

10.   Vasishta and Visvamitra worshipped them all in appropriate manner. They, in turn, worshipped Vasishta and Visvamitra with fervour.

11.   With sincere devotion, the king worshipped the group of siddhas; who, in turn, honoured the king by enquiring about his welfare.

12.   They all, both by flowers and words of praise, adored Rama, who stood before them with modesty.

13.   The seers said: "Well, words of great merit and value have been spoken by the prince. They are noble and can generate dispassion.

14.   O great seers! In this heartless worldly life which is the handiwork of the perverse maya, it is difficult to come across anything that is good.

15.   If the question of Rama, whose words of wisdom are such as to generate inquiry in the whole world, is not suitably dealt with by us, our wisdom is not worthy of being regarded as such."

16.   As the great seers spoke loudly thus in the assembly, Visvamitra looked at Rama before him with delight in heart.

17.   *Visvamitra said: "Rama, great among the wise, there is nothing that is to be known by you. By your own keen intellect, you have known everything.*

18.   *You have an intellect similar to that of Divine Vyasa's son, Sukha. Even after one gets enlightened, the mind has the need to attain repose."*

19.   Sri Rama asked: "Divine seer! How was it that Vyasa's son Sukha, though enlightened, had not attained repose and attained it later, as a result of perfected understanding.

20.   Visvamitra said, "The story which I narrate is similar to yours, Rama. Listen to the story of Vyasa's son. It puts an end to repeated births.

21. As Sukha contemplated about the course of worldly life, discernment arose in his mind, as it did in you.

22. By his own further rational inquiry for a long time, he knew what is the Truth.

23. Though by himself he had attained the knowledge of Truth, he could not abide in peace. His mind had not attained the conviction, 'This is the Truth.'

24. His mind merely withdrew from the craving for sense-pleasures, which are fleeting in nature, like chataka birds after drinking to the full, turn away from the rain.

25. Once, he of pure intelligence, devoutly requested his father and seer, Krishna Dwaipayana when he was seated alone in the Meru-

26. "O seer! How has this extravagant spectacle of worldly life manifested? How does it subside? How vast is it? Whose work is this? When does it end?"

27. Queried thus, the seer, who has known the Truth, told the son all that could be told about the pure Consciousness.

28. "I have already known this"-with this thought, Sukha, in his wisdom, did not value much the instruction of the father.

29. Vyasa, knowing this opinion of the son, told him again, "Son, I do not know really.

30. There is a king called Janaka on the earth. He knows the Truth as It is. From him, you will obtain all instructions."

31. Thus informed by father, Sukha left the Meru and came to the city of Videha, ruled by Janaka.

32. The noble-minded Janaka was informed by the gate-keepers, "O king! Vyasa's son is at the entrance."

33. As if to study Sukha's mental state, Janaka simply told them, "Let him be there," and remained indifferent for seven days.

34. Thereafter, Sukha was taken into the inner mansion. As before, he remained there for seven more days absorbed in meditation.

35. Then, Janaka had him brought to the inner apartment. Sukha was told that the king would not see him during the next seven days.

36. Janaka treated Sukha of moon-like face, to all kinds of delicious foods and pleasures through infatuating and lovely women.

37. Neither delights, nor sorrows could draw away the mind of Sukha, which was firm like a rock.

38. The blemishless Sukha remained lustrous like a moon, calm like a sea, with a mind pure, silent and joyous.

39. Janaka had Sukha, who had understood the Truth, brought to him. Seeing his delightful countenance, Janaka bowed to him.

40. After welcoming Sukha, Janaka told him, "You have done all that is to be done; you have attained all that you have wished. What is it that you seek now?"

41. Sukha said, "O teacher! How has this extravagant spectacle of worldly life manifested? How does it disappear? Tell me what it really is."

42. Visvamitra said: "Questioned thus by Sukha, Janaka told Sukha what was already told by his father to him earlier.

43 & 44. Sukha said: "Through my own discrimination, I had known this truth before. The same truth was told by my father when requested by me. O master of speech! You have also told me the same truth. This

truth is the import of the scripture as well.

45. This world, which has arisen from one's ignorance, disappears with the extinction of ignorance and worldly life has no other significance.

46. O great warrior! Is it so? Tell me the truth. My mind restlessly roaming all over the world may attain steadiness and from your instruction, attain repose."

47. *Janaka said: "O seer! There is nothing higher apart from this truth to be known. You have known it yourself. You have also known it through the preceptor.*

48. *Immutable, unchanging, consciousness is the reality and nothing else exists. One becomes bound by one's own false thought and one is freed when the false thought becomes extinct.*

49. *The consciousness has been clearly realised by you. That is why you have dispasson towards all pleasures, nay, the entire objective matter.*

50. *You have attained with all your mind that which is to be attained. O seer! You crave not for any objective matter. You are liberated. Abandon the delusion."*

51. Instructed thus by the lofty-minded Janaka, Sukha remained peacefully absorbed in the Supreme Consciousness.

52. Bereft of grief, fear, strain, desires and with a firm mind, he left for Meru for practising samadhi.

53. There, abiding in nirvikalpa samadhi for hundreds of years, he became calm,like the lamp without oil. He attained oneness with the Self.

54. Rid of the blemish of imagination and remaining in one's own pure supreme state, like a waterdrop losing itself into the sea, the noble soul, stripped of all vasanas, impressions, became one with Reality.

55. Visvamitra said: "The taint of ignorance alone had to be removed in the case of Vyasa's son, and the same only is needed to be done in your case as well.

56. That all the sense-pleasures cannot entice the mind is the distinguishing characteristic of the enlightened persons.

57. The contemplation of objects intensifies the bondage though it is unreal; with the desire for objects decreasing, the bondage in the world gets weakened.

58. Rama, attenuation of vasanas, tendencies, is what is called liberation by the wise. Strengthening the tendencies pertaining to objects is called bondage.

59. He who has dispassion towards sense-pleasures, not for the reason that it would bring fame, but as a natural trait is called a liberated soul.

60. Rama, if one knows the reality as the existent principle from the instruction of an enlightened soul, one certainly attains repose.

61. *Let the Divine seer, Sri Vasishta, tender appropriate advice to the noble minded Rama for attaining this repose.*

62. *He has been the preceptor of all the descendants of Raghu. He knows all, witnesses all and sees perfectly all that is past, present and future.*

63 & 64. *O Vasishta! Do you remember the instruction which the great soul Brahma himself gave to both of us, for the pacification of the hatred we had for each other and for our own good? The Lotus-born repeatedly taught spiritual wisdom. That same wisdom do though teach Rama, your pupil.*

65. *That is wisdom, that is teaching of the scripture, that is unsullied scholarship-that which is taught to a*

deserving and dispassionate pupil.

66. That which is taught to one who is not a disciple, not a dispassionate person, becomes impure like the milk kept in a leather cup."

67. As Gadhi's son, Visvamitra spoke thus, seers headed by Vyasa and Narada commended his suggestion.

68. Then spoke the lustrous seer Vasishta, the Brahma's son, who looked like another Brahma and who was sitting near the throne of the king.

69. "O seer! (to Visvamitra) What you have suggested, I shall fulfill without hesitation. Even if one can, would anyone disobey the words of the wise?

70. I·remember perfectly all the truths that were taught to us by the Lotus-born, for the removal of the worldly delusion, on the Nishadhadri Mountain long before."

71. Valmika said: Thus spoke the great seer Vasishta, who summoned the faculties required for an exponent, expounded the wisdom which would lead one to the supreme attainment through the removal of ignorance.

In Visvamitra's opinion, the malady of Rama is similar to that of Sukha and calls for the same kind of remedial step. The story is suggestive of the nature of the teaching that is to follow.

The portion of the original Vasishta Maharamayana summarised in the verses 17 to 71 of this chapter has been included in the bigger work as the first sarga of Mumukshu Vyavahara Prakaranam. In Laghu Yoga Vasishta, this portion has been included in the Vairagya Prakaranam itself.

Section-2
Aspirant's Conduct

Chapter-1

The Conduct of the Spiritual Aspirant

1. *Vasishta said: "Everything, Rama, is always perfectly attained in this world of life by the well-directed effort of jiva, who is Consciousness.*

2. *The effort of the jiva is of two types-that which is not in accord with the scripture and that which is. The former is the cause of sorrow and the latter of supreme happiness.*

3. Through the study of scripture, guidance of the wise, etc., acquired by one since birth and through one's own effort is attained lasting good."

4. Sri Rama said: "I act as prompted by the tendencies of the previous births, O seer! A helpless being I am, what can I do?"

5. Sri Vasishta said: "On account of that very reason, Rama, you will attain eternal beatitude aided by your own personal effort and by nothing else.

6. *The tendencies are two-fold-auspicious and inauspicious. The tendencies of the past lives may belong to both the categories or one category only.*

7. If you are led by auspicious tendencies, those

tendencies themselves will lead you progressively to the supreme beatitude.

8. If inauspicious tendencies drag you to difficult situations, then they have to be vanquished by you, through effort.

9. *The stream of tendencies flows in two directions- towards good and bad. Through one's personal effort the tendencies must be turned towards the good channel.*

10. When the mind is dragged towards the bad channel, O courageous soul, turn it through great effort towards the good one, which is beneficial to oneself.

11. The mind is akin to a child. The mind turned away from the evil attaches itself to the good and vice versa. Therefore draw it away forcibly to the righteous one.

12. Calm the mind, slowly and not at once, by pacifying counselling as though you fondle the child.

13. When the good tendencies manifest in mind, know that the practice of turning the mind away from evil tendencies has yielded fruit.

14. In a doubtful situation, when one is not sure that a particular course is good or not, do that which is known to be good. If more of good tendencies accumulate, no flaw arises thereby.

15. *As long as your inner mind is not awakened, as long as you have not realised the supreme inner principle, do abide by the code envisaged by the scripture and the preceptors.*

16. *Thereafter, when you have evolved and realised the inner Consciousness, all tendencies, including the auspicious ones, have to be discarded by you.*

17. By following a path that is ennobling and adhered to by wise persons, that is good and pleasing, attain the state free from sorrow. Afterwards abandon that path as well and remain at peace.

18 to 20. By discarding once for all the world of thought, by making the mind peaceful and happy, by making the intellect capable of weighing the pros and cons of a viewpoint, remaining in Consciousness, do thou listen, O Rama, to what was taught by Brahma. His counsel wipes away all sorrows and endows the mind with poise."

21. Sri Rama asked: "Why did Brahma give this counsel and how was it sought by you, tell me, O great preceptor!"

22. Vasishta said: "There exists Infinite Consciousness-all-supporting, all-pervasive and capable of manifesting all objects. It is the immutable Self.

23. From that, which is both pro-active and non-active, arose Vishnu and from the lotus-heart of Him arose Brahma.

24. And Brahma created the entire cosmos, as mind generates thoughts. After seeing that the humanity, especially in this Bharata-varsha is steeped in misery, the Creator-God was moved by compassion, as a father is moved by son's distress.

25 & 26. He thought intently for a while. How could these short-lived people, with their desires unfulfilled, end their sorrows? Penance, charity, japa, pilgrimage, etc., do not completely remove one's sorrows.

27. Therefore, let me teach the supreme wisdom for transcendence of sorrow.

28. Deliberating thus, the Progenitor, seated in the lotus,

by his mental resolve, created me.

29.   With the water-jug in my hand, I prostrated to Him, who was holding in His hands water-jug and rosary and sought His blessings.

30 & 31. "Come child. Thus calling me, the unborn God seated me in the northern petal of the lotus and spoke, "Let your mind be under the spell of ignorance for a few minutes and be unsteady like a monkey, like a water-drop on mirror."

32.   Thus admonished by him during the talk, I forgot my inherent pure nature.

33.   I began to feel miserable and restless in mind. Like a person in abject condition, I was plagued by sorrow.

34.   Then, He came to me asking, "Why are you grief-stricken? You can seek remedy for sorrow from me and attain happiness."

35 & 36. Thereafter, I duly sought instruction from the Divine Creator, the anti-dote to worldly existence. 'How, O God, the worldly life full of misery has come upon one and how does it get terminated?' The noble soul taught me completely the supreme wisdom. Having got the wisdom, I now remain happy.

37.   After I became enlightened and steady in the attitude towards life, the Creator God spoke these words full of import.

38 to 42. *Though you were wise, I made you an ignorant person and seek wisdom so that all the people may benefit by this essence of knowledge. Now you are freed from the curse and are in the exalted state of Realisation. Go to the earth and to the Bharata-Varsha in the Jambu-dwipa for the benefit of mankind. Those who are attached to the performance of ritual have to*

be taught by you about the proper method of doing it. On the other hand, those who have an inquiring disposition and are dispassionate have to be taught by you wisdom that leads to attainment of bliss.'

43. *Instructed thus by the father, the Lotus-born, I remain here on earth for over ages fulfilling the task.*

44. There is nothing to be done by me here. All the same, I remain on the earth because I have been so directed. With a mind fully calm, as though asleep, I keep doing the task of performing or non-performing certain acts.

45. What is wisdom? What is ignorance? Who is capable of enlightening the seeker? He who knows after due deliberation all these subjects and puts question to the preceptor is a real aspirant.

46. The enlightened seer should proceed to teach wisdom to the person who is capable of understanding the subject in the context of what has been said before and after and not to a one who is dull like an animal.

47. *At the entrance of the mansion of liberation there are four gate keepers-tranquility, inquiry, contentment and wise company.*

48. *All these four-or three or two of them-should be acquired by one with great effort As in the royal mansion they open up the door of liberation.*

49. At least, do thou cultivate one by abandoning everything else. If one is won, all the four are won in due course.

50. Through study of scripture, guidance of the wise, penance, self-control etc., develop desire for the attainment of liberation.

51. O Rama, the disease caused by the poisonous worldly life is dreadful. It is annihilated by the efficacious

Garuda mantra of yoga.

One who is bitten by the poisonous serpent gets cured by the mantra associated with Garuda. Samsara, worldly life, is represented as a poisonous disease and yoga of identity of the Self with the Supreme is the appropriate Garuda-mantra that can cure it-V.C.

52 & 53. The disease caused by the poison of the sense-objects is fierce. If not cured in time, it leads to extra-ordinary suffering in the hell where one is subjected to sharp cuts by swords, blows by stones, burning in fire. bathing in ice, severance of limbs, grinding into paste, exposure to continuous rains, severance of head, denial of sleep, gagging of mouth etc.

54. Therefore, one should attach importance to scriptural study, one should investigate its meaning and understand the teaching. The inquiry should be done in such a way as to lead to the realisation of Truth.

55. *If by steady practice one understands that one's self-experience, teaching of the scripture and the teaching of the preceptor are in perfect accord with one another, one will abide always in the Supreme Consciousness.*

This is an important teaching of Vasishta. By study of scripture, one arrives at the purport of the scripture. One's own reflection attains culmination as experience. The preceptor's teaching conveys the nature of Reality. All the three modes of understanding should lead to an identical experience. Such experience is perfect experience of Reality.

56. If this scripture-Maha-Ramayana-is studied by persons of even limited understanding it removes their stupidity, as no other scripture does.

57. It is better to walk along the slums with a bottle of

liquor and a begging bowl than be born as a stupid person.

58 & 59. Wealth saves not, friends, and relations help not. Nor physical exercises like asanas or pilgrimage or fasts or holy waters help a man to attain goodness. Only through conquest of mind, supreme beatitude is attained.

60. Listen, who the four gate-keepers in the mansion of liberation are. Acquaintance with even one of four gains for you entry into the mansion of liberation.

61. *Sorrows, desires, afflictions get destroyed like darkness before sun, in the case of persons with calm minds.*

62. All creatures, cruel and otherwise, repose faith in him, as they do in the kind mother.

63. A person does not experience that kind of happiness, either through drinking of elixir or embrace of Lakshmi which he gets through a mind imbued with tranquility.

64. While hearing, touching, seeing, eating, smelling pleasing or painful things, he who does not get elated or grief-stricken, can be said to be a calm person.

65. He whose mind is as serene as the full moon and who remains unagitated, during occasions like death, festival, etc., is said to be a calm person.

66. Among persons great in penance, learning, performance of vedic rites, royal power, physical strength, virtue, it is the person who possesses calmness that receives recognition.

67. Tranquility, cherished by the wise, is what those who have reached the supreme state, have relied upon and you may also develop calmness and tranquility to achieve the goal.

68. By an earnest seeker should be done constantly enquiry with a mind that has been rendered pure by the blemishless teaching of the scripture.

69. Intellect, rendered sharper through inquiry, cognises the Supreme. For the prolonged malady of samsara, the worldly life, inquiry is the effective medicine.

70. Who am I? Who is experiencing this worldly life?-thus even during dangerous situations a person must keep reflecting, as he explores the means to counter the problems of life.

71. Inquiry equips one with a wonderful vision, which fails not, even during darkness, which does not get neutralised by effulgence and which enables one to see even distant things.

72. *Who am I? How has this worldly life come upon me? - to reflect on these questions in a rational way, is called inquiry.*

73. Contentment leads one to supremely beneficial state. Contentment gives happiness. A contented person attains supreme poise.

74. For those who have attained great fulfillment through the elixir of contentment, the worldly pleasures, as it were, are akin to adverse poison.

75. *He craves not for things unattained and in respect of things attained, he remains in a composed frame of mind-a person who does not know elation or grief is a contented person.*

76. In the tainted mirror of the mind, that knows no contentment and is tossed by passions, wisdom does not manifest.

77. He seeks not the unattained and enjoys things already attained in peaceful manner-such a person is a

contented person.

78. O Rama! Even rulers and great saints bow to one who is even-minded and is also endowed with other great attributes.

79. *O great warrior! Especially in the task of transcending samsara, worldly life, that which helps one most in various ways, is the guidance of the wise.*

80. A deserted place is full of persons; occasion of death becomes a festival; and adversity turns into affluence- if the company of the wise is at hand.

81. *What has he, who bathes in the cool Ganga of wise company, to benefit by gifts, holy waters, penance and yoga?*

82. Those wise persons, who have been regarded as such by all and whose knot of ignorance has been destroyed, have to be adored by all means. For they indeed are the saviours of others from the ocean of worldly life.

83. These Sama, Santosha, Satsangha and Vichara, are the four unfailing means for the warding of worldly existence. Those who practise these four climb up the shore of the ocean of delusion.

84. Possessing all these attributes mentioned above in the fullest measure, Rama, do thou listen my instruction which dispels the gloom of the mind.

85. O destroyer of foes! Those who merely listen to the stories concerning means of liberation, even if they do not aspire for liberation, attain high understanding.

86. The evil traits like miserliness, delusion etc., of the intellect get eliminated and mind attains to serenity, as the lake after the rainy season.

87. Helplessness, poverty and other evils do not attack

the vulnerable parts of the person, who has protected himself with the armour of discrimination.

88. Frightful events of life do not scare heroes. A great evenness of temper arises in the person, as after the churning has come to an end, in the ocean.

89. The depth and majesty of the ocean, the firmness of Meru, the coolness of the moon, characterise the one having the inquiring disposition.

90. He delights in the activities that are in conformity with the scripture, as they arise, as a person delights in the company of his chaste wife in the inner apartment.

91. He, in whom all basic cravings have ceased, evolves gradually into the state of jivanmukti, liberation while alive, which is beyond description.

92. He is seen like an ordinary person who gets satisfied with things that naturally come to him. But his mind does not succumb to pleasures and pains, whenever they manifest.

93 to 95. The person who is comfortably seated, who eats what is available, who delights in pleasures that are not opposed to virtuous conduct, who is satisfied with the happiness of the moment, who in the company of the wise undertakes the study of this work, Maharamayana, dealing with the means of liberation, attains supreme awareness, that is capable of giving peace and avoiding future suffering and rebirth.

96. Those who are unafraid of sins, who are immoral in pursuit of pleasures, are fit for wallowing in the dirt and such men need not be considered here.

97 & 98. Study of scriptures, inner peace, tenderness, wisdom, company of the wise-these should be

practised along with other traits that manifest and possessed with these virtues, one should practise enquiry, until mind attains supreme repose in the Consciousness, the bliss of the turiya, the transcendental joy.

99 & 100. For the one-be he a householder or otherwise-who has attained the transcendental repose, emancipation from the ocean of life, there is nothing to be gained by life or death, by action or inaction or by scriptural ramblings. He remains unperturbed like the ocean after the churning has ceased.

101. Rama, listen to the very essence of wisdom, being expounded by me in a thorough measure.

102. *Whatever is in accord with reason should be accepted, even if it comes from a child. Whatever is otherwise should be rejected, even if Brahma were to utter it.*

103. Whatever examples are given by me to illustrate a truth, are relevant only in the intended aspect and not in other aspects. They are relevant in the context of teaching wisdom about Brahman and they are appropriate only in those aspects where there is similarity. Let this idea be well understood.

104 to 106. Even then, stupid men raise theoretical questions of this type-how in respect of transcendental Brahman, empirical examples can be given? One should not question the wisdom arising from experience, by resorting to logic, that does not recognise true Self-experience.

107. *Traits like tranquility enrich wisdom and wisdom enriches the virtues. They lend support to each other as the lotus and pond lend elegance to each other.*

108. Only when wisdom and the practice of virtues are

together pursued effectively, they are productive of result and not when only either is pursued.

109. This scripture will confer on one fame, longevity and attainment of supreme happiness. Hearing it will make the intelligent pure and one will get ushered into transcendental awareness.

110. Having known the Truth that should be known, the mind experiences the supreme peace. The Reality is experienced in its unconditioned and unveiled state and the mind never swerves from this experience.

Section-3
Creation

Chapter-1

Mode of Creation

1.   I have recounted to you the conduct of the seeker. Now, the Creation of the Universe is being described.

2.   The supreme awareness, or knowledge or Consciousness, that is most immediate- -aparoksha- is termed as jiva, soul from the viewpoint of Vedanta.

     The Consciousness that manifests in the aspect of Self, as the immediate principle is jiva.

3.   He is Intelligence; is the being endowed with ego-sense. Whatever will or desire he has, that manifests as the objective thing.

4.   The Supreme Being, through His will and contemplation, turns into manifested world, as the stream of water turns into waves.

     The Supreme Intelligence, at the time of creation, initially assumes, as it were, an objective form, then manifests as chitta, ahamkara, buddhi and manas. This sequence of creation is made clear in the later portion.

5.   That which was really no cause becomes a cause, as it were, through the sportive creation, and the Self is the substrate of this illusory world.

6

6. The word experience comprises of perceptions and concepts and the Consciousness contains them within it, as wind contains with in it movement.

8. The Supreme Intelligence manifests in the form it wills-as external space, time, and internal entities.

9. It is in the nature of sarvatma, all-pervasive being, to manifest in the manner it imagines. It manifests as the very thing.

10. Bondage arises on account of the objective existence and when there is no objective existence, there is no bondage. This objective matter does not exist, and how it is so, I shall describe. Listen.

The objective matter includes the world, the entities referred to as 'I' and 'You.' Cognition of these entails the additional manifestation as 'doer' and 'enjoyer.' Doership and enjoyership constitute the bondage. Bondage will cease to exist when the objective matter is known to be non-existent. The aim of Vasishta's teachings is to progressively lead the seeker to the conviction that the objective world does not exist.

11. All that is seen as world comprising of the movable and the immovable gets destroyed at the time of deluge, as dream gets destroyed in sleep.

12. At the time of the deluge, only the unmoving Reality, the unconditioned Consciousness which is neither light nor darkness remains.

13. Of that Supreme Being, terms like Reality, Self, Brahman, Truth, have been coined by the wise, for the sake of worldly usage.

14. The Self as described above alienating from Itself and appearing as other than that, becomes, as it were, jiva, who is subject to misery.

The method of creation is as follows: Prior to creation what is the non-dual Supreme Self, assumes at the time of creation, indistinct objective form, thence collective mind, collective jiva, ahamkara, buddhi, manas, subtle elements and distinct objects-V.C.

15. The being that is referred to as jiva given to imagination and contemplation becomes manas, which through further thinking becomes gross in nature.

16. From the Supreme Self, from the immutable Being, has thus come into existence manas, mind, the everchanging one as wave rises in the water.

17. The manas spontaneously and always keeps imagining and, as a result, the spectacle of world originates.

18. As apart from gold there is no word or thing called bracelet, and as gold does not exist except in the form of bracelet, world and Brahman are causally related.

19. It is the non-existent stream of water that appears to flow with waves in a mirage; it is through mind the delusive panoramic world is fancied as existing.

20. The knowers of Veda refer to this by various names-nescience, worldly life, delusion, bondage, cosmic power, taint, darkness.

21. Listen' to this description of the nature of bondage. Then, O Rama, you will know the nature of liberation.

22. *The assumed reality of the seer and the seen, my dear, is what constitutes bondage. The seer becomes subject to bondage on account of the seen. If the seen becomes non-existent, the seer attains freedom.*

When the seen becomes non-existent, through the comprehension of Reality, the seer also ceases to be the seer and there is liberation.

23. The world (I-you-complex) comprising the created is called the seen. As long as the seen exists, there is no prospect of liberation.

24. As the lotus creeper abides in an unmanifest form in the lotus seed, the unmanifest universe exists in the seer (during dissolution, sleep, etc)

25. The seedling existing in an unmanifest form in the seed, manifests in grown up form, when the appropriate time-space conditons are present. So is the seen universe.

26. As the potency to manifest in the name and form of creeper in future exists veiled in the bosom of the seed, so the future world exists potentially in the bare consciousness.

27. Listen to the story of Akasaja, which is pleasant to hear. Rama, you will clearly understand the subject of the discourse-nature of creation.

28. There is a very righteous brahmana called Akasaja. Always absorbed in meditation, he is devoted to the welfare of all beings. Akasa: Consciousness; Akasaja: One who has emanated from Consciousness.

29 to 31. He has been living for a very - long time and so Mrityu (Messenger of Death) reflected, 'I have been devouring all beings without obstructon; why am I not able to devour this brahmana? My capacity gets blunted when I get into his presence.'

Thinking thus, he went to the city of Akasaja to kill him. Enterprising persons do not discard their chosen task at any time.

32. Even before he reached the abode of Akasaja, Mrityu was surrounded by a raging fire, akin to the one during deluge.

33.   He broke the cordon of the effulgent fire and entered. Seeing the brahmana, he desired to grab him by the hand with effort.

34.   Though the brahmana was before him, he was not able to get at him with any number of hands, as one cannot grab an imaginary being.

35.   Then, returning to his master, who is capable of solving the doubt, he asked, 'How is it, O lord, I am unable to devour Akasaja?'

36.   Yama said: 'Mrityu, thou art not capable of killing anyone by force. The one to be killed gets killed by his deeds of sins, not by anything else.

37.   Therefore, if the brahmana is to be killed, you have to find out through effort, the past deed of sins and with their help you may devour him.'

38 & 39.   Thereon, Mrityu wandered over the earth and looked out for his deeds. Different lands and lakes in all the directions he covered. Despite having roamed over the entire earth, he, through earnest effort, could not find anything anywhere, which were the past deeds of Akasaja.

40 & 41.   Returning to the all-knowing Dharmaraja, he asked, 'For the servants, the masters are the ultimate refuge in matters of doubt. O master, tell me where do the past deeds of Akasaja abide?'

Dharmaraja reflected for a long time and replied thus:

42 & 43.   'O Mrityu, no deeds of Akasaja exist. This brahmana is born of Akasa only. He who is born of Akasa is only Akasa proper. There are no subsidiary causes that bring about his existence as apart from that of Akasa.

44.   When there are no subsidiary causes operating, the one that is born as effect is not different from the main

cause and this fact is borne out of experience like that of dream.

45. 'Mrityu! Do not venture to capture him.' Hearing these words, Mrityu became surprised and returned home.

The viewpoint of Vasishta explained in verses 42 to 45 is this: In the case of clay getting converted into pot, clay is the material cause (upadana karana); pot-maker is the instrumental cause (nimitta karana); and other factors like wheel, water, etc., are subsidiary causes (sahakari karana). Vasishta considers all causal categories apart from the principal one (the material cause: clay in the case of pot) as subsidiary ones. The point that he emphasises is that where there are no subsidiary causes operating and where there is only the principal cause, the effect (karya) is not at all different from the cause. In the case of the Brahman becoming jiva or jagat, there is present the only cause, that is, Brahman and there are no subsidiary causes. In all such cases, what is 'effect' is not really different from 'cause.' In fact, cause itself appears as effect. In the present story, Akasaja is not different from Akasa, that is, he is pure Brahman. This is an essential teaching of Vasishta and will be repeatedly stressed by him.

46. Sri Rama said: "The brahmana referred to by you is only Brahma, the lotus-born, the Cosmic soul who is of the nature of Consciousness, I suppose."

47. Vasishta said: "Great warrior! It is, as you have said, Brahma was spoken about as the brahmana. This conversation of Yama with Mrityu happened in a bygone age.

48. At the time of another Manu, when the all-devouring Mrityu swallowed the people, he acquiring added

strength, and attempted to capture Brahma.

49. At that time, he was duly instructed by Yama (Dharmaraja) thus: "How can Brahma of the nature of Consciousness be ever caught?"

50. "He is akin to an imaginary person manifesting in the space and the Lotus-born is not associated with material elements like earth.

51. He is the self-born, is self-like, infinite, with no beginning and end, is called Brahma, manifesting with form from the point of view of the seer endowed with mind, etc., but in reality, he, like the barren woman's son, has no body.

52. O Rama, the self-born has only ethereal body. A gross body is not an appropriate one for him."

53. Sri Rama asked: "For all the creatures, there is a gross body in addition to an ethereal body. How is it that Brahma has only an ethereal body?"

54. Vasishta said: "For all those creatures who have originated from a causal being, there are two bodies. Inasmuch as the unborn (Brahma) has no such cause, he has only an ethereal body.

55. All others, along with world have sprung from the imagination of Brahma; as for the unborn Brahma, Brahman is the cause and therefore he has only an ethereal body.

56. Brahma is a mental being unassociated with elements like earth. Himself of the nature of the mind, he is the cause of all the three worlds.

From the point of view of Drishti-srishti vada (perception-as-creation theory), mind is the cause of the universe and not the subtle cosmic elements. Mind which is consciousness creates the universe. According to the general theory, normally upheld by advaitic preceptors, the world already created from elements is perceived by the mind (Srishti-drishti vada).

57. The world is formed by Brahma, the self-born, through an act of will and so the world that is perceived is mental only."

58. Sri Rama asked: "O Divine seer! What is the nature of the mind, as it is from the mind, the world abounding in vast evil has emanated? Do explain in detail."

59. Vasishta said: "O Rama, mind is not perceived to have any form. It has only the name. It is like space, which is devoid of all material substance.

60. Mind, which has no substantial form exists neither outside nor in the heart, but O Rama, it exists like space everywhere.

61. O wise man, whatever knowledge arises of whichever object, whether real or unreal, that is manifestation of the mind.

62. The knowledge of any object arises from the mind. Apart from this, there is nothing called mind any time.

63. *Imagining is the trait of the mind. Mind is not different from imagination. Let it be known that where there is imagination, there is mind.*

64 & 65. Imagination and mind are never two distinct entities. O Rama, nescience, worldly life, chitta, mind, bondage, taint, darkness-these are the terms by which the imaginary world-spectacle is referred to.

66. When all these-directions, space, earth, etc., become non-existent, luminous awareness that shines is that of the mind.

67. The entire complex of seen matter-the three worlds, you and I-ceasing to exist, the seer attains to a pure

state and that is the nature of the untainted Self.

68. When the mirror remains as a mere mirror, without carrying reflections of the mountains etc., that would be similar to the nature of the pure Self.

69. When the delusive spectacle of the seen matter (I - you - world - complex) becomes extinct and when the seer no longer sees, there is the pure Self.

70. It is mind that creates the evil of the seen world, perishable in nature, turns the non-existent into the existent, as one dreams within dream.

71. Mind, vascillating by nature, manifests, manipulates, goes, begs, roams about, gets engrossed, withdraws into itself, sinks to a low condition, and at last attains to exalted emancipation and oneness (with Truth).

72 & 73. When the entire seen world gets dissolved in the deluge, the tranquil supreme spirit alone abides. The luminous, blemishless, unborn spirit alone remains. He is the Supreme Lord, the Supreme Self. He is all and the doer of everything.

The nature of the Supreme Reality at the time of deluge and at the time of liberation is explained in these and the following verses.

74. That which words fail to reach, that which is cognised only by the liberated ones is indicated by the terms like Self and these are not descriptive of its nature.

75 & 76. He is known as Purusha by the followers of the Sankhya school, as Brahman by the adherents of the Vedantic school, mere Intelligence by the school of Buddhists called Vijnanavadis, mere Void by the school of Buddhists called Sunyavadhis. He illumines even the effulgent Sun, is ever the speaker, thinker, the

principle of design, the enjoyer, the seer, the recogniser.

77. Although He is existent, He appears to be non-existent. Though He abides in the body, He is different from it. He is of the nature of Consciousness, as the sun is mere effulgence.

78. The primordial matter is the creeper projected by the mind that has grown into the space, with the cosmos as the fruit, mind as the root, the senses as the leaves.

79. That jewel of Consciousness shines in each casket, as it were, of body and bears the city-of-eight elements, (puryashtaka-the linga sarira) as it moves hither and thither.

Five senses of knowledge-(1) five senses of action-(2) the mind-(3)the prana-(4) the cosmic elements-(5) kama (desire)-(6) karma (action)-(7)and tamas (nescience)-(8) constitute the eight elements of the linga-sarira (subtle body), also called as puryashtaka, which carries the jiva from one world to another, after the death of gross body.

80. Inasmuch as he is pure Consciousness, he assumes the form of space by intensely thinking about it. He, as it were, becomes the very object he thinks about.

81. All the three worlds are like the waves that arise and merge in the ocean of Consciousness. They are like the delusive wave in the stream of mirage.

82. Although he conjures up the vast universe, he never creates really anything any time. He abides in the self of unconditioned awareness, ever present and never ceasing to be Consciousness that is his being.

83. "The knot of the heart, of ignorance, is cut asunder, all doubts get dispelled, all actions become extinct-

when the Supreme Being is realised."

84. Sri Rama asked: "O Divine Seer! How could this Brahmanda, the vast universe, perceived by us, be non-existent? Could a grain of stone contain the Meru?"

85. *Sri Vasishta said: "If you betake to the study of the right scripture and counsel of the wise, not in months but in days, you will attain the supreme realisation mentioned above.*

86. *This work (Vasishta Maha Ramayana), is the essence of all the scriptures and if it is properly studied, spiritual liberation ensues.*

87. *The realisation of Truth springs in the heart, if you keep always enquiring into it. The world, though seemingly manifesting, will melt away through enquiry.*

The illusory world has existence, only till its substrate, the Supreme Consciousness, is realised. When that is realised through inquiry, the world, though visible, becomes virtually non-existent.

88. Those human beings who are exclusively absorbed in the inquiry into the self, attain liberation while being alive or after death."

89. Sri Rama asked: "O Divine seer! Do thou describe to me the traits of the one liberated - after - death and the one liberated-while-alive, so that I may aspire to be either one along scripture-guided lines."

90. Vasishta said: "Even when he is attending to the worldly affairs, for the Jivanmukta the seeming world is virtually non-existent and is mere empty space.

91. *The lustre of his face neither brightens nor darkens when joy or grief visits him. He who remains satisfied*

91

with things as they happen is a Jivanmukta.

92. *Though awake, he is in sleep-like condition and there is really no waking-state for him. He whose consciousness is not coloured by past tendencies is Jivanmukta.*

93. Even when he is susceptible to desire, hatred, fear, etc., he is inwardly pure and unaffected like space. Such a person is a Jivanmukta.

94. He who is not ego-tainted and whose intellect is not sullied by attachment, whether he acts or not, is a Jivanmukta.

95. He by whom the world is not frightened and who is not also frightened of the world, such a one, freed from elation, hatred and fear is a Jivanmukta.

96. He, in whom all the restless worldly strivings have become stilled, he who though talented appears to be otherwise, he who though thoughtful, is without thought-such a one is a Jivanmukta.

97. He who goes through all kinds of experiences, as though he is a mere onlooker and remains inwardly cool and whole, is a Jivanmukta.

98. *When the body due to passage of time, drops dead, the seer abandoning the state, attains to the disembodied state of liberation, like the wind discarding its activity of movement.*

99. The seer-in-disembodied state, is neither aware nor unaware, neither existent nor non-existent, neither near nor far, neither identified with oneself nor identified with another.

100. It is the majestic impregnable awareness that he is, he is neither effulgence nor darkness. He is unnamable and unmanifest. He abides as pure existence.

101. He is neither formless nor associated with forms. He is neither the seer nor the seen, nor the cosmic entities. He abides as all-pervasive existence.

102. He cannot be identified, and remains as the perfect absolute. He is not existent nor non-existent, nor both nor thoughtlessness nor conception.

103. He is bare consciousness, unassociated with the seen world. He is the infinite, an unaging and blissful being. He is without beginning and middle and is without disease and blemish.

104. O wise man! By getting absorbed in that consciousness which manifests as the seer, seeing and seen, one attains the Supreme Awareness."

105. Sri Rama asked: "What is the form of the Supreme Reality which is bliss and consciousness? Do thou again describe to me so that my understanding of it may become more clear."

106. Vasishta said: "At the time of the final deluge, the cause of all causes, Brahman alone subsists. Listen to the description.

107. When the mental modifications, become extinct and identification with the gross body ceases, the unnamable awareness that remains is the nature of the Supreme Self.

108. When the individuated consciousness is not inclined towards the objective matter, the consciousness that abides as pure and tranquil is the nature of the Supreme Reality.

109. Because of the non-identification with the body, etc., the knowledge that springs in the mind during sense-experiences (like contact with the wind, etc., which,

93

however, does not cause any sensation) is of the nature of the Self experience.

110. O great soul! That state of the individuated consciousness which is beyond the waking, dreaming, and sleeping states and which is akin to a long sleep, is the nature of the Supreme Self.

111. The beginingless consciousness, which manifests as cognition of the external object and which is aware of the ignorance of oneself is the nature of the Supreme Self.

112. The state of being still, like the inert stone, even when one is engrossed in objective experiences - and appears as conditioned space, though really remaining unconditioned - is the nature of the Supreme Self.

113. That consciousness in which the seer, seeing and the seen together arise and disappear is the nature of the Supreme Self.

114. The inert object which is not associated with mind and intellect and which, if could become imbued with consciousness, can be compared to the Supreme.

115. The non-dual pure consciousness, which follows the merger of Brahma, Arka (sun), Vishnu, Hara, Indra, Sadasiva, etc., which is tranquil and blissful, which is bereft of all adjuncts and therefore is undifferentiated, is acosmic and is the nature of the Supreme Self.

Chapter-2

The Story of Lila

1. Vasishta said: Now, do thou listen to the beautiful story of Mandapa, which without doubt will make your mind attain to supreme repose.

2. There was on this vast earth, a luminous scion called Padma-a lotus as it were of the family-a wise and prosperous king endowed with many sons.

3. In the matter of not transgressing the limit, he was the ocean; to the darkness of hatred, he was the sun; he was a lake abounding in hamsas of good qualities; he was a fire to the grass of all evil.

4. He had an accomplished and charming wife called Lila. She possessed all the signs of prosperity and was verily Lakshmi born on earth.

5. When her husband was worried, she was worried; when he was delighted, she was delighted; when he was despondent, she was despondent. She was, as though, a veritable image of him. But when he was angry, she became simply frightened.

6 & 7. She, who was always of righteous inclination, once reflected: "My husband is dearer to me than even my breath. How can this young, prosperous king be always eternal without being susceptible to old age and death? He can I live happily with him for thousands of years?

8. I shall consult those brahmanas, great in wisdom, penance and learning and ask how death is averted by the human beings?"

9.   Resolving thus, she invited brahmanas, worshipped them and in due humility asked them repeatedly, "O brahmanas, how is immortality attained?"

10.   The brahmanas replied: "All temporal accomplishments (siddhis) are attained through penance, repetition of mantras, discipline, etc., but immortality is not attained by any means."

11.   Hearing thus from the brahmanas, she fearing separation from the beloved plunged into deep thoughts again thus:

12.   'If due to fate I happen to die earlier than my husband then, released from all sorrows I will firmly abide in the bliss of Self...

13.   If unexpectedly my husband dies far earlier, let me so ensure that his jiva (soul) does not leave this abode, this hall.

14.   In the presence of his soul abiding in this very abode and within the range of his vision, I will live happily.

15.   Commencing from today itself, I shall worship Saraswati, the Goddess of wisdom through recitations, fast, spiritual discipline, etc., until she is pleased to fulfill the wish.'

16.   Resolving thus, without even informing her husband, the beautiful lady began practising severe austerity as prescribed in the scripture.

17.   She took food only every third night and worshipped gods, brahmanas, the preceptor, the wise persons and the learned ones during the fast.

18.   She incessantly pursued bathing in sanctified waters, charity, penance, meditation, etc., and attended to all righteous deeds that dispelled physical pain.

19. That young woman completed hundred three-day long fasts, and, disciplined as she was, she adhered to the rigorous austerity assiduously.

20. The Goddess of Speech, Gauri, getting delighted with her austerity in the form of three-day fast continuously for hundred times and worship of her, spoke to her thus:

21. "I am delighted with your uninterrupted austerity born out of your exceeding affection for your husband. Child! Seek whatever boon you desire."

22. The princess replied: "Glory to the Goddess whose moon-like radiance removes the heat of sorrows caused by the fire of birth, old age, etc.! Glory to the Goddess whose sun-like effulgence destroys the dense darkness of the heart!

23. O! My mother and Mother of the universe, Do thou save this abject being. Do grant me the two boons I pray for.

24. The first prayer is that my husband's soul, on death, should not go away from this abode where I am.

25. The second prayer is this: O Goddess, whenever I desire to see you, you should appear and grant me thy vision."

26. Hearing this prayer, the Mother of the Universe said: "Let thy wish be fulfilled," and later disappeared as wave into the ocean.

27. Thereon, the princess with the blessing of her chosen deity became a delighted person and glowed like the full moon filled with elixir.

28. The ever moving wheel of time with fortnight, month and season as the outer orb, days as spokes, year as axle, and minute as hub, rotated.

29. The soul of her husband began to sink in body. When the ruler died, she became extremely afflicted with sorrow and, like the lotus creeper starved of water, became miserable.

30. Suddenly she cried and suddenly she fell silent. Like the proud chakravaka bird, she was keen to court death.

31. When she was thus extremely depressed, the compassionate Goddess appearing in the sky, showered kindness on her, like the first rains assuaging the sorrow of the fishes in a lake gone almost dry.

32. Saraswati said: "My child, did you think of me? Why are you immersed in sorrow?" Saying thus, Jnapti, the Goddess of wisdom, approached her.

33. "Keep this dead body of your husband covered within a heap of flowers and you will get him back again.

34. The flowers will fade not, nor will he die. He will be your husband again.

35. His soul will not go away from the vast space within your abode."

36. After hearing these divine words, she arranged to keep the body under flowers. Thereafter, approaching the Goddess, Lila asked:

37. "Where does reside my husband now? What does he do now? Do thou take me to him, I am unable to remain separated from him."

38. *Jnapti (Saraswati) said: "Beautiful woman, there are chitta-akasa (mind-space), chid-akasa (consciousness-space), and the bhuta-akasa (outer space). The chid-akasa is subtler than the other two.*

In order that Lila may be enabled to see the present condition of her husband within the space of her abode, the Goddess Saraswati explains to her the nature of Brahman, the Supreme Reality. When Brahman is realised and when the mind concentrates on it, one acquires the ability to see things not normally perceived by ordinary persons.

Chitta is also termed as space because of its purity and subtlety-VC

39. *O charming woman, know that when the mind cognises one object after another object, the awareness that manifests between the two cognitions is the nature of consciousness, chid-akasa and that is attained in a minute.*

When the first cognitive mental mode subsides and before the subsequent mental mode arises, the awareness that spontaneously manifests is not related to any object and it is of the nature of consciousness. That which manifests between two successive cognitions and is therefore called the interval is really chid-akasa, the supreme consciousness - VC.

40. *If in that condition you are able to abide absolutely without any thought, you will then attain to the all-pervasive tranquil plane without doubt.*

41. Through the understanding that this world does not at all exist, that state is attained, and not otherwise. You will attain that state, beautiful lady, as a result of my boon."

42. Vasishta said: "After saying this the Goddess returned to Her celestial abode. Lila, as if it were a play for her, rose to superconscious plane in meditation and remained absorbed in it.

Nirvikalpa samadhi is a super-consciousness experience in which all mental activity ceases and in which the cogniser, the cognised and the cognition do not manifest.

43. Instantly discarding identification with the cage of the mind and like the bird leaving the nest and taking to the sky, she soared into the space.

44. In the space of that very abode, she saw her husband happy as a sovereign ruler with several kings as vassals (in a different kingdom)

45 to 47. He was seen seated in a mighty throne. Courtiers sang his glory. The eastern entrance of his mansion was filled with brahmanas and seers. The northern entrance was full of chariots, elephants, horses, etc. The southern entrance was teeming with numberless maidens with attractive looks. She descended into the council unseen before the king.

48 to 50. That same land., those very events, those very bards (who were in Padma's court) as also new persons, scholars, friends, the same land consisting of rivers, mountains, and the king who had ascended the throne in his eighteenth year, when his father had left for the woods-she saw and became extremely surprised.

The princess rose up into the sky and emerged in the abode of hers.

51. She devoutly thought of the Goddess Jnapti and, instantly saw Her in front, sitting on a throne. Lila standing on the earth asked Her:

52. "How did my husband's jiva, incorporeal as it is, transmigrate from one world of creation to another, though illusory. Do thou tell me so that my delusion of the world may be dispelled."

53. The Goddess said: "As on account of the previous memory, this world of illusion has sprung up, the

second world of your husband has also manifested because of memory and how it is so, I shall explain, listen."

The entire creation is only an illusion. The Vedantic view-point is that the previous illusory world is the cause of the present one and the present is the cause of the future one. VC

54.   Somewhere in the chid-akasa, there is the Hall-Mandapa of cosmic creation-which is also vast like space and veiled by its blue colour.

55 to 57. Meru is the pillar of the Hall, Indra and his women are the wooden carvings on the pillar and the created beings are the ants in the heap of mud and hills existing in the corner of the hall. There in it is the house of a brahmana who has become old, having given birth to many sons. The path of the wind is the long wooden beam of the Hall and those swarming in the celestial vehicles are the worms abounding the wooden beam. The siddhas, seers, residing in the celestial space are the bees humming around and around. The devas and asuras are the wicked children indulging in strifes.

58.   In some corner of the space of that abode there is a hill and in its slope there is a village called Girigrama.

59.   In that village surrounded by rivers, woods and hill, there was a brahmana-well-versed in Vedic lore and devoted to worship of Agni. He had abundant cows; He was free from fear of the king and alongwith his wife entertained guests from all sections of society.

60.   He was not Vasishta but was similar to Vasishta in appearance, age, action, manner of doing things, etc. He was also called Vasishta.

61 & 62. He had a wife, beautiful like moon and she was called Arundhati. She too resembled the celestial Arundhati in appearance, age, action, learning and manner of doing things, etc.

63 & 64. That brahmana, once sitting on the slope of the hill amidst green growths saw a king marching with a spectacular retinue below on the earth on an hunting expedition. Seeing the royal fanfare, he reflected thus:

65 to 67. "How glorious is the kingship associated, as it is, with all signs of prosperity! When shall I be a king with my powers extending in all directions and enjoying the paraphernalia comprising of infantry, chariots, horses, and the royal insignia of umbrella, etc.? When shall the wind carrying the fragrance of flowers delight me and relieve the strain of my women in the apartment who are exhausted by their amorous activities?" Thus, from that time onwards, the brahmana was seized with this desire.

68.   He kept performing his religious rites with zeal till the end of his life. Old age began to afflict him as the mist does the lotus blossom.

69.   Ageing struck the despondent man and his wife became gloomy sensing that death was imminent for her husband.

70.   As you did, o beautiful woman, she also adored me. Knowing that immortality is unattainable, she sought this boon from me:

71.   'O Goddess, the jiva of my dead husband should not leave the space of the hall.' I granted the boon.

72.   In course of time, the brahmana passed away. His jiva remained in the very space of the hall of the house.

73.   By virtue of his intense yearning in the previous life,

his soul, space-like in nature, possessing enormous energy, became the ruler of a kingdom.

74. When the brahmana became dead, his wife was much grief-stricken. She became despondent.

75. She also gave up her physical body and attaining the ethereal body, got united with her husband.

76. In that abode of Girigrama, even now exist the brahmana's sons, dwelling, possessions, wealth, etc. Today is the eighth day of death of the brahmana.

77. It is he who has been the ruler of this kingdom and your husband Padma. She, who was called Arundhati is you, o beautiful woman!

78. Both of you, as husband and wife, just like the pair of chakravaka birds, are Shiva and Parvati descended on earth and have ruled the kingdom so far.

79. I have told you about the previous creation, an illusory projection. The entire creation is illusory and what remains is chid-akasa only."

80. Lila said: "Goddess! How false is your utterance? Where is the brahmana in his small abode? Where are we ruling in this vast kingdom?

81. That different world, that land, that mountain, how can all these exist here in this abode where we have been living?

82 & 83. Your statement is as incongruous as the assertion that the wild elephant Iravatha has been imprisoned within the grain of sand, that mosquitoes have vanquished a horde of lions, that the firmly-entrenched Meru has been destroyed by the offspring of a bee."

84. Goddess said: "O beautiful woman, I do not make false statement. Do hear what is real. Persons like us do

not violate the code of good conduct.

85. That village and that brahmana's jiva abide in the same space; this kingdom is also only in the space; the seer of this world is also only the space.

86. The memory of both of you in respect of past life has become erased and a different imagination has seized your minds. O lady, death is akin to a dream in which the memory of normal state is totally absent.

87. As within a mirror exists an image, so this earth exists within the imagination. It manifests as real, within the space of consciousness, as projected in the jiva's mind.

88. Child, these worlds and worlds within worlds, which are mere consciousness, exist within atoms, within jivas and thus in pure consciousness."

89. Lila asked: "Eight days earlier, the brahmana expired, O Goddess, but we have spent several years in this kingdom. O Mother, how can this happen?"

90. Goddess said: "Even as spatial expanse is non-existent, the length of duration of time does not exist, o fair lady! There is nothing beyond the play of consciousness which projects these forms.

91 & 92. O child, how an illusory form manifests, I shall explain. After experiencing the death and the oblivion, the jiva forgets everything about the previous life and imagines different set of things.

93. 'I possess a body comprising of hands and feet. This is mine...I am the father of this person...He is my son...I have a number of years to live...

94. These are my happy relatives...This is my pleasing abode.' Thus he thinks and the delusion arising after the oblivion and death projects the worlds."

95 & 96. Lila said: "O Goddess, a supreme vision has been unfolded by thee for me just now. Before I get established in that vision through repeated practice, do thou dispel the curiosity that keeps my heart restless. O Goddess, do thou lead me to the world where the brahmana and his wife had lived."

97.   Goddess said: "Attaining to the highest state of pure consciousness which is not associated with objective matter, abandon the identification with this physical body and be the pure Being.

98.   If you attain to that state, you will be able to see the other world without hindrance. In seeing the other world, this body of yours is an impediment.

99.   These worlds are incorporeal and because of delusion, are perceived by you to be corporeal, as the gold is cognised as ring.

100. Dear lady, without uninterrupted practice, you will not be able to attain Brahmanhood. You have identified yourself with the physical body. Hence you are not aware of Brahman.

101. Persons who are established in Supreme Consciousness by virtue of repeated practice, cognise that Brahmic awareness always like us.

102. This body is really an ativahika one-a subtle mental body only-and because of intense contemplation of it as an atiboutika, physical body, it has manifested as one.

103. When you are able to abide in the state in which vasanas, tendencies have become attenuated, the physical body regains the subtle form.

104. The solid ice because of heat melts away as water; the mind, bereft of vasanas, turns into pure satvic

nature and transforms into the subtle body.

105. O blemishless woman, strive to attain the state of mind untainted by vasanas. If you are able to firmly abide in that plane, you will be a jivanmukta, a liberated being.

106. As yet, your mind has not become filled with the full moon of cool awareness (of the Reality) and so you may leave here your physical body and go out to see the other world."

107. Lila said: "What is the repeated practice which you consider as necessary for the purpose? How is it done? How does it become fit enough to produce the result? What result does it bestow?"

108. *Goddess said: "Contemplation of the Reality, discussion about it and mutual enlightenment among aspirants, exclusive devotion to the aim-all these constitute Brahmic practice according to learned persons.*

109. They have perfected the practice whose minds are characterised by a loftiness that engenders true dispassion and from whose hearts flow out bliss.

110. *They have stabilised themselves in the practice of Brahmic awareness who have understood that the objective matter does not at all exist and thus endeavour to realise the Truth in accordance with the scriptural teaching.*

111. *'This world was never created, the objective world does not at all exist. This world and I do not exist.'- Those who attain to awareness through such a realisation are well established in the practice of wisdom.*

106

112. When through the realisation that the objective matter does not at all exist, the desire and aversion get eliminated, one gets forcibly absorbed in super-consciousness state and that is called perfect practice of wisdom.

113. The realisation that the objective world does not exist is what is called annihilation of the objective world and when this truth is steadily practised, there results emancipation. Practice indeed leads to attainment of blessedness."

114. Vasishta said: "After conversing thus with each other, during the night, Lila attained samadhi, superconscious state, and remained motionless.

115 & 116. Through nirvikalpa samadhi, super-conscious awareness, she discarded her prior empirical identity. The Goddess Jnapti travelled with her in spiritual body. Lila abandoning the human body assumed the ethereal body through her will and wandered along.

117. Both were intrinsically chit, consciousness in nature and were space-like in external forms.

118. Then the two damsels of elegant looks, travelled through space a vast distance at the perceptual plane.

119. Travelling through long distance, they saw the vast extended space-majestic, pure and infinite.

120 to 127. The wind blowing softly gave pleasure to the body and the siddhas traversed hither and thither at a mental speed faster than that of wind. Somewhere, as waves roll in an ocean, demons and ghosts thronged in a domain. Some other celestials called yogins in strange forms wandered here and there without aim. The wind currents threw up the waters of the celestial Ganga. In a mansion without walls singing Narada

and Tumburu were like the picture of the motion-less clouds on the eve of cosmic destruction. The intoxicated divine mothers had assembled in a realm. Somewhere there was densest darkness as in the interior of a stone and somewhere else was effulgence akin to that of sun and fire. Swimming through planets clustering like insects within a fig fruit, the two great women descended upon an earthern plane.

128. Thus emerging from a different cosmos, the two great women reached the place where the dwelling of the brahmana was situated.

129. The two spiritual adepts saw, without being seen by others, the entire environs in which the brahmana had lived.

130. The people of the family were despondent; their bodies and faces were tainted with tears; they remained scattered in an unnatural condition, like a tree struck by lightning.

131. By now, the beautiful Lila, as a result of her perfected wisdom, became endowed with the powers to fulfil any wish and any desire.

132. She willed, 'Let the people of the family and relations, see the Goddess and me as ordinary beautiful women.'

133. Thereon, the people of the family saw the two women, like the pair of Lakshmi and Gauri illumining the abode with lustre.

134. Jyeshta-sarma, the brahmana's son, saying, 'Obeisance to the Goddesses of the woods,' offered flowers at their feet alongwith other relations.

135. He further said, "O Goddesses, there was a brahmana here with his wife. They were meritorious in the whole world, were solicitous to guests from all sections of

society and were, as if, a pillar of brahmanical tradition.

136. Those couple, parents of mine, leaving kith, kin, home and wealth, went for the heavenly abode and the entire world has become a deserted place for us without them.

137. O Goddesses, kindly dispel our grief. The vision of divine beings never fails to confer a great blessing."

138 & 139. Lila touched with her hand the forehead of her son who spoke thus and because of her touch, he discarded all grief, like the hill getting rid of the heat of the sun with the heavy seasonal downpour. Other persons also overcame the sorrow which was otherwise difficult to do.

140. Then the two spiritual adepts disappeared from view in the very space of the house in the village of Girigrama situated on the mountain slope.

141. The Goddess said: "The Reality that is to be known has been known and the illustrations relating to the falsity of the world have been understood. The nature of Brahman is such. What else do you seek to know?"

142. Lila asked the Goddess: "While I was present in the world where my dear husband is presently ruling, I was not seen by him, but here how am I seen by my son and others?"

143. The Goddess said: "O beautiful woman, because of lack of practice, the conviction that the world exists did not get totally extinguished in your mind on the earlier occasion.

144. The notion 'I am Lila' did not entirely disappear from your mind for lack of practice. Therefore, you did not have then the power to fulfill all wishes.

145. Now you possess the power to fulfill any wish, o beautiful woman! Therefore, your wish 'Let my son see me' materialised.

146. If you, now, go to the kingdom of your husband, you can have dealing with him as here."

147. Lila said: "O Mother of the world, now I am able to recollect everything. My life is a rajasic (passionate) one, not tamasic (ignorance-filled) or sattvic (pacific) one.

148. Descending from Brahma, I have lived about eight hundred lives amongst varied species. I seem to see them all now.

149. In some world before, I was a beautiful Vidhyadhara woman roaming like a bee around the lotuses of different lands.

150. Vitiated by wicked desire, I was later born as a woman amongst human beings. In a different world, I was the beloved of a serpent king.

151. At one time, I was a dark woman of hunting tribe living in the kadamba woods.

152. As a bird, I was caught in the net spread on the earth by the enemy and with great effort I destroyed it like the bad vasanas, tendencies.

153. As a bee, I had tasted the essence of the lotus blossoms and had reposed on the bed of lotus seeds.

154. As a result of acts that would bring about birth as a man, I became the king of the Saurashtra country for a hundred years.

155. I was born as a small bee living with other bees on a grassland with grasses tossing mildly.

156. In that long stream of worldly life filled with mighty

waves caused by the fierce wind, I was born amongst several kinds of species exposed to a hundred hardships and was senselessly dragged into several hurdles.'

157.   Conversing between themselves thus, the two women of beautiful form rose up into the sky through their yogic discipline.

158.   Emerging from that world, they got into another and soon beheld the inner apartment of royal mansion.

159.   The body of the king remained under the heap of flowers. Again, by adhering to the yogic discipline, the two spiritual adepts emerged out from that world.

160.   Lila entered the present kingdom of her husband alongwith Goddess Saraswati.

161 to 173. In the meanwhile, an ambitious king laid seige to that kingdom. The two armies encountered each other in a vast ground and were like another akasa, with gruesome appearance. The two armies resembled two vast majestic oceans. With the two kings facing each other at the centre, the two armies were in full preparedness and glowed like the rising flame. Lila and the Goddess Jnapti surveyed the scene from above. The battle commenced with a roar like that of the ocean at the time of deluge and missiles coursed through like lightning. The huge elephants made the earth shake under their feet. The stones, hurled through mechanised devices, flew past in the sky. The apparels of warriors were torn into pieces by swords. The armours of the warriors got powdered by the blows delivered through fists. The battle-scene was a spectacle in which arrows rained on earth like heavy downpour; headless trunks massed like clouds and

mountain-like elephants rolled over the earth as at the time of deluge. As the intense fight continued thus with warriors braving themselves in the front, the sun had a form beautiful to look at. The setting sun became thin like the warriors, beaten with weapons. After consulting the army chiefs and ministers, messengers were despatched to either side for suspending the fight. The conches blew announcing retirement and the two armies began to leave the battle-ground. Looking like a warrior soaked in red blood, the sun set. Dense darkness surrounded everywhere. The noble-hearted husband of Lila, with a painful heart, deliberated with the councillors on the tasks to be attended to at the next morning and began to sleep in his chambers radiant like the moon.

At that time, the two spiritual adepts-Lila and the Goddess-flew into his chamber, through the window.

174. The wind carrying the fragrance of flowers blew softly in the chamber where the king slept.

175. Because of the elixir-like lustre emanating from their bodies, it was as if the king was drenched by amrita, ambrosia, and, glad at heart, he woke up.

176. He saw two damsels resting peacefully on two seats and reflecting for a while, became extremely amazed.

177. He rose up from the bed, like Vishnu from the serpent-couch, and took in his hands garlands of blossoms.

178. Sitting before them on the ground and exclaiming, 'Glory to the moonlike radiance that wipes away all evils from hearts! Glory to the sun-like effulgence that destroys the darkness of the hearts!' offered at their feet flowers in the form of homage.

179. Saraswati, through thought-consciousness prompted

the minister nearby to reveal the lineage of the king for the benefit of Lila.

180. The two yogins saw the king offering homage through flowers and sitting on the floor reverentially.

182. The Goddess asked, "O king, whose son are you and when were you born here?" and the minister replied as follows, on behalf of the king:

183. "It is the grace of the two Divine Beings appearing before me that enables me to give the details of the birth of my Lord. Do thou listen.

184 to 187. There was a lotus-eyed king belonging to the Ikshvaku family called Mukundaratha, the might of whose arms gave protection to the earth. He had a moon-like effulgent son called Bhadraratha. His son was Visvaratha whose son was Manoratha. Manoratha gave birth to Vishnuratha whose son was Brihadratha. His son was Sindhuratha who gave birth to Sailaratha. His son was Kamaratha whose son was Maharatha. Our Lord of flawless form is the son of this Maharatha.

188. Endowed with exceptional merit of holy deeds, he was called Vidhuratha. His mother Sumitra gave birth to him as Gauri to Guha.

189. He was only ten years of age, when his father gave the kingdom to him and left for the woods and from that time the present ruler has been governing the earth righteously.

190 & 191. After speaking thus, the minister and the king stood still, bowing their heads to the visitors. Saraswati said: "Do thou recollect your past through the mental eye," and touched the forehead of the king with her hand.

192. The darkness and the delusion gripping the heart of

the king disappeared and he was able to recollect the past events spontaneously revealing themselves in the heart.

193 to 195. He remembered his life as the sovereign king with a different body, affection for Lila, etc., and said: "It is cosmic illusion that has projected such wonderful life. I am able to know it now by the grace of the two Goddesses. O Goddesses, only a single day is gone since my death. Here in this kingdom, I have spent seventy years. I recollect many things done here alongwith friends and relations."

196 & 197. The Goddess Jnapti said: "O king, following the swoon, delusion and death in the former world of yours and in the very house, in your mind of akasa, this illusion of a different world originated.

198 & 199. The vast range of activities of this world has manifested and as a short period of time is imagined in a dream to be a period of hundred years, you have the notion that you have spent seventy years of life in the new world which is born entirely out of Maya.

200. In truth, however, you are not born nor dead. You are pure consciousness, abiding in your own self.

201. You cognise the objective world and yet cognise nothing. Since you are all-pervasive, you are simply self-manifesting.

202. He, whose mind is impure and veiled and has not realised the expansive Being, considers the world as unquestionably real, though it exists not.

203. Even as for the ignorant child, the devil imagined by it can be a cause of sorrow to the end of its life, the non-existent world appearing as existent can be for a stupid person.

114

204. Even as mere radiating heat appears as water in the desert stretch for the deluded animal, the non-existent world appears as existent for the stupid person.

205. To an unintelligent person, the golden bracelet is only a bracelet and he does not see the gold.

206. Even so, the unenlightened person who sees only city, mansion, hill, elephant, etc., is a perceiver of an illusory world and not perceiver of the reality.

207. This world comprising the mind, ego, etc., is like a long dream-experience. Those others seen in the waking world are also akin to persons seen in dream.

208. There exists all-pervasive, peaceful, supremely real, space-like Being which is bare consciousness unvitiated by unconscious matter.

209. That Reality is all-pervasive, all capable; it is all and the Self of all. Whatever is willed, it manifests as such.

210. Thus, o king, I have described all these for the sake of Lila's understanding. May good happen to thee! We have understood the illusoriness of the world. We leave now."

211. Viduratha said: "O Goddesses, how can the vision of such an all-bestowing Divine Being like you be in vain for me who is seeking thy grace?

212. O giver of boons! When will I discard this body and remanifest in Padma's body? Do thou tell me the truth.'

213. The Goddess said: 'In this on-going battle, o king, you have to die. You will regain the former kingdom instantly.'

214 to 225. Vasishta said: "As they were speaking to each other sweetly thus, an excited messenger came in haste and spoke: "Master, the enemy's army with all

115

kinds of weapons has established itself everywhere. The city has been set on fire and big palaces are crashing down noisily. Dense dark clouds of smoke rise up to the sky and range through space like garuda birds."

As the messengers hurriedly spoke these words, a big noise was heard from outside the mansion and there was great tumult all around. There was the sound caused by the speeding arrows, the running elephants, the raging fire and the wail of people whose kith got extinguished in fire.

At that midnight, Lila, the Goddess, the king Viduratha and the minister saw from the window the great city causing thunderous noise. It was as if the enemy's strength came in successive mighty waves, all the oceans had become one by the action of the fire at the time of deluge, the smoke of which rose up in huge columns into the sky. The dense clouds and thunder, filled the ear in the form of the people's shouts and the space of the sky got filled with fierce fire balls and the noise of the sobbing people.

226. At this moment, the queen in her pride of youth, looking agitated, entered the chambers surrounded by her friends.

227. A friend of her spoke to the king thus: "Master, the queen has had to flee from her apartment. The gate-keepers of the inner apartment have been dragged away and beaten up by the powerful and proud enemy. Even while they were at a distance, we secretly left the apartment."

229 & 230. After hearing these words, the king setting out for the battles, said to the Goddess, "This is my wife,

a devotee of you both. Do protect her" and left for the battle- front, with eyes red in anger, like the lion rushing out from the cave.

231 & 232. Lila, thereon saw another Lila similar to herself in form, as if she was a reflected image in a mirror and who was beautiful to look at.

233. The senior Lila said: - "What is this, O Goddess, that I am seen in this form of hers? In the very form of mine that formerly was, how is she seen here? Explain to me."

234. Jnapti said: "Whatever your dead husband imagined at the time of his death in that kingdom, the same thing he has experienced in this world.

235. Whatever images remained uncontradicted in his mind, those images have manifested as the things. They are but a reflection in the mirror of consciousness.

236. Dream gets nullified in the waking state and the waking experience gets nullified in the dream. Death gets negated in life and life in death.

237. Thus, all this is neither existent nor non-existent. It is all an illusory manifestation. Among things that are experienced now, some have been experienced before.

238 & 239. Some things are newly experienced. Some are similar and some are dissimilar. It is by the virtue of mental imagination (of Padma) that she appears as Lila who is similar to you in manners and has your conduct, your lineage and your body.

240. This husband of yours, Viduratha, will leave this body, get into the apartment of you and will re-enter that body (of Padma)."

241. Vasishta said: "After hearing the words of the Goddess,

Lila, wife of Viduratha, standing before her and bowing to her, spoke thus:

(Padma's wife and Viduratha's wife will be respectively referred to as Lila, the senior, and Lila, the junior, in the translation of the text that follows.)

242. "O Jnapti, Divine Mother! I have worshipped daily the Goddess and your form is similar to hers.

243. Beautiful Goddess, out of compassion to a distressed soul, do thou give a boon to me. Wherever my husband, after getting killed in the battlefield remains, may I join him there with this very body."

"Let it be so," said the Goddess and now the senior Lila spoke:

245. "O Goddess, how is it that I was not led to the world of Girigrama with my physical body?"

246. The Goddess said: "Beautiful lady, I do not specifically do anything for anyone. The souls acquire everything by their own intense thought."

247. While adoring me, you had this resolve: "Let me get liberated." So you were guided along this line.

248. But she had specifically prayed for this blessing. So I granted the wish. The desire of the people thus materialises as a result of our grace."

249. Vasishta said: "Viduratha, adorned with jewels and accompanied by a retinue, started from the mansion.

250. He looked at the warriors assembled before like a heap of pearls and ascended the excellent chariot.

251. The sound of the bugles blew and it seemed as though the clouds collided with each other and the thunder reverberated through the mountains.

252 to 260. The sound of drums, the noise of weapons

colliding with each other, the songs and shouts and wailings filled the atmosphere. Dust rose to the sky as if to put it out. Darkness spread over quickly like the youth overpowering infancy. The king plunged into his enemy's army. Weapons emitted fire like meteors. Arrows rained like showers. The procession of death, was led by rows of headless trunks. Blood flowing on the ground drenched the rising dust. The dazzling weapons removed the darkness of the night. And now the battle proceeded fiercely. Warriors minded not death. There was not much of noise.

The weapons, armours and missiles thrown together in the battleground looked like a vast ocean difficult to cross."

261. Vasishta said: "As the gruesome battle was being fought, the two Lilas spoke to the Goddess.

262. "O Goddess, why should not our husband win this battle, especially as the enemy elephants are fleeing the battlefield and you are also well disposed towards us?"

263. The Goddess said: "I was worshipped for a long time by the enemy of Viduratha, O my daughters, for the sake of victory in the battle, but not so by Viduratha.

264. That is why the enemy becomes victorious and Viduratha is getting defeated. Viduratha prayed, "Let me get liberated."

265. According to his wish, he will attain liberation. His enemy will rule over the kingdom."

266. Vasishta said: "As the Goddess was speaking thus, the night battle between the two sides went on and the sun appeared in the east as if he was eager to witness the battle.

267. The earth was lifted up from the waters of darkness and was drenched with its golden rays by the sun.

268. The strength of both the armies had been decimated and their presence had become small.

269 to 276. The king encountered the enemy appearing in a defiant mood and aimed a series of sharp arrows at him. The enemy effortlessly countered them and taking the fight to the most fierce level, he harassed Viduratha with strings of arrows. Viduratha, deprived of his flagstaff, chariot, horses, charioteer and bow, and with injury inflicted all over the body, fell on the ground.

"The king has been killed. The king has been killed." The shout filled the air and like the cart with the provisions load breaking down noisily, the capital got thrown into disarray and poeple ran in different directions crying in agony.

277 & 278. At this time, the junior Lila told Saraswati, looking at the body of her husband from which the last breath was to depart, "O Goddess, my husband is about to leave the body. Let me accompany his soul. Be compassionate towards me."

279. After speaking thus, and with the grace of Jnapti, the junior Lila acquired the requisite ability and assuming an ethereal body, flew into space like a bird.

The author of this abridged version of Yoga Vasishta has left out some of the details of the story as described in Brihat Yoga Vasishta. The apparent lack of continuity in narration is due to this reason.

280 to 285. She passed through the realms of clouds, winds, sun and reaching the crest of Brahmanda broke through it and pierced through the veils surrounding

it, reached the primeval consciousness. It was so endless that even Garuda leaping across it might not pass beyond in numberless aeons. Like innumerable fruits in the trees of woods, there are numberless brahmandas in that expanse. She entered into one such brahmanda and reached herein the capital of Padma's kingdom. Strengthened by the grace of the Goddess, she entered into the hall and stood near the heap of flowers covering the dead body.

286 to 288. She saw the body and with her spirit quickened, thought thus: "This is my husband, one of the foremost of the warriors. Because of the grace of the Goddess, I have reached here." Thinking thus, Lila, in sweet elegance, taking a fan in her hand, fanned over the face of the king.

289 to 291. At this time, when the life of the king (Viduratha) became extinct, the senior Lila and the Goddess saw his jiva rising into the sky. The jiva-speck, Lila and the Goddess moved through space, the first not cognising the other two. The two-the senior Lila and the Goddess-followed the jiva-speck from one world to another. Finally, they reached the capital of Padma's kingdom and entered into the apartment of Lila.

292. With the jiva-speck going before, they entered freely into the hall.

Then the senior Lila and the Goddess saw junior Lila standing by the body of the king, having reached the place earlier.

293 to 295. At this time, Jnapti by Her will, restrained the jiva of Viduratha, as one controls the movements of the mind.

The senior Lila now asked the Goddess, "O Goddess, my former body is not seen here, why?"

296 to 298. Jnapti said: "O noble minded Lila, hear what happened to your body. When you entered into samadhi, the body fell on the earth like dead-wood. It became inert like wood. The body became cold like ice. Then, the ministers were brought in and deciding that the body had become lifeless, they placed it on a pyre containing ghee and sandalwood and burnt it.

299. Now, on seeing you here in body, they will think that you have returned to the earth from the heaven. They will get wonderstruck.

300. You are appearing in the ethereal body, which is a mental one, by virtue of your accumulated spiritual powers.

301. You had forgotten this physical body, as the vasanas pertaining to it had become extinct. When one gets established in the ethereal plane, the physical body disappears.

302. Now proceed, Lila. Let us reveal ourselves to the junior Lila. We will follow the course of events."

303 & 304. Jnapti wished, 'Let this Lila be able to see us' and at that, Lila, the junior, beheld before her the Goddess and the senior Lila.

305. She got excited, rose up, offered obeisance at their feet and all of them sat on different seats.

306 to 310. Jnapti said: "O Lilas, fair like the Hamsa birds and of elegant looks, we will restore the king to life." Saying these words, she released his life, like blossom the fragrance. Air touched his nostril and life re-entered the body as wind into a hole. The face glowed and in due course, senses became active, responsive. The eyes opened and there was perception of outside world. He rose up like the elephant emerging out of the Vindhya hill.

311. Looking around, he asked in sonorous tone, "Where am I?" and the two Lilas appearing before him replied, "At your command." He asked, "Who are you? Who is she? Where from is she?" To these questions, Lila the senior replied, "Master, do thou listen to what I say.

313 & 314. I am thy wife Lila living with you since previous life. This is second Lila ushered into life by me for your sake. This auspicious woman of yours is as it were a reflection of mine.

She who is seated in the golden seat near the head, is Goddess Saraswati, who is the Mother of the universe."

315 & 316. After listening to these words, the king rose up, prostrated at the feet of Jnapti and with modesty spoke: "Obeisance to thee, Mother Saraswati." After he spoke thus, Saraswati touched him with her hand and said:

317. "Let all dangers, miseries arising out of wrong perceptions, disappear. Let there be infinite happiness everywhere. Let people be cheerful. Let wise people remain well respected in the country."

318. After conferring this blessing, Saraswati disappeared from view.

The auspicious shouts, 'Jaya, Jaya' rent the air.

The royal mansion became filled with the dear ones and the nobles.

Lila the senior, Lila the junior, and the king - all noble-minded and emancipated- delighted themselves by speaking about past events.

The king, blessed by Jnapti, became enlightened and alongwith two Lilas lived several hundred years and ruled blemishlessly over the kingdom.

Since they were jivanmuktas, liberated souls, the kingdom was absolutely free from strife. After reigning thus, they attained to pure intelligence and freed themselves from bodily association.

Chapter-3

The Story of Suchi (Needle)

1. Vasishta said: "I have told the story of Lila, O Rama, in order to get rid of the fallacious notion that the objective world exists. Discard the notion of the material universe.

2. The world is an illusory reflection. The Self is pure. It is also the Brahman which projects the universe and in itself is characteristicless consciousness. It is majestic, blissful and immovable.

3. The supreme tranquil plenary consciousness is all-pervasive; it is pure being, uncharacterised by attributes. Even by those who have known it, it is indescribable.

4. Know, Rama, that the mild spurt in the Brahmic consiousness - akin to that in calm waters or flame in windless space - to be the jiva, the individual soul.

5. Even as the small spark with the addition of fuel grows into big fire, the mild spurt of consciousness through intense self-assertion becomes ahamkara, the ego.

6. The ahamkara, prone to objective tinge, assumes the form of chitta (mind) which is also called by the names-chetas, manas, maya, prakriti, etc.

7. Manas, mind arose initially from the supreme cause thus. Mind given to objective thought becomes all. The world is formed by it.

8. The Self, Atma, is infinite consciousness and is like waters of the ocean stretching on all directions and

assuming all shapes; It manifests spontaneously as the universe.

9.   Because of the activity of the mind, the samsara has become one long dream, owing its rise to the absence of perfect understanding, vision of the Truth, like the mistaken notion of a post as a standing human being.

10. *As there is no difference (separateness) between chit and Jiva, so there is no difference between jiva and chitta, the mind. As there is no difference between jiva and chitta, there is no difference between chitta and creation, the world.*

11. Vasishta said: In regard to this point, people give this old story as an example containing a vast array of questions covering all aspects of creation raised by a rakshasi, demoness.

Even among beings disposed towards cruelty, occasionally may be seen individuals who do not like cruelty and thus become eligible for spiritual liberation-and this story is given to illustrate this fact-V. C.

12. There lives in the slope north of the Himalayas a demoness called Karkati who looks like a dark mountain or a fierce image of wood.

13. Her eyes are like steady lightning; her knees are like khanjusha trees; her nails shine like sun and emeralds; she is a huge bundle of bones and nerves.

14. Since she had a huge body, and since human flesh which was her food, was not available in sufficient quantity for her, the appetite of her stomach was like that of the raging fire at the time of deluge.

15. She, with a vast belly, never attained satisfaction in the matters of eating. With her tongue shooting up

like the flame, she thought over the matter thus:

16 to 18. "Let me swallow up all the people of Jambudwipa even as the ocean swallows all the waters without even a pause, and even as the rains from clouds destroy the mirage. Then my appetite will cease. Let me perform penance for achieving this aim with an undisturbed mind"-thus with this thought of eating all the beings, she went to a mountainous peak and, after bathing, started doing penance.

19. She, directing her vision to sun and moon, stood on one foot and spent in this manner days, weeks, months.

20. Without getting afflicted by coldness and heat-she was mountainous in nature-she completed penance for several thousand years and the creator-God made his appearance.

21. Even among low-born creatures, there are some who make arduous penance. She remained as she was, and mentally prostrated to Brahma.

22. "Which boon would serve the purpose of quenching the hunger?" This thought engaged her mind. "Ah, I now remember. I will seek a boon from the God."

23. "I shall be a needle, but a non-metallic one, and pierce through jivas. Through such device, I shall eat humans as much as I want.

24. This will quench all the hunger in due course. To have one's hunger quenched is great delight. I will enter into the hearts of all people.' As she thought thus, the Lotus-born said to her:

25. "Karkati, my child, the garland of cloud over the moutain of the rakshasa family, rise up. I am delighted by your penance. Seek the boon you desire."

26. "O Lord, creator of the universe, past and future, let

me be the piercer of jivas, needle-like without being a needle, if you are pleased to favour me with a boon.".

27. The Lotus-born said: "Let it be so." After saying thus, he added, "A suchika (needle) you shall be, but with a qualification and you will be vi-suchika (distinct needle).

28. You shall kill the wicked people who eat evil food, engage in evil acts, have evil disposition and reside in evil places.

29. By merging with the wind and entering into the hearts through their breath, you will torment the hearts and other body parts and be the disease called vi-suchika.

30. You will grab the virtuous and the wicked. The virtuous can be cured through the mantra, mystic chant, I teach you now.

31. Om, hram, hrim, srim, rum, Salutations to the power of Vishnu; the Divine Power of Vishnu! do thou manifest, remove, burn, kill, cut, pound, destroy, throw away. Visuchika, go away to the mountain; O jiva, you have attained to the celestial moon.

This mantra is taught by Brahma, so that Visuchika can cure the virtuous people afflicted with the disease. The entire mantra has not been included in the translation above. The essential sense has been conveyed. Through the mantra, the disease in the form of Visuchika is sought to be driven away to Himalayas from the afflicted individual who is energised to reach the ambrosial moon and get restored to heath.

32. The practitioner who employs the mystic chant must write the letters of the mystic chant in the palm of his left hand and with that hand touch the body of the afflicted man.

Let him contemplate that the disease severely attacked by the mystic chant, has fled to the Himalayas.

33. Let him contemplate that the afflicted soul is abiding in moon and nourished by its elixir, he is completely rid of old age, death and all kinds of ailments.

34. The practitioner must become pure, sip water with holy chant and with a calm mind remove the disease of Visuchika entirely in this manner."

35. After saying this, the Creator-God disappeared. The demoness became progressively smaller in size, became a small grain and then the needle. She entered in the form of air into the body of a weak and emaciated man and became the tormenting disease.

37 to 39. Entering into the body through air, she becomes the tormenting disease.

Thus for several years, she roamed all over the earth and space in dual physical form solely engaged in killing people.

40. After a long time, Karkati, the forest-denizen became disgusted and thought within herself, "What a wrong has been committed by me?

41. I have become the size of a needle. How much food a needle can contain? It becomes full with a minute bit of flesh and blood.

42 & 43. What an ill-luck! Appetite is inwardly tormenting my heart like a needle and it is difficult to appease it. How foolish of me it is to have given up my huge body with limbs spreading like the clouds. My desires have been shattered with the acquisition of the form of needle which cannot contain even meagre food, flesh or blood."

44. Thinking thus, discarding the desire to kill people,

she again went to the Himalayan mountain for penance.

45. She withdrew her mind from all objects and becoming displeased with her needle-like form, she undertook severe penance.

46. She entertained no thought; she ate no food. Her mind was without the least distraction. After a thousand years of penance, she attained to a supreme plane.

47. Becoming sinless through penance, she shone as a pure being. Through her own intellectual enquiry, she had known the Truth.

48. She became intensely displeased with worldly life and remained in penance with a thoughtfree mind for several hundred years.

49 & 50. Finding that she had reached the plane of supreme consciousness, the Creator-God came to her and said, "Child Karkati, you regain the old huge form and roam over the earth. You are a jivanmukta, the liberated one. The ignorance of your heart is gone.

51. Those stupid men, those engaged in wicked deeds, those living in evil places-let them be your morsel of food."

52. After saying this, the Creator-God disappeared from view. She began to abide in existential consciousness without external distractions. She remained in nirvikalpa samadhi, super-conscious state, for a long time.

53. After a very long time, her mind got roused and was responsive to external attractions. She remembered her appetite.

54 & 55. "As long as there is mental essence, the inherent disposition of the body does not get abandoned. Eating

is the natural trait of the species of the rakshasas as ordained by Brahma. Let me look out for stupid people." Deliberating thus, she descended from the mountain slope.

56.   She entered the country of Kiratas situated at the foot of the mountain. In the big woods, somewhere, she began to dwell.

57.   At this time, the maiden of night stretched wide hands of intense darkness all over.

58.   In that frightful night, a king alongwith the minister, proud of their strength, entered into the woods, in an adventurous spirit.

59 to 61. In the woods, Karkati saw from distance the two-king and minister-walking along. They were courageous and ready for encounter with the vetala, the demoness.

She began to reflect, 'O God, something eatable has come my way. They are ignorant of the Self. Their bodies are a burden indeed for themselves. The life of a stupid person is only full of misery, now and later. Since they are sinful people, they are fit to court death.

62.   This practice was established by Brahma at the time of creation. For the people in the habit of killing, the ignorant people are fit food but not the wise, the knowers of the Self.

63.   Therefore, the two are to be killed by me for food. It is only the unwise person who ignores a good thing readily available for enjoyment.

64.   The two persons are, perhaps, not wise men; It is not to my natural liking that wise people should be killed.

65.   Let me now set out to examine them. If they are found to be endowed with virtue, I will not kill them. I shall

not torment the virtuous under any circumstance.

66. By a person who seeks lasting happiness, fame, life, the virtuous people should be honoured.

67. If inevitable, I shall perish for want of food but not eat the wise people. The wise people delight a person even more than one's own life.

68. Even by giving up your life, protect the virtuous. The contact with the virtuous is a herbal medicine and, with its help, even the Lord of Death turns into a friend.

69. If, even I, being a demoness protect the virtuous, who else would not protect them and treasure the merit in his heart like a beautiful necklace.

70. Those noble-hearted souls, who walk over the earth, are really moons descended on it and spread coolness by their company.

71. To kill the wise is to kill virtue; to allow the wise to live is to support virtue. By depending on the virtuous, one gets both happiness and liberation.

72. Therefore, I shall examine these two through a string of questions and shall find out how wise the two men of elegant looks are.'

73. Thereon, the rakshasi who was the fine flower of the rakshasa clan, roared in a loud voice like the thundering cloud.

74. After her roar, she spoke in a frightening voice, like the sound of the falling hail stones after the thunder.

75 & 76. "O, hear me, who are you two striding across like sun and moon in space in this gruesome forest? You look like worms in the crevice of a vast dark mountain of maya. Who are you two? Are you a pair of unwise men who have come here to be the morsel of my food

and to court death in a second?"

77.   The king said: "O demoness, who are you? Where do you stand? Do come out. Is anyone afraid of the noise of a bee?"

78.   "He has spoken well," saying thus, she, to frighten them again, roared and laughed in derision.

79.   When they looked in the direction from which the sound emanated, they saw a huge being with a wide mouth.

80.   Her roar resembled the thunder of the deluge and she was as vast as the slope of a mountain. Seeing such a person, the two warriors stood their ground without any fear.

81.   The minister said: " O great demoness, what is this futile challenge of yours? Are you sporting or serious or seemingly serious?

82.   Desist from the challenging posture. It does not befit you. The wise people intent on achieving their aims, simply set out to act openly.

83.   O helpless woman! Hundreds of persons like you have been pounded by us, as if they were mosquitoes and have been blown away like tiny leaves by the strong wind that we are.

84.   By discarding offensive attitude and by an even-minded and clear-headed approach and intelligence, a wise person achieves his aim.

85.   Do tell us what is it that you seek. None who has sought anything from us has returned with empty hands."

86.   When told thus, the rakshasi thought for a while. "Ha, what a blemishless conduct these lion-like men have!

87.   They are not common folks. They are intrepid. Their words, faces, and looks reveal their inner resolve.

88.   They have almost understood me. I will not kill them. In fact, they cannot be killed by me (as they are men of wisdom).

89.   Let me put questions to them to resolve the doubt that has arisen in my heart. They are indeed unworthy persons, who, having come across wise men, do not endeavour to know the truth from them."

91.   Thinking thus, with a view to discuss the truths, she stopped her thunder-like laughter and spoke: "Who are you that look courageous, faultless men, do tell me?"

92 & 93. The minister said: "Here is the king of the kiratas and I am the minister. We have ventured on nocturnal inspection to punish persons like you. It is the duty of the king during both day and night to destroy the wicked elements."

94 & 95. Rakshasi said: "O King, you have a wise minister. He cannot be a wise king who has an unwise minister. The minister also has a wise king, as a wise king alone gets on with a wise minister.

96.   The wise minister has to educate the king in wisdom initially. Then nobility manifests in him. As the king is, so the citizen.

97.   Lordship and even-mindedness are acquired by the king through Raja-vidhya, the wisdom of the Self. He who knows it not is not a king, is not a minister.

98.   If both of you have known the Truth and if impelled by nature, I eat you up, a great harm will befall.

99.   Boys, having come near me, you can escape from the clutches if you release yourself by answering the set

of questions that I throw at you, through your intelligence."

100. After saying thus, and when the king also said, "Well, proceed with the questions," the rakshasi began to list the questions. Rama, listen to what they are.

101. Rakshasi said: "In which small particle, which is also many, hundreds of universes dissolve as bubbles in the ocean?

102. Which is akasa but without space, which is not anything yet something? Who is he that walks and walks not, that stands and yet stands not?

103. Who is the sentient one that is like stone? Who designs the variegated sky? In which atom abide the worlds, as trees in seeds?

104. How is that nothing dissimilar like stone has emerged from the ocean? How the different things are not distinct from the waters?

105. If, with keen enquiring mind, you are not, at once, able to answer my questions, you will within a minute become the fuel for the fire raging in my stomach."

106 & 107. The minister said: "O lady with lotus-like eyes, you have referred to the Supreme Self through these words in the form of questions and these words are capable of generating knowledge of Brahman.

108. It is not nameable, attainable and is beyond the senses and the mind. It is only consciousness which is also the Self. It is like an atom, subtler than akasa.

109. Within the particle of consciousness, numberless brahmandas, universes exist. The universes arise, subsist and dissolve into it at the due time.

110. The akasa referred to is chit-as, in relation to it, there

is no outside space. It is not anything because it is not nameable. It is something because it partakes the characteristic of existence.

111. This consciousness of the nature of effulgence is akin to stone because nothing exists as object of its knowledge. It is pure Atma, Self who designs the appearance of the variegated universe in the space.

112. This universe is of the nature of the Supreme Reality and is not different from it. The seemingly different universe is really pervaded by that only, and so it is only the supreme.

113. The all-pervading, all-permeating principle cannot go anywhere and so it does not go. It exists not as it has nothing to support it; and since it is existent, it exists as well."

114. After hearing these words of the minister, the rakshasi exclaimed, "What words of superme wisdom have been spoken by the minister! Let the king speak now."

115 to 119. The king said: "That supreme, the knowledge of which is not manifest during the waking state, but which is attained through renunciation of all desires; that supreme whose manifestation and subsidence bring about creation and dissolution of the universe; that supreme which is the import of the Vedantic texts and yet beyond the reach of words; that supreme which is present between subject and object and which permeates both subject and object; that supreme whose projected mind is the cause of all the playful (sport) manifestation of the world; that supreme which though pervading the universe, remains unitary in nature, is the existential essence and the imperishable Brahman and is what, o good woman, has been referred to by you."

120. After hearing these words from the mouth of the king, Karkati, as unsteady as monkey of the forest, became concentrated in thought and discarded the mood of anger.

121. She became cool at heart and attained repose. She was like the peacock at the onset of rains and the kumuda flower at the rise of full moon.

122. The rakshasi said: "How ennobling is the intelligence of you both, which never gets eclipsed and which is illuminated by the sun of wisdom.

123. Persons of discriminating vision like you, are worthy of adoration by the whole world. Such men are to be served. Surely the contact with such wise persons puts an end to samsara.

124 & 125. Would a man holding a lamp in his hands be put to hardship by darkness? In this wilderness to which I have come, you are earthly suns. You are worthy of my worship. What is your blessed desire?"

126. The king said: "O, the fine blossom of the clan of the rakshasas. I pray to thee that no one's life should be harmed by you hereafter."

127 & 128. Fully pleased, Karkati, monkey-like in nature, said, "O Lord, let me act so from now on without fail. No life would be harmed by me hereafter."

129. The king said: "O, lotus-eyed woman, if it be thy resolve, how would you sustain the body? If the flesh is thy only food, how can you comply with my request?"

130. The rakshasi said: "After very many years spent in samadhi-I have not counted the years-when I rose up, desire to eat seized me.

131. Now, I shall again go to this mountain and, resuming meditation, remain happily rooted in it to the end of my life like an idol.

132. I shall practise concentration, dharana and sustain the body till death and give up the body when the time comes.

133. When I behold everything permeated by the auspicious Being, it is not proper for me to harm the souls."

134. When she spoke thus, with upsurging friendship in her heart, and was about to leave the two, the king said:

135. "The affectionate friendship between us should not come to an end in this way. The affection of the good people further grows only when there is the opportunity to see each other.

136. O good lady! Assume a small and auspicious form, pleasing to look at, and come to our mansion and live happily."

137. The rakshasi said: "How would you be able to feed a woman of elegant form but really a rakshasi by birth and have you the strength?

138. The food of the rakshasas alone can satisfy me, not the food of normal people. This trait has been ordained by nature and cannot be abandoned."

139. The king said: "O blemishless woman, adorned with golden garlands and ornaments, do thou remain as a maiden and live in my mansion as long as I want.

140. I will bring from all over the country wicked men, thieves, etc. in hundreds and deliver them to you to be eaten up.

141. You may discard your elegant form and taking all of them with you to the Himalayan crest eat to your satisfaction.

142. Those who have to eat much are happy when they can eat alone. With that satisfaction, you may sleep for a while and again resume meditation.

143. Rising up from meditation, you may again come here in the elegant form. You may take with you others who deserve to be killed. Injury caused as per the dictates of dharma is not injury.

144. When injury is done in accordance with the precepts of dharma, it is not injury at all but great compassion. When you rise up from meditation, do thou come to us. Friendship even among the wicked is not got rid of easily."

145. The rakshasi said: "O king! You have spoken wisely. Friend, I shall do likewise. Who cannot but respond to the suggestion arising from esteem?"

147 & 148. Then they all went to the king's mansion and spent the night in conversation cheerfully.

During the day, the rakshasi merrily spent the time in the inner apartment with the queen.

149. The king and the minister attended to their normal work.

150. By evening the king had collected from his kingdom and neighbourhood hundreds of people deserving death and offered them to her.

151 & 152. During night she became a fierce dark demoness, took the people in her arms and taking leave of the king, sped towards the Himalayan crest.

153. From then on, the rakshasi, emerging from samadhi comes regularly to the Kirata kingdom and takes away people deserving death.

BYV ends the story on a happier note. People of the Himalayan kingdom develop devotion for Karkati and build shrine for her. Worshipped thus, she bestows prosperity on the people for long years to come.

Chapter-4

The Story of Aindava

1. Vasishta said: "I have now completed the story of Suchika, Needle. Only the Self is the supreme reality; there are no worldly projections–are its teachings.

2. It is only the mind that manifests as all entities. In this connection, do thou hear the story of Aindava, which is amusing to hear:

3. Rama, I shall tell this good story. You will understand from the story that the world is a manifestation of the chit, consciousness.

4. Chitta, mind, is the boy that sees the vetala, devil, on account of wrong perception, but when it becomes enlightened, it sees only the blemishless Supreme Self.

5. *The mind, tainted by desire and aversion, contributes to worldly life; the very mind, stripped of them, is said to bring it to an end.*

6. Once, Brahma, after withdrawing into Himself the entire created universe, at the end of the day, was deeply absorbed in sleep.

7. At the end of the night, He fully woke up, did Sandhya worship and with the intention to create people, spread His looks all over space.

8. At that time, He saw with His mind in the vast space several universes magnificently existing without any obstruction.

9. Seeing them all with his subtle vision, He became

141

immensely surprised and asked within Himself, 'What are all these and how have they come into existence?'

10.   After watching them for a long time with his mind, He summoned the sun from these universes and asked him thus:

11.   "O splendrous one, who are you? How has this universe come into existence? If you know it, worshipful one, do thou tell me."

12.   Addressed thus by the Creator-God, the sun with devotion offered obeisance to Him and said in flawless words thus:

13.   "Of this perceived world, you are the eternal cause. Not knowing it yourself, why do you ask me?

14.   O all-pervasive one, if you intend to have fun at my expense, I shall describe how this creation took place. Listen.

15 to 21. In the slope of Keelaja mountain, there lies in some corner Jambudwipa and a region has been formed under the name of 'Suvarnathata' by people descended from your sons. This is a prosperous and beautiful country. There was a brahmana who was a knower of Brahman and exclusively dedicated to dharma. He was called Indu and this supremely pious soul belonged to the family of Kasyapa. That noble-minded person had a wife dear to him like his own breath.

Like the desert land without a tree, they did not have a progeny. The anguished couple went to Kailasa for penance. The two, practising all austerities, reached an uninhabited place in the Kailasa range. Without food and water, they performed severe penance and stood like trees.

Thereon, the crescent-wearing Shiva became pleased with them. He came to the place where the couple performed penance and said, "O learned man, seek a boon; I am pleased."

22. The brahmana said: "O worshipful one, God of Gods, let ten sons endowed with great intelligence and virtue be born to us and let us have no further grief."

23. The God, after saying, "Let it be so," disappeared from view. The couple, blessed with the boon, went home happily.

24. In course of time, the brahmana woman gave birth to ten healthy sons. They also grew up.

25. After a long time, the aged parents left their bodies and attained their destined celestial sphere.

26. Orphaned by the parents and bereft of relations, the ten brahmanas left their home, went to the Kailasa mountain and reflected with a heavy heart:

27 to 30. "What would be the wholesome good for us? What would rid us of sorrow? What is the richness of the people who are subservient to the ruler? What is the greatness about the riches of the ruler who is under the lordship of a sovereign? How great is the sovereign who is ruled over by Indra? What is the greatness of an Indra whose lifetime is but an hour of Prajapathi, Brahma? So that alone which would last the entire kalpa-the life-period of Brahma-would be the wholesome good for us."

31. The eldest said: "My brothers, of all the glorious riches, that which does not perish till the deluge, that is, the state of Brahma alone is worthy of attainment."

32. Others said: "Dear, you have said the right thing. That alone will alleviate all sorrow. Let us attain the state

of Brahma. You are our guide on the path."

33. The eldest said: "Let us all meditate for long time on the lines 'I am the lotus-born effulgent Being and by my intelligence I create and dissolve the universe.'

34. Approving the instruction given by the eldest, the lofty men lost themselves in meditation and appeared like pictures on the wall.

35 & 36. They fervently contemplated within themselves: I am Brahma, the creator, doer, enjoyer, and ruler. With the aid of lokapalas, cosmic agents, I created the fourteen worlds and I dwell within them.'

37. Those brahmanas, totally identifying themselves with Brahma through contemplation, discarded the identification with the bodies that came into existence as a result of the earlier imagination.

38. Those bodies assailed by wind and heat became famished and lifeless like the dry leaves.

39. All the ten, by virtue of their concentrated contemplation, became Brahma and worlds, ten in number, manifested as a consequence.

40. Those ten remain in the mental plane in ethereal form. I am the sun of one of them functioning as the creator of day and night."

41. Saying thus, the sun left for his abode. Brahma, the Lord of the universe, also began to attend to his work."

ॐ

Chapter-5

The Story of Indra

1. *Vasishta said: "It is mind that is the creator of the world; mind is the real person. That what is done by the mind is considered as really done and not that which is done by the body.*

   That which is done by the mind is regarded as perfectly done. It is productive of the intended result V. C.

2. Those who were ordinary brahmanas-the sons of Indu-became Brahmas because of mental contemplation. See how potent is the mind.

3. Only because of the appropriate contemplation, the possessor of the body becomes an agent of actions and when he does not identify himself with body, he is free from the afflictions, the body is heir to.

4. When the yogi's mind gets interiorised (and lost in super-consciousness), he does not experience pleasure and pain. The story relating to Indra and Ahalya proves this point.

   The mind of the Yogi is not aware of pleasure or pain because it gets interiorised. In the case of the normal actions of a person, it will be seen that the real doer is the mind and not the physical body."

5. Sri Rama asked: "Who is Ahalya? Who is called Indra by you? O, Divine Seer! How does this story help my mind to reach a higher plane?"

6. Vasishta said: "It is said, that in the kingdom of Magadha, in bygone times, there was a king called Indradyumna, as famous as the other Indradyumna.

There was a former ruler of Pandya kingdom called Indradyumna and he was a great devotee of Vishnu. V. C.

7. He had a wife who resembled the moon in lustre and the lotus in eyes. She was unto him like Rohini to Sasanka, the moon. Her name was Ahalya.

8. There was residing in that very city a man of loose morals, much known among the people and he was called Indra.

9. That Ahalya, having heard about Indra's fascination for Ahalya from the Puranas, became enormoured of this ordinary Indra.

Valmiki Ramayana narrates how Indra in disguise, sought the company of Ahalya, the wife of the sage Gautama and invited the sage's curse V. C.

10. The deep attachment that arose between them and their open dalliance and immodest conduct reached the ears of the king.

11. Seeing the natural attachment that subsisted between them, the king adopted several tactical means to punish them.

12. Both of them were abandoned in the waters. They happily sported together but did not become miserable.

13. They were tied to the feet of the elephant and yet they did not feel pain. Their bodies were beaten with stick, but they knew not any sorrow.

14 to 23. Thrown into fire, they remained cool as if they were surrounded by snow. The king, thereon, asked them, 'O, wicked people, are you not aware of pain?'

With happiness, surging in their hearts, they told the king:

"We are fascinated by each other and we keep looking at each other's beautiful face. Our minds are so much filled with each other's form that we are not aware of ourselves. We do not, therefore, grieve even when our limbs are injured. When a person's mind is totally absorbed in the object of love, the ordeals to which the body is subjected to cannot affect him. That in which his mind is intensely absorbed, that alone he sees everywhere. He does not cognise his own body. No action of any external agency, not even the curses of the sages, have the capacity, to draw away the mind that is intensely absorbed in a single object, o king! He is impervious to anything, as the Meru mountain to any number of blows.

O king! The body is a mere outer manifestation. It is the mind that is the real being. As water is the vital element in the creepers of the woods, the vital element in the creeper of the body is mind,

O king! If the body is harmed, the mind is capable of making a new one. As in the dream, a person creates new individuals. But if the mind is harmed, the body cannot come to its rescue. Hence, take care to nurture the jewel of the mind in a proper way."

24. Vasishta said: "When the king was told like this by the two, he said to the seer Bharata who was nearby:

25 & 26. "O seer! knower of all dharmas! These words, though of persons blinded by passion, have pregnant truth and delight the hearts. They have been punished according to the scriptures. Let me now expel them from the land." Saying thus, the great king had them expelled from the kingdom."

Chapter-6

The Story of Chitta (Mind)

Vasishta said:

1. "Thus I have told you, o Rama, in the form of a story the fact that everyone in the world has in fact two bodies.

2. One is the mental body, which is quick to act and ever unsteady. The other one is composed of flesh and is a helpless entity."

3. Sri Rama asked: "O seer! Do thou describe in detail about mind which is of the nature of sankalpa (thought) and which is dwelling in the body that is inert and is without an independent form."

4. *Vasishta said: "The infinite supreme self is omnipotent and that form of it which is characterised by the power of thought is known to be mind.*

5. *It is a thing which is both existent and non-existent and is changing in nature. That which is given to contemplation (imagination) of things is known as mind.*

That which is both existent and non-existent, that is, both self and non-self, and assumes the form of the seer and the seen is mind. That it is mind which assumes the forms of the seer and the seen, is known by the fact that in deep sleep when the mind does not function, the seer and the seen are not cognised V. C.

148

6.   Arising from ignorance, chitta (mind) is only seemingly attractive. For the sake of your own liberation, do thou train it in the discipline that leads to liberation.

       Mind, owing to its origin in ignorance, is the cause of bondage and the same mind by becoming extinct through enquiry, is the cause of liberation. V. C.

7.   In this connection, I narrate to you the story of chitta (mind) which was narrated before by the Lotus-born God.

8.   There is a vast land extending to hundreds of miles-uninhabited, deserted and frightful. A tiny corner of it has a characteristic of its own.

9.   There dwells an individual with a confounded mind, frightening form, unnatural body and a thousand arms and eyes.

10.   Through hundreds of hands, he picks up numberless maces and striking his back with them, flees of his own accord.

11.   He strikes at himself with mighty strength and becoming fierce in form, he runs hundreds of miles.

12 & 13. He cries aloud, runs a long distance hither and thither, becomes tired and with limbs falling apart, helplessly falls in a huge dark pit-immense and fearful like dark night.

14.   After a very long time, he rises up from the pit and again beats himself and flees.

15.   Again, after running a vast distance, he goes into a jungle abounding in thorny bushes, as the moth into the fire.

16.   He emerges from the deep forest in a second and again beats himself and flees on his own accord.

17 to 19. Again he goes long distance, enters into a cool plaintain grove with a happy smile and coming out of it again, he beats himself and runs and falls again into the same dark pit.

20. With bruised limbs, he rises up from within the dark pit and speeds towards the plaintain grove.

21. From the beautiful plaintain grove to the dry jungle and from the jungle to the pit and again to the plaintain grove-thus he beats himself and goes to these places one after another.

22 to 24. After seeing him in this act for a long time, I seized him forcefully and making him self-conscious for a moment, asked him, 'Who are you? What is this activity? For what reason are you indulging in it? What is your aim? Why do you roam around in vain?' Thus questioned by me, he replied:

25. "I am not anything nor do I practise anything, o seer! I have been enslaved by you. How fine? You are my enemy.

26 & 27. I have been awakened by you. O, I am almost dead now, both happy and miserable.'

After speaking thus, he saw his bruised limbs and cried aloud with a despondent mind and like the thunder of the raining clouds.

In a second, he stopped crying and after looking at his limbs, laughed for a while.

28 & 29. After the roaring laughter, he became calm before me and discarded the limbs gradually. First fell the fierce head, thence arms, then chest and finally the belly.

30. In a second, leaving these limbs to be merged with the elements, the person, guided by the forces of cosmic necessity, was ready to go somewhere.

In this allegory described from verses 8 to 30, what each concept stands for is indicated below:

Vast land, etc.	: Samsaric existence characterised by sattva, rajas and tamas.
Individual	: Mind.
Hundreds of hands	: Desires for objects.
Maces	: Mental and physical afflictions.
Flees	: Runs from sorrows.
Dark pit	: Vast hell.
Jungle	: Earthly existence.
Plantain Grove	: Heaven.
'I' seized forcefully	: Viveka takes possession of mind.
Discarding of limbs	: Dis-identification with body as a result of enlightenment.
Was ready to go	: Attainment of liberation-Jivanmukti.

31.   Again, I found another person beating himself and roaming around alone with an anguished mind.

32.   I invited his attention and questioned him. He alternatively wept and laughed and discarding his limbs, he totally disappeared from view.

The suggestion is that this individual attained enlightenment and videhamukti.

33 to 36. I saw yet another person, fully blind, running alone and falling into a big pit. I waited for a long time looking for him. The wicked man did not come out of the pit for a long time.

I saw another person running around and seizing him, I asked, 'O wicked man, do you not recognise me?' He shouted back at me, 'O wicked man, get away' and minded his work.

37. Thus, in that vast forest, there are a number of such individuals. They keep roaming and such a land exists even now.

38. That land, infested with various kinds of thorns, filled with dense darkness, is being frequented as if it is a garden-house, by people who have not got the repose attainable through self-knowledge."

39. Sri Rama asked: "What is that vast land, o seer and where is it seen? Who are those individuals? What was it that they set about to do?"

40 to 58. Vasishta said: "O Rama, listen, Let me explain everything. That land is not far away nor are those referred to are human beings. Know that vast deserted land to be the worldly existence, frightful and limitless. Those who are stated to be individuals roaming around there are minds which keep inviting misery. He who saw them there is viveka, the discriminating vision. They were sought to be awakened by viveka. Because of my grace and instruction in the form of viveka, some of them got peace of mind and liberation. Some deluded persons disregarded me, the viveka, and as a result, they again fell into the pit. That which is spoken of as vast and dark pit is hell; the plantain grove is heaven and the jungle is earthly existence. Those who fall into the pit are persons who have committed grievous sins and remain forever in hell. The jungle is also associated with happiness of life and also misery and desire, the characteristics of human existence.

Those who insulted me as wicked brahmin are ignorant of Self and have disregarded their own discriminating wisdom.

Those words that were spoken-'that I have been enslaved,' 'I am lost,' 'You are my enemy'-are the outcry of the conceited mind.

That wail emanating from the men is the cry of the mind that has to give up the pleasures of senses.

Piteous cry arises from the mind that is only partially enlightened and that has not fully attained liberation, when it has to discard pleasures.

The happy smile put up by some who had been ignorant and later attained discriminative vision is a reflection of the happiness their minds have attained. When one has attained discrimination, rejected worldly life mentally, hapiness grows within.

That I seized him forcefully is indicative of the fact that viveka takes possession of the mind in a compelling way.

When the person is stated to beat himself and flees, the mind is seeking to run away from the attack of its own vasanas, tendencies.

Mind by its own sportive indulgence in the vasanas binds itself in fetter like the spider that weaves a web around it.

59.   I have now told you, Rama, the significant story of the chitta. With the help of the chitta, understand the Truth and having understood it, be firm in renouncing chitta."

Chapter-7

The Story of a Child

Vasishta said:

1. *"For the enlightened souls, Rama, mind is of the nature of Brahman only and nothing else. The Supreme Brahman is omnipotent, eternal, all pervading and imperishable.*

2. There is nothing which does not originate in the expansive self. Whatever its sakti (power) wills, that form it assumes.

3 & 4. It is the power of Consciousness of Brahman that manifests in human bodies.

   It is the power of movement that manifests in the wind, power of firmness in the stone, power of fluidity in the waters, power of burning in the fire, power of emptiness in the space, power of destruction in the death.

5. All this world exists in the self, as the peacock feather in the fluid of the egg, as the fruit, leaf, tender shoots, flowers, branches, trunk, root, etc., in the seed of the tree.

6. As various crops arise from the earth at different seasons, various powers arise from the self at some time or occasionally.

7. That self, O Rama, is all-pervasive and is ever-manifest; through contemplating, the faculty of contemplation arises and it is called the mind.

8. Initially, the mind manifests; the capacities for

bondage and liberation manifest in it; it creates the world; known as earth; - such a creative sequence has come to stay like the story narrated to a child."

As the events of the story are believed to be true by the child, this sequence of creation is believed to be true by one at the stage of ignorance. Neither the story nor the creative process is real.

9.   Sri Rama said: "O great seer! What is the nature of the story told to the child? Tell me in detail; how does it explain the nature of mind?"

10.   Vasishta said: "O Rama, some innocent child asked the foster-mother, "O mother, tell me something interesting to hear."

11.   O wise man, in order to delight the child, the foster-mother told a story in simple charming words.

12 to 26. "Somewhere, three good princes-virtuous and valorous-are born to a great king in a city that does not exist at all. Of the three two were not born and the third was not conceived.

Once, the three, with great desire, set out from their city of void to achieve some great goal. As they went, they saw tree in the empty sky with fruits. Resting now and then and eating the tasty fruits, the three princes went on merrily.

They reached in due course, three beautiful streams-one among them was totally dry and in the other two, there was no water. Exhausted as they were, they bathed in the waters to their delight. They sported in the waters for a long time and drank the milk-like water.

Then the three, in the evening, reached the city which was still to come into existence. They heard even at a distance the funny talk of the people. They saw there three dwellings. One was without wall and pillars. The other two were yet to be constructed. The three princes entered the house without wall and acquired three golden vessels. Of the three vessels, two broke into two parts and third one turned into powder.

The three wise persons took the vessel that was in powder. In that vessel, they cooked three measures of food and the food was also short by three measures.

The food was taken by many brahmins without mouths. The food that was the residue, after the brahmins had eaten was eaten by the princes. In that city that was still to exist, the three princes thus lived happily and went on hunting expeditions often.

O Rama, this story was narrated by the foster-mother to the child and the child, incapable of rational analysis, believed the story to be true. Now I have told you the story relating to the child. This world is real only to the minds incapable of rational enquiry. Such were also the events of the story told to the child.

27.   *The entire world is the play of the imagination. It is the imaginative inclination that projects the mind. Abandoning this kind of imagining tendency, O Rama, rise up to super-conscious plane and experience sure bliss."*

Chapter-8

The Story of Sambarika

Vasishta said:

1. "The ignorant person becomes a prey to delusion by virtue of his own imagination but not the wise person whose mind is trained in rational analysis and is not prone to stupid fancy.

2. Enquire into what is real. Discard the unreal. You imagine yourself to be bound when you are not bound. Why do you grieve needlessly? How is the infinite self bound and by whom?

3. When the blissful undifferentiated consciousness abides as a single infinite being and when there is no second entity, who is bound and who is liberated?

4. *It is only through its own fancy, mind becomes bound. When the mind becomes extinct, liberation certainly results.*

5. When the mind is adventurous in pursuit, even long distances appear as small leap. Similarly, a second becomes an aeon and an aeon a second.

6. Here, in this connection, hear this excellent story. It will reveal how the magical worldly spectacle has its origin in the mind.

7. There exists in this vast earth abounding in huge forests, a prosperous big country called Uttarapandava.

8. There ruled a very righteous king called Lavana. He belonged to the family of Harishchandra and was, like a sun on earth, splendrous.

9.   His fame rose up like the pollen of flowers which pervade the trees adorning like gardens in the mountains.

10.   He knew not deceit, possessed not craving. He was noble both in speech and deed.

11.   Once he happened to be seated on the golden throne in the council amidst learned men in state-craft.

12.   Then, with much fanfare, a juggler entered the hall and he saluted the king shining like the crest of a mountain.

13.   With raised head like the flower, he addressed the king, "O king, do thou see now a wonderful magic display, sitting in your throne like the rising moon on earth."

14.   Saying thus, he waved a bunch of peacock feathers which contained a hundred deluding potencies and which, like the Maya of the Supreme being, was capable of generating illusion.

15.   The king saw a luminous spectacle and at the same time the king of Sindhu kingdom entered the hall.

16.   A horse calm but fast-footed followed the king and showing the horse, he told the emperor Lavana:

17.   "O great Lord, this horse, a jewel among horses, is as glorious as Uchhaisravas of Indra. My king has sent this as a gift to thee, the emperor.

18.   A glorious thing shines all the more when it is offered to a noble being." When the visiting cheiftain spoke in this manner, the magician said:

19.   "O Lord, ascend on this good horse and go on a happy ride." Told thus, the emperor looked at the horse.

20.   In less than a minute, the emperor looking at the

horse, became motionless like the picture on a wall.

21. He remained in that condition for two hours like a person absorbed in meditation of Self. The councillors, getting surprised at this development, began to contemplate.

22. The ministers were plunged in doubt. The ostentatious activity of the royal assembly came to a halt.

23. As the magician was proud of his magical skill, as the councillors and people were drowned in fear, doubt and sorrow and as the king remained with his eyes open, the assembly looked like a cluster of lotus buds."

24. Vasishta said: "After two hours, the king woke up. Shaking off from the unconscious state, he became alert now.

25. The king saw the councillors in an anxious mood. Then the councillors and the ministers enquired him.

26. After the king had perfectly regained consciousness, they, with due humility, asked, "How is it that your agile mind has succumbed to illusion? The mind of a noble person does not get so deluded."

27 & 28. The king, becoming surprised and with eyes closed, said, 'O assembled nobles, hear this wonderful spectacle. I saw the peacock feathers waved by the deceitful magician.

29. Ascending on the horse, with an unclear mind, I set out with great fanfare on the hunting adventure alone.

30. By this interpid horse, I was taken too far, like the fool by his own mind exposed to physical pleasures.

31. With the horse getting exhausted, I reached an endless forest which was frightful like a place burnt by fire at deluge, without birds, mist, trees and water.

32. After reaching that forest, my mind became distressed. With a sad heart, I roamed around till the sun set.

33. Like the wise man transcending worldly existence, after great suffering, I got beyond that forest and reached a wood.

34. In that wood, filled with groups of jackals, was heard the cooings of the birds and the trees appeared like relatives to a traveller.

35. Riding on the horse, I reached a place with tambira trees.

36. As I firmly caught the creeper, the horse fled away just like the sins from a person bathing in the Ganga.

37. Being tired of travel over a long distance, I took rest. I was confused in mind and the night I spent looked like a kalpa, aeon.

38. I did not bathe, nor worship God, nor ate food. Caught in a dangerous situation, I somehow spent the night.

39. Attacked by cold, my teeth began to tremble and chatter and the night filled with dense darkness passed away.

40 & 41. I went into the vast land and in that wilderness, I could not see any creature, in much the same way as we cannot see any good trait in a wicked man. Birds flew here and there without fear and spoke in their language.

42. As the sun was about to reach the mid-day, I saw, as I wandered, a girl of dark complexion and eyes, in soiled clothes, carrying food with her.

43 to 45. As moon encounters the night, I encountered her and told her, 'Woman, give me food. For one who gives food to the needy in distressed and dangerous

condition, prosperity accrues. The hunger of my stomach grows mightily.'

46. In spite of my request, nothing was given to me, as to the wicked man by Lakshmi, however much he prays to her for wealth.

47. I followed her a long distance, as she walked from that place to another, like her own shadow.

48. She then told me, 'Know me to be chandali, low-caste woman and Harakeyuri is my name. O king, you cannot get food from me by merely asking for it.'

49. Saying thus, she slowly walked and rested, again and again, under shrubs and creepers, looking for fruits. Then with gesture, she said:

50 & 51. "I shall give this food if you agree to be my husband. My father, endowed with great strength, tills in a land nearby. This food is intended for him. If you take the position of husband, I give it to you, as beloved husbands are worthy of worship even at the cost of life."

52. I told her, "O woman of good resolve, I shall be your husband." When one is in danger, does one care to consider class, caste, family, etc?

53. Then she gave me half the food that was with her. I drank the juice of Jambu fruits and ate the food of the low-caste home.

54 & 55. I took rest for a while without any anxiety. Then she took me-who was dear to her as her own breath- by her hand and led me to her father who was fierce-looking, uncouth in conduct and monumental in size, as one is led to the hell.

56. I was introduced by her to her chandala father. "Let it please you, father, He will be my husband."

57. He told her, "Well, let it be so" and at the end of the day, set us free like the master freeing his servants.

58 to 60. We roamed around in the misty environs and in the evening returned to the dwelling which was filled with fleshes of animals and birds with flies all around.

61. I remained there in the new father-in-law's mansion and he with red eyes called me endearingly as 'son-in-law.'

62 & 63. Where is the need to dilate much? In course of time, the dark daughter was given to me as wife as dark sin begets hell.

64. With much noise, they celebrated the marriage occasion and the dog-eaters drank intoxicating drinks. It was as if wicked deeds indulged in a celebration of their own.

65. From then on, I became a hefty chandala. The celebration lasted for seven nights and another spell of eight months was gone.

66. She became pregnant and gave a daughter like disaster bringing forth some danger.

67. That daughter grew faster like the scheme of a wicked man. In another three years, she gave birth to an evil boy, as a wicked mind given to likes and dislikes giving rise to misery.

68. The chandali woman gave birth to another child.

69. Thus in her company I spent many years-in various states and amidst sufferings caused by cold, wind, heat, etc.

70. Oppressed by the thoughts of the wife and tormented by the anxious mind, I experienced all miseries and there was as though conflagration in all directions.

71.   Long time pased this way. I became old with fatigued limbs. Hot tears gathered in my eyes.

72.   There was great famine. All the grassland became utterly dry. Untimely deaths stalked everywhere.

73 to 85. When the land went dry without grass, leaves and water, when there was no downpour of rains and when people started dying, when the fiery planets clashed in the space and when winds set in, there was an unexpected blaze in the woods. The fire burnt vast areas and all the grass and creepers were reduced to ashes. Miseries multiplied when fate became adverse.

Some people, along with their well-wishers, left the place once for all for Vindhya mountain. Some got destroyed in the fire. Some fell in the pits and some others fell unconscious.

Taking with me the wife and the three children with great difficulty, I left the place and walked slowly and reached the shelter of a tree. I took the children-embodiments of misery-from the shoulders and placed them on the earth. I felt as though I had come away from the rourava hell and rested for a while.

The two chandala girls embracing mother fell asleep in the cool shade of the tree. My son called Pricchaka-he was young of lovable speech and was dear to all-stood before me and with tears gathering in his eyes, asked in piteous tone, 'Father, give me flesh to eat and blood to drink at once.' My little son asked me thus, again and again. His life was nearing extinction and so he cried again and again.

Seeing his distress, my grief got intensified and I decided to solve the suffering by courting death, a true friend in the circumstance and thus enable my son to eat the flesh of my body and survive. I gathered the woods and lit the pyre. The fire creating the sounds greeted me.

86. When I was about to throw myself in the pyre, I felt a tremor in the body. I found myself rudely shaken from the throne on which I was sitting. The sounds of the bugles and the greetings of the courtiers brought me to senses.

87. Thus, an illusory spectacle has been created for me by Sambarika, the juggler, in a minute. Surely, it is the jiva's own ignorance that creates a hundred varied situations for him.

88. As the radiant king Lavana spoke thus, Sambarika disappeared from view in a second.

89. The assembled men said, 'O king, this is not Sambarika, as he has not shown desire for money.

90 & 91. It is some divine cosmic power that has manifested in that form to teach the real nature of worldly life. That power reveals that it is mind that manifests as samsara. Mind as well as the world are but the projections of the Infinite Omnipotent Being."

Chapter-9

The Story of Lavana

Vasishta said:

1. *"Know Rama, that which is done mentally is really done; that which is renounced mentally is really renounced.*

2. If the mind remains bereft of mentation and vascillation, then it has attained to a lofty plane and the meditation has been fruitful.

3. When the mind is restrained, the worldly illusion subsides, as when the churning rod of Mandara mountain gets stilled, the milky ocean becomes calm.

4. Whatever are the modifications of the mind born out of desire for sense-pleasures these really turn into the seedlings of the poisonous trees of worldly existence.

5. Let me tell you what is the supreme and efficacious medicine, readily and easily available for treating the great disease that afflicts this mind.

6. *The mind has been won by the person who discards the objects the mind creates for him and remains unaffected inasmuch as the mind's outgoing tendency gets curbed.*

7. Wretched is the person, who finds it very hard to discard the desired object inasmuch as this is an act which he can himself do and which is entirely beneficial to him.

8. With the help of mind, sharpened by study of scripture, cut the mind already hot on account of worldly

thought, as an iron is cut by an iron.

The blacksmith with the help of a sharpened iron tool cuts the iron that has been heated; even so with the help of a mind sharpened by viveka, the mind rendered hot by worldly worry can be easily cut. V. C.

9. *Except through the extinction of the mind brought about by the renunciation of the desired object-which is within the person's capacity to do-there is no way to attain the blessed state.*

10. When the mind is cut by the weapon of asankalpa, non-imagination of object, the all-pervasive blissful Brahman is attained.

Sankalpa means imagining an object as pleasing or painful and this kind of imagination leads to desire or aversion of the object and by doing away with sankalpa, imagination, one gets rid of desire and aversion and brings about the extinction of mind. With mind getting extinguished through enquiry, the blissful self manifests.

11. Do thou attain to that unique exalted state and abiding in that state for long, let the chitta, mind, get swallowed up by the Chit, Consciousness and go beyond the mind.

Chitta getting swallowed up by the Chit means abidance as the residual Chit. V. C.

12. Release yourself from the worldly identification; be fully absorbed in the contemplation of the Supreme. When the Self is contemplated upon with ease, the mind gets swallowed up by it.

Contemplation of the Self leads to the extinction of mind.

13.   *Summoning up your will, by reducing the mind to naught, rise to the supreme state where there is none-neither you nor anyone else.*

You will attain to the Brahmic state which is non-dualistic in nature.

14.   *Absence of impatience is the means to prosperity. It is absence of impatience that brings about the individual's conquest of mind in relation to which even the victory over all the worlds is insignificant as straw.*

15.   As you contemplate on Chit, the Consciousness in the heart, with the help of the chakrayudha of Chit, kill the mind and no more mental afflictions will torment you.

16.   If what was regarded by you as attractive is now well-understood by you as despicable, the limbs of the mind, in my view, can be said to have been cut away.

When the desire for object regarded as attractive is destroyed by the understanding of the real despicable nature of the object, the mind gets weakened.

17.   'I am so and so,' 'this is mine'-such imaginations alone constitute the mind. By the negation of such thoughts, the mind gets destroyed, as a tree is cut off by the saw.

18.   Even as the dense cloud gets scattered and destroyed by wind in the summer, the mind gets destroyed by asankalpa, non-imagination.

19.   Let the wind blow as if in a deluge, let all the oceans get merged into one, let all the twelve Adityas, suns, burn together; for one whose mind is extinct, there is no harm.

20.   The supreme state which fulfills all the wishes is attainable only through asankalpa, non-imagination,

and do thou remain established in that state of asankalpa.

The state of asankalpa is the state of nirvikalpa samadhi where one abides as Brahman. V. C.

21. The enemy, that is, mind, rises by virtue of mere sankalpa, imagination, and by getting engaged in the perception of a variety of objects, you are defeated by it.

On the other hand, you can conquer the mind through mere santosha, contentment, and with the help of non-craving for objects, attain to the eternal state of happiness.

Sankalpa creates the mind and santosha destroys it. Santosha leads to vairagya and nirvikalpa samadhi.

22. Even-mindedness is a cool, blessed state and as a result of practice of it by the wise man, when the ahanta, ego, gets totally erased, the state of plenary existence manifests and may you abide in that awareness."

23. Vasishta continued: "Mind devoid of the trait of vascillation exists nowhere. As heat is the attribute of fire, vascillation is the attribute of mind.

24. The trait of vascillation is really the spanda sakti, capacity for movement abiding in the chit, consciousness. Know it to be the mental power that is responsible for the world spectacle.

25. The mind bereft of the innate trait of vascillation is virtually a dead mind; such a dead mind is what penance, study of scripture, spiritual doctrine aim at. It also leads to liberation:

Penance, scripture, spiritual doctrine are the means to the attainment of mind's extinction and the latter is the means to Moksha, liberation.

26. Rama, it is this vascillation of the mind that is called avidya, ignorance. Vasana, tendency, is its another name. Destroy that avidya through vichara, enquiry.

Since mind is caused by avidya, it is termed as avidya itself. V. C.

27. By virtue of renunciation of the desired object, avidya, vasana, the inner mind, etc., get dissipated and the supreme beatitude is attained.

28. That which is aligned to both the existent and the non-existent, to both the chitta and the inert matter, that which is dual in form, is known as mind.

29. Chit, vitiated by contemplation of the inert and propelled by it, becomes inert itself, as a result of such intense practice.

30. By contemplation of the spiritual nature and by its innate spiritual tendency, it becomes one with Chit following intense practice.

Mind, being dual in nature, becomes the objective matter or the subjective consciousness in accordance with the intensive practice. Mind has the conscious subjective principle (called 'anidham') and the unconscious objective element (called 'idham') with the former contributing to liberation and the latter to bondage.

31. Through effort, unite the mind to that supreme state and with practice that state is certainly attained.

32. Therefore, exert yourself and by overcoming the mind, by the mind, attain to that state untainted by sorrow and remain established in it.

33. It is only mind that is capable of decisively

vanquishing the mind. O Rama, can anyone other than a king conquer a king?

34. For those drowned in the ocean of samsara, caught in the grips of the crocodiles of desires and carried far by the current, one's mind alone is the boat which can save them.

35. Restrain the mind by the mind and severing the bonds of attachment, redeem yourself from the ocean of existence and no one can do it for another.

36. Whenever the mind is activated by vasana-tainted parts of it, counter the vasanas and that will result in the obliteration of avidya, the nescience.

37. Renounce the desire for pleasure and renounce the sense of difference. Renouncing the perception of manifest and unmanifest things, remain established in superconscious blissful state.

38. It is the annihilation of mind brought about by renouncing every desired object that is known as annihilation of avidya, ignorance.

39. Absence of craving for pleasure is the state of liberation; craving is fraught with misery. Through this practice, Brahman is realised immediately.

40. Avidya, nescience, is surely non-existent. It exists only for the ignorant. When its own name reveals its non-existence, how can it exist in a perfectly realised man?"

41. Sri Rama asked: "O Divine Seer! How does the dense darkness arising from the power of avidya, nescience, get destroyed? Explain to me again."

42. Vasishta said: "Avidya alongwith the embodied jiva keeps revolving in the slope of samsara infested with the thorny bushes until the rise of the desire for the

realisation of the Self which is capable of destroying the delusion and avidya.

43.   When the Supreme is cognised, the avidya gets destroyed. When awareness in all-pervasive form arises, the avidya gets dissolved.

44.   It is desire that is the inherent nature of avidya and the destruction of desire is what is called liberation. Destruction of desire is accomplished by ceasing to imagine that the objects are attractive.

Avidya is destroyed if desire is destroyed and desire is destroyed when one ceases to imagine things as attractive. Sankalpa means sam + kalpa, thinking of things as pleasurable. Asankalpa, non-imagination of objects as pleasurable is the weapon that destroys the desire.

45.   When the night of vasanas is brought to an end in the space of the mind, the dark avidya gets annihilated by the sun of Chit.

Vasanas: Night. Mind: Sky. Avidya: Darkness. Chit: Sun.

47.   Rama asks: Through the contemplation of the Self, does avidya get destroyed, as long as there is objective matter? What is the nature of the Self?"

Rama questions Vasishta's statement in Sl.43 that desire for Self-realisation destroys the avidya.

48.   *Vasishta said: "That consciousness which is not characterised by objective association, which is all-pervasive and supreme is the Self that is supreme good.*

49.   *All this indeed is Brahman which is immutable mass of consciousness. The imaginary entity called mind does not at all exist.*

50. In all the three worlds, nothing arises, nothing perishes. The changing objects do not have real existence.

51. There is only Consciousness-unassociated with objective cognition-which is unconnected with anything, which is spontaneously self-revealing and which is all-pervasive.

52 & 53. In that bare, untainted, pure consciousness which is blissful, all-pervasive and immutable, there arises the tendency, contrary to the innate nature on the part of undefiled chit, consciousness, to become chetyam, object and it is this mentation that causes it to become mind.

54. From this all-pervasive, all-capable Supreme Self arises the power of differentiation. Asankalpa, counter-imagination, destroys it as wind which helps the fire to grow also destroys it.

55. *Intense thought that 'I am not Brahman' serves to bind the mind. Intense thought 'All this is Brahman' frees the mind.*

56. The individual is bound by the activities fostered by the notion 'I am sad, miserable,' 'I am the body' and 'I feel bound.'

57. 'I am not miserable,' 'This body is not mine,' 'Who is bound?'-Such a faith and the activities caused by it, free the man.

58. 'I am not the flesh and the bones,' 'I am different from the body and I am the Supreme'-he who has this conviction has vanquished avidya and is liberated.

59. O Rama, this avidya of the nature of cognition of the non-Self as Self is a figment of imagination and exists only for the unenlightened and not for the enlightened.

60. Avidya brings about adhyasa, superimposition, which causes the non-self to be cognised as Self, the objective body as the subjective consciousness.

61. Whatever the mind wills, the senses carry out, as the king's orders are being carried out by the ministers.

62. Relying on your effort and with supreme will, uproot from the mind the desire for pleasure.

63. 'These are my sons; This is my wealth; I am so and so; This is mine'-through the magical web of relationship, it is vasana that acts.

64. Do not be an ignorant person, be an enlightened person. Conquer this samsara, worldly existence. Why do you cognise the non-self as Self and, like an ignorant person, weep?

65. 'O Rama! Who is this man-mere inert, lifeless body-for whose sake you are helplessly tossed about by pleasures and miseries?

66. *What a wonder it is? That which is real has been forgotten by people; that which is not real and is called avidya is asserting its presence.*

67. *As you keep engaged in your activities, do not get attached to anything, in the same way as the crystal does not hold on to the reflections that arise and pass away."*

68. Valmiki said: "As the great soul Vasishta spoke thus, Rama of awakened intelligence, made a submission.

69. Sri Rama asked: "It is surprising indeed that the threads formed out of the lotus-stalk, have been able to bind the mountain. Avidya, which does not exist (by definition) has wrought the havoc of the world.

70. Through the work of avidya, the creation forges the

strongest bonds. The three worlds which are but a straw-bit are as impregnable as Vajra weapon.

71. There is another great doubt tormenting my heart. How is it that noble-minded Lavana had to undergo hardship?"

72. Vasishta said: "Listen Rama. Let me tell a significant matter. That will explain why Lavana had the deluded experience of being a chandala.

73. From the story, it will be apparent that mind is the doer and the enjoyer of the fruit of action and not the body. Now listen.

74. Once, Lavana born of the lineage of Harischandra, sat alone for a long time and kept reflecting as below:

75. 'My grandfather is a great person, having performed the Rajasuya sacrifice. I am born in his family. Let me perform that yaga at least mentally.'

76. Thinking thus, the great ruler mentally brought together the accessories and got initiated (mentally) for the performance of the yaga.

77. He invoked the presence of the Devatas with the help of the priests and prayed to them through chants and prepared the consecrated fire.

78. Thus in the mental wood-land of the performer, a whole year passed away in the worship of devas, rishis and Brahmins.

79. After honouring the deities and giving away all his wealth as fees to the priests, he woke up from that wood-land at the day's end.

The performance of the yaga for one full year in the woodland was entirely Lavana's imagination.

80.   Thus it is that the king Lavana performed Rajasuya sacrifice. Since he did it mentally, he experienced the fruit of such sacrifice also mentally.

81.   Therefore, know Rama, that mind is greater than the body and is the real enjoyer of pleasure and pain. Unite the mind with the means that lead to reality and blessed life.

82 & 83. Now listen Rama, to the deed of Sambarika, the magician. When Sambarika entered the assembly hall of Lavana, I was there. I saw everything directly.

84.   After Sambarika's departure, I was asked about it by the persons in the assembly and also by the king.

        I reflected on it and saw the fact.

85 & 86. Listen to what I told them, Rama, about Sambarika. Those who perform Rajasuya sacrifice have to undergo various kinds of ordeals for twelve years.

87.   Therefore, for the sake of giving sorrows to Lavana, Indra had sent a celestial messenger in the form of the magician Sambarika.

        After giving hardships to the performer of the Rajasuya, the celestial messenger discarded the form of Sambarika and passed through the sky frequented by the celestials and seers.

88.   Vasishta continued: Let me further proceed. There are seven planes of ajnanam, ignorance and the planes of jnanam, wisdom also are seven only.

89.   There are any number of intermediate planes between these seven planes. These planes give distinct fruits to the concerned persons stationed in them.

90.   *Abidance in the intrinsic state is liberation, to swerve from it is to get seized by the 'I' notion. This, in a*

nutshell, is the characteristic of the enlightened and unenlightened person.

91. Those who are not drawn away from the state of pure intelligence by the feelings desire and aversion, are not subject to ajnanam, ignorance.

92. Those who swerve from the state of pure intelligence and get involved in objective matter are verily under the sway of delusion.

93. *Leaving one distant object, when the mind cognises another distant object, the state that manifests between two such acts, which is bereft of mentation is abidance in Self.*

The practice recommended in this verse is referred to again and again in the Yoga Vasishta. To know what is the nirvikalpa swarupa, the consciousness not characterised by verbalisation, one has to notice the interval between two cognitions and during that state, consciousness abides in pure form. A similar technique is recommended by Sri Adi Shankara in the minor work, 'Laghu Vakyavritti.'

94 & 95. The state in which all desires have become extinct, in which one remains motionless like stone, in which one is free from inertness and dream, is known as the state of abidance as Consciousness.

When the mind frees from the waking, dreaming and sleeping conditions characterised by delusion and inertness, it attains to the turiya, the fourth state, of pure consciousness.

96. When the 'I' notion has been erased and when the duality has been got rid of by the restraint of the mind, the illumining consciousness that manifests is known as Self.

97 & 98. *The seven planes of ignorance are: 1) Bija Jagrat;*
2) Jagrat; 3) Mahajagrat; 4) Jagrat Swapna; 5) Swapna;
6) Swapna Jagrat and 7) Sushupti.

By getting combined with each other in several degrees, they become very many. Hear their characteristics.

99 to 108. Bija Jagrat is the state of cosmic consciousness (chithi) assuming the form of chetana which is unnameable and pure and which subsequently acquires the appellation and the attributes of jiva. Bija Jagrat is the state in which the waking condition remains as potential. This is the first evolution of jnapti, consciousness.

Listen to the description of jagrat. When with the newly-risen cosmic consciousness, notions of externality and ego arise simultaneously, not flowing from previous cognitions, that state is jagrat.

When the consciousness is characterised by the strong impressions, 'I am so and so,' and 'this is mine' aroused by the vasanas in the previous life, that state is known as Maha Jagrat.

The state of consciousness which is absorbed fully in fancies, intentionally or otherwise indulged in by the mind, is called as jagrat swapna, the condition that can happen during the waking state.

That which is recollected or not during the waking state with the thought 'I saw it a brief while' is called swapna, dream. Because the dream is not seen for a long time and because the objects do not have gross and clear manifestation, the dream experiences are so called.

That is known as swapna jagrat which causes the experience to linger on as if in the waking state by virtue of dreaming for a long time.

That is known as the sushupti, sleep, which is attained by passing beyond the other six states; which is inert; and which is the mass of future sorrows in a potential form. In that state, the world gets merged in tamas, ignorance.

109. Thus O Rama, I have described the seven states of ignorance. Each one is capable of manifesting in a hundred modes."

110. Vasishta said: "Now, do you hear the seven planes of enlightenment. O faultless man, he who knows these planes does not get drowned in the mire of delusion.

111. Enlightened persons speak of yogic planes from differing view-points. My own preference is only for these seven planes which are capable of giving happiness.

112. Self-realisation has these seven stages. The realisation itself assumes the form of reality when one has gone beyond the seven planes.

In the opinion of the commentator of BYG (Refer 3-117-Sl.3), jnanam, knowledge itself at the highest level is seen as the jneyam, the Reality.

113. *Subeccha-desire for beatitude, is called the first plane; vicharana-enquiry, is the second; and tanumanasa-the attenuated mind is the third plane.*

114. Sattvapatti-attainment of purity is the fourth plane; asamsakti-non-attachment, is the fifth plane; padartha-abhavana non-contemplation of objects is the sixth plane; and turiya-transcendental awareness, is called the seventh.

115. At the end of these stages remains liberation. On the attainment of it, one does not have to grieve. Do thou hear what these seven planes refer to.

116. 'Why do I remain a stupid person. Let me try to know the Self with the help of scriptures and wise persons'- when such a resolve is made and it is associated with vairagya, detachment that is the plane called subeccha, desire for beatitude.

117. When a person pursues the wise conduct of studying the scripture under enlightened persons alongwith the practice of detachment, that plane is called vicharana, enquiry.

118. When, through practice of enquiry and desire for liberation, a detachment towards sense-objects develops and the mind gets attenuated, this plane is called tanumanasa, state of attenuated mind.

This third plane, according to the commentator of LYV, corresponds to Nididhyasana, concentrated contemplation of the Self. The mind at this plane becomes attenuated because the desire which makes the mind gross has been overcome.

It should be noted that these first three planes pertain to the realm of sadhana, practice, because the sense of duality has not been eliminated. For this very reason, the three planes together constitute the jagrat state among the jnana bhumis.

119. When the practices relating to the three planes are adhered to, and when on account of the detachment, mind abides in the pure Self, the plane is called sattvapatti, attainment of pure Self.

This fourth plane, called swapna stage represents the state in which there is immediate cognition of Self. It is not combined with the first three planes which constitute the realm of sadhana.

120. When the disciplines relating to the four planes are followed, the mind gets established in sattvic purity and becomes totally detached, that plane is called asam-sakti, perfect detachment.

The fifth plane corresponds to sushupti stage in the jnana bhumis and at this stage, the person gets rid of notions of duality and experiences the advaitic state.

121 & 122. When through practice of the previous planes and when out of fervent devotion to Self the person does not cognise any other internal or external entity, he attains to the (samadhi) state called padartha-abhavana, from which he can be drawn away only by other's efforts. This plane, in which objects are not cognised, is sixth.

123. When the practices relating to the six planes are followed for a long time and the difference is not cognised and when the person abides wholly as the Self, that plane should be known as the turiya plane, the transcendental awareness.

As aforesaid, the first three planes belong to the realm of the sadhana. In the fourth plane, there is immediate realisation of Self. The planes, 5th, 6th and 7th represent different levels in the experience of jivan-mukti, liberation-in-life. The seventh plane is akin to videha-mukti, liberation after separation from body. The distinctions in the level of jivanmukti arise on account of the differences in the practice of asamprajnatha-samadhi and the degree of spiritual poise that flows from it.

124. The seventh plane represents the turiya state of jivanmukta. The state of videha-mukta indicates the plane beyond, turiyatita.

125. O Rama, those who have reached the seventh plane, are adorers of Self, noble-souls and have attained to the most exalted state.

126. The jivanmuktas do not get drawn to the experience of pleasure and pain. They attend to the affairs demanded by the occasion or perhaps not.

127. Reminded by people around, they attend to things as required by convention but remain in sleep-like condition, unharmed by anything.

128. The seventh plane is reached only by the wisest. They who reach this state of enlightenment-even if they belong to the low castes-get liberated, whether they are with their body or not. There is no doubt in regard to this fact.

129. Enlightenment arises on account of the severance of the knot (of 'I' notion) and if the knot gets sundered, there is liberation. That results in a state of peace and is akin to the destruction of the delusion of the mirage.

When the illusory 'I' notion called the knot is dispelled, the Consciousness manifests.

130. Those who have gone beyond the dreadful ignorance have really attained the supreme plane. Those who remain in the other planes are exclusively devoted to the attainment of the Self.

131. Those great souls who have conquered these planes are really worthy of worship, as they have vanquished the enemies of senses and in relation to them, the positions of the emperor or sovereign are insignificant

as bit of straw. Such persons have attained the essence of life."

132. Vasishta said: "The means of restraint of the mind are called yoga and they cover seven planes which I have now described.

133. Through these planes is attained the Brahmic reality in which the entities like 'You,' 'I' and 'other' do not at all exist. There is no sense of distinction and there is not attachment to the existent or the non-existent.

134. All this is eternal, imperishable, auspicious and the blissful Being. It is free from taint, falsity and causal relationship.

135. It is neither the existent nor the non-existent. It is both all and not all. It is beyond the grasp of mind and word. It is the greatest void, the greatest bliss.

136. It is non-cognition of anything else, as all duality has vanished. It is unbounded Self-experience.

137. Vasishta said: "I have now told you the seven planes of enlightenment. Rama, now listen again about the invincible nature of avidya.

138 to 143. The great ruler Lavana, having had the illusory experience, went out on the second day to see the woodland. 'I remember the forest where I experienced hardships. They are vivid like images in the mirror. It is possible that I may be able to see them.' With this decision, he set out alongwith ministers towards the south and reaching the Vindhya mountain, he searched for in all the directions, out of curiosity and strode like sun on the sky.

In one place, it seemed as though fulfillment of his wish manifested in a visible form before him; he saw the dense forest as if it was another planet. He remembered all the experiences he had undergone, talked about them, heard from others and became extremely surprised.

144 to 160. Then he reached the very hamlet pervaded by smoke wherein he had lived as a chandala. He saw the same men, the same women and the same huts. He found the old woman complaining with tears in her eyes about her woes. 'Children, where have you gone leaving my laps? O my daughter, you have been taken away from me by adverse fate? The king who had the lustre of the moon, leaving the women of his harem, had delighted in your company and that too has come to an end.' Thus she cried aloud.

Samsara, worldly existence, is a river with waves rising and falling by the results of actions and if a king got united with a chandala woman, what is the improbable thing that might not happen?

The king consoled the woman who had lamented thus and asked her, 'Who are you? Who is your daughter? Who are the children?' With tears rolling down her eyes, she said, 'This is the hamlet of chandalas. There was my chandala husband. He had a daughter with moon-like face. By a stroke of fortune, she got as her husband a king who was an Indra on the earth. He lived with her for a long time happily and gave birth to two daughters and one son.

After some time, because of lack of rains a famine struck and with great handicap, the village people trying to go away from here met death on the way. That is how we have been left here to grieve for them. Remaining in this deserted place, we are a miserable lot and keep grieving for them.

After hearing these words of the woman, the king

became surprised. He saw the people whom he had known and stood motionless like a picture. The wise king, well-versed in worldly matters, out of compassion, gifted appropriate wealth and reduced her plight. He returned to his capital alongwith the ministers. He thought within himself, 'I have known what avidya is. I have become enlightened.

O Rama, avidya has immense capacity for deluding people. The unreal is made real and the real unreal."

161. Rama asked: "O Divine seer! How is it that what was like a dream assumed real existence? This is a doubt and my mind is unable to solve it."

162. Vasishta said: "O Rama, all these do happen in the realm of avidya. This truth wil become more clear when I recount the story of Gadhi.

163. By a fortuitous combination of vasanas, tendencies, great events are set in motion.

164. When, as a result of Sambarika's act, the same avidya that was responsible for the king's visit to the chandala hamlet on the first day, manifested on the succeeding day as well.

165. That very deluded thinking, which had taken hold of the mind of the king had also imprinted itself in the mind of the chandala of the Vindhya hill.

166. Lavana's delusion manifested in the mind of the chandala as well and chandala's thinking manifested in the mind of the king.

167. All the matter has no reality apart from the knowledge concerning it. In fact, the existential nature of all objects is nothing but knowledge of it.

168. *When the seer and the seen get related to each other, the essential nature of the seer is responsible for such*

manifestation and if it is stripped of the aspects of seer, seeing and seen, it is truly the Supreme.

169. *When between two successive cognitions, manifests luminous consciousness, do remain in that condition always.*

170. *That which is the eternal nature of the mind, when there are no jagrat, swapna and nidra, that is, when it is not sentient and not inert, do retain that condition always.*

171. Like the mindless state of the interior of the stone but unlike its inert nature, remain, o great man, always, as pure awareness.

172. Discard the mind and remain as you are without oscillation. By following appropriate reasoning, release yourself from worldly bondage.

173. Samsara is a revolving wheel tied to a machine and vasana being the rope that serves to bind it. O Rama, tear it to pieces.

174. From the Supreme Reality arises the mind and by the mind is created this vast world with its manifold forms, even as akasa, though it is mere void, displays blueness in a beautiful manner.

175. When through the destruction of sankalpa, mind is destroyed, the darkness of delusion called samsara gets driven away. The sky shines in a clear manner when the summer has set in and even so, the pure Consciousness, unborn and infinite, manifests within.

Section-4
Sustenance

Chapter-1
<u></u>

The Story of Bhargava

1. *Though there is no actor nor stage, a fine spectacle is seen in the space of Consciousness. There is no spectator as well. Further, this dream experience has arisen when there is no sleep.*

    In the previous section, (on creation) that the cosmos is the projection of the mind and with the restraint of the mind the cosmic experience also comes to an end, has been explained. In this section (on sustenance), that the cosmos emanating from the mind rests only on the mind and that the mind abides in its cause, Atma, Self, is established.

    The meaning of the first verse is: The world experience is akin to a picture. But this is a picture without a painter, a wall, the paint and the spectator. It is also akin to dream experience with this difference, that it is experienced even while one is not asleep.

2. *In the Chid-atma, Self-Consciousness, which is pure non-differentiated witnessing principle, the worlds get reflected as in a mirror, in vain.*

3. O Rama, without any cause-effect relationship, this glorious universe appears in the Brahman, as a mere image.

4. *In order to remove the vascillating trait of the mind, do thou contemplate with effort that there is only Brahmic Consciousness-unbroken and all-pervasive.*

5. Like a massive stone, that carries within it the impressions of numerous long and small lines, may the solitary Brahman associated with the three worlds be viewed by you.

6. *As there is nothing apart from Brahman to serve as cause, the world is really unborn. In the vast Brahmic Consciousness, it manifests as an image in it.*

7. O flawless soul, let me now narrate to you the story of Bhargava. Your mind will then grasp that the world is really unborn.

8. Long before, in some slope of the Mandhara mountain abounding in flowers, the divine seer Bhrigu performed severe penance.

9. Sukra, his erudite son, possessing all the effulgence of the moon and spiritual radiance like the sun, worshipped his father.

10. Sukra, having not yet attained the supreme beatitude, was stranded between wisdom and ignorance, as Trishanku was in the mid-space.

    The king Trishanku who had become a chandala, low-caste man, aided by the mystic power of sage Viswamitra, went to the heaven in his own physical body and the celestials having refused entry to him into heaven, he remains suspended in the mid-space. Sukra was not wholly enlightened, nor was he completely ignorant, and so he was in wavering condition.

11. His father was once in nirvikalpa samadhi, super-conscious state of absorption, and Sukra was free from

concern and was alone, just like a king who had defeated the enemy.

12. At that time, he saw a celestial nymph adorned with a mandara garland and with her curly hairs tossed by the wind she was passing through the sky.

13. Seeing the beautiful nymph, his mind indulged in amorous fancies. He kept thinking about her intently, without even closing his eyes.

14. Sukra was totally lost in a world of his creation. This celestial nymph reached the abode of the thousand-eyed Indra.

15. 'I am now here at Swarga where live these celestial nymphs with charming bent gait.

16 to 18. They adore Indra, as the creepers their lord, the tree. Here is Indra's supreme abode and let me offer obeisance to him who is only next to the Creator-God.' Thinking thus, Sukra mentally offered obeisance to Indra, who in turn offered obeisance to one, who was just like another Bhrigu in the sky.

Indra received Sukra with great affection and worshipped him.

19. Sukra began to sport in the heaven, surrounded by the celestials.

There he saw among the celestial damsels his beloved nymph with deer-like eyes. And she too saw him and became instantly drawn towards him.

20. With passionate love manifesting towards each other, they glowed like the sun and the morning lotus.

21. Seeing her in that condition, Sukra, who was capable of fulfilling any wish, wished to be surrounded by darkness like the one created by Rudra at the time of destruction.

22.   As all others went away in their chosen directions, the nymph came before Bhrigu's son, as the peacock before the clouds.

23.   Then, amidst the bunches of creepers, they forgot all their sorrows for a while. They delighted their minds with long loving looks, talks and manifest expressions of endearment. This union gave delight to Sukra. So he began to live with her in the city of Indra.

24 & 25. He lived happily with the deer-eyed beloved for several yuga cycles. At the thought of extinction of merit occuring to him, he fell on the earth.

26.   As he was falling on earth, he remembered his own abode, and entered in the form of jiva into the sphere of moon.

27.   After passing though the deluge, he assumed the form of grain and was eaten by a learned brahmana of Dasarna country.

28.   Attaining the form of bindhu (semen) in the body of the brahmana, Sukra became the son of the brahmana and his wife. By virtue of association with seers, he pursued severe penance.

29.   He dwelt in the cave of Meru happily for the whole period of a Meru's lifetime. At that time he begot a son through the celestial nymph who had assumed the form of a deer.

30 & 31. Because of attachment to the son, he became a prey to delusion at once. He got engrossed in the thought, 'Let my son have wealth, virtue and long life', and swerved from the abidance in the Reality.

Since he had discarded virtue because of attachment to the son and pleasures, his life was coming to an end and the Lord of Death swallowed him as the serpent inhales the air.

32 & 33. Since he had died with a keen desire for pleasure, he was reborn as a king of Madrapuri. He attained several other births also.

34.   Finally, he was born as the son of an ascetic on the banks of Ganga.

35 & 36. By virtue of exposure to wind, heat, etc., over innumerable years, his body-as the son of Bhrigu - in the sitting posture at the hermitage of Bhrigu fell.

Since Bhrigu had great powers accruing from his penance and the hermitage was free from the influences of desire and aversion, the body of Sukra was not eaten up by the birds and the animals.

37 & 38. After several hundred celestial years, Bhrigu, as great as the Supreme Lord, rose up from the state of super-consciousness.

He did not see before him his son imbued with modesty, an embodiment of all virtues and divine merit in human person. He only saw the body, a mere skeleton of bones in an imposing form.

39 & 40. The skeleton appeared like a body that had been subjected to misery; it was poverty in visible form; it was a picture of suffering caused by penance with birds using the holes as nests and the frogs using the belly as their dwelling.

41.   He looked for a long time at the skeleton, which resembled the post to which is tied an elephant, and reflected not upon the possible sequence of events.

42.   Pondering over it for a long time, he understood that his son was dead. He had uncontrollable anger towards Kala, the Lord of Death.

43. 'My son has been taken away even before the due time of death'-saying angrily thus, the divine seer proceeded to pronounce a curse on Kala.

44. Kala who had no visible form and was known as devourer of people, assumed a physical form and appeared before the seer.

45. He wielded in his hands sword and noose; his body was adorned with jewels and armour. He had six shoulders and six faces and was surrounded by his servants.

46. Approaching the great seer who was as majestic and agitated as the ocean at the time of deluge and pacifying him, Kala said these words:

47. "O great brahmana, you have enormous powers of penance. I am but a person appointed to perform duty. I worship you, o holy brahmana, but not for any favour.

48. Do not waste away your penance through folly. I have not been burnt up by the conflagrations even during the times of deluge. Are you going to harm me by your curse?

49. Several Brahmas, worlds have been gulped by me, several Rudras and several Vishnus have been swallowed up, and o seer, what are we not capable of?

50. O divine seer, we are devourers and you and others are the eatable. It is the cosmic law that inexorably cperates and is not the wish of either of us.

51. There is neither doer nor enjoyer, seen from the point of Truth. For seers with a deluded perception, there are very many doers.

52. Flowers are seen in clusters in the branches of the trees and even so, creatures in the world. They come

into the world and go out of it as necessitated by their karma, action, and at the end of a kalpa, even Brahma goes out as ordained.

53. Where is that spiritual vision, the greatness and the courage? When this Truth has been well-ascertained, why are you deluded and blind?

54. Without understanding the course of events caused by one's own karma, O wise man, how, like an ignorant person, do you desire to curse me?

55. An individual is what his chitta, mind is. A thing done by the mind is really done. The mind itself, because it throbs with life, is called the jiva, the soul; and because it has the faculty to be decisive, is called buddhi, the intellect; because it has self-identification, is called ahankara, the ego, and thus it assumes many forms.

56. The mind of your son Sukra, as you were absorbed in samadhi, discarding the physical body went to the heavenly world.

57 to 60. O Seer, there he consorted with the heavenly beauty Visvachi. Thereafter, he was a brahmana at Dasarna country, the ruler of kingdom at Kosala, a fowler in the forest, the hamsa bird in the Ganga's bank, a king called Poundra in the solar dynasty and a preceptor called Soura in the Salva land. He was a Vidhyadhara during one kalpa. He was also a wealthy intelligent man once. He was a sovereign of the Souveera country and a preceptor of Siva's cult in Trigarta. He was a bamboo thicket in Kerala land, a deer in a jungle, a serpent, a cock, etc.

61. In several other species of various types, your son propelled by vasanas, tendencies, attained birth and lived.

62. Presently called by the name Vasudeva, your son, now born as the son of a brahmana, is doing penance on the bank of the river Samanga.

63. With matted locks and beads in hand, he, having controlled all the senses and the mind, remains established in penance for the past 800 years.

64. If you wish, O seer, to see the dream-like illusory phenomenon, open your inner eye of wisdom and see fully."

65. When he was thus told by Kala, the even-minded ruler of the universe, the seer began to see through the inner vision all the deeds of the son.

66. The entire sequence of events concerning the son, he saw in an hour, reflecting as if in the mirror of his mind, as a result of his yogic attainment.

67. He went mentally to the bank of Samanga to see Sukra in his present form and re-entered his own body in the presence of Kala.

68. The seer who was bereft of likes and dislikes, told Kala with a detached mind, after gazing at him with affection and amazement.

69. "O Divine lord, Ruler of the past and the present universe, we are indeed adolescents, with imperfect minds. Only the minds of persons like thee have perfect vision of the past, present and future."

70. When the Divine Being, Kala, was told thus, he smiling, at the nature of worldly life, took the seer by his hand, like the Sun joining with the moon.

71. Now, Kala and Bhrigu-the two celestials-set out to go from the Mandara mountain to the bank of the river Samanga.

72 & 73. In a minute, they reached the Samanga river and on the bank of it, Bhrigu saw his son, with senses perfectly controlled, deeply absorbed in meditation, with the mental oscillation brought to complete still.

74. Seeing Bhrigu's son in that condition, Kala willed, 'Let him wake up,' and the brahmana boy emerged out from the meditation. Opening his eyes, he saw before him Kala and Bhrigu.

75. Rising up from the seat made of creepers, he bowed to them. Conversing among themselves, they sat together on a rock.

76 to 79. The brahmana boy thus spoke to them in serene words: "I have attained great peace by the sight of you both. That delusion of the mind which is not erased by scripture or penance or wisdom or worship, that delusion is totally gone in a minute by the sight of you both. Even the amrita, immortal elixir, does not gladden the heart as the sight of holy personages. Who are you two, who, possessed with the effulgence of the sun and moon, have condescended to render this place holy by placing your feet on it?"

80. After he spoke thus, Bhrigu addressing his own son in a former birth, told him, "Do recollect your past, you are an enlightened person. You are not ignorant."

81. Instructed thus by Bhrigu, he, shattering his ego and entering into samadhi recollected in an hour all the happenings in the previous lives.

82. He, a master of speech, became delighted at heart and with face expressing his wonder, spoke clearly these words.

83. "Ah, what an illusion gets projected by the mind! It is through that illusion, this worldly spectacle is getting enacted.

84. *I have known the Truth to be known. That which has to be seen has been clearly seen. Now I abide in great peace. There is nothing indeed but Consciousnes.*

85. Father, rise up. Let us go to see the body in the Mandara mountain. Let me see the body. I am eager to see the ways of the Cosmic Will. There is nothing here which is particularly to my liking or otherwise."

86 & 87. Sri Vasishta said: "Conversing thus about the ways of life of the world, the three Knowers of Truth, reached in a minute the hermitage in the Mandara mountain and there Bhrigu's son saw his body of previous birth.

88. He said, "Father, this body, which was once fondled by you and fed by you with delicious things, is now a famished one.

89. See how the body remains sleeping without any thought or curiosity and imaginary fancies?

90. All the afflictions and sorrows caused by the darkness of delusion come to an end with the rise of moon and even so, unless one attains to the state of mindlessness, there is no way any creature can attain beatitude.

91. They alone have gone beyond all pleasures of life, who, having attained vision of Truth, remain in a mindless plane.

92. I see the body, by chance, released from all sufferings, devoid of all fevers and all thoughts."

93 & 94. Kala, disagreeing with his statement, told Bhrigu's son, "O wise man, enter into this body, as a king enters the capital city. With the help of this body, you have to function as the preceptor of the Asuras. Let there be happiness to all. Let me take leave of you."

95. As Kala spoke these words, the other two shed tears of joy. Kala disappeared from view.

96. After the Divine Kala had left, Bhrigu's son acting in accordance with Cosmic Will, discarded the brahmana's body acquired on the bank of Samanga and entered into his previous body.

97. As life entered into his son's body, the great seer sanctified it by uttering mantras and sprinkling on it the waters of the water-jug. All the nerves of the body sprouted into life and became active.

98. With prana circulating all over the body, Sukra rose up and offered obeisance to the father, an embodiment of holiness.

99. Thereafter, the two, Bhrigu and Bhargava (Bhrigu's son Sukra) remained happily in that forest without any sorrow like a lake without waves.

100. O Rama, thus have I described to you the experiences of Bhargava (Sukra). After deeply examining the nature of worldly life, do what is proper.

Chapter-2

The Story of Dhama and Others

1 to 5. Sri Vasishta said: "For the seeker who has done proper enquiry, who has stripped the mind of modifications, discarded the mentation, the Self is getting slowly unveiled. He who has discarded the objective matter and has established himself as the witness Consciousness. He is ever alive to the task of realising the Supreme. He is asleep without any thought in the dark delusion of worldly life; he is utterly detached in regard to objects of rich pleasure or no pleasure. When the net of samsaric tendencies, is cut asunder by vairagya, as the net spread for catching birds gets destroyed by rat, the knot of the heart-the ego complex-is destroyed. One's mind, by virtue of wisdom, becomes serene, as the muddy water becomes placid consequent on the contact with kathaka seeds.

6. He who is unattached, unassociated with anything, unassailed by pairs of opposites independent of anything, comes out of the delusion as the bird from the cage.

7. The wicked doubt has been vanquished; no curiosity spurs the mind. The mind regaining its fullness shines like the full moon.

8. For the one, who, after enquiry, has realised the supreme Self and for whom the Self is manifesting within, Brahma, Vishnu, Indra and Sankara really become objects of pity.

9.   The realised soul establishes himself in such an exalted state that he finds the Gods comparatively in lesser state of joy.

10. *He who cognises the Self and other things in all-inclusive perspective, with the conviction, 'All are the luminous Chit only' really knows the Truth.*

11. He who has the inner understanding, 'The Infinite Self is all-capable, all-inclusive, and non-dual', really knows the Truth.

12. *'I am not. Nor is there anything. This is pure Brahman only,'-He who has thus understood the reality in distinction from the non-self, really knows the Truth.*

13. The person with stabilised wisdom attends to the affairs without any desire, just as the mind cognises the things which it casually comes across.

14. *When a pleasure is experienced after understanding its nature, that pleasure gives fulfilment. When a thief is befriended knowingly, he becomes a friend, not a thief.*

15. *The enlightened person sees the objects of pleasure in much the same way as a traveller sees accidentally the functions and celebrations in the villages he passes through.*

16. A person with a restrained mind experiencing even a small object of pleasure is highly satisfied with it and he does not want the experience to be expanded through much pain.

17. A king in bondage is satisfied with three morsels of food; the same king, unassailable by any opponent, does not consider a kingdom vast enough.

18. Strike the hand with the hand, press the teeth with the teeth, crush the limbs by the limbs-thus exert

and initially conquer your own mind.

There is no way to redemption in the ocean of worldly life except through control of the mind.

19. Those are fortunate men, endowed with wise minds, worthy of being spoken amidst congregations-who have not been vanquished by their own minds.

20. I salute that imperishable, tranquil being in whose heart-like hole remains, in a coil, the serpent of mind with the poison of thought rendered powerless."

21. Sri Vasishta said: "In the sovereign domain of the hell,evil deeds are the unruly elephants and they are propelled by the iron rods of desire. Indeed, the senses are too mighty enemies to be conquered.

22. In a mind, which has eliminated pride and hatred, and which has been got rid of through the control of senses, the vasanas, tendencies, seeking more and more pleasures, begin to vanish as the lotus blossoms do in the lake during the winter.

23. *As long as the mind has not been conquered, through the concentrated contemplation of the Self as the sole Reality, so long the vasanas, like the devils in the night, remain active in the heart.*

24 & 25. A disciplined mind of the wise man, I believe, is akin to the servant who executes the given tasks; akin to a minister who performs righteous acts; akin to a sovereign as it directs the senses to function; akin to a perceptor as it gives wisdom; akin to an affectionate damsel, as it gladdens the heart; akin to a father as it protects; akin to a well-wisher as it is trustworthy.

26. Mind, like a father, sacrificing its own existence, presents great siddhis, attainments, when it is examined in the light of scriptural teachings and when

Truth is experienced through one's own understanding.

27. Mind shines like a pleasing jewel in the heart when it is fully cognised, made firm, pure, attractive and is properly disciplined.

28. O Rama, the jewel of mind has been sullied much by the mire and gets back the enlightened vision by washing it through the water of discrimination.

29. Relying on supreme discrimination, intuiting the reality through the intellect, vanquishing the enemies of senses completely, do thou go beyond the ocean of samsara.

30. *O wise man, give up the limited vision caused by the conviction, 'This is myself'; through proper enquiry of your own mind by identifying yourself with the unlimited Consciousness, go about, drink and eat, and, being devoid of mind, you will not get bound.*

31. O Rama, do not adhere to the example of Dhama-Vyala-Kata; you will free yourself from sorrow."

32. Sri Rama said, "O Divine Seer, what is meant by you, whose words are capable of dispelling the afflictions of worldly life, by such expressions as the Dhama-Vyala-Kata example and Bhima-Bhasa-Dhrida example."

33. Sri Vasishta said: "O Rama, do thou know what Dhama-Vyala-Kata and Bhima-Bhasa-Dhrida, respectively, stand for and thereafter do thou act in the way you want.

34. There was in the realm of patala (nether world) which was endowed with attractive riches, an asura-chief called Sambara and he was, as if, a jewel in the ocean of maya.

35. He was the lord of devas as well and had a huge form.

He had a very vast army capable of vanquishing the devas.

36. When he, endowed with magical powers, had been away from his kingdom, the devas finding the asuras vulnerable, quickly defeated them.

37. Thereon, Sambara sent an army led by the ministers Mundika, Anka and Dhruma for ensuring protection of his side.

38. The devas defeated them also after finding out their weakness. Thereupon, Sambara, getting angry, set out for the capital of the devas, himself.

39. The devas, becoming afraid of the magical powers of Sambara, disappeared and with tear-stained faces, they went into the hide-outs in the Meru mountain, forests, etc.

40 & 41. Sambara found the capital of the devas utterly empty, like the cosmos at the time of deluge.

42. As the hatred between the devas and danavas (asuras) got further intensifed, the devas deserted the heaven and hid themselves in various quarters.

43. Whoever was made the chief of army intentionally by Sambara was sought out and killed by the devas with great effort.

44. Sambara became enraged and furious and by his magical powers created three ferocious and mighty asuras.

45. They were like huge mountains without wings, fashioned by magical skill. Thus arose Dhama, Vyala and Kata.

46 & 47. Since they were born for the first time, they were free from past vasanas, tendencies and conceit. They

knew neither attack nor defence nor flight from the battle-field. They cared not for life or death, success or defeat. Whenever they saw warriors facing them, they killed those warriors.

48 to 59. Sambara, delighted with their conduct, began to think over. 'They are free from likes and dislikes caused by vasana. They do not flee even when attacked by the devas.' Deciding thus, the asura-chief sent the army under Dhama-Vyala-Kata for the destruction of the devas.

51 & 52. Daityas (asuras) rose up from their dwellings in mountains and caves with weapons and appeared like hills without wings, sporting with each other.

Suras (devas) also rose up from their hide-outs in mountains and they appeared like mountains on the move. The armies with their respective flags adorning the sides clashed with each other.

53 & 54. It was like a frightful deluge. As the gruesome battle was being fought, the devas suffered enormous injury. The warriors lost their limbs, and blood was gushing out in torrents. They were routed.

55. Dhama, Vyala and Kata shouted victoriously and ravaged all over like the fire on the fuel and looked out for devas.

56. The devas had hidden themselves and could not be traced by the daityas despite their efforts.

57. Dhama, Vyala and Kata, then, left for the Patala, lower world, happily.

58. The devas became grief-stricken at their defeat by Dhama and others. They went to Brahma of supreme prowess, after resting for a while.

59. Brahma appeared amidst them in a red apparel, seated in a red throne. The devas bowed to him reverentially and told him all the plans of Sambara and the deeds of Dhama, Vyala and Kata.

60. After hearing all that they said, thoughtful Brahma pondered over the matter and said words which were of consoling nature to the devas.

61. Brahma said, "My dear ones, after thousand years, the army of Sambara has to be defeated. Do wait for the time.

62. You join battle with Dhama, Vyala and Kata. O Devas, do fight with them, run away and then fight again with them.

63. As a consequence of repeated fights, the ahamkara, the ego, will forcefully manifest in their hearts as image in a mirror.

64. Dhama, Vyala and Kata, when they become victims of vasanas, get easily defeated, as birds caught in the net.

65. It is craving that is the cause of all one's troubles and the absence of craving is the cause of all joys.

66. This world keeps revolving tied as it is by the rope of vasanas; vasanas multiplied cause great agony and vasanas annihilated cause great joy.

67. Whether he be a brave man or a knowledgeable man or a wise man, he, when possessed by desire, gets bound, as a lion gets bound by the fetters."

68. After saying this, the Great God disappeared from view. Devas heard his counsel and retired to their destination.

69. They assembled in the sky and blew their bugles. They and the asuras, emerging from the patala, fought again to bide time.

70. The devas took to flight. Again, they sought out the asuras for fight.

71. Thus the devas resorted to these means to pass away the time and to delude the asuras.

72. By about this time, and as a result of intense habit, Dhama and others got attached to ego and desires.

73. They became victims of vasanas concerning life and vasanas caused by likes and dislikes. Thus they became helpless and weak.

74. As they intensely thought 'Let this body be everlasting, let there be wealth to give me happiness,' their courage of heart failed.

75. The asura chiefs felt diffident in the battle and they were assailed by the thought, 'we will die.'

76. Deprived of vigour, they were incapable of killing the enemy warriors; when there is no fuel, the fire cannot consume the offerings made into it.

77. What is there to describe? The enemies of devas were scared of death and were intent on fleeing for life.

78. In order to enlighten you about this point, O Rama, I said in jest, 'Let the example of Dhama-Vyala-Kata not be followed.'

79. Because of lack of discrimination, the mind gets into the distressing state. It, as it were, wishes to undergo manifold sorrows."

80. Sri Rama asked, "How did Dhama, Vyala and Kata arise from the Supreme Reality-this doubt of mine, O seer, may kindly be dispelled by thee."

81.   Sri Vasishta said: "Even as, O Rama, Dhama and others are illusory projections of Consciousness, we are also such illusory projections only. We have no separate existence.

82 to 86. You are a fictitious being, I am a fictitious being, Dhama, Vyala and Kata have also only an existence that is fictitious.

The Supreme Reality, is a self-cognising Conscious principle which is capable of illusory manifestations and that Conscious principle, acted upon by Sambara's mind, in the act of dhyana, manifested as the three asuras.

Therefore, these Dhama, Vyala and Kata are not real; nor are we. There is real and pure intelligence, flawless and vast like space.

There is the all-pervasive Reality-without origin and eclipse. The manifest form of its potency is what the world is. This is the Truth.

The Consciousness exists everywhere as experience. That which is not experienced does not exist anywhere. It is Reality that manifests as the world. Therefore, discard the doubt and setting aside the notion of separateness, abide as the Supreme."

Chapter-3

The Story of Bhima and Others

Sri Vasishta said:

1. "O great soul, 'Let this be mine,...Let this be mine'- such a notion, arising out of ignorance and sense of difference prevents the manifestation of the Self.

2. The noble soul considers the three worlds as mere bit of grass; all vicissitudes avoid him as deers avoid the dry grass.

3. The gods protect, as they do the vast universe, him in whose hearts throb always awareness of the Reality.

4. They alone, who exult in virtues, desire acquisition of learning, exert for the attainment of Reality, are men and the rest are animals.

5. When a disaster suddenly strikes, one should not at all choose the wrong path. Rahu who drank the immortal ambrosia still met with death, because he did it in the wrong way.

6. Those who are insubordinate become subservient to him; all dangers recede; prosperity never declines, for the one who has risked fame for the sake of virtue.

7. *Relying on supreme effort, and exerting oneself to the utmost, along the path shown by the scripture, without losing patience, who does not achieve fulfillment?*

8. *He who acts in accordance with the scriptures should not be in haste in the acquisition of siddhis, yogic*

powers. When the effort takes a long time to mature, the fruits attained are ripe.

9. *Let one pursue the worldly duties without becoming subject to grief, fear, pain, craving, deceit and in accordance with scriptural teachings. Let not one choose the contrary course and seek destruction.*

10. *The accumulated wealth brings in disasters; the sense-pleasures are harbingers of diseases; all riches lead to dangers. By remaining unattached to anything, one triumphs.*

11. For him - who is endowed with virtuous conduct, self-contemplation, disinterest in the various pleasures and pains of life - fame, virtue, etc, bring forth good fruits along with prosperity, even like the creeper that gives one good fruits in season.

12. Penance, holy rivers, scriptures, japa, do not emancipate a man from the ocean of samsara except through service to the wise elders.

13. He in whom the traits of covetousness, delusion, etc., become everyday less and less and who acts in accordance with the scriptural teaching, is a wise person.

14. *If the ego remains unknown, it is akin to a stain in Supreme Consciousness. If the ego remains perfectly known, it is verily the Supreme Consciousness.*

15. As long as the effulgent Chit remains fully veiled by the ahankara, till then the kumuda flower of Supreme Reality does not blossom.

Chit-moon, ahankara-cloud, kumuda flower-Reality.

16. Ahankara is the sprout of the 'tree of birth' that remains always imperishable; the notion 'mine' is the vast branch; sorrows are its fruits.

17. Sri Rama asked, "What is the form of 'ahankara'? How is it properly discarded? Be it the gross ahankara of the waking state, or the subtle one of the dream state, what does happen when it is given up?"

(The translation of the verse is based on the interpretation in BYV, 4-33-48).

18. Sri Vasishta said: In all the three worlds, the ahankara has three forms. Two are spiritually beneficial. The third should be discarded. Now let me describe.

19. *That is a supreme form of ahankara when it is associated with the firm understanding, 'I am all this universe. I am the immutable Supreme Lord. There is nothing besides.'*

This ahankara seen in the liberated soul does not fetter the soul.

20 & 21. *A second and auspicious form of ahankara manifests in the form, 'I am completely different from all. I am the minute intelligence.'*

This form of ahankara leads one to liberation and is seen in a liberated soul.

22. *'I am only the body comprising hands, legs, etc.'-the ahankara manifesting in such a conviction is the third one. It is gross and false.*

23. This wicked form should be abandoned. This notion is the root of the successive births. The person assailed by him falls to lower and lower levels.

The readings in BYV 4-33-54 are preferable to those of LYV.

24. When this harmful ahankara has been completely discarded and when the other two ahankaras manifest, the person concerned attains liberation.

The two ahankaras conducive to liberation manifest in the form of 'I am all' and 'I am completely beyond all.'-V.C.

25. The first two ahankaras are transcendental and beneficial. The third one is world bound and has to be discarded.

26. This gross ahankara should be discarded. In whatever way he discards this miserable ahankara, on all such occasions, he rises to transcendental plane.

27. O, faultless man, if one ponders over the ahankaras as explained above, and remains pure, one attains to the supreme plane.

28. He who renounces that ahankara also and is absolutely unassociated with any ahankara, he remains at a very high plane and is established in supreme beatitude.

29. The embodied state, bereft of ahankara, is a highly meritorious one. This leads to the greatest good, the greatest state.

The body, when not activated by ahankara, serves to pursue yoga sadhana and therefore is meritorious.

30. Now, hear what happened after Dhama, Vyala and Kata were gone. Though his army was defeated by the devas, Sambara was confident.

31 to 36. The asura-chief thought of joining battle with the devas again.

'Dhama and others who were created by me, deluded themselves by attachment to false ahankara. Let me create through my magical power another set of asura-chiefs. They will be efficient, knowledgeable in scriptures and spiritually enlightened.

Since they will be Knowers of Truth, they will not succumb to false delusion.

They will not get vitiated by ahankara and will conquer the devas.'

After resolving thus, the asura-chief created by his will asura-chieftains. They rose up, like bubbles in the stream. They were knowledgeable, Knowers of Truth, devoid of desires and blemishes.

They, who were known by the names Bhima, Bhasa and Dhrida were excellent persons who only attended to the things that naturally fell to their lot and were self-enlightened.

37. To them who were fire like in glory, all the world was a straw.

Receiving instruction from the asura-chief, they pervaded the sky and fought the devas for several years.

38. Whenever the vasana, 'This is mine' rose up in their mind, it got annihilated through the enquiry, 'Who is this ahankara?'

Since they were knowers of Brahman, the notions 'I' and 'mine' could not enslave them-V. C.

39 to 41. Thus, by the asura-generals Bhima, Bhasa and Dhrida, who were untainted by ahankara, unscared of old age and death, mindful of only duty, valorous, devoid of desire and hatred, and even-minded, the army of the devas was defeated, humiliated, vanquished and scattered, as food by eaters.

42. The army of the celestials, maimed by Bhima, Bhasa and Dhrida, ran like Ganga leaping in bounds from the Himalayan crests.

43. Like the cloud driven by the wind seeking shelter under mountain, the army of the devas ran to the God reclining on the serpent couch in the ocean of milk.

44. Thereupon, the asura-chiefs were fought by Vishnu in a gruesome battle and were burnt by the fiery chakra and sent to the world of Vishnu.

   (The asura generals killed by Vishnu attained liberation.)

45. O Rama, mind is bound when associated with the vasanas and is liberated when it is freed from the vasanas. Therefore, do thou, through discrimination, free the mind from the vasanas.

46. *By perfect vision of Truth, vasanas get extinguished. When the vasana has been eliminated, the mind becomes tranquil, like the light of the lamp without oil."*

Chapter-4

The Story of Dashura

1. Sri Vasishta said: "For the sorrow caused by the tormenting worldly life, there is only one cure and that is the control of one's mind.

2. *Do thou hear about wisdom in its fullness. After hearing about it, do thou contemplate on it. The desire for happiness is bondage and renunciation of such desire is liberation.*

3. Of what use are the extensive scriptures? Let this alone be accomplished-whatever is thought of as pleasing be known to be like poison and like fire.

4. The sense-delights are spurious and after repeatedly reminding oneself of this fact, let the person mentally discard the things and experience them. Such kind of experience produces joy.

5. Existence of the mind destroys happiness but the destroyed mind ushers in bliss. An enlightened person's mind is as good as dead and to an ignorant man, the mind is a binding chain.

6. The mind of a realised soul is neither blissful nor otherwise, neither moving nor unmoving, neither existent nor non-existent nor the combination of these."

Since the mind of a realised person is unvitiated by vasanas but is responsible for the interaction of the senses, it cannot be correctly described. Therefore, the mind of the realised person is stated to be anirvachaniya, indescribable-V. C.

7.   Sri Rama asked, "O seer, how does this world abide in the transcendental Conscious Self? Do thou explain to me, so that my undestanding becomes more perfect."

8.   *Sri Vasishta said: "Even as the external all-pervasive akasa, space, because of its subtlety is not cognised, the all-pervasive Chit, Consciousness, because of absence of parts in it is not cognised.*

9.   The Consciousness, imperishable in nature and called by the name Atma, Self, is bereft of thoughts and names.

10.   The Consciousness, a hundred times subtler than the space, abides as a partless whole in the case of realised persons, but in respect of the ignorant, manifests along with the impure ignorance and the world as one undivided whole.

11 & 12.   As the waves, varied and vast do not manifest apart from the ocean, the notions 'I' and 'Thou,' varied and vast, do not manifest apart from the pure Consciousness.

13.   In the case of the cognisant persons, the Consciousness manifests in the form of likes and dislikes and contains the seed of samsaric sorrows. In the case of the realised persons, it appears like all-inclusive effulgent existential oneness.

14.   The Consciousness, by virtue of empirical involvement, illumines the karmas, deeds, enjoys the tastes of all things and experiences all sense pleasures.

15.   The Consciousness manifests not, disappears not; rises up not, sets not; it comes not, goes not; it is here and not here.

16.   This pure blemishless Consciousness abiding in itself,

O Rama, projects itself in the form of universe and called as such.

17. It is intrinsically Consciousness, all-pervading and self-revealing; it is intrinsically luminous and partless but illusorily dark and made of parts.

18. By its own imagination, it abandons the exalted infinite plane and by the sense of identification, 'I am this,' tends to be ignorant in course of time.

The translation is based on the correct reading of the verse in BYV 4-36-18.

19. With the manifoldness intensifying as a result of further identification, when the tendency to accept or reject objects existing or non-existing gets stabilised, the Consciousness shapes or shapes not through a hundred fancies the subtle body.

20. Thus, the jivas assuming fixed strong forms and engulfed in empirical process emerge from the natural form of Brahman and pass away.

21. Even as a stream of water appears to flow in the space, because of heat radiation, creation and dissoluton are seen in the existential Chit.

The translation is based on the interpretation of the verse in BYV, 4-37-4.

22. As a drunkard sees himself as another, so does the Chit, Consciousness, under the influence of avidhya, nescience, cognizes itself as something else.

23. O Rama, that Self which as Consciousness cognises sound, taste, form, smell, etc. is the Supreme Brahman, that is all-pervading.

24. It is Brahman that is known by the name world and apart from Brahman, there is not the stained entity, ajnana.

214

It is the waters of the ocean that manifest as the furious waves and nothing else.

25. *A second thing-or an imagination of it-does not exist, O Rama, apart from Brahman, as in fire nothing exists apart from heat.*

26. *Initially, awaken the disciple by inculcating sama, control of mind, dama, control of senses and other virtues; thereafter teach him, 'All this is Brahman and you are pure Consciousness.'*

27. *He who teaches the ignorant and partially enlightened person that 'All this is Brahman' pushes him into vast hells.*

28. For only an enlightened person-like unto you-whose desire for pleasure has vanished and who has no thoughts, the Truth that the dirt of avidhya does not exist is intelligible.

29. Lamp existing, there is illumination; Sun existing, there is day; if there is flower, there is fragrance; if there is Chit, there is jagat, the world. But the world is only a semblance and is not absolutely real."

30. Sri Rama asked, "I have been awakened by your words, picturesque and impressive, and as cool and pure like the ocean of milk.

31. I feel pushed into a realm of darkness now and in a realm of light another time like the partially cloudy day of the rainy season.

32. How has the infinite and incomprehensible effulgent Consciousness that does not eclipse, come to be endowed with world-conception?

The all-pervasive, non-dual Consciousness being ever self-luminous in nature, how is it characterised by ignorance that causes bondage, since light and darkness do not co-exist?-This is the doubt raised by Sri Rama-V.C.

33. Sri Vasishta said: "All my utterances truly mean what they say; they are never incorrect nor contradictory.

34. When perfect realisation of Truth dawns and gets expanded, abiding in that state, you will know the import or its absence of my words.

35. Through the excellent avidhya, nescience, which is embarking on self-annihilation, vidhya, realisation of Truth, which brings about cessation of all sorrow, is attained.

Vidhya, which brings about the extinction of avidhya, is also only a modification of it.-V.C.

36. *A missile is countered by another missile; a taint gets removed by a counter-taint; a poison is neutralised by counter-poison and an enemy is killed by another enemy.*

37. Such is the nature of maya, cosmic power of illusion, which by its act of self-annihilation confers joy; it has no cognizable form and when rationally examined, it ceases to exist.

38. 'The avidhya does not really exist'-with such a conviction, let the wise person experience the knowable and thus he will know the actual form of avidhya.

39. *Until you have not attained the realisation of Truth, have the conviction, on the strength of my utterance, that the avidhya does not at all exist and remain firm.*

40. *He who has the inner conviction that all this is Brahman, he is worthy of attaining liberation. Avidhya, nescience, is of the nature of cognition of separateness. At all cost, avoid that.*

41. The river of avidhya is not crossed except by attaining to Self-realisation. O Rama, Self indeed is the imperishable attainment.

42. *O Rama, enquire not how has this avidhya come into existence; do thou only enquire, 'how shall I conquer this?'*

43. *When this avidhya has attained annihilation, O Rama, you will doubtlessly know fully 'whence it came, how it was and how has it suffered annihilation?'*

   We find Rama himself dismissing the question in his enlightened state-BYV.

44. Do thou make effort to cleanse this breeding ground of disease so that it may not again push you into the distress-filled birth.

45. Even as wind moves about in space on its own support and induced by its own nature, Atma, Self, by its own strength and propelled by its own nature assumes the form of the world.

   That Atma is both the material and instrumental cause of the world is the meaning of the verse-V.C.

46. Let it be firmly contemplated within, the spurt of consciousness sustains itself and though characterised by movement, is of one existence and is unconditioned by anything.

47. In the ocean of chit, the chit-sakthi, power of consciousness arises as a result of a stress in it; yet as the wave arising in the ocean is nothing but pure water, the power of consciousness is nothing but the pure consciousness.

48. During the short moment the divine infinite power manifests in the ocean of chit, she sets on job her other friends-the powers of space, time, action, etc.

217

49. Although the chit-sakti, the divine power, abides in
     expansive space, she succumbs to forgetfulness of her
     nature and identifies herself with limited forms.

50. When the beloved chit-sakti identifies with limited
     forms, other goddesses pertaining to name, number,
     etc. follow her.

51. O valorous man, the imaginary form of chit given to
     mentation and as associated with space, time and
     action is called as kshetrajna, knower-of-the-field, that
     is, jiva.

52. Again, with the disposition to imagine vasanas, he
     assumes the form of ahankara. Ahankara, swayed by
     the vasanas and endowed with the faculty of decision,
     is called buddhi, intellect.

53. Buddhi, vitiated by the tendency to think in terms of
     'either this or that' becomes manas, the mind. Manas,
     as a result of intense imagination assumes the forms
     of senses. The body characterised by feet and hands
     is known to be only an association of the senses of
     action.

54. Thus, the jiva fettered by the rope of imaginary vasanas
     gets entangled in the web of sorrows and in course of
     time, becomes miserable.

55. Thus the chit endowed with powers becomes stabilised
     as ahankara. Like the cocoon, it binds itself of its own
     accord.

56. By becoming a victim of its own desires, it remains
     caught in the web and becomes extremely diffident
     like the lion bound by iron chain.

57 to 59. It is Chit, Consciousness, that at different times,
     is called by various names-manas, buddhi, jnanam,
     (knowledge,) kriya (action) ahankara, puryashtaka,

(the subtle-body comprising of the eight principles), prakriti, maya, malam (impurity), karma, bandha (bondage), avidhya and iccha (desire).

By virtue of the different traits it exhibits, the Consciousness itself manifests in different forms.

60. This worldly life, full of fettering desires, bears a fruit that is devoid of juice as the fruits of the banyan tree.

61. Burnt by the fire of worry, cut into pieces by the serpent of anger, and beaten by the waves of the ocean of desire, the mind has forgotten the Atma, its progenitor.

O Rama, do thou drag out this mind like the elephant from the mire.

62. O Rama, he, who is not aroused by the condition of the mind and does not act to save it from the scorching torment by the constant pulls of the righteous and unrighteous deeds it has to contend with, is nearly a rakshasa in human form.

63. Thus the jivas are chit only ensnared by the worldly contemplation. They are only imagined forms and countless such forms exist in the Brahman.

64. Infinite number of such entities were born, and even now are born. In future also they will be born-like the bubbles in the waters of the falls.

65. Some are born for the first time; some have been born a hundred times before; some have been born countless number of times; some have had various kinds of lives.

66. Some are born as kinnaras, gandharvas, vidhyadharas, maharajas. Some have emanated from Sun, Moon, Varuna, Siva, Vishnu and Brahma.

67 to 69. Some are born as brahmanas, kings, merchants, servants, etc.

Some are born as holy herbs, leaves, fruits, roots and insects.

Some are born as kadamba, jambira, sola, tale and tomba trees.

Some are born as mahendra, malaya, sahya and mandara mountains.

Some are born as reservoirs of salty waters, curds, ghee, milk, cane-juices, and water.

Some are born as sky and some as rivers.

70. Some merrily go up and some fall down to rise up again, like balls, as if they are ceaselessly tossed about by the Lord, the God of Death.

71. After experiencing several lives in the worldly pool some ignorant souls fall lower below and become inert matter.

72. The vast ceaseless flow of the three worlds, caused by Maya, in the river of Supreme Truth, remains full now or becomes extinct purposelessly, like the wave in the ocean."

73. Sri Rama asked, "O Divine Seer, how does the jiva, abiding at the plane of mind attain to the plane of Brahma, do thou explain in detail."

74. Sri Vasishta said: "O valorous man, let me explain the process by which the body of Brahma is attained. In the light of that explanation, you will know the cosmic order.

75. The Reality of Self unconditioned by space and time, by its own natural propensity, acquires the form conditioned by space, time, as if in sport.

76. The manas, by virtue of intense play of vasanas, becomes what is known as jiva and is susceptible to imagination and negation of it.

77. Initially, the mind-power contemplates on the seed-essence of sabda which leads to the formation of akasa.

78. Attaining a grosser form, the mind contemplates on the seed-essence of vayu, air, leading to the emergence of vayu.

79. Because of the mental interaction between akasa and vayu and because of the friction with their intrinsic forms, the fire element arises from the mind.

80. Mind getting endowed with the essence of sabda, sparsa and rupa, contemplates on rasa, the essence of taste and in a second, knowledge of water characterised by coolness arises, that is, the water element emerges.

81. Endowed with other essences, the mind contemplates on smell and the knowledge of earth arises, that is, the earth element gets formed.

82. Associated with the essences of the elements, mind discards the subtle body and contemplates the body similar to the form of fire and manifests in the space.

83. The same body associated with the aspect of ahankara and the essence of buddhi, called as the puryashtaka-the city of eight constituents-comes to dwell like bee in the lotus-like heart of the creatures.

84. Dwelling therein and by virtue of intense contemplation on the luminous form, mind attains to the gross form like the ripened bilva fruit.

85 & 86. Shining like the molten gold within the moulds, the naturally luminous entity, puryashtaka, assumes different forms, the form of head above, the feet below,

hands on sides and stomach in the middle.

87. Growing distinctively with time, he attains a flawless full form-endowed with buddhi, consciousness, strength, enthusiasm, knowledge and lordship over elements.

88 to 90. It is He that is the God Brahma, who is the creator of all the worlds.

Seeing His own form lovable and excellent, the all-knowing seer contemplated thus, 'In this vast space-like and limitless Consciousness, what was there before?'

91. The all-knowing, first-born seer saw all the worlds and creations of the past and remembered them along with their intrinsic nature and characteristics.

92. As if in sport, He created through imagination, the various creatures displaying varying kinds of behaviour akin to a dream-land.

93. To provide them with both pleasure and liberation and to enable them to pursue dharma, virtue, artha, acquisition of wealth, and kama, attainment of pleasure, He composed endless number of sciences.

94. O Rama, creation of various beings and the world occurred in this manner from the collective-mind of Virinchi, as the flowers grow out from the honey essence.

95. The devas, asuras and other celestials came into existence as a result of sankalpa, imagination and with the sankalpa ceasing, they also cease to exist like the lamp without oil.

96. O wise man, all are the same as akasa and have their forms only as a result of imagination. Know the worldly life to be a long dream experience.

97.   Nothing is born or dead at any time. O wise man, all this worldly existence is really false.

98.   The extravagant worldly life is an abode of snakes of desires-abandon it. Knowing it to be non-existent, do not place trust in it.

99.   Whether the dream city is decorated or defiled, whether the imagined children are happy or miserable, is there anything to be done?

100.   When wealth, wives, etc., get multiplied, it would be more proper to be despondent than to be happy. When the darkness of delusion gets intensified, who would be at peace.

     The verse as in BYV, 4-46-4, is more correct and the translation is based on it.

101.   Those very pleasures which generate greater desire in a fool, bring about dispassion in a wise person.

102.   *Therefore, Rama, let the enlightened person engaged in worldly task, ignore whatever gets lost and accept whatever that comes his way.*

103.   *Not to desire the pleasures that do not befall one's lot and to experience the pleasures that have come without being sought is the characteristic of an enlightened person.*

104.   The non-existent avidhya does not enslave the enlightened person who does not think 'let this be mine' and who has no desire towards any object.

105.   Do thou discern through intellect the plane of pure Consciousness which sustains the manifest and unmanifest things and by abiding in it, neither seek the material objects, within and without, nor reject them.

106. The wisdom of the enlightened person who abides in his place discharging the natural tasks, who has neither likes nor dislikes, does not get sullied like the lotus-leaf by the water-drop.

107. O Rama, if the sense-pleasure does not cause any relish in the heart, you have attained the wisdom and saved yourself from the ocean of life.

108. Endowed with dispassion, O Rama, do thou through keen perception, separate the mind from the host of vasanas, like the scent-dust from the flower, for attaining the liberated state.

109. In the ocean of samsara filled with the waters of vasanas, only those who have betaken to the boat of wisdom get emancipated and others are drowned in misery.

110. *They discard not, nor seek involvement in world affairs. The persons who have known the Supreme follow the natural course.*

111. Even in a desert they do not experience misery; they do not get attached even to celestial gardens. The wise men swerve not from the cosmic law, like the sun from its course."

The translation is based on the reading in BYV, 4-46-28.

112. Valmiki said: Thus was Rama spoken to by the noble minded Seer in flawless words. Rama examined and understood the nectarine words and became cool at heart like the full moon.

113. Sri Rama asked, "Is creation of similar form? Or is it in dissimilar forms? Do thou explain. By knowing its nature, the nature of Maya will become clearer."

114 to 119. Sri Vasishta said: "Sometimes the creation is

224

authored by Shiva, sometimes the creation emanates from the lotus-born Brahma; sometimes the creation proceeds from Vishnu; sometimes the seers also bring about creation.

Brahma at times is born from the lotus; at times from the waters; at times from the egg and at times from the space.

At one time during creation, the earth was densely filled with trees; at another time, it was full of people; and yet another time it was covered by mountains.

In one creation, the earth was full of clay; in another it was filled with small stones; in some other, it was full of gold and in yet another, it was complete copper.

During one creation, space came into existence first; during another, earth was first; during yet another, it was water; during a particular one, it was fire and during another one, wind was the first.

The creations made by one Prajapati, progenitor, have been described by me as an example. Really, there is no conformity in creation, even to a small extent.

120. Krita yuga comes again, Treta comes again; Dwarapa and Kali come again. Everyone of these comes again and again. But not the immutable Reality.

121. In order to explain to you the illusory nature of the world, let me tell you the story of Dashura. Do thou listen.

122. The country of Magadha, with vast people, is like a beautiful flower-tree in this great earth.

123. It has large forest of Kadamba trees and with various species of birds abounding in it, it is a wonderful place and most fascinating.

124 & 125. In a particular hill-slope, which was full of plantain groves, there was one noble-minded saint given to austere penance. Called by the name Dashura, he did arduous penance.

126. O Rama, his father, called by the name Saraloma, was akin to Brahma and he lived in the same hill.

127. He had only one son, like Brihaspati, whose son was Kacha. Alongwith that son, he was living his life in the woods.

128. After living several yugas, Saraloma, discarding the body, left for the heavenly abode, like the bird flying out of the cage.

129. The only inhabitant of the wood, Dashura, began to sob, in a pitiable manner, like the cuckoo bird, having been left alone by father's death.

130. Because of separation from mother and father, he became afflicted with sorrow and misery, like the lotus blossom at the fall of snow.

131. "O son of a great seer! O wise man! Why do you weep like an ignorant person?

132. Why do you not understand the transient nature of worldly life? O wise man, the worldly life is ever fleeting in nature.

133. One arises, lives and dies away necessarily later. Do not needlessly fall into gloom because of father's death.

134 & 135. That which rises up must necessarily set like the sun."

After hearing these words of one who did not have physical form, the boy with reddish eyes gathered up courage like the peacock after the thunder.

Rising up from the dejected state and after performing

the obsequies for the father earnestly, he concentrated on doing penance for the attainment of nobler ends.

136. He began to do intense tapas in the wood, following the mode of a brahmana, and became a victim of multitudinous desires.

137. Though learned, he had not known the Truth and so his mind did not attain peace.

138. Though the entire earth around was very pure, he saw it as utterly impure and was not at peace in any place.

139 to 141. Thinking along these lines, he resolved, 'Only the top of the tree is pure enough. It is proper that I abide there only. Let me now perform penance. As a result, I shall reside, like the bird, on the tree and its branch.'

Deciding thus, he prepared the holy fire and began to offer the flesh of his own body into it.

142 & 143. 'Let not the brahmana's entire body get reduced to ashes on account of its being offered into my mouth'- thinking thus the God Agni appeared before the brahmana, like the effulgent sun before Brihaspati.

144. He said, "Brahmana boy, take the boon sought by you. O wise man, you will shine like jewel in the jewel box."

145. The God Agni, who spoke thus, was worshipped with fine flowers and songs of praise by the brahmana boy.

146. He prayed, "O God, in this earth filled with creatures, I do not obtain a holy site. Therefore, let me reside in an abode at the top of a tree."

147. When the God of Agni was requested thus by the ascetic boy, He who was as it were the mouth to all

the Gods, said, "Let it be so" and disappeared.

148 to 150. The God disappeared like the clouds during twilight. In the midst of the wood was a kadamba tree which kissed the sky. The brahmana climbed up the tree and reached a branch which remained suspended, as it were, in the high sky. Sitting in the soft leafy branch, he plunged into penance without any mental disturbance.

151 to 154. He looked around in all directions out of curiosity. The entire wood appeared like a well-adorned damsel, with the stream flowing like a garland on the breasts of mountains and with curly hairs of clouds moving about.

Sitting in the bower on top of the tree, he looked at all sides.

Thereafter, he sat in padmasana posture, withdrew the mind from all the directions, and desirous of particular aims, he mentally performed yajnas, since he had not known the Supreme Truth and was addicted to performance of sacrifice.

Remaining in that abode, he mentally performed sacrifices for propitiating the Gods with the aid of cows, horses, human-beings, etc., and vast cash-gifts for ten years.

155. In course of time, his mind became vastly pure and supreme wisdom born of Self-realisation, forcefully manifested itself in it.

156. The veil that enveloped his vision was destroyed; the impure vasanas were totally annihilated.

157. Once he saw standing before the bower the forest-nymph, with wide eyes and adorned with flowers. The damsel with elegant looks stood bending her head

down and the ascetic asked:

158. "Who are thou, with eyes resembling the petals of utpala flower and whose beauty is capable of destroying the peace of even Manmatha, the God of Love?"

159. Questioned thus, the deer-eyed, white-coloured nymph, with large breasts, told the ascetic these sweet, mind-captivating words:

160 to 165. "Whatever unattainable is longed for in this vast earth is certainly attained by the favour of great men.

I am the Goddess of this forest in which abides your hermitage.

The Goddesses of the forest assembled at Nandana on the occasion of the festival of God of Love on the thirteenth day of the bright fortnight of the Chitra month.

I went to the assembly of the damsels from all the three worlds and there I saw my companions in amorous delights.

Being without a son, I was exceedingly distressed at heart.

When in this forest, like the wish-fulfilling kalpatharu tree, you are there, capable of granting any wish of the seeker, O Lord, why should I grieve, as though I am without saviour for want of son? Do thou, O seer, give me a son. If not, I shall throw myself into the fire here, so that the sorrow on account of the absence of son may get quenched.

166. When the woman of slender-waist spoke thus, the seer smiled and gave her a flower with love and compassion.

167. "Do thou go, slender-waisted lady, in a month's time you will beget a son, worthy of love and worship, like the creeper bringing forth a new one.

168. However you were willing to court death when you made the request and because of the distress you underwent, your son will with difficulty become a knower of Truth."

169. After saying thus, the seer permitted her, the radiant-faced, who had offered to serve the seer, to leave.

170. She reached her abode and the seer attended to his own duties. The wheel of time kept rotating and years passed.

171. After a long time, the woman with beautiful eyes took the son of twelve years age to the seer.

172. After offering obeisance to the seer and sitting before him the woman with moon-like face, spoke to him tenderly, like the she-bee to the mango-tree.

173. "O Divine seer, here is the virtuous son of both of us. He has been made proficient in all arts by me.

174. But through this, the auspicious wisdom is not attained. Without the wisdom, he will get tormented in the cycle of samsara without any escape.

175. O Master! Out of compassion, you may yourself impart the spiritual wisdom to him now." When she said this, the seer told her:

176. "Do thou leave him here," and then permitted her to leave.

After she left, the wise boy remained as the disciple of the father with rigid self-control like Aruna before Sun.

177 & 178. The seer enlightened the son for a long time

through interesting speeches and a hundred stories, real and imaginary, and examples that were capable of generating wisdom.

179. He taught likewise, itihasas, vedas, vedantic truths patiently and elaborately in due order."

180. Sri Vasishta said: "Once I went along the path of the siddhas in the sky, for taking bath in the Ganga at Kailasa mountain in an invisible body.

181. Getting out from the Abode of the Seers, I happened to reach the tree of Dashura during the night.

182. There I heard from the bower within the tree, words like the sound of the bees from the bosom of the lotus blossoms.

183. Dashura said: "Listen, my child, an interesting story that is similar to the worldly life. I shall describe it to you.

184. There is a king, known in all the worlds for his valour by the name Swottha who is prosperous and has the capability to enslave the world.

185. Whose commands are obeyed by all the chieftains of the world and are adorned by them as if they are crest-jewels.

186. Who is always of daring acts, is delighting himself in various wonderful sports and there is no great soul in all the worlds who has not been enslaved by him.

187. Whose deeds, innumerable in number, like the waves of the ocean, bring forth immense pleasure and misery.

188. Whose prowess is not countered by any missile or fire or by anyone and it is impossible to assail him like the space by the arm.

189. Whose delightful deeds and manifold achievements

are incapable of being imitated by even Indra, Vishnu and Siva.

190. He has three bodies capable of sustaining all directions and with this three fold nature as superior, inferior and intermediate, he dominates the whole world.

191. This three-headed person is born only in the vast expanse of space, is living in it and finally like sound, gets dissolved into it.

192 & 193. In that very space a vast city has been designed by him, with three divisions and fourteen big approaches, encircled by woods and parks, mountain-crests as pleasure-spots. It has a necklace around it of white pearls; it is adorned with seven wells and is illumined by two lamps-one hot and another cool-that do not ever get extinguished.

194 & 195. In that very vast city by that Swottha has been formed rows of houses; some are placed on the top, some in the middle and some at the bottom. They are covered by black overgrowths and have nine holes.

196. With wind ceaselessly passing through it, it is endowed with a number of windows. It has five lamps; three pillars and white trees.

197. It is soft-coated with clay, has number of junctions of roads-all these have been designed by the great-souled king.

198. There are protectors who have vast sway and are frightful to look at.

199. In the rows of houses, the great ruler sports in various ways, like the bird in the nest.

200. O son, the three headed ruler playing within it

alongwith friends and living within it gets out of it at some time.

201. Possessing a mind of fickle-nature, he occasionally gets the strong desire, 'Let me construct a new city, let me go out.'

202. As if he is possessed by some spirit, he rises up and leaps away and attains to a new city, designed, as it were, by the celestials.

203. My child, he occasionally gets the desire, being unsteady in nature, 'Let me die' and so, he becomes extinct.

204. He rises up again like the big wave from the waters; he sets about to do things in a big way and by his own actions, he gets disheartened.

205. 'What can I do? I am ignorant. I am miserable.' Thus he grieves at one time. Becoming happy another time, he grows fat.

206. He drinks, goes, plays, grows, dazzles, shines. He can assume luminous forms. Child, that ruler has great capacity, even as the ocean, the lord of rivers, has.'

207. Sri Vasishta said: "In that dead of night at Jambudwipa, the son asked the noble-hearted father, seated in the branch of kadamba tree.

208. "Who is, O father, the ruler called Swottha endowed with excellent form? What for have you told me about him? Do explain truly."

209. Dashura said, "Listen, child, what was this about, let me explain. Through this you will understand the nature of the cycle of worldly life.

210. Only this samsaric state, worldly life, was described by me thus. It owes its origin to a non-existent entity and is itself non-existent.

211. That Sankalpa, thought, which arose from the Supreme Consciousness is called Swottha. He arises of his own accord and disappears into the cause on his own.

212. This vast world of experience is his manifestation; the world existing when he exists and the world disappearing when he disappears.

213. Brahma, Vishnu, Indra, Rudra are only his limbs. In the void-like space, he has set up these three worlds.

214 to 237. By mere will and contemplation, he assumes the form of Virinchi. In Him, these vast fourteen lokas and lokaloka manifest-with woods as parks and gardens, mountains of Sahya and Mandhara as sport-centres, the Sun and Moon as hot and cool lamps, unextinguished even by fierce gales, waves radiating sun's rays as pearls and the rivers as necklaces of pearls, cane-juice, milk, etc., as water, with various precious jewels as lotus-sprouts, seven great oceans as wells.

In that city of the world, designed by the ruler of sankalpa, thought, for the sake of his sport, the bodies of rows of houses have been created. Some of them associated with celestial abode are placed on the top; some are human beings at the middle level, and some like serpents are in the lower level. The bodies comprising of the clay of flesh are driven by the device activated by prana.

The white bones are the trees and the soft coating on the impure flesh is that of the ointment. Some have their heads covered by attractive hair: The ears, eyes, nostrils, etc., are the nine entrances, the windows. The arms are the junctions of roads and the five senses are the lamps.

O wise man, sankalpa has brought into existence this body, by its own power of maya.

The ahankara, etc., are the dreadful yakshas and in the non-existent house of the bodies, alongwith the friends ahankara, etc., the ruler sports merrily.

He is happy and prosperous in one second and thoroughly gloomy like the oil-less lamp in another. In the body arises thoughts like waves in the ocean. To whichever plane he goes, a new city gets formed.

Whatever he thinks manifests within a second and whatever he un-thinks gets destroyed at once. This world has been invested with his own reality and it gives only endless misery and never happiness.

Being non-existent in nature, he destroys everything like darkness the twilight.

By his own actions, he gives rise to sorrow and weeps. When a small delight born of thought possesses him, he is in high spirits. The ignorant person has three bodies-inferior, superior and intermediate. They are called as tamas, sattva and rajas and are responsible for worldly process. The tamasic form of sankalpa by his constant mean action, attains to a miserable state and becomes worms and insects. The sattvic form of sankalpa, devoted to the pursuit of virtue and knowledge, attains to the state of solitariness and has an empire of his own. The rajasic form of sankalpa engaged in worldly affairs, remains caught up in life, and attains wives, sons, etc.

Discard all forms of thought, restrain mind through mind, and bring about the extinction of all sankalpas, desires, for external or internal objects. Even if you do penance for innumerable years, whether in the lower world or on the earth or in the heaven, there is no way to emancipation except through the extinction of sankalpa, desire.

238. *For attaining the non-distressing, non-changing blissful supreme state through the extinction of sankalpa, make your own supreme effort.*

239. O faultless son, it is only in the long thread of sankalpa, desire, all things of the world have been knit together. When the thread is cut to pieces, we know not where the destroyed things have gone.

240. Without any attachment, be inclined to attend to the affairs on hand. When the desire gets destroyed, chit ceases to get externalised through mentation.

241. By realisation of the Supreme, by discarding the mental fancies decisively, get established in the non-dual plane for the sake of endless happiness, as in sleep state.

242. The son asked, "What is the nature of sankalpa, O father, and how does it originate? How does it become stronger and how does it perish?"

244. Acquiring an existence of its own in a small measure, slowly it becomes strong and veiling the Consciousness of the existential Self, it becomes a dense mass like cloud.

245. The chit, consciousness contemplating the chetya, the object as different from itself becomes, as it were, the sankalpa, in the manner seed grows into a sprout.

Chit contemplating the chetya as different from itself is sankalpa. V.C.

246. It is willing the non-existent object that is called as sankalpa and it arises on its own, grows strong on its own and produces both misery and happiness.

247. Do not allow sankalpa to arise. Do not interest yourself in the external objects. Through this attitude alone, you will be worthy of liberation.

248. It is not necessary to make too much effort to destroy sankalpa. By unwilling the objects-by not thinking about objects-this sankalpa is conquered.

249. In plucking a fresh flower there is perhaps some effort but in destroying sankalpa through easy negative-will, there is none.

The translation of the verse is based on the interpretation of Tatparya Prakashika of the verse in BYV, 4-54-14.

250. *Destroy sankalpa by sankalpa, mind by mind and abide in the Self. Would that be difficult to accomplish?*

251 & 252. Even as the space is void-like, the world is also void-like, inasmuch as both owe their origin to the imagination of the non-existent. O son, even as the husk of the grain and the taint of the copper, get removed by effort, the ajnana of the Consciousness is also removed by effort.

The imprint of ajnana in the Consciousness is removed by the action of sravana, manana, etc.-V.C.

253. Like the husk of the grain, the ajnana of Consciousness is a natural impurity and can be totally destroyed and therefore exert yourself.

254. Let there not be the delusion in you that 'my riches are great and superior,' as you and all the riches and all this worldly form are only chit, Atma, the Self-Consciousness."

255 to 259. Sri Vasishta said: "O Rama, the moon of the akasa of Raghu clan, after hearing their conversation

237

in the night, I descended on the kadamba tree from the sky. On seeing my arrival, Dashura seated me on a leafy branch and worshipped me with great ardour in proper manner. The night was spent by us, similar to a beloved pair, in interesting conversation as if it was an hour. I took leave of Dashura and went away for bath in the celestial Ganga. I have told you the story of Dashura, O Rama, and do thou understand the world in the manner taught by Dashura.

Chapter-5

The Spiritual Instructions

1.   Sri Vasishta said: "In the infinite stretch of time, very trivial is a period of hundred years, and if that is the longest span of human life, with what hope can man evince longing for life?

2.   The external riches are mere figments of imagination and by renouncing the inner craving for these, remain what you are and go about in a sportive manner in this world.

3.   *Even if the jewel wishes not, lustre emanates from it; even so, in the mere presence of the Supreme, the worlds keep functioning.*

4.   *Therefore, indeed, Atma is characterised both as a doer and as a non-doer. Since he does not wish anything to happen, he is a non-doer; he is a doer, inasmuch as, in his presence, things move.*

5.   *O faultless son, there are two kinds of Atma-one is a doer and the other a non-doer. To whichever you are inclined, do thou firmly attach yourself to it.*

6.   *With the firm thought, 'I am a non-doer,' in all condition, if a person keeps doing things that befall his lot, he is not tainted through the acts.*

7.   When the individual does not engage in external actions, his mind gets stripped of all desires. Therefore, always let there be the keen awareness that 'I am a non-doer.' If so, there results the supremely nectarine experience of mental equipoise.

8. O Rama, if you wish to get stabilised in the thought 'I am the doer of all,' then the great sense of doership is also preferable.

9. When there is the notion that I do everything in the world, how could there be desire or aversion, as there is none else?

10. My body is to be burnt by someone; it has been fondled by someone else–all these happen as a result of my own past karma. Where is the need for happiness and sorrow?

11. 'In regard to the pleasure and pain, rise and decline of worldly prosperity, I am the author'-if a person thinks in this manner, where is the need for happiness and sorrow?

12. In regard to all the experiences of pleasures and pains resulting from one's own acts when one's desire subsides, there is only mental equipoise.

13. *The equanimity towards all happenings which arises on account of abidance in the plane of reality, when attained by the mind, the individual no longer undergoes rebirth.*

14. Otherwise, O Rama, abandon all notions of doership or non-doership, abandon all and by merging the mind totally in Consciousness, be what you are, with firm attitude.

15. The mental perspective characterised by external thoughts of the kind, 'I am this...,' 'I am not this...,' 'I do this...,' 'This does not exist'-is not conducive to bliss.

16. The notion 'I am the body,' is the path to the hell Kalasutra, is the trap called Mahaveechi, is life in the forest of Asipatra.

Kalasutra, Mahaveechi and Asipatra are names of different hells.

17. Even if one has to meet with total destruction, one should abandon with all effort such identification. She is an uncultured woman and should not even be touched, like the dog's flesh, by the person aspiring for liberation.

The sense of identification with the body is akin to touching an uncultured woman.

18. O Rama, when the sense of identification with body, blinding one's vision, is cast away finally, a supreme vision, arises like a radiant moon in a cloudless sky and when this vision arises, the ocean of samsara is surely crossed.

19. By realising in a firm manner either as 'I am not the doer nor I am all' or as 'I am the doer, I am all' or as 'I am not any particular entity, I am beyond all,' do thou abide in that plane in which wise men of excellent knowledge abide.

20. *Bondage is really bondage caused by the vasanas; liberation is the annihilator of vasanas. Abandon all vasanas and also the desire for liberation.*

21. *At the outset, discard the mental vasanas pertaining to sense-objects and acquire pure vasanas like the sense of friendliness, etc.*

The desires for objects are impure vasanas and these must be discarded. Pure vasanas like friendliness must be acquired and this is conducive to the serenity of mind. What the pure vasanas are have been indicated by Patanjali in the Yoga Sutras (1-37), according to which one should practise friendliness towards happy persons, compassion towards the distressed, happiness towards the virtuous, and indifference towards the wicked, and such a kind of contemplation leads to mental poise.

22. *Even these pure vasanas you should inwardly renounce, though outwardly you keep practising them and with a mind bereft of all attachment, be exclusively attached to Chit, Consciousnesss.*

23. Renounce that attachment to Chit also, and with mind and intellect integrated, abide firmly in Chit, Consciousness and discard even the least effort of renunciation of vasanas.

24 & 25. Chit, manas, imagination, form, ignorance, vasanas, objects, prana's movement-do thou discard all these without exception and be as serene and tranquil as space. O wise man, if you reach this plane, you are established in your real nature.

26. He who discards all things totally from the heart, O great soul, and remains without sorrow is a liberated soul, is the Supreme Lord.

27. *Let him practise samadhi, concentrated contemplation or pursue karma, action or let him not do these. He who has totally abandoned all craving of the heart is a liberated and noble soul without doubt.*

28. *He has nothing to attain by renouncing karma or by performing karma; nor has he anything to gain through samadhi and japa-if only his mind is totally devoid of vasanas.*

29. *The scriptures have been examined thoroughly; the teachings have been discussed with others for long. There is no greater state than silence attained through total renunciation of all vasanas.*

30. All that has to be seen has been seen; all quarters

have been roamed about again and again. There are only very few persons who have known the Truth as it is.

31. Whatever deeds are begun and whatever wrong things are done-all these are for the sake of bodily care and none of these is for the Self.

32. All over, there are only five elements and sixth element does not exist-be it in the nether world or earth or heaven. Where can a wise soul find peace?

33. *For a person conducting himself in accordance with spiritual instructions, samsara is as small as a footprint of the cow to cross; for one who has thrown away the reason, it is a vast ocean.*

34. *The unique things of earth cannot provoke the curiosity of the enlightened seer-even as a country girl cannot entice a city-bred man of refinement.*

35. Of the vast ocean of pure waters of Brahman, huge mountain ranges are, as it were, the foam. Brahman is the big effulgent Sun and the worldly glory is a mirage.

36. In regard to this truth, O Rama, our ancestors quote the holy song sung by Kacha, the son of Brihaspati.

37. Kacha, rising up from samadhi, with a serene mind, and remaining in a solitary place, sang this in a touching tone.

38. "What shall I do? Where do I go? What do I take? What do I give up? The whole world is filled with Self, as the earth with waters at deluge.

39. Within body, and without it, above it, and in all directions, there is Self only and there is nothing which is other than Self anywhere.

40. There is no place where I am not; there is nothing which is not in me; when all this is intelligence, what else is there to desire"-

Here ends the song of Kacha.

41. O Rama, the sattvic ones among human beings are endowed with great virtues. They are always happy, like moon in the sky.

42. They do not suffer any danger as the golden lotus during the night. They do not seek to do anything but the natural duties and adhere to the path of the wise.

A natural lotus shrinks during night, but the golden lotus does not shrink and so is the wise man during danger.

43. They are inwardly full and unagitated always, like the beautiful moon. Even in dangerous conditions, they do not abandon their coolness like the moon.

44. Endowed with lovable virtues like friendliness, they have a glorious appearance. They are even-minded, calm and always of wise conduct.

45. Possessing a large heart, they, like ocean, keep themselves in bounds. That is why, Rama, they are beyond the reach of danger.

46. One should enquire into the spiritual truths with effort in the company of wise persons-'Who am I? How has the world spectacle come into play?'

47. The wise people must be followed always and one should not walk into danger.

Some of the verses found in this portion of the text are not complete verses taken from BYV. Single lines have been taken from BYV and put together in the form of verses.

48. The all-devouring Death should not be ignored.

49. The body comprising bones, flesh, blood, etc., is entirely impure and has to be abandoned.

   Do perceive only the Consciousness, which like thread, permeates the row of cosmic bodies.

50. That very Chit which manifests in the luminous bodies adorning the sky, manifests in the hallows of earth, in the swarms of insects.

   Those who belong to the categories of tamasic and rajasic human beings and other such beings, only by virtue of their own effort, attain to sattvic birth."

Section-5
Dissolution

Chapter-1

The Story of Janaka

1. Sri Vasishta said: "O Rama, this samsara, a spectacle of maya is sustained ever by people of rajasa-tamasa type, like a hall by strong pillars.

2. By persons of sattva class, like you, who are courageous and virtuous, this maya is discarded casually, as the slough by the snake.

3. *All this indeed is Brahman; everything is only the expansive Self. Discard the deluded notion 'I am different and this is different.'*

4. In the massive Brahmic Consciousness, thoughts do not arise. O Rama, the distinctions that appear in the water surface on account of the waves are not absolutely real.

5. *Sorrow exists not. Ignorance exists not. Birth exists not. One which is born exists not. That which always exists, that alone exists. Rama, be free from all anxiety.*

6. Being free from the dual notion, abiding in sattvic trait, be unconcerned with your welfare, and Self-conscious. Be the non-dual Self free from sorrow and anxiety, O Rama.

7. Be calm, self-possessed, firm in mind, serene, contemplative, silent and pure like the precious jewel

and O Rama, be free from feverish anxiety.

8. *By enjoying those experiences that naturally come to you, by being dispassionate towards everything, by neither seeking nor avoiding anything, be free from all anxiety, O Rama.*

9. O great soul, like the pearl entering into the oyster of special quality, pure wisdom enters the heart of the person whose present birth is the last one.

10. *Like women thronging in the inner apartment, virtues of nobility, tenderness, friendliness, serenity, freedom and scholarship make him their abode.*

11. All people are fond of him who is mild in manners and sweet in speech, like the deer in the forest desiring the sweet tune of the flute.

12. I have thus spoken about the normal mode of realisation seen in ordinary people. O lotus-eyed Rama, do thou now listen about the mode that is extraordinary.

13. For those born in the world, O Rama, there are two excellent modes that are capable of leading one to worldly pleasure and liberation.

14. One is the steadfast practice of the precepts of the Guru and thus one attains realisation in one life or in a series of lives.

15. Another is attained through exertion, by one who is already awakened. Attainment of Realisation in his case is akin to the accidental fall of fruit from the sky.

16. In regard to the attainment of Realisation, like the fruit fallen from the sky, let me tell an event which happened before.

17. There was a great energetic ruler called Janaka in the

Videha country, who was noble-hearted, who had triumphed over all darkness and won to himself all rich possessions of the earth.

18. He was like a kalpa vriksha, wish-fulfilling-tree to those afflicted and poor who sought his help and a sun to the lotuses of friends.

Once, he went to the charming garden in which passionate cuckoos sported, like Indra to the Nandana Garden.

19. In that beautiful garden filled with the fragrance of flowers, as the attendants remained at a distance, the king was strolling amidst bowers.

20. As he was in the grove of tamala trees, he heard the invisible siddhas speaking amongst themselves about their own viewpoints.

21. These are the songs of the seers who lived in seclusion and roamed amidst hills-in which their modes of Self-contemplation are described.

22. *The manifest delight that arises at the contact between the seer and the seen is that of the Reality of Self-such is my decisive conclusion'-so said a seer.*

23. 'Abandoning the seer, the seeing and the seen alongwith vasanas pertaining to them, the primal Consciousness that manifests all these is the Self-such is my conclusion'-said another seer.

24. 'That which serves as the substrate of the existent as well as the non-existent and which illumines other luminous objects is the Self-such is my mode of contemplation.'

25. 'The mantra with 'ah' as the first letter and 'ha' as the last letter represents all the letters which have formed the whole universe and the Consciousness which is

constantly uttering this mantra is the Self, such is my mode of contemplation'.

The translation is based on the verse 5-19-13 in BYV and the comment in T. P. The author of TP approves the reading of LYV also.

26. Those who ignore the Lord present in the heart and worship external form discard the kaustubha jewel in their hands and go after ordinary jewel.

27. By discarding all desires, one gets at the Consciousness which uproots the poisonous creepers of desire.

28. He is not a man but an ass, who, in spite of the repeated experience that the sense-objects are permeated by sorrow, attaches himself to them.

29. As Hari strikes at the mountain with vajra, let the aspirant strike at the inimical senses again and again, with the stick of discrimination, regardless of whether they are manifest or not.

30. *Let the aspirant crush the hand with hand, grind the teeth with teeth, crush the limbs and thus overpowering one's mind, conquer it.*

31. Let the aspirant secure the holy calm that comes from the control of senses. Mind becomes calm easily for the self-controlled person. The calm mind abides in the Self and such abidance brings in lasting happiness.

32. Hearing these words of the siddhas, the great ruler became very contemplative and sad like a timid person at the battle-cry.

33. Leaving behind the surrounding retinue, the king entered alone into his abode, like the lion into the cave.

34. There, reflecting on the ways of the world which are as wavering as the wings of the birds in flight in space,

he lamented thus:

35. 'Alas! What hardship are the worldly ordeals. I remain tossing around like a stone amidst stones.

36. In the infinite stretch of time, a tiny portion happens to be my life-time. I am clinging to it. How foolish it is of me!

37. That object which is real, which is charming, which is laudable and infinite, does not at all exist in the world. Then, what is the thing that my hope rests on?

39. Those who are at the glorious height of the world are thrown down in matter of days. O mind, with such a lot befalling the glorious, how could you have trust in life?

40. They who were most renowned and were surrounded by host of relations have become objects of memory. Why then trust the present happenings?

41. Where have gone the wealth of kings? Where have gone the Brahmas of bygone worlds? Things material pass out of our existence. How can I have trust?

42. Countless Brahmas have gone by; numberless creations have passed through; Mighty rulers have become part of dust. What hope can I have in my life?

43. Samsara is an evil dream in a long night in which attachment is formed towards the unreal body. How stupid is my perspective?

44. A number of days have gone by and are passing on even now. But that day has not come in which an imperishable thing has been obtained by us.

45. There are things that are attractive at the initial stages or at the middle stage or at the final stage but all become finally impure and unfit for experience and they perish.

46.   The rustic becomes, with every passing day, more sinful, more cruel and necessarily more sad. What states has he to pass through?

47.   The child is blinded by ignorance; the youth gets waylaid by thoughts of maidens. In the rest of life time, a person is victim of worry. What can an ignorant man do?

48.   Existent things end in destruction. Happy beginnings carry unhappy endings. Joys turn finally into sorrows. Which of these am I to rely upon?

49.   When there are persons whose opening and shutting eyes bring about rise and fall of worlds, where are persons like me?

50.   Those attractive possessions lauded by the mind, I think, my dear, are only the forerunners of great disasters.

51.   Samsara is the greatest of sorrows, it is said, and how can the body caught in it, be expected to be happy?

52.   If this tree of samsara, which has countless number of sprouts, branches and leaves, mind is said to be the main root.

53.   That mind, I think, is of the nature of sankalpa, thought. By extinguishing sankalpa, thought, I shall so dry up the tree of samsara that it withers away.

54.   Awakened I am. Awakened I am. The thief has been identified as mind. Let me kill it. The mind has long enslaved me.

55.   Till now the mind has not been tutored. Now it has been tutored and is fit to be treasured.

56 & 57.   I have been properly enlightened by the words of the wise siddhas. I am on the path to the Realisation

which is the means to supreme bliss.

58. O discernment, obeisance to thee. This mind, which fancies itself to be everything, which is a very powerful enemy but which is unreal I have vanquished. I am now serene.

59. Reflecting in this manner, Janaka became silent. With mind discarding its restless activity, he appeared like a picture on the wall.

60. Remaining absorbed for a long time, Janaka, who infuses life into others, woke up and again contemplated with a mind that was exceptionally calm.

61. Janaka said, 'What is there for me to acquire? What have I to achieve through effort? How can there be kalpana, imagination, in a mind that is stablised and pure?

62. *I seek not the unattained and the attained I discard not. Let the Self abide as Self. That which is mine, let it be mine."*

63. Sri Vasishta said: "Thinking thus and with a mind utterly unattached to things, Janaka rose up to perform his daily duties like the Sun at the morn.

64. He does not anticipate the future nor grieves over the past. Attending to the present work on hand, he remains smiling.

65. O Rama, the lotus-eyed, by virtue of his own enquiring spirit and not by any other pursuit, everything has been attained by him.

66. O Rama, by the favourable, beautiful and pure wisdom and not by pursuit of the unreal everything has been attained.

67. That great effort which is undertaken by the people to acquire external fortune, that same effort should be undertaken by them to acquire inner wisdom.

68. Do thou destroy the folly which is the greatest of sorrows, the abode of all darkness and the seed of the tree of samsara.

69. *Intelligence is the wish-fulfilling gem in the heart of the wise. Like the wish-yielding kalpalatha creeper, it gives what is wanted.*

70. As arrows do not attack a person ready with his weapons, various faults associated with desires do not surround a person, who is discerning, intelligent and wise.

71. The dark cloud of ego-dense, vast and insensitive- which veils the supreme sun of Self, gets annihilated by the wind of wisdom.

    The reading of the verse in BYV, 5-23-49 is correct.

72. Those who want to attain to the highest beatitude form this resolution primarily. For, is not the land properly tilled at the outset by the farmer, who wants to reap a rich harvest?

Chapter-2

The Story of Punya and Pavana

1. All wrong perceptions-alike caused by the bunches of seeds of ignorance and wicked intentions multiplying into dangers-vanish when there is realisation of the Supreme.

2. For one, who is always inwardly reflecting, like Janaka, on the transience of worldly life, Atma, the Self, spontaneously reveals Itself in course of time.

3. *The only refuge for those scared of samsara is one's own effort and not fate, not karma, not wealth, not relations.*

4. When the identificaton with the body manifesting in the conviction, 'I am this body' is erased, the Consciousness gets enlarged and transcends the universe.

5. When the darkness manifesting in the thought 'I am this body' becomes extinct, all-pervasive effulgence sets in.

6. O Rama, only the tendency of the mind to grab the desired object and totally avoid the object not liked is what constitutes bondage and not anything else.

7. Do not experience pain when you have to part with desired things nor seek out things you desire. Abandon the thought of acquisition and rejection and be established in equanimity.

8 & 9. Desirelessness, fearlessness, sense of permanence, equanimity, learning, thirstlessness, actionlessness,

serenity, thoughtlessness, firmness, friendliness, contentment, softness, tenderness in speech, absence of likes and dislikes-all these, without attendant vasanas, manifest in the man of wisdom.

10.   The net of vasanas containing the catch of fishes of desires that has been cast over the waters of samsara is woven with the thread of thought.

11.   My dear, through the sharp tool of intellect, cut the thread and destroy the entire net as if by the wind the cloud, and abide in supreme plane.

12.   Vanquishing the mind by mind, like the tree by the axe, attain to the lofty plane at once and abide in it.

13.   As you stand, walk, sleep, keep awake, breathe, jump, fall, have the firm inner conviction that all this is false and give up attachment towards them.

14.   Mind, by nature inert, seeks to unite with Chit, Consciousness, like cat, out of desire for meat, that befriends the lion.

       Cat seeks the friendship of lion with the hope of getting meat for itself and its offsprings. The translation of the verse is based on the interpretation of the commentator of BYV, 5-13-47.

15.   The minion of the lion eats the meat got through the valour of the lion. Mind seeks to feed upon the object obtained with the help of Chit.

16.   *If you remain attached to the objective matter, you have an active mind and you are in bondage.*

       If you do not remain attached to the objective matter, your mind is dead and you have attained liberation.

17.   Resolving that 'I am not the seen objective matter,' remain steady like the all-pervasive Lord within the heart.

18. Between the Self and the world which have assumed the forms of the seer and the seen, there is the awareness that is called seeing and contemplate that awareness as Self.

The practice prescribed in this verse is frequently stressed by Vasishta in different forms.

19. The residual experience of taste - what remains after taste and the object of taste have been ignored, that is not connected with both and yet sustains both - contemplate that experience as Self always.

20. When there is experience of the desired object, even as you keep experiencing it, ignore the experiencer and the object and contemplating on the experience alone, be absorbed in it.

21. Do sever this unholy 'I' notion by the tool of the thought 'I am not' and by overcoming the ordeals of life, abide in contemplation of Self, which is all glory."

22. Sri Rama asked, "O Divine Seer, thy words of instruction are of frightful import. You have asked me to discard the 'I' notion.

23. O master, if the 'I' notion is to be abandoned, I have also to totally abandon the body with which I am associated.

24. If the 'I' notion gets erased, the body also necessarily perishes, like the great tree when its root is severed by axe."

25. Sri Vasishta said: "O lotus-eyed Rama, the renunciation of all vasanas is of two kinds-Dhyeya, Contemplative and Jneya, Spiritual.

26 to 28. 'I belong to these things,' 'They give life to me,' 'I do not exist without them,' 'None of these can exist without me'-discarding such convictions, and after

rationally understanding, 'I do not belong to the thing' and 'nothing is mine,' and performing sportively all activities with a cool mind, he has made the kind of renunciation of vasanas, O Rama, that is called Dhyeya, Contemplative.

29. Regarding all things as essentially one in nature and discarding the body with the thought 'It is not mine,' he who annihilates all vasanas is known to have made the renunciation, Jneya, Spiritual.

30. Dismissing the companion of 'ahankara' and the vasanas, he who makes the dhyeya tyaga, contemplative renunciation, is called a jivan mukta.

31. Uprooting all vasanas, he who has become one with Consciousness, has made the jneya tyaga, spiritual renunciation and is a liberated soul.

32. Both, who have made such renunciation, are liberated alike. Both have become one with Brahman. Both are free from the samsaric fever.

33. He who is not elated or despondent when fortunes or misfortunes happen at different times, is said to be a liberated person.

34. He whose inner vision is not coloured by likes and dislikes and who performs acts, as if he were in sleeping condition, is said to be liberated.

35. He whose thinking is not influenced by elation, jealousy, fear, anger, lust, miserlines, etc., is said to be a liberated person.

36. He whose mind remains stilled as if in sleep, even during the waking state, who is endowed with all talents but appears to be without any and who is always happy is considered to be a liberated person.

37. O Rama, the desire aroused by the vasanas of the

external objects is bondage and the desire bereft of vasanas of external objects is said to be liberation.

38. O Rama, the thought, 'let this be mine' in the inner heart, know to be the desire-and also the fetter.

39. He whose exalted mind is always indifferent to the existence or otherwise of worldly things, attains to a supreme state.

40. Abandoning likes and dislikes, state of bondage and liberation, the real and the unreal, abide as an unperturbed ocean.

41. Further, O Rama, in the mind of the inquisitive soul manifests the conviction which enlarges the vision in four ways.

42. I am the body comprising of feet and hand, brought into existence by my father and mother-Such conviction based on illusory perception, leads to bondage.

43. I am beyond all entities and subtler than the subtlest fibre of lotus-stalk. Such conviction leads to liberation and arises in those who are wise.

44. I am the Self which is imperishable and Self of all beings, pervading the whole world-O Rama, such a conviction which is the third also leads to liberation.

45. This world is unreal and void, like the void-like space-This fourth kind of conviction also leads to liberation.

46. Of these four, the first pertains to desire of the kind that leads to bondage. The desire of the other three types is pure and is being displayed by jivanmuktas.

47. 'All this is Self which I am'-acquire such a conviction, O noble soul and your mind will not be subject to grief again.

48. The Self is spoken of as void, primordial matter, maya, knowledge of Brahman, Shiva, Purusha, Ishana, etc.

49. *It is truly the supreme power of the non-dual Brahman that manifests as the dual and non-dual universe, created as if in sport.*

50. Do not get swayed by happiness or sorrow, whether in respect of oneself or another or all, when there is something fortunate or otherwise.

51. He who contemplates what is beyond the world, who is as full of coolness in the heart as the full moon, who is neither too anxious nor too contented, does not fall into grief in life.

52. He who is equal to friend and foe, who is endowed with compassion and tolerance, who attends to things that the situation brings up does not fall into grief in life.

53. He praises not, hates not, grieves not and desires not. Bereft of likes and dislikes, he does not fall into grief in life.

54. He tells what is acceptable to all; when questioned, he speaks tenderly. He knows the hearts of people. Such a person does not fall into grief.

55. Acquiring the vision of the whole, renouncing the vasanas through contemplation, and abiding in the Self like the liberated soul, do sport in the world, O Rama.

56. *Internally renouncing all desires, attachments and vasanas, externally attending to all tasks, do sport in the world, O Rama.*

57. Preoccupied externally with worldly affairs, unconnected internally with all things, be a doer

externally, a non-doer internally and thus sport in the world, O Rama.

58. With 'ahankara' discarded, mind still as though in sleep, a lustre like that of the moon, but without the taint, do sport in the world, O Rama.

59. Be noble-minded, tender-hearted, devoted to the pursuit of religious duties, and renouncing everything internally, do sport in the world, O Rama.

60. Internally be dispassionate. Externally be earnest to fulfill. Be outwardly anxious and internally cool and thus sport in the world, O Rama.

61. Let the false notions-'He is my relation,' 'He is an outsider,' 'I am this,' 'It is you'-totally disappear from your heart, O Rama.

62. Only the petty-minded think in terms that 'he is a relation' and 'he is not' for the noble-minded, the entire world is a single family.

63. The experiences in various kinds of previous lives cause the perception, 'this is a relation,' 'this is not,' in the world, but this happens during the phase of delusion. In reality, no one is either a relation or not.

64. In regard to this matter, there is an ancient story relating to the conversation between brothers, who were the sons of a seer, on the banks of Ganga.

65. There is in some corner of Jambudwipa a mountain infested with huge forests, called Mahendra.

66. In a broad slope of the mountain, attractive and filled with jewels, there was an illumined seer, who was noble-hearted and interested in the pursuit of penance.

67. Called by the name Dhirgatapa, he looked an embodiment of penance. He had two sons beautiful like moon.

68.   The two, known by the names Punya and Pavana, were as intelligent as Kacha, the son of Brihaspati. The seer lived alongwith the sons for a long time.

69.   O Rama, as days passed, the elder of the brothers, Punya became a knower of Truth and was endowed with virtues.

70.   Pavana was only partially-enlightened, like the not fully blossomed lotus in the pre-dawn period of the day. Being within the grip of crass ignorance, he had not attained Realisation and was tossing around.

71 & 72. With the all-devouring Time passing on without pause, tired of old age and life, the seer Dhirgatapa discarded the nest of the bird of imagination the body, in the manner of fuel-gatherer unburdening himself in the home.

73.   Like the fragrance of the flower dissolving into the sky, the seer attained to the serene realm of Consciousness, unexternalised and unattached.

74.   With father dead, Punya performed the obsequies dutifully, but Pavana was overwhelmed with grief.

75.   He was sorrow-stricken and depressed. And roaming in the woods, Pavana without mature understanding, remained weeping over father's death.

76.   After performing the obsequies of the father, a staunch follower of dharma, Punya came to the grief-stricken Pavana in the woods.

77 & 78. Punya said, "My son, why are you a prey to intense grief that blinds one's vision. O wise man! A person of great wisdom, your father has attained to one's own state of Surpeme Self which is liberation. When some natural thing has happened, why do you grieve?

79.   O child, you have seen in previous lives hundreds of

fathers and mothers. Sons and relatives surround one in every birth.

80. If the dead father, mother and child should be mourned over, why are the thousands of fathers of previous lives not mourned?

81. In the vast deserted stretch of ajnana, ignorance, the illusory stream of water caused by the radiant rays flows with good and bad deeds as waves and this stream is endless.

82. The worldly life is pervaded by friendship, hatred and delusion towards relations, friends and children and all these are merely imagined.

83. *If one is thought of as a relation, one is a relation. One is an outsider if thought so. Like poison turning into nectar, objects are determined by attitude.*

84. As there is only the non-dual, all-pervasive Self, how could there be the imagination 'he is a relation' and 'he is not?'

85. Son, do thou enquire with your own mind whether you are the aggregate of blood, flesh and bones, called body.

86. From the viewpoint of the Absolute, neither you nor I exist. It is false cognition that projects Punya and Pavana.

87 & 88. You had number of relations born amongst animals in the holy centres and why do you not grieve for them? Did you grieve for those born among lions on the mountain slopes?

89 & 90. You were born a dark wild monkey in the Dasarna land, a prince in the Thushara land and a wild crane in the Poundra land. You were an elephant in the land of Mehayas, an ass in the land of Trigartas, a dog in

the Salva land and a bird of the forest.

91. In these and many other species and as a human being, you were born before in the Jambudwipa times without number.

92. Countless number of fathers have come and gone as also countless number of mothers, like leaves appearing in tree.

93. Do thou calmly contemplate the Self which is unassociated with real and unreal things and which is bereft of old age and death. Do not fall a prey to stupidity.

94. O son, through great discrimination remove the taint of desires from the pure Self by contemplation of the Self in the heart and by completely discarding the delusion, attain to beatitude now itself."

95. Thus enlightened by Punya, Pavana attained Awareness, like the earth becoming effulgent at dawn.

96. Both of them became perfect in knowledge and realisation and they roamed in the forest without sorrow.

97. O faultless man, numberless are the relatives of your previous births. Are you for multiplying the desires arising on account of them or for discarding them?

98. Thought feeds thought, as fuel feeds fire. Thoughtlessness extinguishes the thought as the absence of fuel the fire.

99. O Rama, ascend the chariot of the renunication of vasanas through contemplation and endowed with the vision of compassion, look at the world and abide in peace and bliss.

100. This is Brahmic Consciousness, natural and bereft of

desire and sorrow. Attaining this, even an ignorant man does not get deluded.

101. Do thou acquire the one well-wisher, viveka, the discrimination and the one female companion, the intellect and keep sporting. You will be free from delusion all through creation.

102. Unless it is through courage, by which one sets aside all desired objects and keeps away all relations, one cannot pull oneself out of the ordeal.

103. Uplift your own mind through effort, through dispassion, through study of scripture, through practice of virtue for saving yourself from the danger of samsara.

104. That which is attained through a refined and trained mind is not attained through the wealth of the world, through all the jewels or treasure.

105. If there is fullness of mind, the world is saturated with the blissful nature. If only a man has footwear on the feet, is not the entire earth covered by leather?

106. Through dispassion, mind attains fullness but not through desire. Desire sullies the mind, as summer, the waters of the lake.

107. The heart enslaved by various desires becomes empty and its deep interiors get exposed like those of ocean, when its waters have been drunk by Agastya.

108. *The full moon is not so effulgent, the milk-ocean is not so majestic, the face of Lakshmi is not so attractive, as the mind bereft of desire is.*

109. The devil of desire vitiates the inner mind of the individual, as the shred of cloud the full moon, as the black stain the painted picture.

110. He is an exalted soul in whom all desires have become extinct and do thou throw away the fetter of life and be such an emancipated soul. When the ropes of the desires that chain the mind get severed, who does not get liberated?

Chapter-3

The Story of Bali

1. "O Rama, the full moon of the sky of Raghu's family, do thou attain pure wisdom through the kind of enquiry pursued by Bali.

2. Sri Rama asked, "O master! Tell me the manner of Bali's attainment of wisdom, for wise people readily show consideration to seekers who are humble."

3. Sri Vasishta said: "There is in this universe, at some corner of it, the region called patala, which is below the earth.

4. In that region was, as the ruler of the mighty empire of asuras, the danava, Bali, the son of Virochana.

5. The kingdom covering all the three worlds won by him with ease, was as if the ornament of the king, who ruled over the daityas for ten crores of years.

6 & 7. As countless number of yugas passed, as the mighty waves of suras and asuras kept rising up and falling down, with all the pleasures of the three worlds experienced again and again, the danava chief Bali became disgusted with the pleasures.

8 & 9. Once, standing on the top storey of the mansion, he reflected 'what has finally accrued to me from the enjoyment of the immense pleasures in my kingdom of the three worlds? They are seemingly pleasant and inevitably short-lived. They give momentary delight. Is this real happiness?

10. The beloved is embraced again and union with her is

again experienced. This kind of sport culminating in birth of children is shunned by the wise.

11. Why is not the intelligent person disgusted with same kind of acts repeatedly done everyday, with the object losing its charm?

12. Again the day follows, the night follows. Man indulges in same acts again and again. I think the intelligent man is indulging in a farce.

13. By repeatedly doing the acts whose purpose has been served, what is achieved that has a lasting value rendering further acts useless?

14. Apart from the passing experience of pleasure, what is there that is lasting and imperishable? Let me contemplate over it, so thought Bali.

15. The king of asuras said instantly, 'Ha! I do remember now,' and knitting the brows, he began to think deeply.

16. 'Indeed, the Divine Virochana, who was a knower of the Self and well-versed in worldly matter, was questioned by me on this matter long time before.

17 to 19. "O father, what is the ultimate experience attaining which all illusions about happiness and sorrow finally cease? When does this delusion of the mind get dispelled? Which is the state that is beyond all desires and dispassion where mind can experience the quiet for long? If there is a thing which has lasting bliss and beauty, please tell me so that I can remain immersed in it for long?"

20 & 21. My father said, "There is, my son, a vast land, in which countless number of worlds keep manifesting, but in which really, there is no earth, no space, no ocean, no mountain, no port, no holy centre, no river and no lake.

22. There is one who is great and all-powerful. He is the king who is doer of all, and who is all but he remains quiet.

23. Brought into existence by the will of the king, the mantri, minister, is actively indulging in mental fancies and makes impossible things possible and possible things impossible.

24. He does not know enjoyment, does not know anything. He keeps constantly doing things for the sake of the king.

25. It is he who acts for the great king in all conditions. The king simply remains still in solitude."

26. Bali asked, "O Lord, what is that land which is free from all the afflictions-mental and physical? How is it attained? Who has attained it?

27. Who is that mantri, minister, and who the valorous king, who has not been conquered yet by me, who has dragged the world at will?"

28. Virochana said, "O child, the mantri is a powerful man and he cannot be overpowered by any number of devas and asuras combined.

29. Sword, spear, missile, thunderbolt, chakra, etc., are powerless against him and get blunted like the knife that strikes against stones.

30. That mantri is easily won only by his master, if at all he is won. Otherwise, he is unshakable by any.

31. O son, he can however be brought under control in no time through appropriate counsel. But if he is unthinkingly handled, he burns up one, like the infuriated serpent.

32. Son, let me tell what that land is even at the outset.

What was described as land is only the state of liberation which is beyond the reach of sorrows.

33. The king is Atma, the Self, who is beyond all empirical entities. O wise man, he who has been made the minister by the king is the intelligent mind.

34. The appropriate discipline by which the mind is conquered, my son, is the practice of extreme detachment towards all sense-objects in all circumstances.

35. This is the supreme discipline, and it is by this only the mad elephant of mind is quickly tamed.

36. The uninitiated person entering on the path of spiritual quest, should thus fill the four parts of the mind-two with experience of sense-objects, one with the study of the scripture and the rest with the service of the preceptor.

37. One who has already progressed on the path should fill one fourth of the mind with sense-experience, two fourths with the service of the preceptor and the rest with study of scripture and reflection.

38. One who has progressed far should fill two-fourths with scriptural study and dispassion and two-fourths with meditation and service of the preceptor.

39. O son, one who is established in enquiry and wisdom has to practise self-control always. Let him contemplate on the Self and discard all cravings of the mind.

40. Enquiry gets strengthened by dislike of pleasures and the latter by enquiry. Both strengthen each other, like the clouds and the ocean.

The ocean becomes full with rain-waters and the cloud gets formed with the waters of the ocean. S. T.

41. By conforming to the prevailing environment and by flawless means, acquire wealth. With that wealth, honour the wise knowers of Truth. Association with such persons leads to dispassion and proper enquiry, which culminate in Self-Realisation.

42. Bali further recollected, "This was stated by my father who had properly investigated into the spiritual truth. By chance, I remember it now. I have become enlightened.

43. I have now complete dispassion for sense-pleasures. I begin to experience the bliss of tranquility which is natural and cool like amrita.

44. The blissful calm is really attractive because of coolness. All experiences of pleasure and pain become dissolved when there is inner calmness.

45. Let me seek to know from the preceptor Suka, the knower of Self, 'Who I am' and 'what is the Self,' so that my ajnana may get destroyed."

46. Sri Vasishta said: "Thinking thus, the powerful Bali with eyes shut contemplated on Sukra, who was always in Brahmic plane.

47. The all-pervasive chit that Sukra was, he understood Bali's thought and arriving at the mansion entered it through the jewel-decorated window.

48. There, Bali offered jewels and mandara flowers and prostrated at Sukra's feet and worshipped him.

49. Bali said, "The effulgence that arises in my heart, on account of thy grace prompts this speech of mine, as the sun's rays prompt one's task.

50. What is it that is here in world? What is its exact nature? What is it full of? Who am I? Who are you? What are these worlds?-do thou tell me without fail.

51 & 52. Sukra replied, "I am on the way to Swarga. Where is the need to expatiate much? O chief of danavas, hear the essence of wisdom. *All this is pervaded by Chit only. Chit you are. Chit I am. All these worlds are Chit-This is the essence of wisdom.*

53.   If you are earnest and humble, you will obtain everything from this teaching of Truth. If not, any amount of instruction would go in vain like the oblation in the ashes.

54.   *Chit-chetya, subject-object relationship is bondage and release from that is liberation. Chit unexternalised is Atma, the Self-this is the essence of entire Vedanta.*

55.   With such a conviction and through the purified mind, see the Self and you will attain the infinite plane.

56.   Let me go to the heaven. The seven seers are to meet there. I have to be there in connection with a celestial affair."

57.   Sri Vasishta said: "After saying this, Divine Sukra ascended to the sky. Bali began to realise that the universe is chit in content.

58.   Bali said, "The Divine Seer has spoken only what is in conformity with reason. All the three worlds are chit only. Chit I am. Chit is world. Chit is desire. Chit is action.

59.   That which is bereft of objectivity and cognition is pure Self. He is ever manifest and self-luminous. I am Parameswara, the super-seer.

60.   I am chit unrelated to chetya, object. I am all and am pervading all. With all cognisable object disappearing, I am pure unrelated intelligence.'

61.   Thinking thus, the supremely wise Bali contemplated on the matras of 'OM' upto the ardha-matra

(representing turiya) and remained absorbed in Consciousness.

62 & 63. With all thoughts perfectly stilled, with all imaginations fully eliminated, with all seer-seen relationships totally cast away, with all distractions of meditator-meditation-object erased, the mind remained stripped of vasanas and shone like the unflickering lamp in a wind-less place. Bali had attained the supreme beatitude.

64.   With the cravings eliminated through perception of the whole, all mental fancies wiped away, Bali shone like the luminous cloudless sky."

65.   Sri Vasishta said: "Thereon, other danavas who were the followers of Bali, ascended instantly to the top storey of the crystal mansion.

66.   After remaining absorbed in super-conscious state for long, the noble-minded Bali rose up from the state, when the ministers were also present.

67.   Bali, the son of Virochana renouncing the vasanas, through contemplation attended to all the affairs of the kingdom.

68.   He saw both fortunes and misfortunes in the same plane. His attitude manifested no joy or depression in conditions of happiness or sorrow.

69.   Bali happened to know many views desirable and undesirable, many things real and unreal and yet he did not get attached to any.

70.   Therefore, O Rama, withdrawing the mind that rushes after things of this world and the other, restrain it in the cave of the heart.

71.   *Wherever mind, like child, gets stuck up in mire, raise*

up the mind from all such situations and unite with
Reality.

72. By the person who practises this discipline, the proud
elephant of mind is completely tamed and the
supreme beatitude is attained."

Chapter-4

The Story of Prahlada

Sri Vasishta said:

1. "Do thou hear about this supreme mode of attaining Realisation. Listen how the chief of daityas, Prahlada became an enlightened soul.

2. When Hiranyakasipu, the enemy of the devas got killed, Prahlada, stricken with sorrow, began to reflect.

3. 'Father and other asura chiefs have been killed by Vishnu, like the groups of mountain by the mighty wind at the time of deluge.

4 & 5. Many asura chiefs equal to huge mountains, fought valiantly.

   Of these frightful and mighty chiefs of asuras, if there is any who remains unafraid, he will undoubtedly become afraid soon (of Vishnu).

6. Therefore, there is only one way of conquering the mighty and unexcelled warrior Vishnu and I do not see an alternative mode.

7. He is the final saviour, to be sought with all the heart, with all the energy and with all the requisite rituals and there is no other refuge.

8. From this very moment I take total refuge in the eternal Hari. I am entirely filled with Narayana.

9. 'Obeisance to Narayana' is the mantra that is capable of achieving all the aims. As wind does not leave its abode of space, this mantra will not leave my heart.

10. Any one other than Vishnu, by propitiating Vishnu

274

does not obtain the result of worship. By becoming Vishnu yourself, worship Vishnu. So I am Vishnu already.'

11. Sri Vasishta said: "Prahlada, thinking thus and transforming his body into one similar to that of Narayana, again thought of Vishnu, the enemy of asuras, for the sake of worshipping him.

12. 'Let me for the sake of worship invoke His supreme form in the external idol, similar to Vishnu, through imparting of prana.

13. Let me worship Him surrounded by His retinue, in the appropriate manner, with all ingredients mentally conceived.'

14 & 15. Thinking thus, Prahlada offered mental worship to Madhava, the Lord of Lakshmi with all the ritualistic paraphernalia-jewelled vessels, sandal paste, lamp, camphor, scented sticks and other holy ingredients and ornaments.

16. Then, in the divine sanctum, the danava chief, Prahlada, collected all materials fully and worshipped Janardhana.

17. From that time onwards, Prahlada worshipped, with a fullness of heart and devotion, the Supreme Lord.

18. In that city of the daityas, all the citizens became devotees of Vishnu for truly the king sets the code of conduct for others.

19. The news reached the denizens of the heavens that the asuras had discarded their hatred of Vishnu their enemy, and became the devotees of Him.

20. All celestials including Indra, became wonder-struck and asked, 'How have the daityas become worshippers of Hari?'

21. The celestials, getting amused, left the heaven and sought Hari, skilled in war, reclining on the serpentine couch in the ocean of milk.

22. *The celestials submitted, 'What is this strange occurence that daityas who oppose you have become totally your worshippers? We are seized by wonder.*

23. Where are the wicked asuras who have destroyed mountains? Where is devotion to Janardhana which is attained only by a human being in his last birth?

24. This is similar to the happening that a rustic has become a virtuous soul. In fact this development, like the blossom in wrong season, makes us not happy but suspicious.

25. Where is the low-born danava, a despicable soul of uncultured and undesirable conduct and where is the devotion to the Universal God?

26. The Lord said, "O celestials, do not become gloomy. Prahlada is a great devotee. This is his last birth. A destroyer of foes, he deserves liberation.

27. A virtuous person becoming wicked is fraught with harm to others. But a wicked person becoming virtuous is a desirable development.

28. O celestials, do thou return to the excellent worlds of yours. Manifestation of great attributes in Prahlada will not cause any harm."

29. Saying thus, the Lord disappeared amidst the waves of the milk-ocean, like the flower-bunch of the tree on the bank in the rising waves.

30. The devas, having worshipped Hari, returned to their celestial abodes. They became very friendly with Prahlada from that time onwards."

31. Sri Vasishta further said: "Prahlada being a great devotee worshipped the God of Gods Janardhana every day in thought, word and deed.

32. Devoted as he was to the performance of worship, his mind did not evince interest in pursuit of pleasures which are only maladies.

33. He had renounced the pleasures but not attained the repose. His mind remained suspended like a swing.

34. Lord Krishna, being all-pervasive and deeply concerned, understood the state of Prahlada even from his abode in the milk-ocean.

35. Through the subterranean path, Vishnu who is foremost in delighting the devotees entered into the puja room of Prahlada.

36. Knowing that the Lord has come, the danava king, with increased devotion and fervour, worshipped Vishnu.

37. Prahlada, getting immensely delighted, extolled in excellent words, Hari, who had directly manifested Himself in the puja-room.

38. Prahlada said, 'In the delightful treasure of all the three worlds, in the supreme effulgence which wipes away all taints, in the saviour who is the resort of the helpless and worthy of surrender, in Him who is unborn and immutable, in the Lord who is Hari-I take refuge.

39. In Him, whose colour resembles that of the heap of blue lillies, who is as pure as the vast summer sky, whose black eyelids resemble the dark bees, who wields the lotus, chakra and gadha in His hands-I take refuge.

40. In Him, whose body has the lustre of the bees, who has the conch similar to the white lotus bud, whose lotus-like form has the bee of Brahma, the creator of Vedas, humming around, who is like the water that supports the lotus of my heart-I take refuge.

41. In Him, whose nails look like stars strewn around, whose smiling face resembles the whiteness of the radiant full moon, whose chest creates the illusory notion of the flow of Ganga, who is like vast summer sky-I take refuge.

42. In Him, who is like the fragrant pollen of the lotus of the three worlds, who is like the lamp that dispels the darkness of delusion, who is Chid-atma that is entirely Conscious, who is a remover of the afflictions of the distressed, in that Hari-I take refuge.

43. In Him, whose chest is adorned by lotus-born Lakshmi, who is as white as the pollen dust of the lotus that has just blossomed, whose limbs are red like the declining sun and who is beautiful like the sky of golden colour-I take refuge.

44. In Him, who is constantly engaged in the play of creation, who is unborn, immutable and all-pervasive, whose body despite its existence for countless number of yugas looks like the one just born, who, as a child is reclining in the banyan leaf-I take refuge.

45. In Him, who is like mist to the lotus of daityas, who is eternal sun to the lotus of the devas, who is like the sustaining water of the lotus-born Brahma, who abides in the lotus-like heart of mine-I take refuge.'

46. Extolled thus by words full of virtues, Hari, the killer of asuras, with the chest inhabited by Lakshmi, delighted like the peacock with the clouds and with

the blue taint of the lily, spoke to the asura-chief who was devout.

47. The Lord said, "O priceless jewel of the family of the daityas! Treasure of that family! Seek the boon that gives relief from the sorrow of life."

48. Prahlada said, "O Supreme Lord, do thou give unto me that alone which is capable of fulfilling all aims, which contains all the world, as it were, within itself and which is the most exalted."

49. The Lord said, "O faultless soul, that which puts an end to all delusions, that which confers on one the supreme good, is attainable only through enquiry which culminates in the experience of oneness with Brahman and let this kind of enquiry manifest in you."

50. Sri Vasishta said: "Saying thus to the scion of the Dhithi family, Vishnu disappeared from view, making the sound which resembled that of the waves of ocean.

51 & 52. As Vishnu disappeared, Prahlada made a final offering of flowers and recitation of stotras to complete the worship, left the seat bedecked with jewels and sat beside in the padmasana posture and began to reflect.

53. 'I have been told by the Lord, who is the annihilator of samsara, 'to pursue only enquiry.' Let me now enquire into the Self.

54. What indeed am I, who, in this worldly drama speaks, goes, stands, exerts and plays about?

55. This world, comprising of tree, mountain, grass, etc., is not myself. How can I be that which is exterior and insentient?

56. I am not the inert body which has manifested through

the action of vayu, and which gets destroyed in a short period of time.

57. I am not the inert sound which is perceived by the organ of ear momentarily, which is of the nature of void and which arises from void.

58. I am not the touch-experience, which is cognised by the skin in momentary spells, not by itself but by the grace of the conscious self.

59. I am not the experience of taste, which is insignificant, momentary, abiding in substance and brought into existence by tongue again.

60. I am not the form which remains latent in the object and vision, not lasting beyond a second and ultimately merging in the seer himself.

61. I am not the experience of smell, which is manifested by the nostril, insignificant and not sentient in nature.

62. I am indeed pure Consciousness, bereft of the illusory five sense-perceptions, without the notion 'mine,' without mentation, conception and imagination.

63. I am indeed the illumining Consciousness which is bereft of chetya, objective form. I am pervading all, within and without and am partless and pure existence.

64. Ah! I remember the teaching. This experience is real. I am the undifferentiated Self-Consciousness pervading all.

65. All these objects, pot, cloth, including sun are illumined by Self-the consciousness, the supreme light.

66. The different sense-cognitions manifest because of Self-luminous effulgence within-like the row of sparks.

67. My form of Consciousness keeps extending beyond

the abode of Brahma and beyond even the deluge.

68.　When my being is unbounded and unconditioned how could there be the limited identification caused by the notion 'I.'

69.　Infinite blissful experience, extremely tranquil and pure, prevails over all limited perceptions.

70.　My salutations to Myself who is one with all existence, who is bereft of change, the object and who is innermost Consciousness.

71.　Various kinds of strange powers are manifested by the pure Supreme Consciousness, which is unchanging and bereft of taint.

72.　When the three periods of time, past, present and future are ignored, when the bondage caused by the chetya, object, is erased, when the object itself is totally uncognised, there is only the residual equanimity.

73.　Since that state is beyond the description of words, it is as though non-existent; it is identical with the state in which there is no self, as it were.

74.　When the chit, Consciousness, is tainted by desire, hatred, etc., it is not able to get liberated like the bird bound by fetters.

75.　Human beings, because of the delusion caused by the pairs of opposites like desire and aversion, become indistinguishable from the creatures thriving in the holes of earth.

76.　I salute the expansive, unbounded Consciousness, which is my Self. A jewel of this and the transcendental world you are, O God, I have realised the Truth after a long time.

77. I have reflected upon you, attained you, realised your ultimate form, understood you distinctly from imaginary entities and my salutations to you who is of such nature.

78. Salutations to my Self, who is infinite. Salutations to you, the auspicious Being. Salutations to God of Gods, to the Supreme Self.

79. I salute my Self, which is blissful, self-manifesting, self-realising and self-abiding, which shines effulgently with the removal of the veil, like the full moon with the removal of the dense cloud.

80. Though he remains standing, he is not there; though moving he moves not; though calm he is active; though acting he is untainted.

81. As the tender leaves get tossed about by wind, the senses are activated by It. As the horses are driven by the charioteer, the group of senses is driven by It.

82. He alone should be constantly sought after, praised and contemplated upon. One gets emancipated from old age, death, maladies and delusion.

83. He who is like the bee in the lotus of the heart is too easy to attain and can be won over like an intimate relation.

84. I have no craving for the host of pleasures nor have I aversion towards them. What is to come, let it come. What is to leave, let it leave.

85. Till now, with my discriminative sense snatched away from me, I have been harmed by the enemy ajnana, ignorance.

86. With mind destroyed by mind, when one attains to ego-less plane and worldly thought is discarded

through contemplation of Brahman, I abide in pure Self.

87. My being remains motionless as pure Consciousness, when there is no conception, no 'I' notion, no thought, and no desire.

88. Where has gone the evil bird of ahankara, I do not know, from the cage of my body after the binding ropes of desire have been cut away?

89. The abundant objects of pleasures, though exist, exist not for you, as the beauty of a maiden exists not for the man without vision.

90 & 91. Victory to the Frightful! Victory to the Beatific! Victory to that which is beyond the Scriptures! Victory to the wisdom of the Scriptures! Victory to the Born, Victory to the Unborn, Victory to the Perishable, Victory to the Non-perishable! Victory to the Existent, Victory to the Non-existent! Victory to the Conquered! Victory to the Unconquered!"

92. Sri Vasishta said: "Thinking in this manner, Prahlada, conqueror of the foes, passed into super-conscious blissful awareness.

93. Remaining in the super-conscious state, he looked like a picture. He remained wholly absorbed in consciousness for five thousand years.

94. Because for such long duration, the patala world remained without a ruler, there was confusion with the law of the fishes prevailing, that is, the stronger fishes swallowing the smaller ones.

95. Hari reclining on the serpentine couch in the milk ocean, whose being is for the sake of the protection of worldly order and who is like the sun for the lotus of the three worlds, reflected thus:

96 to 103. 'When Prahlada has withdrawn into the plenary beatitude, and the patala world is without a ruler, the cosmic process is caught in impasse. For the cosmos will be without daityas, and if there are no daityas, devas will not bestir themselves to be victorious over them. They will become a quiet lot and unswayed by success or failure, they will attain to liberation. With the devas attaining liberation, the sacrifices, penances and austerities done in the earth for soliciting their favour will be fruitless. When these rituals become extinct, the world will also become extinct. With the world ceasing to exist, the cosmic process, samsara, will get terminated. In such a case, as sun, moon and stars disappear, I too will have to withdraw into my serene state. If the world were to come to an end at the wrong time in this manner, I do not see any good accruing to the souls. I feel the danavas should live on. When they become active, devas will exert to conquer them. Sacrifices, penances and rituals will be performed on the earth. The cosmic process will proceed unhindered. Otherwise, the samsara will come to an end. To the end of deluge, Prahlada has to carry on with this body. Such is the divine law already ordained by the Supreme.'

104. Thinking thus, the Universal Soul emerged from the milk ocean and reaching the capital of Prahlada, entered into the mansion.

105. He was seated on Garuda; Lakshmi was by the side fanning the Lord; His attendants wielded the appropriate weapons; the seers were offering prostrations to Him.

106. 'O lofty soul, wake up,' saying so, Vishnu blew Panchajanya, which filled the directions with the reverberation.

107. The ruler of the danavas woke up in stages as a result of the explosive sound caused by Vishnu's effort.

108. The power of prana abiding in the Brahmarandra, leaving the centre pervaded the nadi-channels all over the body of Prahlada.

109. When the consciousness activated all the nadi-centres; it became inclined towards the chetya, by virtue of reflection in the prana-mirror.

110. Getting inclined towards chetya, the object the chit assumed the form of chit-chetya complex, called mind. O Rama, this is akin to a beautiful face doubling itself at the contact with a mirror.

111 to 113. It was as if the seed had sprouted and the eyes were mildly throbbing like blue lilies. Prana and apana ranged through all nadi channels and like the lotus getting swayed by the wind, his body experienced movement. Instantly, the mind assumed gross form and the eyes, mind, prana activated the entire body.

114. When his eyes opened, mind became externalised, the Lord of the three worlds told him as the rain-bearing cloud the peacock.

115. "O wise man, remember thy glorious sovereignty and stature. Why do you withdraw your body-consciousness at the inopportune time?

116. Rise up, what is the harm that can accrue from bodily activities to one who is devoid of likes and dislikes and conceptions of real and unreal?

117. This body is to be sustained by you till dissolution by managing the affairs of the kingdom in the spirit of a liberated person.

118. It is no deluge time for you to think of discarding the body, for the twelve adityas, have not arisen, the tall

mountains have not become submerged and the earth has not become red-hot. O wise man, why do you choose to leave the body in vain?

119. He is fit to die, whose mind is pillaged by the thoughts, 'I am miserable,' 'I am despondent,' 'I am stupid,' etc.

120. He, whose mind is dragged by the fetters of desires, whose mind is prone to pleasure-seeking, is fit to die.

121. It is proper that the person who is bereft of ego, who views all creatures in the same manner, and whose mind is not attached, continues to live.

122. He, whose heart is cool and free from desire and hatred and who remains a witness of all the world, should continue to live.

123. He, who having attained perfect vision, is free from notions of desirable and undesirable things and who has merged the mind in Consciousness, should continue to live his glorious life.

124. When the subject-object contact ceases, peace manifests in the heart fully and when that beatific state gets established, it is said to be realisation.

125. Rise up, O asura chief, ascend the royal throne. Let me myself perform the coronation ceremony.

126. Those seers, siddhas and celestials who have come here in response to my panchajanya call-let them shower the auspicious benediction."

127 & 128. Then Vishnu with waters brought from Ganga and other holy rivers and oceans, ceremonially bathed Prahlada, who again was extolled by both devas and asuras and then Madhusudhana told Prahlada:

129. "O flawless soul, as long as there are Meru, the solar and lunar mansions, be thou the king with all the noble virtues in full measure."

130. Sri Vasishta said:"After saying thus, the lotus-eyed Lord alongwith the humans and celestials, disappeared from view, as if it was another act of creation.

131. Sri Rama asked, "How did the mind of the noble and divine Prahlada, which had merged in the supreme plane get aroused by panchajanya?"

132. Sri Vasishta said: "In the heart of the liberated souls, exist pure vasanas, akin to burnt seeds, as they cannot lead to future rebirth.

133. The holy, lofty, pure sattvic tendencies, conducive to Self-contemplation exist in the person, who is seemingly asleep.

134. Even after a thousand years, with the inner existence of seed-like vasana, the liberated souls return back to the normal world, if only the bodies remain unimpaired.

Chapter-5

The Story of Gadhi

Vasishta said:

1. O Rama, this maya called by the name samsara, has an endless sweep. It is brought under control only through one's chitta, mind, and not by any other means.

2. In order to enable you to understand the strange and manifold nature of maya and the world, I shall tell a story. O faultless soul, listen intently.

3. There is a region called Kosala kingdom in this vast earth. There was a virtuous brahmana living in it, called Gadhi.

4. With some aim in his mind, he left his relations for the wood to do penance.

5. He saw a lake filled with lotus blossoms. Standing in neck-deep water, he took to penance.

6. Eight months passed since he commenced the penance in the water of the lake. When he was thus undergoing arduous hardship, Hari appeared before him.

7. The Lord said, "O Brahmana, come out from the waters and seek the desired boon. Your endeavour has achieved the intended aim."

8. Gadhi said, 'Obeisance to Vishnu, who is, as it were, a bee in the lotus-like hearts of the countless creatures of different worlds, who is, as it were, the single lotus in the lake of universe.

9. I desire to see the nature of maya, in its supremely

real form, which is your handiwork and the samsara which is wondrous."

10. Sri Vasishta said: "This maya you will behold and then discard," saying so, Vishnu disappeared like the illusory celestial city.

11. After Vishnu left, the great brahmana came out from the waters. He was supremely delighted with the vision of the Lord of the Universe.

12. A few days passed as he remained in the wood, immersed in the happiness of the divine vision and in the performance of brahmana's duties.

13. Once, as the lotus in the lake blossomed, the brahmana started taking bath in the lake, thinking all the while, the words of Vishnu in the mind.

14. He was bathing in the waters in the ritual manner and as he performed this rite, his mind forgot the mantra and the contemplation.

15. He saw himself as dead in his own prior home as a result of pain. With prana and apana ceasing to move, he passed into oblivion.

16. He was surrounded by distressed relations, with wife near the feet, and mother caressing the chin lined with hair.

17. With the kind of wailing aloud appropriate to the occasion and other activities of the people, the body was taken to the cremation ground shrouded with cloth, etc. In the funeral pyre, the body was reduced to ashes.

18 to 27. Thereafter Gadhi saw with his distressed mind, himself lying as a child in the womb of a woman of a tribe who ate dog's meat living in a village on the border of the kingdom of the Hunas. In course of time,

the woman gave birth to the boy. The boy grew as a
darling of the tribal family. He became twelve years
old and afterwards sixteen years old. He had fat,
robust limbs and looked like a dark cloud. A tribal
girl, attached herself to him like a creeper, with bud-
like breasts and shoots-like hands. They played around
and roamed amidst forests. They slept under bowers
and lived in caves. He brought forth sons who were
typical men of the tribe. After sons were born, he had
lost his youthful vigour. He lived on with his withered
limbs until his relations were overtaken by death.
Stricken with grief, he lamented over their death and
with tear-stained face, left that land and thinking over
his lot, passed through several lands.

28 to 35. Once, he happened to reach the kingdom of Kiras
and their prosperous capital, teeming with vassals,
damsels and important citizens. He reached the royal
gateway of the capital resembling that of the heaven.
The entrance was decorated with jewels and there
was the adorned royal elephant looking like a mountain
gazing hither and thither.

As the king had died, the elephant was commissioned
to look out for a king and when Gadhi was looking at
it, the elephant took him by the beautiful trunk and
placed him on its head. He appeared on the elephant,
like the sun at the crest of Meru. Bugles blew and
trumpets were sounded.

The cry, 'Victory to the king' filled the air. Like the
sound of the birds that have risen from sleep in the
morn, there was joyous sound. The maidens began to
attend on him, and adorned him with royal insignia.
All nobles and people followed suit. Thus, the eater
of dog's meat became the king of Kira kingdom and

his lotus–like feet were caressed by the hands of Kira women. The renown of the new king reached the far ends of the kingdom; his command was obeyed everywhere; in a few days, he was able to impose his will on the people; his ministers carried the burden of governance-thus continued the reign of the king who was known by the name Gavala.

36 to 43. Surrounded by lovely women, obeyed by the circle of ministers, revered by the vassals of the kingdom, adorned by the ceremonial umbrella and fan, the eater of dog's meat ruled the Kira kingdom for eight years.

Once, by chance, he happened to be without the royal dress and ornaments. Alone, with the bare body, he went out from his mansion. He found a large crowd of dark persons of his tribe. They were playing on the veena-like contrivance, made of creeper with hands which were like leaves. From among them, one old person with reddish eyes recognised him, rose up and at once accosted the king with the words, "O Katanja, where are you? By chance have I seen you. Long live my relation. In which wood were you living all these years?" As the fellow-tribesman uttered these words, the king made some gestures and concealed his discomfiture. But at the same time his women and ministers who were witnessing this occurrence from the balcony of the mansion realised that the king was really of low-caste and became completely broken-hearted.

44 to 51. The king immediately returned to the woman's apartment, in which all were found immersed in sorrow. The ministers, citizens, women did not go near him and touch him, as if he were a corpse.Even while he was amidst people, he was alone and was kept

away from the paraphernalia, like a way-farer from a different land.

All the people, including the ministers, important citizens, etc., feeling that they had become so impure because of the long contact with the low-born and that they cannot purify themselves through any atonement, prepared fire on all sides and entered into it with their relations.

Because of the contact with wise persons he had as a king, Gavala's mind was pure and he began to reflect alone with sad heart. 'A great misfortune has befallen the people on account of me. Of what use is painful life for me? Death will be a happy event.' Deciding thus, Gavala like a moth, threw his body into the fire before him, and got scorched by fire, as it were. Gadhi woke up from the delusion at the very time and also emerged from the waters.

52 to 58. Within less than two hours, Gadhi became free from delusion. 'Who am I? What do I see? What did I do?'-reflecting thus, he came out from the midst of waters. Mind, getting intoxicated by illusory fancies, like the tiger freely roams in the forest-Deciding thus, he ignored the delusion and spent a few days in his own hermitage.

Once, a lovable visitor happened to come to the hermitage of Gadhi. He became delighted with the offerings of fruits, flowers and seat. Thereafter, the two performed sandhya worship and practised japa. Reclining on their beds, they conversed about holy things. In the course of the talk, Gadhi asked the visitor, 'O brahmana, why do you look pale and exhausted?'

59 to 64. The visitor said, 'There is on this vast earth, in the

northern part, a big prosperous kingdom called by the name Kira. There I lived for a month honoured by the people of the town. There, in the course of conversation, it was told by a person, "O brahmana, here was a low-born ruler for eight years. He was known to be such at the end. He entered into a huge fire. At that, hundreds of brahmanas entered into fire." After I heard thus from him, I came out of that kingdom and performed bath and japa at Prayaga to purify myself. I performed the rigid fasting of chandrayana for three spells (as an atonement) and after breaking the fast I have come here. Hence I am pale and exhausted."

64 to 71. Sri Vasishta said: "Hearing these words of the brahmana, Gadhi thought, 'The events of my life have been similar. Let me try to know without any sorrow my life as the low-born.' Leaving his hermitage, he passed beyond several lands and reached the region of the Hunas. He saw the environs similar to the ones he had experienced, the house he lived in and other dwellings here and there. As he recollected the events, he also remembered his own activities as a tribal. He was amused at the act of creation of the Lord.

He left the Huna region and reached the Kira kingdom. Here he saw things which he had seen and experienced before. He also heard from the people on the same lines. 'I remember everything. It is all the great play of maya without doubt, which Vishnu has revealed to me.'

72 & 73. Thinking thus, Gadhi left that kingdom and ascended to the cave of a hill, like a lion. Taking a palmful of roots as food, he performed penance for one and half years, to please Vishnu.

74.   Then, there came to the abode of the brahmana in the hill, Vishnu, appearing like the beautiful rain-bearing cloud.

75.   The Lord said, "O brahmana, you have seen the mighty maya of mine. Doing penance on this hill, what else do you want?"

76.   Offering flower and waters in the form of worship and after coming around, prostrating with all his body to Him, he spoke to Vishnu like the chataka bird to the rainy cloud.

77.   Gadhi said, "O Lord, maya which is of most confounding nature, has been revealed to me. I am not able to know its significance. How did the illusory spectacle become real?"

78 to 97. The Lord said, "O brahmana, the earth etc., exist in the chitta, mind and do not exist externally any time. This fact is experienced by all in the occurrence of dream. Wherein the whole worldly phenomenon exists, what is there to be surprised at, if by that chitta is revealed one's birth as the low-born, etc?

You saw yourself as a low-born by an illusory projection. In the same way, the brahmana's arrival was also an illusory projection. So was your decision 'let me go to Huna region.' So was the spectacle of Katanja's former house. So was your visit to the Kira country. In the Kira land, you saw the kingship of the low-born.

It is through an accidental association-like the fall of fruit from the palmyra tree when crow sits on it-there was the appearance of the low-born in your mind. The illusory spectacle manifested in the same manner in the case of all at Huna and Kira lands. Occasionally same illusory manifestation arises in several people. The ways of the mind-being the result of an accidental association-are variegated.

In the way in which you saw, there was a Katanja, of the low-born caste in the Huna land. With his lot becoming miserable, he went to other lands. He became the king of the Kira kingdom and then jumped into fire. What manifested in your mind was illusory identification with him and his activities.

'This is myself...this is mine'-such notions possess an ignorant person. The knower of Truth thinks, 'I am all this' and does not get deluded.

O brahmana, this maya is limitless in its dimension and is called samsara. Only through Self-contemplation, it is brought to an end and not otherwise.

The knower of Truth does not get deluded, because he does not have the conditioned deceptive vision of existence as separate things.

Since you do not have total vision, it is difficult to overcome the mental delusion and the delusions enslave the mind in an instant.

It is chitta, that is the nave of the wheel of the entire samsara and if you are able to prevent its rotation, through exertion, the maya cannot harm you.

Rise up, do perform penance for ten years in the hill top and you will attain complete wisdom."

After saying this, Vishnu disappeared there itself. Gadhi attained supreme dispassion as a result of his discriminative vision.

With compassion-filled heart, he went to the hill-top to practise austerity. He did intense penance for ten years without getting distracted by thoughts, and as a result, attained knowledge of the Self.

The noble soul attaining his real Being, bereft of fear, grief, desire for pleasures, etc., became a serene liberated soul of universal vision, like the untainted full moon.

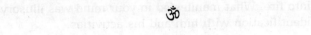

Chapter-6

The Story of Uddalaka

Vasishta said:

1. "The maya of the Supreme Being, o Rama, is infinite, incomprehensible, vastly deceptive and terribly harmful.

2. Therefore, O valorous man, I say that this harmful maya engulfs a restless mind in difficulty everyday.

3. Except through the supreme medicine of overpowering the chitta, mind, as a result of intense effort, the great malady of samsara is not cured.

4. By experiencing externally at the moment the things that naturally encounter him, and by not thinking about the past and future pleasures, the chitta tends to be inactive.

5. If you constantly avoid thought, desire, memory concerning pleasures, every second, you have attained to the exalted mind-less plane.

6. Consciousness pervading the chitta is called pratyak chetana, the individual soul. Consciousness unassociated with mind is not vitiated by the taint of desire.

7. That state, where mind has been extinguished, is the reality, the bliss, the omniscience, the fulfillment and the ultimate existence.

8. The mind must be turned away through effort decisively from indiscrimination and forced to pursue study of scripture and contact with the wise.

9. As you prattle, abandon, receive, open and close the eyes, be free from all thought and remain as bare intelligence.

10. 'This is mine,' 'He is this,' 'I am that'-Discard such vasanas through single-minded absorption and remain as mere intelligence.

11. Discarding the impurity of objectivity and by making the mind pure, cut asunder the fetters of desires and be established in Self-awareness.

12. Bereft of notions of good and bad, with afflictions of desires completely removed, with happy and unhappy perceptions cast away, be exclusively absorbed in bare intelligence.

13. Setting aside the thoughts of mine-ness and other-ness and all worldly distractions remain established firmly in Self like the sacrificial post.

14. At this, the ignorance, cause of samsara, gets dispelled. With impurities and desires gone, one gets stabilised in Self-awareness.

15. When one is absorbed in Consciousness, when one is enveloped in bliss, even the elixir is as displeasing as poison.

16. When chitta becomes gross, Self-awareness gets removed to the farthest, as when dark clouds envelop, light disappears.

17. Mind becomes gross when the body, the non-self is regarded as self, when attachment gets formed towards one's body, son, wife, family, etc.

18. Mind becomes gross when through the play of notion, 'mine,' ahankara gets strengthened and manifests in such forms as 'this is mine.'

19. Mind becomes gross because of mental and physical afflictions, attachment to wordly life, notions of desirable and undesirable.

20. Mind becomes gross with the acquisition of seemingly pleasing things like wealth, jewels and women.

21. The serpent of mind becomes stronger through drinking the milk of wicked desires, inhalation of the wind of sense-experience and movement around in the form of faith in worldly life.

22. By the vivisection and destruction of the five cosmic bodies, Do thou, like Uddalaka, again and again, O courageous soul, enquire into inner Self."

23. Sri Rama asked, "Oh Seer! In what manner was the cosmic body destroyed and enquiry into Self done by the seer Uddalaka?"

24. Sri Vasishta said: "Listen, O Rama, how by enquiring into the nature of the cosmic elements, unchanging supreme vision was attained by Uddalaka.

25. There is a great mountain called Gandhamadhana abounding in trees with fragrant flowers.

26. In some slope of the mountain filled with fruit laden trees, there was a seer called Uddalaka pursuing arduous penance.

27 & 28. Initially he was not well-educated and proficient in vichara, enquiry.

But he, in course of time, through the practice of study of scripture, austerities, acquired discernment.

He reflected thus: 'What is it that is most worthy of attainment so that one will not grieve afterwards?

29. When will I attain repose, like the cloud on the cliff of Meru mountain, and abide for long in supreme

beatitude, leaving mental fancies?

30. When will the craving for sense-experience become quiet in the heart and the mental oscillation like, 'having done this, I have to do something else' cease?

31. When, with the boat of lofty intellect, I will have crossed the river of desire with turbulent waves?

32. When will I abide in peace, in the self-luminous plane of Consciousness, bereft of likes and dislikes, desirable and undesirable?

33. When, through practice of nirvikalpa samadhi in the mountain, with the tranquil mind, I will look like stone nearby?

34. When after I have become dumb through the practice of nirvikalpa samadhi, birds will construct grass-nests on my crest?'

35. Thinking constantly thus, the brahmana Uddalaka sat again and again and practised meditation.

36. When the mind, monkey-like, ran after objects, he was not able to get established in happy samadhi state.

37. When he discarded the external objects of sense-experience, the monkey-like mind resorted to internal imaginary things of sense-experience.

38. When the internal pleasure was denied, the mind ran after external objects. His mind flitted like a restless bird.

39. Sometimes he perceived effulgence rising all around him; sometimes the bare space and someother time intense darkness.

40. Getting distracted in the pratice of meditation and distraught by constant thought, he became very sad

at heart and roamed over the hill without peace.

41. He once reached a cave-like a seer attaining liberation-which cannot be reached by other people and which was absolutely free from all human contact.

42. The virtuous soul entered into that cave of Gandhamadhana mountain and prepared a seat with leaves, keeping the bunches of buds in the fringe.

43. He spread on it a beautiful deer-skin. He sat on it with determination and disciplined mind.

44. Sitting in firm padamasana posture, facing east, with heels supporting the kidneys, he offered obeisance to Brahman.

45. Drawing the deer of mind from the mire of vasanas, he pursued this enquiry for attaining nirvikalpa samadhi, super-consciousness state.

46. 'O stupid mind, what gain is made by the worldly activity? Wise persons do not pursue the activity that ends in sorrowful results.

47. He who jumps at sense-objects discarding the elixir of tranquility, rushes into a jungle of poisonous weeds, leaving behind the wood of mandara trees.

48. Even if you go into the earth or to the abode of Brahma, without drinking the elixir of tranquility, you cannot attain peace.

49. All the various real and unreal objects can lead only to sorrow and fear and not happiness any time.

50. O stupid man, of what use are sense-cognition like sound, which do not give any joy? Why do you not have recourse to mental tranquility, which gives serene peace?

51. O stupid mind, do not identify yourself with sense-

organ, ear and getting attached to the cognition of sound, become like the deer and court death.

52. O stupid mind, do not identify yourself with the skin and getting attached to the sensation of touch, be not the elephant that is enticed by the she-elephant, to bondage.

53. Do not identify with the organ of tongue and getting attached to tasty dishes, do not get killed like the fish that jumps at the meat in the hook.

54. Do not identify with the visual organ and getting attached to beautiful forms, get not burnt like the moth attracted by fire.

55. By getting attached to the fragrance and drawn by it, do not, like the bee, get imprisoned in the lotus of the body.

56. Deer, bee, moth, elephant, fish-enticed by even one sense, each of these met with destruction. How can there be happiness for the ignorant man who is a victim of all the senses?

57 & 58. Why do I have to give instruction to you and for what purpose? For one pursuing enquiry, chitta itself ceases to exist.

The translation is based on the reading in the BYV, 5-52-25.

59. The infinite Self cannot exist within the finite mind, as the elephant cannot exist within a bilva fruit.

60. From the foot to the head of the body, every cell has been investigated. He who is projecting as 'I' has not been found.

61 & 62. I see only the all-pervasive presence of self-revealing Consciousness premeating all the directions and the three worlds.

It has no form, no name; it is neither many nor one; it is neither gross not subtle.

63. O mind, I am self-luminous Consciousness and you are only a source of misery. By discriminating vision, I now destroy you.

64. This is flesh, this is blood, these are the bones of the body, this is the movement of the vital breath. What is it that abides as 'I'?

65. Flesh, blood, bones, knowledge, movement of prana-all these are other than self. O mind, which of these is the self?

66. Nose, tongue, skin, ears, eyes, movement of prana-all these are objects of cognition and as such other than self. Which of these is the self?

67. 'I am everywhere' and 'I am nothing'-this kind of vision embraces the real Existence. There is no other way of realisation.

68. For long have I been waylaid and harmed by the wicked ajnana in the form of ahanta, ego, as a cow is attacked by the deceptive jackal in the forest.

69. By chance I have now clearly identified the thief of ajnana. I will no longer trust him who steals away the wealth of Self.

70. Even if they are not prompted by vasanas, eye and other sense-organs, of their own accord, interact with the sense-objects. Vasanas are not the cause of their activity.

71. Therefore, O stupid sense-organs! Do thou discard vasanas and pursue the usual activity. You will not experience sorrow!

72. The senses, like children, spoil themselves through

desires, as spiders get destroyed by the web of their own making.

73. Therefore, O chitta, you are the driving force of all the senses. Know that alongwith the senses, you do not exist. There is only Consciousness free from the taint of sorrow.

74. By thoroughly dispelling the innumerable afflictions caused by desires of objects and the notion of 'I', through the mantra, mystic chant, of renouncing the desired object, do thou attain the plane, O Divine Seer, where fears do not intrude.

75. By cutting away the tree of thought, and the creeper of desire and thus destroying the forest of mind, I have gained a vast land in which I roam as I please, delightfully.

76. I have attained to the plane where I am all alone. I am victorious. I am liberated. I am partless, desireless.

77 to 79. Purity, perfection, firmness, friendliness, singleness, all-inclusiveness, fearlessness, freedom from opposites-these ever-joyous, healthy, fortune-showering beautiful maidens are the beloved who have won my heart and delight me always in seclusion."

80. Sri Vasishta said: "Deciding thus, the seer with a pure mind and with eyes half-closed remained in the firm padamasana posture.

81. He uttered the liberating mantra, 'Om' in such a manner, that it reverberated in the crest of head, like the sound of the bell when pulled fast by the rope.

82. As he uttered 'Om,' the principle of Consciousness was revealing itself and expanding with reverberation continuing in the crest.

83 & 84. When, of the three and half parts of pranava, the first part was uttered, the prana-current was flowing in a measured manner. As a result, of rechaka, the prana issued out and emptied the body, as Agastya drank the waters and emptied the ocean.

85. As the prana lingered in the outer sphere permeated by the chit, the fire in the heart shining effulgently burnt up the impurities of the heart.

86. He remained in that first aspect of prana as long as desires persisted, and not by force. To restrain prana by force is fraught with harm.

87 & 88. When the second part of pranava was concentrated upon, kumbhaka pranayama manifested. There was no movement of prana either outside or inside, either above or below. It was like a bladder filled with air.

89. The fire which burnt the body before, like the thunder, died. The body appeared like white ashes, white stone.

90 to 92. In the camphor-white ashes, the white unmoving bones appeared like sleeping. The ashes driven to the sky and united with bones appeared like a cloud driven by whirl wind in an instant and disappeared in no time like a tiny cloud in the summer. This condition persisted as long as the desire lasted in the contemplation of pranava. Again this is not achieved through force, for force is fraught with harmful consequences.

93. In the third phase of the contemplation of pranava, tending to make the mind tranquil, the prana currents assumed the form of puraka, which means filling up.

94. In that phase, prana currents flowing amidst chid-amrita pervaded space, became very cool, soft like snow and beautiful.

95. From the space they entered into the region of moon and appeared like streaks of clouds in the sky bearing cool water particles.

96. In that region of moon filled with the essence of life, the pranic currents turned into an ambrosial flow.

97. That ambrosial essence fell from the sky on the residual ashes of bones, like the waters of Ganga on Hara's head.

98. Then manifested the body of Uddalaka-moon-like and four-armed, in the blissful form of Narayana.

99. The alchemic prana currents filled that body completely and permeated the interior of kundalini.

100 to 123. Seated as he was in padamasana posture, he kept under restraint the senses, like iron-fetters the elephant, and restrained through thought the oscillating mind in the lotus-heart, like dam the waters. He half-opened the wing-like eyes and like the stillness in the sky and the lotus-pond during the late evening, there was calm in the movement of prana and apana. Absorbed in silence he dissociated the senses from the objects with effort and the courageous soul kept at long distance the external sense-objects and destroyed the inner thoughts by isolating them from gratification. He restrained the anus and other nine outlets of the body and practised kumbhaka pranayama filling the nerve channels with prana.

Like the Meru mountain bearing aloft the cliff, the courageous soul carried in heart the reality of Self flowering effulgently. Like the proud elephant trapped in a pit in the Vindhya hill, he tamed the mind through appropriate yoga and the fully restrained mihd shone elegantly in the lotus-heart.

Remaining in the plane similar to that of vast, pure and calm sky, whatever thoughts manifested, he destroyed and such thoughts which did not leave so easily, he killed them through mind, like the warrior killing enemies through the sword. As thoughts left him, he found in the inner heart, sun-like effulgent consciousness veiled by cloud. He removed that veil as well and there was perfect effulgence like that of the sun. The manifestation subsided and he saw attractive, pure, luminous being. He mentally cut it off, like the calf-elephant the lotus blossom.

When that lustrous effulgence also subsided, and the mind too was not fully at rest, he fell into sleep like the lotus at night. He cast aside the sleep as well. When the sleep had disappeared, pervasive intelligence manifested in him. When that pervasive intelligence disappeared, the mind experienced dullness. The noble hearted soul dispelled the dullness from the mind. Then, attaining to the plane of Consciousness which was free from darkness, dullness and delusion, the mind enjoyed perfect peace for a while.

After being at rest for a while, the mind attained cosmic intelligence, like the waters resisted by the dam returning to their place.

By virtue of long contemplation of chit and self-cognising experience, the mind turned into chit, like gold the form of anklet. The chitta abandoned its chetya nature and became chit, like pot, emerging from the clay. Chit, abandoning association with chetya, object, became pervasive chit. Like the waves-filled ocean becoming distinctionless sheet of water, there was pervasive awareness in place of countless cognitions.

Attaining Realisation, he discarded totally lurking thoughts of sense pleasures and reached the purer plane of Consciousness embracing the universe. Then he attained the ocean of bliss, bereft of distinctions of seer and seen. It was an ocean of elixir, infinite and excellent in taste. That consciousness transcended the body and reaching indescribable state, was of the nature of satta-samanya, all-pervasive existence. He was himself an ocean of bliss. The brahmana's soul was like a hamsa bird sporting in the lake of bliss; he shone in the sky like the full moon. He was an unflickering lamp, a painted picture on the wall, a waveless calm ocean, a still cloud that had emptied the rain.

124 & 125. Thus remained Uddalaka in a transcendental world for long. He saw siddhas and other celestials in countless numbers, passing through sky. Strange siddhis, powers came to him from all sides. The brahmana did not evince any interest in them.

126 & 127. He kept away the siddhis, powers and revelling in the abode of bliss of Self, he remained at the hill-top for six months. He attained the state of jivanmukti, liberation in which siddhas, celestials, Brahma, Hara, etc., ever remain.

128. Since the happiness in that state was also susceptible to change, he went beyond the state of bliss. It was neither happiness nor the lack of it. It was bare awareness.

129 & 130. That is the highest plane in which Shiva abides. That is beatitude, imperishable and auspicious. Reaching that plane, whether for a minute or for a long duration, wise persons do not get swayed by worldly cognitions that lead to rebirth.

131 to 137. After neglecting the siddhis, Uddalaka remained absorbed in samadhi for six months and waking from it saw celestials of moon-like lustre-vidhyadhara women accompanied by vidhyadhara husbands.

They offered obeisance to the seer, Uddalaka, and appealed to him thus, "O Divine Seer, do look at us with favour. Ascend this celestial vehicle and come to the heaven. Heavenly pleasures are the highest of pleasures in the world. Experience thy chosen pleasures till this creation-cycle comes to an end, O Lord."

The seer received the visitors, who spoke those words, and offered worship to the celestials. Without becoming excited, the courageous seer neither approved nor rejected their offer and the delights. He simply said, 'O siddhas, do return' and reverted to his own pursuit.

Thereafter, the siddhas offered worship to the seer, who was disinterested in pleasures and immersed in Self-experience and returned to their abode after sometime.

138 & 139. The seer, a jivanmukta, a liberated soul, roamed among woods and hermitages happily. He remained in samadhi sometimes for a day, sometimes for a month, sometimes for a year, sometimes for years and then rose up.

140. By intense contemplation of all-pervasive chit for a long time, he attained the state of all-pervasive existence.

141. As a result of attainment of vision of oneness , the mind became calm and free from needless lament and doubt; like a calm, vast and luminous summer sky,

he was clear-minded and blemishless. Renouncing the mind, he was bare Consciousness."

142. Sri Rama asked, "O seer! the sun of the day of Self-realisation, fire for the grass of my doubt, cool nectarine moon that assuages the affliction of ajnana!. What is called satta-samanya, all-pervasive existence?"

143. *Sri Vasishta said: "When the mind becomes extinct as a result of the contemplation of the absolute non-existence of the external world and when there is all-pervasive awareness, that is called as all-pervasive existence, satta-samanya.*

144. When the mind, deprived of object, dissolves into Consciousness, because it has no real form, there is clear manifestation of all-pervasive existence.

145. When the mind negates all existence, outer and inner, there is manifestation of all-pervasive existence.

146. When the objects are negated, they get merged in the seer, as the limbs of the tortoise get merged in it and there results all-pervasive existence.

147. This is the supreme vision that surely characterises the liberated souls-whether they are associated with body or otherwise and this state is called turiya-tita, trans-turiya plane.

148. O blemishless soul, this vision arises, whether he is awake or in samadhi, in respect of an illumined soul. But this vision arising from supreme awareness does not visit the ignorant.

149. It is in this plane, all the great liberated souls abide, O Rama, including all of us, like Narada.

150 to 163. It is in this plane of vision abide Brahma, Vishnu and Ishvara. By attaining this plane, which is beyond

all fears of life, Uddalaka lived as long as he wanted in this home of world.

After a long time, he thought, 'Let me discard the body and remain as a videhamukta, without any oscillation.' He sat on a seat of tender-leaves in the cave of the hill in firm padmasana posture with half-closed eyes. He restrained the anus and other outlets mentally and disassociated the senses from the objects and contemplated the Self as bare mass of Consciousness.

With prana controlled completely, with body-neck-head remaining erect, the root of the tongue raised upwards, behind the jaw, with vision not directed towards any object, outer or inner or void, with the rows of teeth not in contact with each other, with face exuding calmness, with limbs experiencing thrill, he meditated on intelligence as permeating the limbs and as a result attained to the state of all-pervasive chit.

As a result of that practice, he experienced superior bliss welling up within; withdrawing the mind from its experiences, he contemplated on the infinite universal Consciousness and attained to all-pervasive existence. By practising contemplation of pure intelligence, he got established in all-pervasive chit. Remaining in that state of oneness and tranquility, he attained complete repose.

Passing beyond the states of bliss, non-bliss, tranquility and transcendental bliss, with a benign radiant face, he attained the plenary state.

With the extinction of all mentations as a result of mental control for a long time, he became a mere presence, a picture on the wall.

164. Having gone beyond samsara, he, in a matter of few days, slowly withdrew into his pure Being-like the juice of tree, at the end of summer, returning to its source-the effulgence of sun.

165. With all mental imaginations removed, with his own form beyond all transformation, with all fears destroyed through the annihilation of the adjunct, he attained the kind of plenary bliss, which flowing full, makes Indra's happiness a tiny grass floating upon it.

166. The brahmana became the Reality-the Infinite, the Bliss, the Primordial Being, the Eternity-pervading the extensive sky and the internal, and supporting the universe. He transcended all qualities and became worthy of worship by all who seek to be wise."

Chapter-7

The Story of Suraghu

Sri Vasishta said:

1. "O lotus-eyed Rama, pursuing enquiry into the Self with the help of Self, and conducting yourself in befitting manner, do thou attain repose in the supreme plane.

2. With the help of scripture, preceptor, one's own reflection, enquiry is done until, through the extinction of all objective matter, supreme beatitude is attained.

3. The holy state is attained either through dispassion, practice of contemplation, study of scripture, preceptor's instruction and self-discipline, etc., or through supreme discernment.

4. If the intellect is pure and sharp and blemishless even if other qualifications the person does not possess, still he attains the imperishable beatitude."

5 & 6. Sri Rama asked, "Among the enlightened knowers of past and future, there is one, who has obtained samadhi, realisation of Truth and repose and is engaged in external activities; there is another who is resorting to seclusion and practice of samadhi. Of the two, who is greater, kindly tell me."

7. The coolness of heart, which the enlightened person - who sees the aggregate of three gunas, attributes, as non-self - possesses is stated to be the condition of samadhi.

8.   There is a jivanmukta who with coolness of heart understands that he is not in any way connected with the objective matter and is engaged in the external activity. There is another who is always immersed in contemplation.

9.   O Rama, if both are cool at heart, both are liberated, without doubt. The coolness of heart is the fruit of long intense penance.

10.   If the mind of the person sitting in meditation is restless, then his meditation is comparable to uproarious activity.

11.   If the mind of the person engaged in uproarious activity is bereft of vasanas, his uproarious activity is the same as the samadhi of the awakened person.

12.   The two-the realised person engaged in activity and the realised person engaged in contemplation in the forest-are equal and both have attained liberation without doubt.

13 & 14.   Even if he is engaged in action, if his mind is without vasanas, he is a non-doer like the person whose mind is elsewhere, though he is seemingly listening to discourse.

Even if he is not engaged outwardly in action, if his mind is heavily coated with vasanas, he is a doer of action, like the person whose body is actionless in sleep but who dreams of falling into mire.

15.   The sense of non-doership is itself the supreme samadhi. That is the state of kaivalya, aloneness. That is supreme beatitude.

16.   It is mind that is both calm and restless that is the cause of the state of meditation or otherwise. Therefore strip the mind of vasanas.

17. The mind that is not activated by vasanas is one-pointed. That is meditation. That is the kevali-bhava, aloneness. That is also the lasting beatific peace.

18. The attenuation of vasanas takes the mind to a high plane. From that condition results the extinction of vasanas.

19. The sense of doership represents dense vasana. This condition gives rise to all hardships. Therefore, endeavour to eliminate the vasanas.

20. Renouncing mentally multifarious vasanas, remain as you are-whether in contemplation in the wood or in performance of work at home.

21. For the house-holders with one-pointed mind, who have also got rid of the blemish of ahankara, the home itself is the unpeopled wood.

22. As the casual by-standers moving around in a market-place are not taken note of because they do not make transactions, for the enlightened, the village is similarly non-existent.

23. The enlightened person with in-drawn mind is asleep, as it were, and even if he moves in a city, he sees it as a forest.

24. For the one abiding in self-consciousness, the external world is only vacant space. For the one cool at heart, the world is cool. For the one whose heart is turned hot by desire, the world is hot.

25. For all creatures, what exists within exists without. The sky, earth, wind, space, mountains, streams, directions, are all parts of the internal organ projected outside.

26. He is said to be abiding in samadhi, when he delights in Self while outwardly doing all activities with the

sense-organs and is swayed by joy and sorrow.

27. He naturally sees everything as Self, others' riches as lump of clay and not out of fear. Such a person really sees Truth.

28. Let death occur to him now or at the time of deluge, he does not get affected as the gold in contact with mire.

29. All this is serene, unborn, non-dual, beginningless, luminous, blissful, unobjectified presence. To say verbally that all this is serene presence is also only for the sake of enlightening others. All this is 'Om,' for 'Om' is Brahman.

30. In this connection, is cited the story of Suraghu, the king of Kiratas, which is wonderful to hear.

31. There is the peak called Kailas on the Himalayan mountain. At its foot, is the kingdom of the Kiratas called Hemajata.

32. They had a noble king, who was a conqueror of foes, called by the name, Suraghu, and he was strong enough to defeat even celestial warriors.

33. He discharged the royal duties of helping the virtuous and punishing the wicked. The joy and sorrow caused by such action, however disturbed his mind.

34. What is this torment that my mind undergoes like the sesame grain caught in the crusher? My heart bleeds for all those who are suffering.

35. If I do not punish those who deserve to be punished, orderly society will not exist. There cannot be stream without waters.

36. The mind of the king harrassed by conflicting thoughts did not find peace.

Once the seer, Mandavya came to his mansion.

37.   He worshipped the great seer and told him, "Thy arrival has brought peace to my mind.

38.   I am now at the top of all the virtuous people. O Divine Seer, Knower of Dharma, I trust you have had long spell of tranquility.

39.   Kindly destroy this doubt of mine, as the sun destroys darkness. Whose sorrow does not vanish as a result of contact with noble souls?

40 to 42. Persons who know, consider that doubt is the source of the greatest distress of heart.

The reflections of my heart caused by the acts of protecting the wise and punishing the wicked, often harass my mind in the way the claws of lion pain the elephant.

Show such compassion to me, O great soul, worthy of worship, that oneness of vision arises in my heart, like the sunshine spreading equally on the earth, as a result of thy instruction. I need nothing else."

43.   Mandavya said, "O king, through one's own effort, self abidance and self-exertion, the darkness of the mind, like snow, melts away.

44 to 46. The impurity of inner mind gets removed by one's own vichara, enquiry.

'Who am I?' How did this universe arise? What is this? How do birth and death arise?'

Do enquire inwardly and you will attain to supreme plane.

When through enquiry, you have known the Reality, your mind will discard the feverishness and attain quietude. Mind will no doubt exist but discard its earlier trait.

317

47. O king, only a weak-mind trembles at the smallest dangers, like mosquito getting drowned in the water in the cow's foot-print on earth.

48. Until the Supreme Awareness, the Supreme Self alone manifests, the individual soul must keep renouncing everything.

49. *As long as everything is not renounced, the Self is not attained. When all things have been renounced, what survives is the Self.*

50. As long as other things are not renounced, the desired thing is not obtained in the world ordinarily. If so, where is the need to speak about Self-attainment?

51. For the sake of realisation of Self, renounce all. When all this is renounced, that which subsists is the Supreme Principle.

52. Setting fully aside, the cause and effect manifestation of worldly things and also by dissolving the mind thereafter, that blissful Being which manifests, is the Reality."

53. The Divine Seer Mandavya, after speaking thus to Suraghu, O Rama, left for his own serene silent abode.

54 to 58. After the great seer had left, the king sought seclusion and began to reflect by asking, 'Who am I?,' 'I am not the body comprising of the hands and feet. Let me look into the inner body. I am not also the flesh and bones which are inert. I am not the organs of action nor are these mine. They are also inert. I am not also the intellect. I am not the body and all these. Let me see what is beyond all these? That which remains after the negation of all these is pure Consciousness which is beyond distinction. This Divine Self, like the thread in the pearls, permeates

all the universe, the cosmic elements like wind, etc.

59 & 60. The pure Chit Shakti, power of Consciousness dissociated from the impure object, pervades all directions and has an inspiring form. It pervades all; it is subtle; it is bereft of existence and non-existence. It abides in all beings-from Brahma to grass and is brimming with all potencies.

61. Whatever is seen in the objective world, as belonging to the object, is really the partial manifestation of chit and not any other thing.

62. Bereft of attractive object and of all objects, released from the delusion of samsara and freed from desire, I abide in the Self, which is enduring, serene, all-inclusive, blissful, as in sleep."

63. Thus the king of Hemajata attained supreme beatitude, through practice of discernment like Visvamitra attaining the brahmana status.

64. His mind shone by always remaining in sleep-like condition.

65. He was not cruel nor merciful nor swayed by opposites. He was not unenvious nor wise nor unwise. He was neither seeking nor contented.

66. Listen now to the dialogue between Suraghu who had thus realised the Truth and the royal seer, Parnada, which is wonderful.

67. There was a king of Persia called Parigha, who was a vanquisher of foes. He was like the iron club in the fight of charioteers and so known by that name.

68 to 71. O Rama, he was a great friend of Suraghu. Once there was a great famine in his vast land. People died in vast numbers. Parigha was helpless and pained at

their ordeal he left the kingdom and went to the woods for penance. He had a calm mind and pursued penance and ate dry leaves. Since then, he came to be known as Parnada, eater of leaves.

72.   Through intense penance for several hundred years, he attained supreme wisdom which gave him mental serenity, freedom from dual afflictions and equanimity.

73.   He roamed the whole earth as he pleased. He once reached the mansion of the ruler of Hemajata.

74.   The former friends expressed their happiness at the meeting with each other and were engaged in delightful conversation.

75 to 78. Parigha said, 'As you have attained, I have attained the supreme wisdom. Do you attend to the affairs with a clear and serene mind? Is the creeper like body free from the afflictions, mental and physical, as you perform the necessary duties? Do you remain unenticed by the seemingly attractive pleasures? Do you resort to the practice of samadhi any time which state is free from desire and which is capable of giving good rest and peace to the mind?'

79.   Suraghu said, "O great soul, when does the illumined sage, whether he is keeping quiet or engaged in action, has a distracted mind, tell me.

80.   Those who are ever awake to the Truth, even when they are engaged in actions, are always abiding firmly in Self and so they are in the state of samadhi.

81.   Even if one, seated in the padamasana posture, has offered obeisance to Brahman, if his mind is restless, how can he attain samadhi? What kind of samadhi can he attain?

82. *The realisation of Truth burns up all desires like fire the grass-such state is spoken of as samadhi and not remaining in still condition.*

83. O wise soul! Through the term samadhi, knowledgeable persons refer only to the supreme intelligence, which is one-pointed, self-satisfied, and cognizant of the things as they are.

84. The term samadhi is used to refer to the state which is not agitated, is free from ahankara, is unaffected by dual experiences of pleasure and pain, and firmness like that of the Meru mountain.

85. Samadhi is a state of mental fullness which is free from thought, desire, and notions of desirable and undesirable.

86 & 87. As Time is always cognizant of every second's movement, the wise person is always cognizant of the Self. As wind, moving elsewhere, is aware of its constant movement, the wise person is ever aware of bare Consciousness.

88. Enlightened seers with composed minds keep engaged in external activities regardless of their result. Therefore, the distinction between one-pointed and distracted mind, as stressed in your speech is not correct, O blemishless soul."

89. Parigha said, "O king, you are highly enlightened. You have attained the supreme plane. You have a cool heart and a vast understanding.

90. You are pure and large-hearted. Bereft of the taint of ahankara, you are all-embracing Being. You are always stablised in Self-awareness and you excel in every way.'

91.   Suraghu said, "Enough of extensive discourse. The unique vision that leads to bliss is the experience in which desire is absent, which is equanimity in nature, which is soaked in inner bliss. Such vision is the supreme attainment."

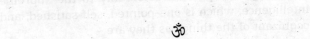

Chapter-8

The Story of Bhasa and Vilasa

Vasishta said:

1. "Suraghu and Parigha discussed thus the nature of worldly life. They respected each other and were delighted with each other. Thereafter they parted.

2. He who is ever steeped in Self-Contemplation, is inwardised mentally and immersed in the thought of Consciousness, is not assailed by sorrow.

3 to 5. O Rama, through supreme exertion, drag out this jiva bull trapped in the pond of samsara, bound by the fetters of numberless desires, feasting on the pleasure of grass roots, fatigued by the huge burden carried before, amidst the mire of ignorance, bitten by the snake of desires, drawn by the strong leather-rope of craving, tainted by the mire of sinful deeds, wandering in the forest of samsara, drawn here and there by thirst but unable to find a cool shade.

6. O Rama, like getting a boat from the boatman, you can get from the wise person the appropriate and unfailing counsel, the means, for crossing the ocean of samsara.

7. Let not the earnest seeker live in that land or mountain, where there is no fruit-bearing tree of wise person which also provides cool shade.

8. Neither wealth nor friends nor scripture nor relations help the people in pulling themselves out of the mire into which they are fallen.

9.   One finds oneself drawn out from the trap in which he is caught by merely discussing with a noble-hearted soul who is living near him.

10.   If the body is perceived as something similar to the lump of clay or wood, the Lord, the Supreme Self is attained by that sense of discrimination alone.

11.   He is like the brimming ocean, beyond the description of words and beyond any comparison. He rushes not towards pleasure.

12.   He is bare Consciousness, luminous and lasting and can be compared with only turiya, the transcendental state, if it is attained.

13.   That state is akin to sleep, and is fullness like the vast space.

14.   When mind and ahankara, ego, get dissolved in the underlying Consciousness, that bliss which wells up in the heart is that of the Supreme.

15.   That is the culmination of the practice of yoga, not much different from the state of sleep. O Rama, this state is indescribable, though it can be experienced at heart.

16.   All this without exception is Atma, the Self. If the gross manifold manifestation is restrained in the mind through the practice of samadhi, the Lord within manifests as the entire universe of movable and immovable.

17.   As a consequence of such experience, impure vasanas get extinguished; then set in pure vasanas; the supreme shines forth effulgently; with the rise of equanimity, there is abidance as Self which cannot be described.

18.   If Atma is not cognised by severing the mind through

324

the mind, the sorrow of worldly life is not annihilated. If the mind is severed, there is manifestation of blissful Self.

19. In regard to this matter, a dialogue between two friends Bhasa and Vilasa in the slope of Sahya mountain, long before, is cited as an example.

20. There is the famous mountain Sahya, known all over the world, which has defeated the sky in height, whose vast base has pervaded the earth, whose depth has invaded the patala, nether world.

21. In the northern slope of it, filled with trees bending on account of the weight of fruits, there is the hermitage of Atri, which alleviates the sorrows of life.

22. In that great hermitage of Atri, were two persons engaged in penance. It looked as though that Sukra and Brihaspati had descended down from the sky.

23. They lived together and had one son each, known by the names Bhasa and Vilasa, who grew up in course of time.

24. They were attached to each other like the affectionate husband and wife. They had one mind, though they were seemingly two.

25. Their parents discarded their bodies. The two performed the obsequies and lamented over their death.

26. Becoming dispassionate, they spent the time separately in the woods. Their penance had withered their bodies and they were extremely disgusted with life.

27. Days, months and years passed. Meeting each other by chance once, they conversed amongst themselves thus:

28. Vilasa said, "Welcome to thee, Bhasa, who is the ripest fruit of the tree of life, the nectarine ocean of mental peace, a great relation of mine in this world.

29. Separated from me, you have spent a number of days. How did you spend the time? Has your penance fructified?

30. Has your mind become still? Have you become self-conscious? Has the learning become fruitful? Are you now fully proficient?"

31. Bhasa said, "O wise soul, welcome to thee. By chance have I seen a worthy soul. How can there be peace for us who are caught in samsara?

32 to 34. *How can there be peace for one, as long as the knowable has not been known, as long as the samsaric ocean is not crossed, as long as all the desires arising from the heart have not been decimated like the tree by the saw, as long as equanimity has not manifested, as long as Awareness has not set in.*

35. This fierce malady of samsara surely arises again if there is no Self-knowledge, if there is not the supreme medicine of wisdom.

36. The soul undergoing several kinds of pleasures and sorrows, old age and death, getting tossed about in the mountain in the heart of the world, becomes destroyed like a dry leaf."

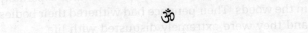

Chapter-9

The Story of Veetahavya

Vasishta said:

1. "The two conversed in this manner and attaining wisdom after a long time, became liberated.

2. Therefore, O valorous soul, there is no emancipation for the fettered mind except through wisdom.

3. The pure, unattached mind, even if it experiences samsara, is liberated. The attached mind, though practising penance for a long time is surely much bound.

4. The individual soul who is free from inner attachment and has agreeable conduct, whether he is externally active or otherwise, is neither a doer nor an enjoyer."

5. Sri Rama asked, "O Divine Seer, what is the nature of attachment? What is the kind of attachment that binds and what is it that liberates? How is attachment got rid of?"

6. Sri Vasishta said: "Discarding the discriminating sense between the body and indwelling spirit, the identification with gross body is sangha, the attachment, that is of binding nature.

7. To regard the infinite Self as confined to body and to have inner craving for pleasure is sangha, the attachment, that is of binding nature.

8. 'All this is Atma, the Self. What is there to be obtained or given up by me?'-this is non-attachment that leads to jivanmukti, liberation-in-life.

327

9. 'I am not. Nor there is any. Let pleasures accrue or not.' This inner detachment takes one to liberation.

10. He has no special interest in action lessness nor gets deeply involved in activities. He who is even-minded and has renounced the fruits of action is said to be unattached.

11. He who has perfectly renounced the fruits of actions mentally but not externally is said to be unattached.

12. My dear, through non-attachment, all the manifold activities with their ramifications get purified and become noble-spirited.

13. Falling down again and again, people become worms and insects and this incidence is only a consequence of attachment.

14. Like waves in the ocean, creatures innumerable are born, and reborn and die and that is the manifestation of attachment.

15. The attachment, O Rama, is spoken to be of two types-barren and laudable. The 'barren' is to be seen in the ignorant and the laudable in the really liberated souls.

16. The firm attachment, not associated with Self realisation, arising in relation to body, etc., leads to samsara again and again and this is called barren.

17. That attachment, associated with Self-realisation arising in relation to Self and born of discrimination does not lead to samsara and is laudable.

18. Vishnu endowed with conch, chakra, mace, through his various activities in the form of avataras protects the three worlds only as a consequence of this laudable attachment.

19. Siddhas and other cosmic Divinities, only as a result

of their laudable attachment, keep doing their cosmic duties.

20. Mind rushes towards sense-pleasures like the eagle towards meat, as a consequence of the barren attachment, in the vain expectation of happiness.

21. The alluring harems, which are really the hells called Raurava, Avichi, Kalasutra have been designed only for those having the 'barren' attachment.

22. People given to barren attachment are like dry fuel and the fires in hell burn more fiercely with this fuel.

23. With the dawn of realisation and eclipse of ignorance, and with non-attachment towards all things-he who remains is a liberated soul.

24 to 31. Let the mind, absorbed in tasting the bliss of Self, remain immune to any other taste, as the enlightened seer remains engaged in all types of activities, at all times , in all manner of conditions and in the company of all types of people. Let him withdraw into chit or be connected with chetya to some extent but not get attached to activities, concepts or objects for concentration-like lower space, higher space, external pleasures, sense-contact, inner mind, prana, crest, jaw, the centre of the eye-brows, tip of nose, face, stars, darkness, reflected image, space of heart, waking state, dream, sleep, purity, blackness, yellowness, redness, maya-vitiated, moving, unmoving, sound, the middle or any other centre, the distant, the near, the front, the object, the self, the sense perceptions of sound, touch and form, the states of delusion and pride, movements, time measurements.

32. Remaining in that state without attachment, the jiva transcends jivahood regardless of whether he pursues worldly affairs or not.

33. Whether he pursues activities or not, the seer abiding in the blissful Self is not affected by results of actions, like the space by the cloud.

34. Or let him discard that chetya, objective element also and remain a mere mass of bliss like the luminous jewel.

35. Those lofty souls, delighting in Self, thoroughly illumined and compassionate are wavering like the end of the feather outwardly but are firm like mountain inwardly.

36. When the chitta is in a state of dissociation with chetya, object, in respect of those who have brought total restraint of the mind, that is a condition in which thought or imagination ceases to arise and that condition is similar to sleep.

37. This is the sleep-like state, O Rama, that arises on account of continuous practice of yoga and the same getting intensified becomes turiya, transcendental state, according to knowers of Reality.

38. Remaining in this imperishable state of turiya, and being exclusively absorbed in the blissful nature, he passes on to the state beyond bliss.

39. Going beyond the state of absence of bliss and the state of bliss, he attains turiyatita, the state beyond turiya and is known to be liberated.

The commentator of BYV (5-71-32) interprets the term 'ananda' as referring to the three states of waking, dreaming and sleeping.

40. With all fetters caused by birth cut asunder, with the sense of self-identification totally eliminated, the noble soul attains to pervasive experiential state like the lump of salt thrown into the water.

41. That which underlies the objective cognition and the self-cognition is spoken of as the supreme reality in the Upanishads like Brihadharanyaka.

42. That bliss which manifests at the contact between the sense and object is of the nature of self-experience and is called Brahman.

43. The bliss that manifests at the contact of the sense and the object, if associated with the objects is of the nature of bondage and if dissociated from objects is liberation.

44. Hold on to the pure experience that manifests at the contact of the sense and the object and remain in that sleep-like state.

45 & 46. Firm adherence in that sleep-like state leads to turiya state.

The Atma, the Self, is not gross, not subtle, not immediate, not mediate, not sentient, not insentient, not non-existent, not existent, not the ego, not the other, not the one, not the many.

47. It is beyond whatever is cognised by the senses and the mind here and O Rama, it is not like anything here.

48. *Liberation is not abidance in heaven or nether world or earth. The extinction of mind as a result of the extinction of all desires is known to be liberation.*

49. If there is the thought, 'Let there be liberation for me,' the mind has arisen. With thought mind becomes gross, and there results sure bondage.

50. In that, which is beyond all or which is all, how could there be bondage or liberation? Root out all thought and mind.

51 to 53. With mind absorbed in Self and heart permeated by bliss, fullness and sanctity, with the taint of lust removed, with the bondage of delusion destroyed, he is freed from the blemish of dualities and has crossed the ocean of samsara. He has attained supreme repose, the unattainable state.

He has attained the state from which there is no return. Since he has attained all, he desires not anything, exerts not to attain anything.

54.   Do thou hold the red hot iron blade representing supreme detachment as also the flower bunch of desirelessness of the tree of self-control.

55.   O Rama, for one who is adorned with the ornament of desirelessness, all things of the world-cow, earth, Meru, jewel-box and the three worlds-are like a straw-bit.

56.   For the discriminating seer who sees the Self as distinct from the body, even if his body is severed, he is not severed at all.

57.   The experience of Self by the seer does not get affected or alienated, if his body gets burnt or severed, even as his relish of jaggery is not affected by such harm to the body.

58 & 59. The woman who, even while engaged in household chores, keeps remembering at heart her rapturous experiences in the company of her illicit paramour, the seer who has established in Supreme Truth and attained repose, keeps remembering the same experience, even if he has to engage in external activities.

60.   The inner coolness of heart, as a result of the detachment towards objects, is the state of liberation.

That state manifests whether one is with body or without it, if one is sinless.

61. He who lives without any sense of attachment is called a liberated being. He who lives with attachment is in bondage. He who is without attachment and without body-identification is also surely liberated.

62. He anticipates not the future, is not attached to the present, does not recollect the past, but keeps doing everything.

63 to 65. He remains unattached to those who attach themselves to him; he is affectionate to the devoted and crude to the wicked. He is a child, when he is with children; an old person in the company of old people and a courageous soul while associated with the courageous. He is an youth among the youth and he is sad in the company of sad people. He is courageous, ever happily disposed, tender-hearted, fond of praising holy men. He is wise, serene and deep. He is without diffidence and desires.

66. Even if sun turns cool, moon emits scorching heat, fire moves downwards, the liberated soul is not seized by wonder.

67. All these strange powers flow from chid-atma and therefore he does not show curiousity towards these wondrous spectacles.

68. Even as the circular ripple-formations appear as different from the waters, the world appears as different from the activity of chitta.

69. Even as due to defective vision, a cluster of luminous specks appear in space the unreal world appears as real on account of the activity of chitta."

70. Sri Rama asked, "What causes the activity of chitta

and what makes it still, O Divine Seer? Kindly enlighten me about this, so that I can achieve the aim."

71. Sri Vasishta said: "As whiteness in snow, and oil in sesame are seen intertwined, chitta and spanda, activity, are intertwined.

72. O Rama, there are two modes, yoga and jnanam, of bringing about mind's destruction. Yoga is control of mental modifications. Jnanam is total perception of Reality.

73. Chitta is actually prana's movement, according to those proficient in the scripture. If prana is controlled perfectly, mind becomes restrained.

74. With the mind and spanda getting constantly restrained, samsara disappears, as the worldly activity comes to an end like the sun's movement coming to an end in the evening."

75. Sri Rama asked, "How is the ceaseless movement of prana, etc., which pervade the body and which are difficult to understand, to be arrested?"

76 & 77. Sri Vasishta said: "The prana's movement is restrained through study of scripture, association of the wise, dispassion, practice of yoga, disinterest in worldly affairs, contemplation of the nature of the desired object, and intense concentration on Consciousness.

78. Prana's movement is restrained through intense practice of puraka-pranayama in a manner that does not cause pain and exclusive practice of dhyana, meditation.

79. By the contemplation of the meaning of the final half syllable in the utterance of 'Om' and by self-revelation

334

occuring in sleep, prana is restrained.

80.   By the restraint of the protruding flesh at the root of throat through the tongue, if prana is made to flow upwards towards crest, prana gets restrained.

81.   By concentrating on the pure space between the tip of the nose and dwadasanta the cognition dissolves into Consciousness, prana is restrained.

82.   When from the brahmrandra, crevice at the crest, prana is made to flow towards dwadasanta, prana's movement gets restrained.

83.   When the cognition of luminous world arising on account of the concentration between the eye-brows disappears and the cognitive world merges in Consciousness, prana is restrained.

84.   When super-normal cognition suddenly takes place, and the cognitive mode is separated from bare knowledge, prana is restrained.

85.   When the space within heart is contemplated for a long time, and when through vasana-free mind, meditation is done, prana is restrained.

86.   Through these various means, and also through methods instructed by various teachers, prana is restrained.

87.   Through continuous unhindered practice, these methods become the means for the transcendence of worldly life in the case of the earnest seekers.

88.   When through practice, the prana and its variations become fully controlled, mind become's extinct and liberation results in."

89.   Sri Rama asked, "You have described, O Master, the serenity of mind that results from the practice of yoga.

Do thou explain to me out of compassion, how it is attained through perfect wisdom.

90. Sri Vasishta said: In all the three worlds, to know the Self as the world and attain all-inclusiveness is cognition of the Reality.

91. When the dispassion strengthened by repeated practice of pranayama erases the vasanas of the mind, the control of prana has yielded desired result.

92. When the thoughts of creatures swayed by all kinds of fancies become extinct, that residual state, from which words return, manifests.

93. To know that all these objects like pot, cloth, etc., are only the Self and nothing else, is to have perfect vision of Truth.

94. To have the conviction that there is the vast luminous Supreme Self without beginning and end is to have perfect wisdom.

95. If all this is Self, where is the question of the real and the unreal, the bondage and the liberation? O Rama, what is there to feel sorry about?

96. There is no chetya, objective entity. There is no chitta, mind. It is Brahman that manifests as all these. All this is the non-dual Brahman. What is liberation? What is bondage?

97. It is Brahman that has assumed the vast magnificient form. The duality has totally vanished. Be the Supreme Self by thy own self-contemplation.

98. When objective entitites-wood, stone, cloth-are cognised perfectly, they are not intrinsically distinct from one another. How can there be objective mental inclination?

99. O Rama, the blissful Presence which is there both at the beginning and after the end is imperishable, is the self of the object and the subject; is inseparable from that Being.

100. Like the ocean itself manifesting in the manifold form of waves, the Self itself by its own play projects dual and non-dual distinctions and delusions of old age and death.

101. How can pleasures bind one who remains as pure Being always, who is ever with inwardised mind?

102. As wind cannot harm the mountain, the enemies of sense-objects cannot torment even to a small extent, the mind of one who has properly pursued enquiry.

103. The manifoldness in conceptions are not of distinct realities and are just like the manifoldness in the appearance of waters-he who has this firm conviction is a liberated soul. He has perfect cognition of the objective reality.

104. O Rama, you may hear another viewpoint which is also capable of leading to beatitude and which was whole-heartedly practised by the seer, Veetahavya?

105. The seer Veetahavya, living in the cave of Vindhya mountain, was devoted to the pursuit of rituals for a long time.

106. Caught in the trap of delusion of unending performance of ritualistic chores and harassed by mental and physical afflictions, he became impatient at one time.

107. He discarded all rituals and for the pursuit of nirvikalpa samadhi, went to a new dwelling place.

108. There, on the seat of the deer-skin, he remained in the firm padmasana posture with palms placed above the testicles.

109. He withdrew the mind slowly from all external distractions. He removed all objects of thought, external and internal, steadily from mind.

110. Then the seer, in order to make the mind more resolute, began to reflect with a clear mind thus:

111. 'Ah! How unsteady is the mind! Though withdrawn from the object, mind does not become steady. It wavers like the leaf tossed by the wave.

112 & 113. Like the monkey jumping among the trees, the mind chases objects, hops from the pot to the cloth and from the cloth to the cart.

The five senses and the mind cognise the objects. These senses are cognised by witness-Consciousness which is all-knowing. These objects and the senses and the witness-Consciousness are totally unrelated to each other like the nether world, the sky and the earth.

114. O restless mind who goes to all the four directions for objects of pleasure! thy search is fraught with pain; do not run around in the world.

115. Thy notion that 'I am sentient' is illusory. The two totally distinct entities like Consciousness and mind can never be one and the same.

116. 'Jiva I am,' 'I am this'-all such notions arise from the evil ahankara, ego. It is false. It produces only sorrow. Discard the illusion.

117. O mind! This lack of enquiry alone contributes to thy existence. Like darkness getting destroyed by fire, your identity gets destroyed through enquiry.

118. You were non-existent before. You are non-existent now. You will never exist in future. O mind, leave me at peace.

338

119. I am free. I am blissful. I am free from misery. I abide in Self alone, in turiya state.

120. The Supreme Consciousness, the Lord, is doing everything all along remaining as witness. O sense-organs, why do you become needlessly restless?

121. The pure and blemishless chit remains distant from the senses like the wayfarer from the snakes, like the brahmana from the eater of dog's flesh.

122. The inclination of the Consciousness towards external object, akin to memory, gives rise to sorrow.

The cognition of the body or the mind or other inert object, bereft of objective inclination is only bare Consciousness and there is nothing beside. The cognition bereft of objective inclination, of the body, or the mind or in other inert object, is only bare consciousness de-objectified and there is nothing beside.'

123. Thus deciding, the seer Veetahavya, ridding the mind of vasanas, controlled it and remained motionless.

124. The regular prana movement got arrested slowly, like the raging fire after burning out the fuel.

125. With eyes directed towards the tip of the nose slowly closing, he was like the beautiful lotus blossom closing into bud form.

126. That great soul, holding the body, neck and head erect, remained still, like the idol sculpted out of a rock or a picture painted on the wall.

127. As he remained in that state thus in the Vindhya mountain, three hundred years passed away like a few minutes.

128. Through passage of time, the body of the great seer,

carried by the waters of the rainy season, got buried in the soil.

129. After three hundred years, the luminous seer woke up to normal consciousness, but the body deeply stuck in the mire did not move.

130. His intelligence however left the body buried under the soil. There was no movement of prana as prana channels remained closed.

131. The thought, pulsating with life, in the form of mind began to experience in diverse ways in the heart itself.

132. He spent a hundred years as a liberated soul in seclusion in the forest of Kailasa at the foot of a kadamba tree.

133. He was for a hundred years a vidhyadhara free from all cares. He was for a full five yugas as Indra served by the celestials.

134. He was one of the ganas, attendants of Shiva for a kalpa, the period of one cycle of creation. Veetahavya had all these experiences in spiritual form.

135 to 137. Thereafter, the all-pervasive Self manifesting in the mind of Veetahavya desired to review the happenings in all previous lives. He saw all previous bodies of his-that remained destroyed and undestroyed. He saw that the body called by the name of Veetahavya remained undestroyed. His mind remaining within the buried body wanted to raise it.

138. He thought, 'This body is completely stuck up in soil. To raise it, let me enter into sun.

139. His attendant will raise my body.' Thinking thus, the seer entered into sun in the form of air. His subtle body integrating itself with air, entered the sun, as wind entered in bladders.

140. The Lord Sun, who knew what to do, realising that the seer had entered into his heart, issued suitable instructions to the attendant.

141. Permitted by the Sun, the subtle body of Veetahavya entered into the body of the attendant, who set out for Vindhya forest.

142. The attendant leaving the sky reached the forest which was beautiful and dense like the sky of the rainy season.

143. He saw the body of the seer in the forest grove and lifted it up from the mire-pit by removing the upper soil by hand.

144. The body of the seer was as shining as the lotus stalk in the lake.

145. The subtle-body of the seer entered into that body. The attendant returned to the space. The seer left for the lake of pure waters.

146 & 147. He bathed, did japa and worshipped Sun. His body getting united with the mind again became resplendent.

148. The seer, endowed with the traits of friendliness, equanimity, supreme ability, profound wisdom, happiness, compassion and richness, and being free from all attachment, roamed on the river banks in the Vindhya hill for a number of days.

149. Having seen all aspects of worldly life, the seer's mind once again thought of entering into samadhi.

150. 'The senses had suitably been disciplined by me already. I don't need to think of the problem which has already been solved.

151. Even the notions of 'existence' and 'non-existence,' let

me destroy like the tender creeper and let me remain stabilised in the residual awareness and be motionless like the peak of hill.

152. Though manifest, yet not active, though non-manifest, yet active, I am uniform luminous awareness that is exceedingly pure.

153. I am awake and yet asleep; I am asleep and yet awake. Attaining transcendental plane, I remain in the inner heart absolutely motionless.'

154. Thinking thus, he again remained in samadhi for six days. He rose up from it like the wayfarer after a second's nap.

155. Thereafter, the Divine Veetahavya, a jivanmukta, kept roaming around for a long time.

156. After all notions of desirable and undesirable, attachment and detachment had died, the mind of the seer Veetahavya went beyond the states of likes and dislikes.

157. He, reaching the final phase of the karma-rebirth sequence, decided to discard samsara finally and attain the unexcelled disembodied state.

158. At one time, the seer who wielded lordship, entered the cave of a mountain. Remaining in padmasana posture, he told himself:

159. 'O Attachment! Be rid of thy nature. O hatred! Be rid of that nature. For a long time, you have both played on me.

160. O pleasures! I offer countless salutations to you. I have been fondled by you like the children by their elders.

161. O happiness! I salute again and again thee, who has made me forget the holy state of liberation.

162. O sorrow! I salute thee! It is the affliction caused by you that drove me to enquire into Self and this path of mine was shown to me by you.

163. O activity, my friend! I am parting from a long associate of mine. Having led me to the realisation of Self, you have killed yourself.

164. O desire, my mother! Obeisance to thee. You are grieving alone with my extinction. You should not give into sorrow.

165. O divine kama! The faults arising out of unexpected lapses have to be forgiven by you. I seek quietude. Bless me.

166. Obeisance to thee, O God of the virtuous deed, I have been drawn out from hell and ushered into heaven by you.

167. These pranas are my well-wishers since birth. I take leave of them, as they rise up. May all be well with you. Let me leave.'

168. Thus deliberating within and with mentation and desire getting extinguished, he slowly uttered the liberating 'pranava' and attained the supreme plane.

169. He cast away all conceptions of things of all worlds, external and internal, gross and subtle.

170. With the long unbroken utterance of pranava coming to close, he discarded the subtle aspects of the senses, like wind the fragrant particle.

171. He discarded the darkness enveloping the space all around, as a wise person the rising anger.

172. Thereafter there was effulgence. He reflected a second and discarded it as well. There was neither darkness nor effulgence.

173. Attaining the state beyond gunas, through the mind, he cast away the cognitive element within a split second.

174. Then he attained pure chaitanya nature bereft of all vitiating vasanas like the just born child.

175. Within a moment, he dropped the chetya, objective aspect, like the wind discarding the trait of movement.

176. He attained the all-pervasive, existential state, called 'pasyanti,' and remained, as if in sleep, like the unmoving mountain.

177. After getting established in the sleep-like state, he passed into Turiya state.

178. He was in the state described by the terms, 'not this, not this'; though not blissful, yet blissful, existent though non-existent, filled with Consciousness and yet not.

179 to 181. Then the pure state ensued which is indescribable by words.

That which is void, according to proponents of Sunya, Brahman, according to the knowers of Brahman, bare Intelligence, according to the followers of Vijnanavada, Purusha, according to Sankhya school, Ishvara, according to the Yoga school, Shiva, according to the followers of Shiva religion, Kala, according to believers in Kala, Atma, according to the knowers of Self, Formless, according to such believers, the Madhyam, according to the Budhdas and all for those who have attained oneness of vision-that he was.

182. He remained as that which is the teaching of all scripture, which pervades all hearts, which is all, permeating all and related to all.

183. That which was supremely more effulgent than luminous beings and which is cognised by Self-experience alone, that he was.

184. That which is one and many, is tainted and untainted, is all and not all, that he was.

185. He, who was unborn, eternal, beginningless, non-dual, both variegated and homogenous, remained purer than space and was the Supreme Lord.

186. The seer Veetahavya, remaining on earth happily in this manner for innumerable number of years, passed into Peace thus and was never to be born again."

Chapter-10

The Powers of Flying in the Sky

1. Sri Rama asked, "Why are the powers of flying in the sky not seen in relation to jivanmuktas, the liberated souls, who have known the Self."

2. Sri Vasishta said: "O Rama, a person, though not a knower of Self, though not liberated, attains the powers of moving in the sky, as a result of the potencies of materials, mantra, ritual and time.

3. These are not the aims of the knower of Self. The knower of Self simply knows Self. He is totally satisfied within himself and does not pursue false aims.

4. The knower of Self is beyond all. He has discarded all cravings. He is fully happy with Self. He does not do anything, seek anything.

5. Those worldly attractions that exist are known to be false. How can the knower of Self, who has destroyed ignorance, revel in them?

6. He who is noble-hearted and yet wants the powers, strives to attain them through appropriate means.

7. Materials, mantra, ritual, time, etc., which help one in attaining powers, do not help anyway in the attainment of Supreme Beatitude.

8. To the knower of Self, who has attained to all-pervasiveness, desire for siddhi does not arise anytime. If desire arises any time, he acquires it by the proper means.

9. The desire for Realisation of Self arises only when

desires for all powers, etc, cease. How can that be attained by one, who has burnt the desire for powers?"

10. Sri Rama asked, "O Divine Seer, how do seers live for a very long time? Do thou clarity the doubt."

11. Sri Vasishta said: "The movement of the pranas causes the movement of body; when that movement gets arrested, they are akin to stones. When they abide in that state through concentration, the bodies do not age or become old.

12. Transformation of body and death do not exist for one who does not have the movement external or internal of the prana or the mind.

13. When prana and mind become tranquil both externally and internally, the components of the body do not lose vigour.

14. Those noble-hearted souls, who have known the Truth and are without desire, have the knots of ignorance completely destroyed and such persons remain in the body at their Will."

15. Sri Rama asked, "Owing to the rise of discriminative wisdom, with the chitta getting dissolved, where do the qualities like friendliness, etc., abide?

Since the chitta ceases to exist in the case of the seer, where do these noble qualities abide is the question.

16. Sri Vasishta said: "The destruction of chitta occurs in two ways: form-associated and formless. In the case of the jivanmukta, it is of the form-associated (Sa-rupa) type; in the case of videhamukta, disembodied one, it is the formless one (A-rupa).

17. The existence of chitta causes only sorrow. The destroyed chitta brings in happiness. Therefore strive to bring about the non-existence of chitta.

347

18. The ignorant person values highly the chitta characterised by the attributes of Prakriti and regards it as 'mine.' The chitta so regarded by the ignorant person is what is termed as jiva.

19. That which is the support of happiness and sorrow, which always sustains the notion, 'I am,' which nourishes the tree of samsara, is known to be mind.

20. O Rama, I have described to you the nature of chitta. Let me describe the process of destruction. Listen.

21. His chitta may be known as dead, if conditions of joy and sorrow do not disturb that courageous person from poise, even as winds cannot disturb a mountain.

22. His chitta is dead, if danger, misery, exhilaration, pride, dullness, excitement, cannot upset him.

23. When the veiling trait of chitta is destroyed, the extinction of chitta comes about and purity manifests.

24. Noble vasanas of the type of friendliness, etc., manifest and they do not bring about the rebirth of the jivanmukta.

25. The destruction of chitta in the case of jivanmukta is form-associated. Like flowers in the spring season, noble virtues like friendliness blossom in him.

26. The destruction called formless one, O Rama, described by me occurs in the case of videhamukta, disembodied one, and he is characteristicless.

27. The sattvic element, which is the abode of all great virtues, also gets extinguished, in the case of videhamukta, who abides in the supremely pure plane.

28 to 30. In the case of the videhamukta, whose chitta has attained the formless destruction, nothing at all exists.

There are neither gunas nor their absence, neither richness nor poverty, neither rise nor decline, neither elation nor distress, neither effulgence nor darkness, neither twilight nor night, neither existence nor non-existence nor the intermediate. His state is beyond all these.

31. Those who have gone beyond the mind and the samsaric panorama, for them the state of videhamukti is the vast plane of repose, like the space for air.

32. With sorrow getting extinguished, Consciousness manifesting as in sleep, bliss overflowing without being tainted by passion, the souls expansive like vast space with and without body, whose minds have totally dissolved abide in exalted plane.

33 & 34. Sri Rama asked, "Of the vast grape-vine of samsara, what is the seed? Of this seed, what is the seed? What is the seed of last seed? What is in turn its seed? O excellent speaker, kindly explain all these in a nutshell so that my experience may become more perfect and I may also know what is quintessence of wisdom."

35. Sri Vasishta said: "O Rama, know the body to be the seed of the vastly grown creeper of samsara in whose main sprout lie embedded potencies of countless virtuous and non-virtuous actions.

36. Of this body, the seed chitta, is the abode of manifest and unmanifest experiences, is the container of the jewels of sorrows and is totally subservient to the sway of desire.

37. This body of manifest and unmanifest features most strikingly arises from the mind only. That this is a fact is understood from one's dream experience itself.

38. This tree of chitta which as an enormous growth of

ramifications has two seeds-one is prana's movement and the second is strong vasana, tendency.

39. When prana moves, by coursing through nadi channels, then the cognitive mind certainly is born.

40. The latent all-pervasive intelligence is awakened. Therefore, O Rama, restraint of the cognitive mode is conducive to one's good.

41. The intelligence activated thus becomes the knowable and from the cognition of it, endless sorrows manifest in mind.

42. When the intelligence remains, as it were, asleep and without future rise, the attainable becomes attained and the pure state manifests.

43. Therefore, if the intelligence is not drawn out towards object through the movement of prana and the propelling of vasanas, then you are the unborn spirit.

44. Intelligence hardened is known to be chitta, which in turn has spread the vast net of snare to catch the jivas.

45. Yogis seek to control prana to get mental calmness through pranayama, meditation, and such other rational methods.

46. The control of prana is known to give mental calmness, great equanimity and keeps intelligence as the self-illumining principle.

47. The other factor which brings about the rise of mind is vasana, and Rama, let me describe this process explained by men of wisdom and experienced by them as such. Listen.

48. That is called vasana which is responsible for one's response to an object with intense feeling and without any prior or posterior investigation.

49.   Whatever is intensely contemplated by Atma, leaving aside other thoughts, that it becomes, O valorous soul.

50.   Enslaved by vasana, the person assumes that form, sees that as real and gets deluded.

51.   Through the overpowering influence of vasanas, the soul abandoning its natural form and becoming deluded, sees false things like the one who is drunk.

52.   That which is the cause of imperfect vision, the cause of cognition of non-self as self, the cause of illusory perception of the unreal as the real, know to be mind, O Rama.

53.   The vacillating chitta arises as a result of intense practice, exclusive contemplation of the object, and leads in turn to birth, old age and death.

54.   When nothing is contemplated upon, either as agreeable or otherwise, when one remains without any thought, then chitta does not manifest.

55.   When, through elimination of vasanas, mind does not keep thinking, a-manaska, mindlessness arises, which is capable of giving supreme tranquility.

56.   O Rama, this is the nature of mind, which keeps thinking of objects as real and joyful.

58.   If one does not find any object worthy of contemplation spontaneously and if one is as pure as space, whence could chitta arise?

59.   Disinterested cognition, non-cognition of the existent, cognition of the real as it is-if these are there, chitta does not manifest.

60.   Renouncing everything inwardly and remaining cool at heart, even if one's chitta has modifications, that chitta is considered as non-existent.

61. He who does not have thick vasanas which lead to rebirth is a liberated soul. He abides in Reality. He is functioning like the rotating wheel because of past karma.

62. Those vasanas which are akin to burnt seeds, which are not capable of leading to births and which are bereft of the element of pleasure are known to be those of the liberated souls.

63. They have attained the highest wisdom and since the chitta they possess is only of the form of sattva, they are said to have no chitta. When the body falls, they remain as space-like Consciousness.

64. O Rama, the tree of chitta has two seeds- prana's movement and vasana. If one of them is annihilated, both of them get destroyed.

65. Vasana causes prana's movement and, because of the latter, vasana arises and thus chitta manifests. Seed-sprout succession is kept up in the manner.

66. Of vasana and prana's movement, the seed is samvedhya, the knowable, since both are caused by it.

67. By discarding samvedhya, the knowable, both prana-movement and vasana get totally destroyed, like the uprooted tree.

68. Know samvid, object-oriented intelligence, swerving from its state, is the seed of samvedhya, the knowable and without it, samvedhya cannot exist, like oil seed without oil.

69. Samvedhya does not exist independently either, outwardly and inwardly. Samvid imagines and becomes the samvedhya, the object.

70. Samvedhya is the creation of samvid, like the cognition

of one's death or of one's existence in some other place arising from mind endowed with the faculty of imagination.

71. Whether it has been seen before or not, whatever the nature of object, what samvid wills manifests. Therefore, a wise person through effort should erase the samvid.

72. Samvid not properly erased results in manifestation of the vast samsara. Samvid properly erased is experienced as state of liberation.

73. Samvedana, cognition of the knowable, leads to the rise of endless number of sorrows. A-samvitti, negation of samvedana, resulting in sentience leads to natural bliss.

74. Discard samvedana, and passing beyond bliss, attain sentience. The de-objectified awareness culminating in Self-realisation is what you are, O Rama."

75. Sri Rama asked, 'What is de-objectified cognition which is not insentient? How is insentience resulting from the negation of cognition avoided, O master?"

76. Sri Vasishta said: "He, who is not attached to any object and does not dwell on any object, who does not cognise any object, he has attained the state of de-objectified and non-insentient awareness.

77. He, who is not characterised by cognitions of 'this' and 'that' is in the state of de-objectified awareness, even if he indulges in a hundred acts.

78. His mind is not vitiated by the object. Such a one remaining in de-objectified awareness is called a jivanmukta, a liberated soul.

79. Having got rid of vasanas, when he does not contemplate on any object and when his condition is

characterised by mere awareness as in the case of a child or a dumb, he lives long.

80. His awareness is free from objectivity and remaining in that expansive state of awareness, he is not born again.

81. By the practice of nirvikalpa samadhi, super-conscious state, let him cast away all vasanas. As blueness permeates the sky, he will be pervaded by bliss.

82. When the yogis remain absorbed in the awareness free from objective cognition, even the bliss-experience gets merged in Consciousness.

83. As he walks, touches, smells, he remains bereft of feeling and objective cognition, in a state of awareness and happiness.

84. By adhering to this vision through effort, do thou cross the limitless ocean of sorrow caused by the attributes (of sattva, rajas and tamas).

85. Of this samvid, Rama, san-matra, bare existence, is said to be the seed. It is from bare existence, cognition arises, as effulgence from light.

86. The bare existence has two forms. The first is variegated and the second is homogenous. Know their distinction.

87. That has multiple forms in which the existence is cognised as associated with pot, cloth, that and this.

88. Discarding all the distinctions, that which remains as bare existence, which is uncoloured, universal, is known to be the homogenous form.

89. *Discard all notions pertaining to time, knowledge and object and be aware of bare supreme existence.*

90. Existence as associated with time, self, even if it is

bereft of verbalisation, is not ultimately real, though of exalted character.

91. The distinct perceptions lead to different experiences and differences in objects, and as such, how can that be the most blissful state?

92. *Contemplating bare homogenous existence alone as all-pervasive, remain saturated in bliss and as all-pervasive being.*

93. The bare universal existence in its ultimate form, O learned soul, is the seed of the tree of samsara and it is from that only, the tree has grown.

94. Of that state of bare existence, eternal, bereft of all conception, there is no seed.

95. In that plane, existent matter gets dissolved and there is no trace of any distinction. The person attaining that state is not born again in the world of sorrow.

The teaching of spiritual realisation expounded in this portion of YV is a very significant one. The concepts are exclusive to YV and are not found in general Vedantic works. And these key-concepts have endowed Vasishta's technique with a rationale that is distinctive.

96. That state of bare existence is the cause of all causes and that itself has no cause. That is the essence of all existence and there is no essence apart from it.

97. In that vast mirror of chit, all things are seen. They are reflected images, as images of trees in the waters.

98. That is pure, non-ageing principle of Self. On realisation of it, the mind gets extinguished. You have known that vast Being and have already gone beyond the fears of life."

99.   Sri Rama asked, "O worshipful seer, you have mentioned the various causes, seeds, as it were. How are they to be transcended and how is the supreme plane to be attained quickly?"

100.   Sri Vasishta said: "I have told you the various seeds of sorrow. By tracing each condition to its seed in an exclusive manner, the supreme plane is quickly attained.

101 & 102. If in the aforesaid ultimate satta-samanya plane, the state of bare existence, you are able to remain for a while by discarding all the vasanas at once through supreme personal effort, O wise soul, in that very second, you have attained the imperishable state.

103.   With some little effort on your part, if you are able to attain to the plane of satta-samanya, bare existential state, you will attain to the supreme plane.

104.   O Rama, if you are able to stay contemplating the cognitive principle samvid with some great effort, you can reach the supreme plane.

105.   O Rama, it is not possible to exclusively meditate on objective matter, samvedhyam.

106.   Because, Consciousness is always present in all forms.

     The point made is that an object cannot be separated from the Consciousness.

     The second line of verse 105 and the entire verse of 106 have been printed again as the second line of verse 109 and as the entire verse of 110.

107 & 108. If effort is made by you to totally discard vasanas, the mental and physical afflictions will get destroyed instantly.

109.   The discarding of vasanas, which is more effective than

other disciplines mentioned above, is difficult to be achieved, is more difficult than uprooting Meru mountain.

110. As long as mind has not merged, so long there is no complete elimination of vasanas. As long as vasanas have not been eliminated, mind does not become serene.

111. As long as there is no Realisation of Truth, so long there is no extinction of mind. As long as the mind has not become extinct, there is no Realisation of Truth.

112. As long as there is no elimination of vasanas, how can there be Realisation of Truth? As long as there is no Realisation of Truth, so long there is no elimination of vasanas.

113. *Realisation of Truth[1], extinction of mind[2], elimination of vasanas[3]-they are mutually related to each other and so they difficult to be accomplished.*

   1. Tattvajnanam, 2. Manonasam, 3. Vasanakshayam.

114. O Rama, therefore, through great effort and discrimination, cut away desire for sense pleasures and practise all the three.

   Since each one of them cannot be separately practised, they have to be practised together.

115. As long as the three are not practised effectively again and again, so long Truth is not realised, even in a hundred years.

116. O noble soul, elimination of vasanas, Realisation of Truth and extinction of mind, practised together for a long time by the seer becomes fruitful.

117. If these are practised separately even for a long time,

they do not attain fruition, like the interrupted utterance of mantras.

118. By the continuous practice of all the three, the mental knots (of ignorance) get completely destroyed, like the rope getting destroyed with the destruction of fibres in it.

119. This samsaric experience has been experienced during several hundred births and it does not come to an end, except through practice of yoga for a long time.

120. The control of prana also is known to be equal to elimination of vasana. Therefore, practise that as well.

121. Through elimination of vasana, chitta becomes non-existent. Control of prana also brings about the same result. Do as you deem fit.

122. Through intense practice of pranayama, adherence to preceptor's instructions, practice of asana and fasting, the movement of prana gets controlled.

123. By practice of non-attachment, by avoidance of worldly imagination, by contemplation of the prospect of body's destruction, vasanas get eliminated.

124. When the vasanas do not any longer overpower, mind is not active. When there is no wind, the dust particles also do not move.

125. The movement of prana is the same as the movement of mind. Wise persons should make great effort to conquer prana.

126 & 127. Except through the flawless practice of single-minded repeated attempt the mind cannot be controlled, even as the angry-elephant is not controlled except through ankusa, goad.

128 & 129. *Study of scripture about Self, company of the wise, elimination of vasanas, control of prana,-these*

disciplines are conducive for the effective conquest of mind. Through these the mind is completely conquered, even as through downpour of rain, dust gets settled quickly.

130. When these disciplines are available, those who attempt to control the mind through force, they throw away the lamp and resort to other means for driving away darkness.

131. Those fools who try to control the mind through force, are attempting to bind a riotous elephant by slender threads.

132. Mind, distracted and distraught by the pracitce of Hata Yoga, like the deer that has strayed into the village, does not attain peace.

133. Maya, through various delusions of sacrifice, austerity, charity, holy pilgrimages, worship of Gods, etc., torments the people, as the various maladies torment the animals.

134. Therefore, O Rama, abandoning those false disciplines, get established in the plane of pure awareness and be free from all desires.

135. O noble soul, by contemplating the supreme samvid principle bereft of all conceptions and the objective entity, remain stabilised in the inner heart without sense of separation; and while doing duties, be a non-doer immersed in equipoise.

136. A person has attained the fruit of life only if he has made enquiry and has made some attempt at control of mind.

137. If the seed of enquiry gets lodged in the heart, as a result of practice, it grows into a mighty tree with numberless branches.

138. The winds of worry cannot destroy the tree having flowers of enquiry, when it is firmly rooted in the earth.

139. He, whose mind, as he walks, stands, remains awake or asleep, is not constantly engaged in enquiry is almost a dead person.

140. What is this world? Who am I?-Enquire thus everyday in the light of your inner Self, or in the company of wise persons.

141. Wise people consider enquiry as part of the wisdom of the scripture. As sweetness is found in milk, the wisdom of the knowable is found through enquiry.

142. One who has attained the vision of Truth becomes the same Truth. He is not afraid. He is never in a helpless or miserable condition.

143. A person who drinks wine becomes intoxicated with it. Even so, the knower of Brahman becomes the blissful pure Being. The Self manifests itself through mere realisation of It.

144. Even if he eats unholy, unfit, poisonous, impure, rotten, tasteless dishes, he digests them like good food.

145. The knower of Truth, detached as he is, finds poison, counter-poison, salty waters and food to be of the same taste.

146. He looks with cool and compassionate eyes, both the men who deprive him of livelihood and the men who give him livelihood.

147. The wise person, because his mind is free from love and hatred, does not, at any time, show attachment to anything within the range of his sense.

148. Senses swallow up the man, like the deers the tender shoots, who is not a knower of Truth, who is restless, who has not realised the Self.

149. Attachment is the cause of all evils, the cause of samsara, the cause of all desires, and the cause of all dangers.

150. Renunciation of attachment is liberation, freedom from rebirth. Renounce attachment towards all objects and be a liberated soul."

151. Sri Rama asked, "O Seer, you are the mighty wind that drives away the cloud of doubt. Tell me in a nutshell what is attachment."

152. Sri Vasishta said: "Those impure vasanas relating to real and unreal objects which give you joy and sorrow are called attachment.

153. The vasanas of the liberated souls, which do not cause rebirth, elation or sorrow, are called pure ones.

154. The vasanas of the ignorant people who are miserable and stupid are called by the term 'attachment' and they cause future birth.

155. If you are susceptible to the experience of elation, sorrow and distress, then, vasanas capable of fettering the soul will arise from such experience of elation and sorrow.

156. O Rama, if you are not susceptible to the experience of elation and sorrow, you will be free from such desires, fears, angers, etc., and therefore you will be detached.

157. O Rama, if you are not saddened by pain or excited by pleasures, you will be unswayed by ambition and you will be a detached soul.

158. O Rama, if you remain the same whether fortune befalls or misfortune and if you keep doing things that come in a natural way, then you are a detached soul.

159. Be the one who has the same disposition towards all objects while internally remaining free from attachment. That which comes your way, do it without attachment and remain happy, O Rama.

Section-6
Liberation

First Half

Chapter-1

The Story of Busunda

The Nirvana Prakarana that commences here contains 15 stories. The story of Busunda tells the manner in which the contemplation of the course of prana leads to mental poise and liberation.

Sri Vasishta said:

1 & 2. "I am naught else but that Brahman which is not limited by space and time and which knows no origin and destruction and which is the non-decaying Consciousness-, tranquil and non-dual;' thinking thus internally and experiencing both real freedom and ostensible bondage, remain still and silent, experiencing the bliss of Self. (BYV 6A-2, 23 25).

S. T. interprets the phrase muktamuktavapu thus: free on account of the absence of identification and non-free on account of the force of prarabdha.

3. *As long as there is ajnana, as long as there is the notion, 'I am not Brahman,' as long as there is the conviction that the phenomenal world exists, till then there is the play of the mind, etc. (BYV 2, 30).*

4. The chitta exists not, nor ignorance, nor manas nor the individual soul. O Rama, Brahman only has been

imagined to be these things. In fact, it is Brahman bereft of origin and destruction that exults like the ocean (assuming various forms of words). (BYV 2, 26 & 2, 29).

According to S. T., Chitta is the faculty of the internal organ in which the pure sattva is preponderant; manas is the faculty of the internal organ in which the rajo guna is preponderant.

5.   As long as there is identification with body and as long as one refers to perceptible things as 'this is mine,' there is the play of the mind etc. (BYV 2, 31).

6.   *With an interiorised mind, when the seer offers as oblation the entire world in the fire of Consciousness, the mind and other fancies get burnt up. (BYV 2, 46).*

When a person contemplates himself to be all-pervasive, the mind gets interiorised and the world becoming as useless as dry grass gets negated in the Consciousness of the Supreme Self, because all that is seen is not existent apart from the seer. S. T.

7.   *You are self-consciousness, partless whole, devoid of beginning and end. Recollect thy expansive form and do not become a limited being by virtue of ignorance. (BYV 2, 56).*

8.   He who entertains natural friendliness even towards an inveterate foe intent on killing him at once is really even-minded. Such a person knows the Self. (BYV 2-16)

9.   He who uproots attachment and aversion alongwith their basic cause, even as the river waters uproot the tree on its bank alongwith its roots, has vanquished pleasure and pain (BYV 2,17).

10.   *The poisonous venom of desire gets destroyed, as mist*

by autumn when the mantra of the scripture pertaining to self is contemplated upon. (BYV 4, 4).

The TP says that this portion of BYV describes the secret spiritual practice called pratyagdrshti, cosmic subjectivity. The comments of S. T. on verses 1 to 7 of the sarga 4 are very significant.

11. Where the instruction of the preceptor has been viewed by one's mind as most worthy of acceptance, that instruction thoroughly permeates the disciple's mind, as water in the utterly parched land. (BYV 4, 12).

12. Those who have not reflected upon the meanings of the scripture concerning the self and who have not intuited the Consciousness are lifeless and dull beings that merely toss about like grass. (BYV 6, 22).

13. In fact, all the souls are only Consciousness, chit-by nature. But by virtue of ignorance-unawareness of their true nature-they have descended to the miserly state. (BYV 6, 26).

14. The frightening sounds of the idiotic men, like those that emanate from the bow strung with arrows, are the result of lack of self-awareness and only entail death for others. (BYV 6, 28).

15. Whatever is offered to such a man is something thrown into a pit. Talking to him is like the barking of dog in empty space. (BYV 6, 31).

16. Ignorance is the root cause of all disasters; what disaster does not wait on an ignorant man? This cycle of birth and death (samsara) keeps rotating only because of the negligence of the ignorant man. (BYV 6, 32).

17. The world, which, for a wise man, is only as small as

a water-pool of the size of the foot of a cow, becomes an endless stretch of deep waters that cannot be crossed for the ignorant people. (BYV 6, 47).

18. Prior to creation, pure Being, all-pervading and of the nature of sat, chit and ananda-untainted by objective matter and creative potency, exists (BYV 9, 2).

19. From chit arises, of its own accord, creative mode, kala, basically of the nature of creative potency, kalpana. That creative mode is regarded as of three types-subtle, small and gross. (BYV 9, 3).

The kala that arises in the chit is likened to the lines that get formed in the flowing waters. The point is that with the rise of kala, chit does not undergo any real transformation in its form. According to S. T., kala refers to avidya.

20. It is this kala that is referred to as the primordial matter, prakriti, comprising of sattvam, rajas and tamas. This engenders the cycle of birth and death, samsara, for the soul and the state of freedom, kaivalya, is beyond it. (BYV 9, 6).

21. Each of the three gunas, attributes, pertaining to prakriti, is again stated to be of three forms. So this avidya which merely consists of gunas, is divisible into nine types. (BYV 9, 7).

22. O Raghava! Know that Rishis, Munis, Siddhas, Nagas, Vidyadharas and Suras constitute the sattvic category of avidya. (BYV 9, 9).

23. Even among these relating to the sattvic category, nagas and vidyadharas comprise the tamasic sub-division, munis and siddhas, the rajasic sub-division, and the gods Hara and others, the sattvic sub-division. (BYV 9, 10).

24.   Thus it is only part of avidya, ignorance, that has come
        to be regarded as vidya, knowledge. The pure sattvic
        portion of avidya is called as vidya. (BYV 9, 15).

        The S. T. says that the pure sattvic aspect of causal
        avidya is vidya and it is in this vidya, the manifest
        world, the effect of avidya originates and merges.

25.   Likewise, the creations pertaining to rajasic and
        tamasic gunas also are of three types each. The trees,
        etc., are the embodiment of ignorance as they
        represent the tamasic portion of tamas."

        Rajas and tamas are again sub-divided into sattvic,
        rajasic and tamasic aspects and the trees represent
        the extreme form of tamas.

        This verse is not traceable in the BYV-NS Edition. The
        doubt raised in next verse by Rama is based on the
        statement in this verse and hence it is presumed that
        the text followed by the compiler of LYV is different
        from the one available in NS Edition. The author of
        TP does not seem to be aware of this verse, vide his
        comment on 10, 9 in BYV.

26.   Sri Rama asked, "O Master! How does the hardened
        mass of ignorance assuming the form of trees,
        manifest?" (BYV, 10, 9).

        Rama wants to know the mental state of the trees as
        the discriminating nature is totally absent in them.

27.   Sri Vasishta said: "They had not attained to the state
        of mindlessness and are not also capable of mental
        discrimination. The soul abiding in the trees, etc.,
        assumes an intermediate state. (BYV, 10, 10).

        The mind manifesting in the trees is neither insensitive
        as human mind in sleep nor capable of performing
        the normal functions of reflection and recollection.

28. Sri Rama asked, "If the soul abiding in the trees is not capable of the mental functions, O Seer, I presume that it is not far from the state of liberation."

29. Sri Vasishta said: "Where the soul abides with all its faculties, as if in dormant state and yet manifesting happiness like a mute, blind and inert being, there the chit is merely existent."

The chit abiding as soul in the trees manifests only its existential aspect and the sense of knowledge and action do not attain manifestation.

30. Sri Rama asked, "As the chit manifests itself only in its non-dual existence aspect in the trees, I presume, O Master, it is not far from liberation." (BYV, 10, 12).

The doubt of Rama is that inasmuch as mental functions do not manifest in trees, their state is not different from that of liberation. In BYV, the doubt is presented in clearer terms.

31. Sri Vasishta said: "Through rational reflection and through right cognition, if there is attainment of existential awareness, that is final liberation. (BYV, 10, 13).

The point made clear by Vasishta is that the satta-samanya-bodha attained only through spiritual enquiry and spiritual discipline represents the state of liberation.

32. *Only when the vasanas have been fully discarded as a result of realisation of self, there ensues the existential awareness constituting liberation. (BYV, 10, 14).*

33. Abidance in the existential awareness is realisation of Brahman when it is attained as a result of enquiry, discussion with preceptor, study of scripture

pertaining to the self and contemplation of self. (BYV, 10, 15).

Attainment of existential awareness must be preceded by study of Vedantic works, reflection and contemplation of Reality.

34 & 35. Where the mind has merged in the causal ignorance and the vasanas are dormant, the state of sleep, being inert in nature, is capable of causing manifold sorrows including birth. (BYV, 10, 17).

36.   All these trees, inert in nature, are in the oblivion of sleep and are susceptible to rebirth, again and again. (BYV, 10, 18).

37.   Even as flower, etc., is latent in seed, the pot in the lump of clay, O wise man, the related vasanas remain lodged in the inert trees. (BYV, 10, 19).

38.   Wherein the seed of vasana is dormant, that is only a state of sleep and not liberation; where the vasana is without the seed, that is turiya state and that is regarded as liberation. (BYV, 10, 20).

What constitutes the seed of vasana is mentioned in verse 41 below.

39.   Even a vestige of vasana, as in the case of fire, debt, disease, hatred, attachment, enmity and poison, is productive of harm. (BYV, 10, 20).

In the case of fire, etc., even a small portion of it is capable of causing great harm in course of time. It is so with vasana.

40.   Be he, in whom the seed of vasana has been burnt up, associated with body or not, he has attained the form of existential awareness and is not again subject to sorrow. (BYV, 10, 22).

41. The sakti, potency, of Chit constitutes the seed of vasana for all embodied souls; it is non-cognition of the Chit that is called as avidya by the wise. (BYV, 10, 23, 30).

The veiling power that envelops the Chit, preventing the cognition of it, is avidya and is the basic cause, seed, as it were, of vasana.

42. With the help of the chief part of avidya, the rest is burnt up; by the mutual rubbing of the two, both get destroyed and beatitude manifests.

Vidya serves to destroy avidya and in the end gets annihilated. The verse is not traceable in BYV-NS Edition.

43. *This much alone is the nature of avidya that there is the conviction. 'This is not Brahman.' That is destruction of avidya when there is the conviction, 'This is Brahman.'*

44. May that firm conviction which shines forth in the hearts of Hara and the seers like Narada be yours as well, O Raghava."

45. Sri Rama asked, "Gracious Master! Kindly describe in full the nature of the conviction that enabled these brave and noble souls to remain completely without sorrow." (BYV, 11, 14).

46. Sri Vasishta said: "All this spectacular universal show seen in front is only pure Brahman and is rooted in it. (BYV, 11, 16).

47. The chit is Brahmana; the universe is Brahman; the successive cosmic bodies are Brahman; I am Brahman; my enemy is Brahman; my friends and relations are Brahman. (BYV, 11, 17).

48. For the ignorant, the world is filled with sorrow; for the wise, the world brims with joy. The world is dark to the blind and is filled with light to the man with vision. (BYV, 11, 32).

49. *A man becomes Brahman if he contemplates that all this is Brahman only. Who indeed, after drinking amrita, does not attain immortality?*

50. Bare knowledge, bereft of objective content, illumining all objects and existing everywhere is experienced as Brahmic Consciousness (by the seer). (BYV, 11, 67).

   In the knowledge of any object, if the object content is carefully eliminated, the residual awareness is only chit.

51. The knowledge that a person walking along a path gets about the objects in front, uncoloured by any mentation, while the mind is cognising something else, is Brahmic all-pervading awareness. (BYV, 11, 77)

   The knowledge of an object not vitiated by past impressions and mentations of any kind, is pure Consciousness.

52. 'I contemplate on the Consciousness, that is Self-which fulfills all desires, which illumines all luminaries and which is the highest attainable. (BYV, 11, 92).

53. I contemplate on Consciousness, that is the Self-in which all desires have been quietened, all anger has dissolved and all efforts have been neutralised.' (BYV, 11, 99).

54. Endowed with such a firm conviction, those true and noble souls untouched by sins, abide happily in the supreme state-that is real, unchanging and always the same. (BYV, 12, 1).

55. Their hearts being full and their minds stripped of all

desires, they neither extol life nor condemn death."
(BYV, 12, 2).

56. Sri Rama asked, "O seer! I abide in ease, in the state of jivanmukti, liberation-in-life, by virtue of annihilation of vasanas effected through supreme knowledge. (BYV, 13, 1).

57. How does one abide in the state of jivanmukti by annihilation of vasanas effected through the control of the course of prana, vital breath?"

All the clarifications made in BYV on this vital subject have not been presented in LYV.

58. Sri Vasishta replies: "The means by which the cycle of birth and death, samsara, is transcended is called by the term 'yoga.' It is done through self-knowledge and control of pranas. (BYV, 13, 3, 4).

59. *Although both the means are referred to by the term 'yoga,' the usage of the term in regard to control of prana has come to stay. (BYV, 13, 6).*

60. *For some one, practice of yoga is impossible; for some one else, acquisition of firm knowledge is impossible. Therefore, the Lord Paramesvara enunciated both the means. (BYV, 13, 8).*

The latter line of the verse is not traceable in BYV.

61. I have already explained to you what is supreme knowledge; now hear the method of yoga. In this connection, I recount to you an interesting story.

62. Once I happened to be at the assembly of Indra in the heaven. There, I heard stories about those endowed with longest life from Narada and others. (BYV, 14, 4).

63. While recounting the stories of some persons with

longest life, the seer Satatapa said: (BYV, 14, 5).

64. 'In the north-western part of Meru, atop it, there is a beautiful cliff studded with rubies and in that stands a kalpataru possessing all charms.

65. Atop the kalpataru, in its southern branches, intertwined with golden creepers, there exists a nest of birds. (BYV, 14, 7).

66. There lives the crow called Busunda, well-endowed with riches. He is desireless and vastly learned and shines like Brahma in His lotus abode. (BYV, 14, 8).

67. O Devas! He lives for so long in the heart of the universe that there was none before and there will be none hereafter in the heaven like him. (BYV, 14, 9).

68. He has long life; he is free from disease; he is rich; he possesses great intellect; his mind is tranquil and serene. He is lovable and knows all about times.' (BYV, 14, 10).

69. Thus Busunda was described again by Satatapa when questioned by me in the assembly of the celestials. What he said about him was true.

70. When the discourse came to an end and the celestials dispersed, I went to see the bird Busunda out of curiosity.

71. I saw the Kalpataru, with the branches forming a circle in the most beautiful cliff of Meru in which Busunda had his abode. (BYV, 15, 1).

72 to 75. I found several kinds of birds resting in their nests- in its branches, joints, bunches of leaves and thickets- swans as white as moon reciting sama veda and other vedic mantras, parrots, crows, cuckoos and peacocks proficient in the esoteric wisdom concerning Siva, taught by Skanda.

76. In front I beheld in the vast hole of a solitary branch, crows in an assembly, without exhibiting any immodesty. (BYV, 15, 26).

77. Amidst them stood the accomplished Busunda with an exalted form. He was exceedingly contented, silent, majestic and beautiful. (BYV, 15, 28).

78. By virtue of contemplation over prana, his mind was ever inwardised and happy. He was serene, deep, kind, wise and of endearing speech. (BYV, 18, 32).

79. Thereon, I alighted before his radiant personality and for a moment the abode of birds agitated like the lake studded with blue lotuses.

80. Busunda noticed my arrival and instantly understood that it is Vasishta that has come.

81. The valiant one rose up from the seat of leaves-like the tiny cloud from the crest of hill-and spoke endearingly sweet words, 'O seer! thy coming is auspicious.'

82. He offered me flowers, which came to his hands by mere wish, like the clouds materialising snow.

83. Saying, 'here is the seat,' the wise chief of birds himself brought a new branch of the kalpataru tree.

84. With all the birds eagerly looking at me, I sat on the bunch of kalpataru leaves.

85. After offering me water to wash the feet and hands, the happy Busunda spoke to me in affectionate words.

86. Busunda said, "How blessed we have been by thee after a long time, Gracious Lord. It is as if we, the wise trees have been drenched by the ambrosial waters descending from the clouds of thy look.

87. What for has thy visit taken place today? Why has

your body been put to strain? You may command us, as we are ready to act according to your instructions.

88.   I have come to know everything by a mere sight of thee; you got reminded about us in the course of the talk about persons with long life.

89.   I know about the purpose of the visit; yet, I ask about it because I am impelled by the desire to drink the nectarine words that flow from thy mouth.'

90.   Thus spoke the bird, Busunda of long life who knew well the past, present and future and I replied thus:

91.   "O king of birds! What has been spoken by you is true. I came only to see one with longest life.

92 & 93. Gracious bird, do thou dispel my doubt by recounting the fact. In which family were you born? How did you become the Knower of Truth? How long have you been living? Do you remember or not the events that have taken place in your life? By which far-sighted soul was this abode shown to you?"

94 & 95. Rama, thereon, Busunda was delighted and said submissively: "O seer, whatever you ask, I will tell. Be pleased to hear. Who can disregard such command of persons like you? After replying thus, the king of birds told me everything."

96.   Busunda said, "There exists in this great world the God of all Gods called Hara, who is the greatest among the celestials and who is adorned by them all.

97.   The attendants with whom he sports are persons with curious forms-some have hoofs in their heads; some have hoofs in their hands; some have mouths in their hands; some have mouths in their belly. There are also attendants with the faces of camel, bear, elephant and goat.

98 & 99. There are also attendants who dance before Divine Mothers and before the Lord in cremation grounds, etc. They live in caves of mountains, sky and nether worlds.

100. The Mothers are known by the names, Jaya, Vijaya, Jayanti, Aparajita, Siddha, Raktha, Alambusha and Utpala.

101. These eight are the mistresses of all the various mothers and their followers.

102. O chief of saints! Among these eight mothers worthy of veneration, there is a famous one known by the name, Alambusha.

103. A crow called Chanda, impregnable like Indrasila mountain and with bones as strong as that of vajra, was her vehicle, like Garuda for Vaishnavi.

104. These Mothers endowed with the eight siddhis, intent on doing acts pleasing to Rudra, once happened to assemble in the sky, for some reason.

105. They celebrated a festival, highlighting the glory of Reality and indulged in singing and dancing in an intoxicated state.

106. As they were celebrating thus, their renowned vehicles, (hamsas, etc) drank wine and danced and sang together elsewhere.

107. While they were sporting themselves in the sky, the hamsas who were the vehicles of Brahmi, happened to be with the crow, Chanda, the vehicle of Alambusha.

108. Overcome by amorous feelings, the infatuated hamsas had conjugal union with the crow Chanda.

109. The delighted hamsas became pregnant at once. The Mothers became fatigued by dancing.

110. Thereon, the Mothers and Hara, with their attendants, returned happily to their abodes.

111. O chief of saints! These hamsas, pregnant as they were, told the Goddess Brahmi all about the event.

112 & 113. The Goddess Brahmi, compassionate as she was, told the hamsas, 'Friends, you are carrying children in the wombs and so are not fit for carrying my chariot; enjoy rest as you please,' and got absorbed in Nirvikalpa Samadhi.

114. The hamsas also, in due time, gave birth, at the Brahma lake, to twenty-one sons.

115. The Goddess Brahmi was fervently adored for a long time by us along with the mother-hamsas. She rose up from samadhi.

116. At the appropriate time, we were blessed by the gracious Goddess with wisdom, and that is how we attained to liberation.

117. We were contented and peaceful and deciding to spend our life in contemplation in solitude, we approached our father, Chanda.

118. We saluted our father and worshipped the Goddess Alambusha. She looked at us with great kindness. We said to the father:

119. 'Father, by the grace of Goddess Brahmi, the Reality has been completely understood by us. But we desire for stay a secluded and suitable place.'

120. It is by that all-knowing seer, we have been shown this kalpa tree that is unknown to all hardships.

121. Thereafter, we did obeisance to him and leaving that place reached this Kalpataru and remained here without any worry.

377

122. All the good deeds done by me for a long time have borne fruit today as I have been able to see you, the foremost of saints.

123. Whom does not delight the moon-light of the wise company, which is, so to say, a life-giving drink, and capable of giving peace and supreme bliss?

124. *I do not think of anything else as the index of a person's well-being, excepting that the wise men bereft of all desires should be visiting him.*

125 & 126. Though I have realised the Supreme Truth, I am inclined to think that by the sight of Thee, my wrongs have been condoned and my life has attained fulfilment, for the wise company wards off all dangers."

127. Sri Vasishta said: "O Rama, when after speaking thus, Busunda offered me water for ablution and drink repeatedly, I asked him:

128. "O king of birds, why is it that your brothers of noble descent are not seen but you alone are seen here?"

129. Busunda replied, "Since we started residing here, O seer, a long time has passed away; yugas and kalpas rolled by.

130. During this long period, all my brothers have thrown away the body, as if it is straw, and attained oneness with Siva.

131. All-those with long life, mighty men, wise men, strong men-get swallowed up by Time most certainly."

132. Sri Vasishta asked: "When during Cosmic dissolutions fire rages, waters inundate, winds blow and suns burn, alternately, how do yo manage to remain unharmed?"

133. Busunda replied, "When at the close of a kalpa, aeon, the world-order ceases, I abandon this nest like an ungrateful man, the friend.

134. Bereft of all thoughts and with a mind stripped of all vasanas, I stay in the sky with my entire being rendered still.

135. When the Suns burn, remaining in the sky, I get immersed in the contemplation of Varuna, the deity of waters and thus firmly secure myself.

136. When during dissolution mighty winds blow, I get immersed in the contemplation of mountain and thus remain unmoved.

137. When the whole world including Meru gets engulfed in waters, I pursue the contemplation of Vayu and contrive to float on the waters.

138. When the cosmic elements have dissolved, I station myself on the edge of the Brahmanda and remain as if in sleeping state.

139. When again Brahma, the lotus-born, undertakes the creation, I enter into the Brahmanda and abide in this nest of birds.

140. It is only through the force of my sankalpa, thought, in every kalpa, again and again, this tree grows up in the same mountain.

141. Sri Vasishta said: "O king of birds! Like the way you have been able to survive through steadfast contemplations at the time of dissolutions, why have not other Yogis been able to survive the dissolution?"

142. Busunda replied, "O knower of Brahman, this is due to the Cosmic Will set in motion by the Supreme God and cannot be transgressed. I have to contemplate the way I do. Others contemplate in a different way.

143. That which has to happen cannot be made to alter the course. This is the way of Nature."

144. Sri Vasishta asked: "Thou are versed in the wordly and transcendental wisdom. Thou art brave and endowed with a mind steeped in Yoga. Fortunate Soul, what are the curious things you have noticed in the three worlds?"

145. Busunda replied, "I remember times when a huge tree appeared on rock; when there was not even a blade of grass on earth; when there was neither mountain nor forest nor tree.

146. For thousands of years, the entire earth was only filled with dust.

147. In one cycle of yugas, the earth was filled with trees and plants; in another cycle, it was studded with mountains.

148. I remember another cycle of yugas, in which, the Vindhya mountain, (Agastya being absent), had expanded so much as to cover the whole earth.

149. I remember a creation cycle in whch Brahmins were addicted to drink, non-Brahmins scorned the Brahmins and family women lived in a permissive way.

150 to 153. The birth of sun and moon, the ascent of Indra and Upendra, the coveting of earth by Hiranyaksha, the recovery of earth by Varaha, the assignment of rulers over earth, the restoration of Vedas, the uprooting of Mandara mountain and the churning of ocean for amrita, the birth of Garuda, the formation of oceans-all these events, even those much younger in age, can recollect. There is nothing extraordinary about my narrating them.

154. Of the seers like you who were born-Bharadwaja, Pulasthya, Atri, Narada, Indra, Marichi, Sanatkumaa, Bhrigu, Siva, Skanda, Ganapati, Gowri, Sarasvati,

Lakshmi, Gayatri-I have seen so many till the current creation, that I cannot even count.

155. O seer, for you and the mind-born son of Narada, this is eighth birth. I am meeting you for the eighth time.

156. Sometime you were born in sky; sometime in water; sometime in mountain; sometime in fire.

157. O seer, on five occasions, the earth disappeared in the waters and was lifted up by Kurma only.

158 & 159. I remember twelve occasions of churning the ocean of amrita; three times of carrying away of the earth into nether region by Hiranyaksha.

160. Hari incarnated as Parasurama, the son of Renuka, six times; in hundred Kaliyugas, Hari appeared as Buddha.

161. I recollect that Tripuras were destroyed by Siva thirty times; the sacrifice of Daksha was destroyed by him twice; ten Indras were humbled by him; eight times he waged war for the sake of Bana.

162. I noticed the disparity in the men's intelligence-in the form of increase and decrease and the different variations in the Vedic texts.

163. Several puranas containing the same message appear and several also lapse away.

164. I also remember the existence of another Ramayana, containing one lakh verses, expounding the supreme wisdom.

165. I have noticed yet another Ramayana composed for the twelfth time by Valmiki or by an ordinary person bearing that name.

The comment of S. T. on this verse is significant.

166 to 167. I remember another similar composition called

Bharatam, originally written by Vyasa and later forgotten, recomposed for the seventh time by Vyasa or someone bearing that name.

168. Shortly there will be eleventh appearance of Rama, the incarnation of Vishnu on earth for the destruction of Rakshasas.

169. Oh chief seer, there is going to be sixteenth incarnation of Vishnu in the house of Vasudeva for the removal of earth's burden.

170. This delusive appearance of world does not really exist any time; or it exists some time as bubble on the water.

171. This unwelcome illusory spectacle, existing potentially in intelligence manifests and subsides as wave in sea.

172 & 173. This northern direction and this mountain were in a different place in a former creation. The direction and the location are dependent on the movement of Sun and Stars and the location of Meru etc., and if the latter change, others also change.

174. In Kali manifests the conduct appropriate to Krita Yuga and in Krita that of Kali. A similar juxta position between Treta and Dwapara I recollect.

175. Vasishta said: "Out of curiosity, O Rama, the crow was questioned by me thus on the top branch of the Kalpavriksha: 'For one abiding and acting in the heart of the world, O King of birds, how is body not assailed by Death?'

177 & 178. Busunda said: "Oh the omniscient seer! even though you know everything, you ask for love of wisdom. Masters like to draw out the tongue of servants. Anyhow, I reply to your question. The real worship of the wise ones is obedience of their command.

179. Death does not attack a man whose heart does not wear the pearls of evil traits strung together by Vasanas.

180. Death does not attack a person, who is not haressed by mental afflictions, which are, as it were, the worms abounding in the creeper of the body, capable of eating away the tree of hope.

181. Death does not attack a person who is not bitten by the serpents of desires, who live in the tree of the body and whose hoods are thoughts.

182. Death approaches not the man who is not preyed upon by the vermin of desire and hatred and by the serpent of greed for which the mind is the abode.

183. Death approaches not the man who is not the victim of anger that is like a Vadava fire, drying up the waters of discrimination.

184. Death approaches not the man whom kama does not oppress as the oil-extracting machine oppresses the gingely seeds.

185. Death approaches not the man whose mind finds repose in the exalted, non-dual, pure Consciousness.

186. All these great evils, aforesaid, cause the disease of samsara but they do not torment the man whose mind gets absorbed in the contemplation of non-dual Reality.

187. All the pains arising from mental and physical afflictions are born from illusory fancies and they do not torment the man steeped in contemplation of all-pervasive Being.

188. The mental afflictions caused by lust and anger that blind one's vision do not torment the man steeped in contemplation of the single Reality.

189. Wrong possessions, wrong deeds, wrong attitudes, wrong postures and wrong reactions do not harm the man whose mind is steeped in contemplation of the single Reality.

190. That state which does not lead to bondage, which is lasting, unassociated with prakriti, untainted by ignorance and beyond the travail of samsara-let the mind attain that state.

191. Let the mind be made to attain the state which is untainted by ignorance that leads to manifold miseries by giving rise to the devilish sense of multiplicity.

192. The contemplation of Self puts an end to all afflictions. It is easily attained by persons like you, but not by persons like us.

193. How can dull-minded persons attain to that which is beyond all mentation and which is the very extremity of non-dual existence?

194 & 195. *Of the various methods identical in nature to the contemplation of Self, I have adhered to the Contemplation of Prana, the One that puts an end to all sorrows, conducive to one's good and supports the life."*

196. When Busunda had spoken thus, I, impelled by curiosity, again asked the seer, though I was well-versed on the subject.

197. Sri Vasishta asked: "O long-lived one! Dispeller of all doubts! O wise soul! Tell me in detail what is meant by the contemplation of prana."

198. Busunda replied, "O seer, hear from me about the contemplation of prana which makes the body a beautiful house to live in. (BYV, 24, 4).

199 & 200. O seer, the air going up and down in the body is

known by two names. They are rooted in the lotus-like heart in the centre of the body. They are called by the well-known names of prana and apana. By contemplating always on their courses, I remain alive.

201 to 203. Through the contemplation in all the states of waking, dreaming and sleeping of the two bodies always orbiting in space, which represent heat and cold, which are Sun and Moon manifesting as Agni and Soma in the inner space of the heart, which called as Prana and Apana respectively sustain the life-machine and alleviate the pain, days are spent away, Oh seer, in sleep like condition.

204. Their movements, though existing, are very difficult to identify. They are subtler than the thousandth part of the fibre of the lotus stalk.

205. O divine seer, this prana, representing the power of unceasing movement, within and without the body, has an upward course.

206. O divine seer, this apana, representing power of unceasing movement, within and without the body, has a downward course.

207. Do thou now hear for the sake of your enlightenment the supreme mode of prana-control which takes place in an enlightened seer, whether he is awake or asleep.

208. The egress of prana from the lotus-like heart, with ease and absence of least effort, is inner Rechaka, exhalation.

209. When the prana exhaled remains pervading the dwadasangula region, twelve finger-breaths, that is from the tip of the nose and gets integrated into whole, that is called Puraka, external pervasion.

210. When from the supreme state, apana enters into the

system with ease and activates the inner parts, that is also called Puraka, inhalation.

The phases described in verses 209 and 210 are both puraka-but, in the first, it is exterior and in the second, it is interior.

211. The state which is consciously experienced by the Yogis when the apana merges and the prana has not risen in the heart is Kumbhaka, suspension of breath.

212. Rechaka, Puraka and Kumbhaka-in this three-fold manner, prana has manifested. Kumbhaka is akin to the state of pot, prior to its manifestation, within the clay.

213. The abidance of apana in space at dwadasangula distance from the nose-tip is known to be Kumbhaka by the wise.

214. The inner abidance of prana with the nose-tip as the outer limit, is known to the adepts of Yoga as one form of outer Puraka.

215. Leaving the nose-tip, if the prana remains within dwadasangula, it is also known by the wise as another form of outer Kumbhaka.

216. When prana has merged and apana has not still risen in the outer space, that is a state of fullness and is known as outer Kumbhaka.

217. The rise of apana and its downward movement is known as outer Rechaka and contemplation of it leads to liberation.

218. Arising from the dwadasangula region, the downward course of it in expanded form is another form of outer Puraka.

219. Both outer forms and inner forms of Kumbhaka,

Rechaka and Puraka, ceaselessly practised, lead to the control of prana and apana and the person is liberated.

220. These eight forms of control of prana during day and night, O wise soul, are considered by me as conducive to liberation.

221. By unhasty practice of these and by avoiding the external proclivities of the mind, in matter of days only, one reaches the state of beatitude.

222. One who practises these modes of control of prana does not get attracted by sense-pleasures as a brahmana by food in leather-bowl.

223. Those who adhere to these practices are of steady mind. They have attained all that is to be attained. They are beyond all sorrows.

224. If a person adheres to these practices as he walks, stands, keeps awake or sleeps, he does not get fettered.

225. The rise of prana happens in the lotus-like formation in the heart. In the outer fringe of dwadasangula, from the nose-tip, prana subsides.

226. O great seer, apana arises at the outer fringe of dwadasangula and it subsides in the centre of lotus-like heart.

227. Apana, representing moon, flowing from outer, cools the physical system. Prana, representing sun, burns the body within.

228. By attaining the state wherein the apana, the moon aspect, is devoured by prana, the sun, one is not born again.

229. Similarly, by attaining the state wherein the sun of prana is devoured by the cool moon of apana, one is not born again.

230. By remaining in that state of function where apana swallows prana, one is not born again.

This state of function represents the witnessing state of Consciousness.

231. That principle of Chit which is in between apana and prana, between the disappearance of apana and the appearance of prana is the Self which I adore.

232. I adore the principle of Chit which is free from the taint of apana and which manifests at the function of apana's disappearance and prana's subsequent appearance.

233. I adore that principle of Chit vibrating in dwadasangula and manifesting when apana has not risen and prana has subsided.

234. In that principle which is free from all taints of ajnana, which in jiva aspect is permeated by ajnana, which reveals fully to an aspiring mind, which is the highest state worshipped by all the celestials-in that principle, I take refuge.

235. This is the repose in Chit that is practised by me through the means of Prana Contemplation. In this way one is led to the abidance in pure Self.

236. I think not of anything of the past or the future. Abiding in Consciousness, I concentrate on the present.

237. 'I have attained this today,' 'I will get this beautiful thing'-such thought I never indulge in. Hence, I remain living happily for long.

238. I praise not, I censure not, anywhere, anything, any time, of myself or others. Hence I remain alive happily for long.

239. *I feel not elated when some good thing is obtained; I*

feel not sad when some harm befalls me. My mind remains in the same condition. Hence I remain alive happily for long.

240. I have remained at all times, an all-inclusive being and as I practise the supreme sacrifice, I remain alive happily for long.

241. O seer, my mind is exceedingly calm, as it is free from cravings, sorrow and desire. Hence I remain alive happily for long.

242. O divine seer, I do not see anyone as relative, anyone else as outsider, one as dear to me and another as otherwise. Hence I remain alive happily for long.

243. I am always composed and my mind is not assailed by desires. Hence I remain alive happily for long.

244. When fortune befalls, I am joyous and I am sad when I am in the company of distressed. I am dear and friendly to all beings. Hence I remain alive happily for long.

245. In grave danger, I remain undisturbed and in times of fortune, I am a friend of the universe. I do not get attached to real and unreal things.

246. O Divine Seer, Supreme Knower of Wisdom, I have now told you how I live happily for long. This audacity of mine manifesting as speech was but only for the purpose of carrying out your command."

247. Sri Vasishta said: "O, you have spoken interestingly things which one longs to hear. You have spoken about your own life which causes great wonder.

248. May all be very auspicious for you! Do thou enter into the cave of Self. This is noon time. Let me get back to the celestial abode.

249. O king of birds, do not trouble yourself and follow me for seeing me off." Saying thus, I left the tree and took to the sky like a bird.

250. In the sky, he followed me over for a long distance. With difficulty, I persuaded him to stay behind. Truly, the attachment to the wise is hard to give up.

251 to 254. At the commencement of the past Krita Yuga, I had a meeting with Busunda in the Meru mountain. O Rama, Krita Yuga is over and now Treta Yuga is on. In the middle of Treta Yuga, you were born. In the eighth year of your life, my meeting with him again took place on the top of the great mountain and Busunda was there without any sign of advanced age.

Thus the interesting story of Busunda has been told. After hearing this and reflecting upon it inwardly, do what is proper."

Chapter-2

The Worship of Ishvara

Sri Vasishta said:

1. "This body is only seemingly so. It is cognised as 'This is mine' and 'This is myself' and it is illusory.

2. Discard the deluded notion that 'I am the body' as the body is an aggregate of flesh and bones. There are a hundred bodies arising from imagination.

3. O Rama, the person who has gone to sleep on a beautiful couch, in dream, goes to various distant directions of the world. Where is that dream body now?

4. When in that dream-world, you happen to visit the heaven or Meru mountain, where is that body to be seen now, in the waking state?

5. O Rama, do know samsara, worldly transmigration, to be a long dream or a long delusion or a long mental fancy.

6. 'All the three worlds are but mere illusory manifestation. They are neither real nor unreal'-with such a conviction to discard all objective conception is total comprehension of Truth.

7. One's death is a necessity-such is the decree of nature. If so, why do you needlessly wail when you have to encounter death?

8. Any person born in the world meets with some fortune in life. If so, why should there be pride, when some wealth accrues to one.

9. In the illusory and variegated objective universe, do

not see things distinctly from one another, but see them as distinctionless, bare existence.

10. But this illusory objective existence is vitiated by material conceptions and so, disregarding all material projections, attain to undifferentiated awareness.

11. Desire and hatred are two serpents in the hole of a person's heart. If they are not lurking, what great good cannot be attained from that person, who is akin to a kalpataru, wish-fulfilling tree?

12. Wretched are those honoured asses who are proud of wisdom who are learned in scripture, but are imbued with desire and hatred.

13. This wheel of life has as the central hub, sankalpa, thought, O Rama. If that hub is rendered motionless, the rotation of wheel comes to a halt.

14. If the hub of mind is activated, the wheel, even if prevented from moving, speedily rotates with added momentum.

15. By summoning supreme effort, by the use of intelligence and inner strength, control the chitta, the hub of the wheel of life by all means.

16. Through wisdom, good qualities, knowledge as envisaged in the scripture and personal effort, if something is not attained, it is not attained by any means.

17. That which is attended with fear, with undesirable consequences, with loss of confidence or wealth, is the demon of mind and, casting it away, remain as you are.

18. Neither scripture nor relative nor preceptor nor any one individual can save a person who is completely enslaved by the demon of chitta.

19.   On the other hand, preceptor, scripture and relatives can save easily a person like dragging out a deer from a small pit if he is not enslaved by the demon of chitta.

20.   Great and small pleasures have to be discarded. The path of the wise should be adhered to. By enquiring into the nature of the Supreme Truth, get established in the non-dual Being.

21.   In this connection, hear about another viewpoint which is capable of destroying the great delusion, which was unfolded to me by Lord Shiva, who wears the moon in crest, for the sake of destruction of samsaric fear.

22.   There is the luminous celestial abode, as white as moon's rays, which is called Kailasa mountain and which is the abode of the Lord of Gowri.

23 & 24. In that abode resides the Supreme God, Hara who wears the moon on his head.

In that same mountain and on the bank of Ganga, I lived in a hermitage, rendering worship to Him as a penance which I practised for a long time.

25 & 26. O Rama, a long time was spent by me in the company of seers, in the composition of works on scriptural truths, in the gathering of flowers in baskets and in the collection of books, in that hermitage at Kailasa.

27 to 32. Once, on the eighth night after the full moon in the month of Sravana, when the first half of the night was drawing to a close, when total darkness and stillness prevailed all around, when I too, emerging from the samadhi state was lost in the enchanting external environment, I saw with wonder a bright effulgent shaft intensely luminous like a host of moons

manifesting suddenly in the forest and illuminating all the space around.

As I tried to understand what it was through inner vision, appeared on the mountain slope the crescent adorning Lord with his hand held by Gowri and with Nandi in the forefront leading them.

33 to 38. I alerted the disciples and, taking water and flowers, walked with humility towards Him. I offered flowers to the three-eyed God and arghya, pure water, and made prostrations to Him. At that, His moon-like cool, kind and tender glances which wipe away all sorrows bathed me over a long time. When the Lord was seated on a flower-bedecked slope, I approached him in due manner and again made offerings of water, flowers, etc. I offered bunches and bunches of mandara flowers. Repeated prostrations I made and I sang His praise in various ways. The Goddess Gowri, alongwith her divine attendants, was also worshipped by me in almost the same manner.

39.   At the conclusion of worship, in words as cool as that of moon's rays, the Lord spoke to me who was sitting before Him.

40 & 41. 'O Divine Soul, have you attained the repose in the Supreme that quietens all thoughts? Are thy perceptions lofty and ennobling? Does your penance proceed without hindrance? Is your mind satisfied and have all your mental fears subsided?'

42 to 44. O Rama, as the Lord, who is the sole cause of all the universe, spoke words with such tender concern, I replied, 'Supreme Lord, for those who are blessed to contemplate on you, there cannot be anything unattainable, there cannot be fear of anything. There are not beings in all the worlds who do not prostrate

before persons whose hearts are filled with bliss arising from thoughts of Thee.

45. There are lands, there are human habitations, there are country-sides and mountains in which people exclusively contemplating on Thee live.

46. O All-pervasive Being, contemplation of Thee is at once the fruit of past meritorious deeds and the nourisher of the present and future meritorious deeds.

47. Thy contemplation, O Lord, is a pot of ambrosial elixir, an effulgent mass that destroys the darkness and is the pathway to the city of liberation.

48. With the possession of the supreme wish-fulfilling jewel in the form of your contemplation, I have placed my foot on the entire store-house of dangers, O Lord of all beings!'

49. When I spoke thus, the Lord was delighted with me. O Rama, again I prostrated to Him and made this submission, which you may hear now.

50. O Supreme Lord, by thy grace all my desires remain completely fulfilled. Yet I seek thy clarification in regard to a matter.

51. Be pleased to tell me patiently the mode of worship of Ishvara which is blemishless, which is capable of destroying all sins and is the promoter of all auspicious qualities.

52. Maheshvara said: "O chief of the knowers of Brahman, listen to the excellent manner of worship of Ishvara.

53. *The Supreme Lord is not the lotus-eyed Vishnu; nor He is the three-eyed Shiva. The God is not a physical person nor is He a mental entity.*

The Luminous Consciousness that is unborn and eternal is called Deva, God.

54. How could this characteristic be found in a conditioned limited being. The unborn eternal self-revealing Consciousness is known to be Shiva.

55. The question 'Who is God?' has been answered thus. Do perform worship to the same Consciousness that is called God.

56. *Formal worship of God-in-form has been suggested only for those who cannot cognise Consciousness as Shiva. A short path is suggested only to the one who cannot undertake the long path.*

57. Space-like Chit alone exists without any boundary limit and without any objective externalisation and the same principle abides even after deluge.

58. That Shiva who is pure Chit is to be worshipped, according to those proficient in this knowledge, through the three important flowers of awareness, oneness, mental stillness.

59. If the God of the Self is worshipped through the flowers of serenity, awareness, etc., know that to be the proper worship of God. The worship done to the form is not so.

60. The Chit is unborn, eternal, non-dual and unconditioned. The bliss of liberation is not attained by any external mode of worship of such Being.

61. The self-cognising Chit is beyond all kalas, partial aspects of Truth, is the inner essence of all things, is the substratum of all manifest and unmanifest things and is of the nature of bare existence.

62. Swerving from the state of pure Chit, the same principle becomes vitiated by desire and in the natural course, it imagines inert matter and itself turns into objective entity.

63. Due to the interaction of the forces of space and time, the principle gets further enveloped by matter and becoming jiva, soul, assumes progressively the forms of intellect, ego and mind.

64. Having identified with mind, he gets completely immersed in samsara, like a brahmana becoming a chandala consequent on his thinking himself to be one.

65. The awareness, 'I am this body,' makes the knowledge tainted and immerses one in the mire of delusion and the soul has to experience one sorrow after another.

66. This misery which the soul has to undergo is entirely due to his sankalpa, thought. That being the case, by mere negation of sankalpa, thought, the misery can be wiped. Why do you feel helpless?

67. The individual, through imagination, drowns himself in sorrow and by avoiding all imagination, he experiences all happiness.

68. Through the wind of discrimination, scatter away the clouds bearing the water particle of sankalpa and, as sky of the summer, be the pure expanse.

69. Do thou attain serenity of mind and supreme bliss by removing the stain of thought in Self through the effort of Self.

70. The Self, though formless and is mere Consciousness, is the embodiment of all powers and as such is capable of contriving the appearance of samsara and its disappearance through the interplay of such powers.

71 & 72. The powers of the Supreme Self are endless. Such powers arise from, or are related to, desire, space, time, cosmic necessity and universal existence. These are powers that give rise to jnanam, wisdom and kriya,

activity, sense of doership and its absence.

73. Its power of display causes the samsara to manifest and its power of restraint brings to an end this samsara.

74. Of the several features of worship, the consecration of the body in fire is a purifying feature. Abandoning the physical and accepting the spiritual body through conscious effort is a holy act.

75. This Consciousness is God. He is supremely worthy of worship by all the wise, always. Worship of Him is of the nature of meditation on Him in the inner heart. There is no other form of worship of Him.

76 to 81. Therefore, through meditation, worship Him who is the support of all the three worlds, who is Consciousness, as radiant as a thousand suns, and who is the illuminator of all luminous things, who is the inner effulgence, who is the Self and the essence of the principle in heart, who has the infinite space as the upper neck, who has endless space for chest and feet, who has endless directions for arms and who has various worlds as different weapons, who has numerous unborn worlds in the corner of his heart, who is infinite mass of permeating light, who is pervading above, below, and in all sides always, is ever associated with Brahma, Indra, Hari, Rudra, and others; and all these cosmic manifestations may be contemplated as hairs in a row on His Being.

82. The various rope-like forces which operate the machine of the three-worlds, may be contemplated as the powers of desire, etc., pertaining to His body.

83. He is pure Chit, self-revealing Consciousness, all-pervasive and all-supporting. He is the God. He is the Supreme worthy of worship by the wise always.

84. He is infinite, the ultimate support, of the nature of bare existence, the author of world-spectacle. Time is His door-keeper.

85 & 86. His vision spreads in all directions; His capacity to smell permeates all places; His capacity to touch and taste is everywhere; He hears at every point. His mind is associated with everything. Also He is beyond mental reach and is everywhere. He is manifest as Shiva. Thinking of the Supreme as above, render worship in an appropriate manner.

87. This conscious Self who is God is not worshipped by external articles like fruits, flowers, etc. He is worshipped only through one's own awareness, which is attained without difficulty, which is eternally cool and which is ambrosial elixir.

88. Uninterrupted cognition of the pure inner Consciousness is what is supreme meditation, is what is supreme worship.

89. Be pure Chit as you see, hear, touch, inhale, eat, walk, sleep, talk, acquire and discard.

90. *Atma is worshipped by the article of meditation. Meditation represents the offering of flowers to Him. Without it and through other means, Atma is not at all attained.*

91. O wise man, through such meditation for thirteen minutes, even a stupid person gains the merit of having gifted a cow.

92. The person doing such worship of the Supreme for a hundred minutes, gains the merit of having performed asvamedha sacrifice.

93. Worshipping the Lord of Self for a duration of three

hours, a person gets the merit of a thousand asvamedha sacrifices.

94. He who worships the Self through the Self, through the offering and through the article of meditation for more number of hours, attains the merit of Rajasuya sacrifice.

95. Through such worship up to noon, one earns the merit of several Rajasuya sacrifices.

Through such worship the whole day, one abides in the supreme beatitude.

96. This is supreme yoga. This is supreme rite. I have told thus the external excellent worship of the Self.

97. Whether you are asleep or walking or standing, do contemplate always on the Supreme Principle immanent in the body.

98 & 99. Whether he is having sense contacts or is without them, whether he experiences rich pleasures or discards them, he is-by virtue of contemplation of the innate nature of sense knowledge-Consciousness, pure. Let him, through continuous awareness, worship the Lingam of Spirit.

100 to 105. Let him contemplate the luminous Consciousness which is present in mind, as mental faculty; which activates prana and apana; which is manifest in the centres of heart, neck and throat; which shines forth in the pedastal in the centre of the eye-brows; which is beyond the thirty-six categories of principles; which is beyond the mindless state, which has endless number of feet and other limbs and the features of hair, nail, etc., as the supreme God. Let him contemplate as follows:

The various strange powers, and different talents serve

me constantly as many wives do their great lover. The mind is the door-keeper who keeps me informed of the three worlds. Thought is my orderly at the door. Various sciences are the different ornaments that beautify me. Senses of action and knowledge are the various entrances. I am an infinite Being unconditioned by any object. I am the all-pervasive and all-inclusive Absolute.

106. By worshipping this imperishable Being with the oneness of vision, uniform attitude and identical form, serenity manifests in full measure.

107. *With the oneness of vision and uniform spirit, let him worship the Pure Consciousness through all experiences that accrue to him in the natural course.*

108. Effort should not at all be made to acquire anything specially. By renouncing the desire, let him worship the Shiva of Consciousness.

109. Let him worship Him through all acts of eating, drinking, diverse activities, sleeping, sitting and flying as they occur.

110. By cognising the Self through all delightful experiences of the nature of beloved's company, drinking, eating, etc., and other kindred pleasures, let him worship.

111. With such painful experiences caused by mental and physical maladies and ignorance and other distressing experiences that naturally happen, let him adore the Self.

112. Through poverty or kingship, whatever befalls in the natural course and through flowers of odd actions, adore the pure Self.

113. Through pleasure, righteous, or sinful, gratified or renounced adore the awakened luminous Self.

114. Whatever has passed away, forget; whatever comes your way, accept with an unexcited mind. And that is the true adoration of the Self.

115. May the person who is absorbed in the adoration of the Self convert every object into Self, be it seemingly delightful or seemingly disturbing.

116. All that exists in all forms is beneficial and all this is Brahman-with such a conviction, let him adore the Self.

117. By the seer's experiences, all things, as they are, attained or not attained, and all experiences, have to be undergone by him like the ocean receiving all kinds of rivers.

118. No excitement should be evinced in matters, big or small, and all have to be ignored like formations of clouds in the sky.

119. Adore the Self by accepting, with an even disposition, whatever good or bad things happen as a result of the interplay of space, time, action, etc.

120. All those articles of worship which have been stipulated in the adoration of Self, having different tastes, become wholly sweet, when contemplated upon as Chit-rasa.

121. Whether they are saltish or sour or astringent or bitter or a combination of different tastes, if they are contemplated upon as Chit, they all become sweet.

122. Oneness is sweet and delicious and its taste is beyond the sense. When a thing is contemplated upon as permeated by Chit-essence, it becomes the elixir.

123. Whatever is contemplated upon as permeated by Chit, the spirit of oneness, that becomes sweet as if it is a part of the nectarine moon.

124. The Self should be wholeheartedly contemplated by the seer, as a full moon, as a mass of pure Consciousness, as unmodifying as stone.

125. Abide as the supreme master of the body, with all desires erased away from the mind, and propitiated by all kinds of pleasures and sorrows, real or otherwise, brought about by factors of time, space, instruments, etc.

126. The wise man, by employing pure avidya eliminates impure avidya as a clever person removes the stain on the cloth by contrary stain.

127. Although they are not causative, the pure aspects of avidya like preceptor, his instructions, etc., turn out to be the means for dawn of Self-realisation.

128. With Guru's instruction intended to impart the means of Self-realisation to the disciple taking place although the Truth cannot be taught and the Self cannot be seen the Self spontaneously manifests.

129. *The Self is not awakened by the understanding of scriptural teaching, nor also by the word of the preceptor. The Self gets awakened on its own as a result of its inherent capacity of revelation.*

130. The Self is not awakened except with the help of preceptor's instruction, scripture, etc. United together these elements bring about the revelation of Self.

131. With the existential union of preceptor, scripture and disciple over a long time, Self-revelation takes place, like worldly activity after dawn.

132. O Chief of Seers, by doing such worship of God everyday, the enlightened soul reaches that state wherein we Divine Beings as well would be regarded as only servants.

133. O Seer, these three worlds, though non-existent, appear as existent. They are mere illusory projection. There is nothing else.

134. That which is called by such terms as Brahman is Samvid, Intelligence. This Pure Intelligence turns, as it were, into the knowable and assumes various names.

135. Because of contemplation of it as knowable for a second, the Chit assumes the form of ego like the man becoming woods and elephant in a dream.

136. This ego is joined by space and time, as if they are its companions, though they are non-existent.

137 & 138. Enveloped by such elements, the same principle comes to be called as jiva. Ever rooted in ignorance, the jiva-consciousness acquiring determining faculty, becomes intellect. Moreover, the jiva gets associated with the powers of sound, activity and wisdom.

139. The jiva, united with all such factors, very soon becomes inclined to imagination and as a consequence, becomes mind, the seed of imagination.

140. That mind becomes worthy of being called by the wise as ativahika, ethereal body. It has the proclivity to reflect upon, and limitless are its powers. It assumes the form of space and manifests as worlds.

141. Like the imaginary devil, the vasana of chitta is really non-existent. It brings forth the world. With its extinction, there is peace that is endless.

142. In the ego, in the world, in the water of mirage, he who has trust stands as a condemned man. Such a person is not worthy of being instructed.

143. The enlightened seer gives instruction only to the deserving wise soul and not to the light-hearted, deluded, unwise person. He who instructs the stupid

gives his beautiful daughter in marriage to a dream son-in-law.

144. What you have enquired, I have explained, O seer, may you be happy. Let me leave for abode. O Parvati, rise up.'

145. After saying thus, the blue-necked Shiva received the salutation offered by me in the form of flowers and swept across the sky alongwith the attendants.

146. Since then I am doing the same kind of worship of the Self till now and I keep doing it without neglect.

147. Through this method of propitiation, O Rama, those vasanas, though they generate activity, are borne by me with ease.

148. By propitiating the Self through flowers in the form of natural activities, as ordained by time, day and night, I ensure that the worship is done always, even when seemingly interrupted.

149. The contact between the sense and the object is natural for all creatures. But the contemplation of the Self pursued by Yogis turns the sense-experience into worship of Self.

150. O Rama, through such vision of natural detachment, do thou roam around the earth wherein worldly travail does not exist and you will not experience pain.

151. Sri Rama said, "O Divine Seer, my doubts remain completely cleared. All that has to be known has been known. Supreme fulfillment has arisen in my heart.

152. The mind has acquired immense strength, like that of an elephant, capable of fighting the war of samsara, which cannot be assailed by anyone else and which has vanquished the enemies in the form of desires.

153. The mind has cast away the fancies and thoughts.
The desires have been extinguished and there is
supreme confidence. An extraordinary serenity which
is not seen in all the worlds floods into the inner heart
of mine."

406

Chapter-3

The Story of Bilva Fruit

Vasishta said:

1. Sri Rama asked, "Drinking the nectar of your words never satiates me. O Divine Seer, do tell me again the mode of realisation of Truth."

2. *Sri Vasishta said: "Who has not experienced the truth that a thing newly acquired does not give to the person, during the next second, the same delight which it gives during the first second?*

3. A thing which is gratifying when it is just acquired is not so thereafter. Only a child, and not anyone else, gets attached to such a thing which is pleasing for a second only.

4. For the happiness that one gets from the thing at the stage it is desired, the desire is the real cause. Happiness always terminates in unhappiness. Therefore, discard the desire.

5. Let desire cease to be so, let contemplation of things get annihilated. Let mind become no-mind and let life be lived in a detached manner.

6. With the inner senses cleansed by vasanas while performing external actions, you will not get agitated, like the space remaining unaffected by a hundred changes.

7. The manifestation and subsidence of thought represent creation and dissolution of the world. Through elimination of vasana and control of prana, render the mind lifeless.

8.   The rise and subsidance of prana is the creation and dissolution of Universe. Through practice of prana-control, prevent the manifestation of prana.

9.   The presence and absence of ignorance is the cause of performance of karmas and the non-performance of them. Through resort to preceptor, study of scripture, self-control, etc., destroy the ignorance.

10. By mere prevention of cognition, mind is turned into no-mind. It is also brought about by control of prana. The plane attained by such means is beatitude.

11. The happiness that arises at the contact of the sense with the object is really Supreme Reality. By contemplation of the inner Consciousness Brahman, the mind can be rendered non-existent.

12. When the mind has not manifested, there is experience of supreme bliss, which neither increases nor decreases, which rises not nor sets.

13. The mind of an enlightened person is not called mind. His mind is called Sattva. Mind assumes the nature of diverse objects. Sattva becomes Brahman through realisation-like copper becoming gold.

14. Chitta, after indulging in worldly pursuits, passes into turiya state when it becomes the principle of Chit, and turiyatita state is also experienced thereafter.

When the mind pases from the experience of waking, dreaming, sleep state into the transcendental state, it is called turiya, fourth. When the mind remains always in the transcendental state, it is called tiriyatita. When the transcendental state alternates with other states, it is turiya; when the transcendental state remains uninterrupted by other states, it is turiyatita. S. T.

15. The non-dual Brahman only, through manifold delusions in the form of vast universe, etc., manifests in diverse forms. My dear, there is nothing else like chitta. All this is only an appearance, as in a dream.

16. O Rama, hear this brief interesting story, which will cause wonder, for a better understanding.

17. There is this mighty Bilva Fruit, several thousand miles vast which is beautiful and ripe and unshrinking despite its existence for several yuga-cycles.

18. Though old, it is fresh like tender shoots and pleasing to look at. It remains unshaken even by the mighty winds of the deluge time.

19. Huge distances covering lakhs of miles do not in any way condition it. It is the ultimate cause of the universe.

20. Inside the Bilva fruit, even huge brahmandas, universes, get arranged in rows like small pebbles at the foot of a hill, as if in play.

21. The fruit never attains that ripeness which makes it fall. Though it is always ripe, it does not become decomposed.

22. The essence of the entire fruit gets condensed into majja, the pulp of intelligence, that has wondrous vigour.

23. The Intelligence that pervades it wholly casts over itself this creative look.

24. 'This is endless space...this is the aspect of Time...this is Necessity ever active...this is Activity of the nature of movement.

25. This is the great hall of Brahmanda...these are its creation...This is the mode of creation.'-Thus all these

are manifestations of the wondrous power of the Bilva's essence."

26. Sri Rama said, "O Divine Master! Knower of all! I think that in the name of Bilva fruit, the vast essence of Consciousness has been described by you.

27. In the pulp of Chit comprising 'I' and 'This,' there is absolutely no difference caused by notions of duality and non-duality.

28. Just as the essence of pumpkin of Brahmanda manifests as Meru, etc., so the essence within the Bilva manifests as Brahmanda and other worlds."

Chapter-4

The Story of A Block of Stone

Sri Vasishta said:

1. "O Rama of lotus face, hear another interesting story which is beautiful, to be described by me now.

2. There is a huge block of stone, dense, soft, shining, concentrated and massive.

3. Within it, O Rama, there are a number of lotus blossoms as in a pond.

4. Some of them are inter-locked. Some of them are totally disconnected with each other. Some have roots above and some below. Some have no roots.

5. Near these lotus blossoms are innumerable conches as also groups of chakras in huge lotus-like forms."

6. Sri Rama said, "I have truly seen such a block of stone. In the place Salagrama, such a stone exists over the head of Hari."

7. Sri Vasishta said: "I have spoken to you about the stone of Chit in which worlds exist. The chit is also a stone because it is a concentrated homogenous mass.

8. Although it is dense and concentrated in form, there exists within it a number of worlds, as air in space.

9. Heaven, earth, wind, sky, mountain, different directions, exist within that stone, though there are no space-zones within it.

10. The pictures of sankha and chakra drawn on the stone do not exist independent of the stone. The worlds,

past, present and future, manifest within the Chit Block and are, therefore, not different from it.

11. Though the inner configurations of a stone may be of various forms, it is still a single mass. Even so, the Chit containing within it worlds, does not cease to be a single mass.

12. Just as the lotús, visualised within the stone, is not different from the stone, the world manifesting within Chit is not different from Chit any time.

13. The forms of lotus within the stone, as the radiation within the mirage, neither come into existence nor go out of existence. So is creation in Chit.

14. As there is child within the womb of woman, as there is ‘pulp within the Bilva fruit, so there are endless number of worlds within Chit.

15. As there are chakra and padma forms within the stone, there are worlds in sleep-like condition within Chit.

16. That which the Chit imagines, the Chit becomes. Brahman is all and manifests in different forms, as if in sleep-like condition.

17. Various huge manifestations which are caused by the world-delusion are really in a sleep-like state, like the lotus within the stone.

18. This world-spectacle abides in sleeping state in the tranquil spirit which is Self. Creations, etc., exist in Chit as lotus in stone and do not become objectively real."

Chapter-5

The Story of Arjuna

1. Sri Rama submitted, "The Truth that has to be known has been known. The Truth that has to be seen has been seen. However I ask further only to improve my understanding.

2. That which is capable of creating the world, that which is pure as mirror, that which is called the puryashtaka- the eight-centred city-O Divine Master, what is its real form?"

3. Sri Vasishta said: "The beginningless and blemishless Brahman which is the cause of the universe, the same associated with imagination is called jiva, soul.

4. The pure chit is bereft of imagination; and the same externally inclined, is called jiva.

5 & 6. That jiva manifesting in the body acts further and gains in form; through self-identification, becomes ego; through imagination becomes mind; through decisiveness, the intellect; through imagination of senses, the senses. Thinking of body, chit becomes body and of pot, becomes pot. This is the nature of Self and jiva is known as puryashtaka.

7. That Consciousness which is called jiva, which manifests as knowership, doership, enjoyership, witnessing tendency is known as puryashtaka.

8. Only through the influence of puryashtaka, the soul moves on from dream to dream and sees unreal things. So is the world.

413

9 & 10. O lotus-eyed Rama, it is by adhering to the auspicious detachment as taught by Hari, Pandu's son Arjuna, the liberated soul, will live happily and spend the life without sorrow."

11.   Sri Rama asked, "O Seer, when is that great soul, Arjuna, Pandu's son, to be born? What kind of detachment Hari is going to teach about to him?"

12 to 15. Sri Vasishta said: "The Divine Yama sometimes performs penance at the conclusion of each four-yuga period to ward off the sin of killing people. He performed penance for ten or twelve or sixteen years. When he remained indifferent to his functions, he did not kill people of the world. As a result, the earth was filled with living creatures completely, like the elephant with flies in the rainy season.

16 & 17. O Rama, the celestials resort to strange means to remove the excess burden of the earth and decimate the population. Thus hundreds of yugas, innumerable events passed off as also countless number of worlds.

18 to 22. Vaivasvatha Yama, the God-head representing the ancestors at the end of some yuga-cycles, will perform penance for the eradication of the sin of killing people for twelve years in Nirvikalpa Samadhi. This earth, getting filled with living creatures and oppressed by heavy burden, will undergo hardship. Tormented by the weight, the earth will take refuge in Hari. Hari will descend on earth assuming two bodies-one as the son of Vasudeva and called Vaasudeva and the second as Pandu's son, Arjuna.

23.   When Arjuna has to fight the most gruesome battle against the sons of Dhritharasthra, all the relations will join the battle.

24. Seeing all his relations in the battlefield in the jaws of death, Arjuna will get despondent and decline to fight.

25. Hari, with his enlightened body will teach Arjuna through appropriate counsels for achieving the intended aim.

26. "O king among lions, know the Self as infinite, unmanifest, unborn, eternal Consciousness without any stain. You are unborn, eternal and blissful.

27. The Self is not born, does not die any time; after coming into existence, He does not cease to be. He is unborn, eternal, everlasting, ancient. He is not dead when the body is killed.

28. O Dhananjaya, abide in yoga and do the duties without attachment. Consecrating every deed in Brahman, you become Brahman instantly.

29. By surrendering all things to the Supreme Ruler by cognising the Supreme Ruler everywhere, be the Supreme God, the Self of all beings, adorning the earth.

30. By renouncing all thoughts, by attaining oneness of vision, by the contemplation of Self through the practice of renunciation, be a liberated soul."

31 & 32. Arjuna asked, "O Divine Master, for destroying the vast delusion of my heart, do explain in proper sequence what is renunciation of attachment? What is concentration in Brahman? What is consecration in God? What is Sanyasa? What is jnana? What is yoga? How are they distinct?"

33. Supreme Lord said, "When all desires have become extinguished, when the strong vasanas have been

eliminated, the formless Consciousness that subsists is known to be Brahman.

34. The effort to attain that wisdom is known as jnanam and yoga according to wise people.

Brahman is all, the world as well as My-self-such attitude is consecration in Brahman.

35. The renunciation of fruits of actions is known by the wise as sanyasa.

36. To regard all thoughts and manifestations as pervaded by God and to be rid of all notions of duality is self-surrender to God.

37. Exclusively contemplate on Me, be devoted to Me, do sacrifice for My sake, prostrate unto Me. By being devoted to Me thus, you will reach only Me.

38. Ordinary, transcendental-two such forms I have, O blemishless one. The one endowed with hands, conch, and chakra, etc., is ordinary.

39. The transcendental form of mine is beginningless, all-pervasive and taintless. This is called by such names as Brahman, Atma and Paramatma.

40. As long as you are not awakened, there is identification with non-self; till then be devoted to the Godhead with four hands.

41. In course of time, getting illumined, you will know the Supreme Being-which is my transcendental form-and you will not be born again as a consequence thereof.

42. Those who have cast away pride, delusion, attachment, are devoted to contemplation of Self, are devoid of desires, are beyond pairs of opposites of pleasures, pain and sorrow-such persons freed from ignorance reach the imperishable Supreme.

43.   He whose actions are bereft of desire and motive, whose deeds have all been burnt by wisdom is called a pandita, a man of wisdom, by knowledgeable persons.

44.   Do free yourself from notions of good and bad, and remaining stabilised in sattvic nature, do not think of your welfare and be stablised in Self. Attending to things as they arise, be an adornment of the earth.

45.   Let the Vindhya hills break into pieces; let the mighty wind blow as in deluge. The path taught by the Guru and the Sastra is not be abandoned by the intelligent person.

46.   *It is due to the ignorance of the Self, vasana gets formed. With the awareness of the Self dawning, the vasana gets extinguished."*

47.   As the Lord of the three worlds spoke thus, Arjuna was lost in silence for a while, like the bee in the lotus cluster. Pandu's son again spoke thus:

48.   Arjuna said, "All despondency has gone away, O Divine Master, my mind has experienced great enlightenment, as a result of thy words, even as the worlds get awakened by the Lord of the day, Sun."

Chapter-6

The Story of Hundred Rudras

Vasishta said:

1. "O Rama, listen to an ancient story of an ascetic who was capable of pursuing deep contemplation.

2. There was a hermit who was devoted to the practice of samadhi and he was spending the entire day through such self-contemplation.

3. His mind perfected by samadhi had become so pure that whatever it thought, it became the object instantly, like the waters assuming the form of wave.

4. Once he took respite from samadhi and sitting on his seat contemplated on the worldly process.

5. As he was contemplating, a thought arose in his mind spontaneously-'for the love of it, let me act like a common man.'

6. Thinking thus, his mind took the form of another individual, like the waters assuming the form of wave by mere discarding of the former state.

7. After assuming through imagination, the existence of an individual, he also named himself, 'I am jivata,' through sheer accident.

8. That imagined individual roamed around for long in a dream-city among its streets.

9 & 10. He drank intoxicant drinks and passed into oblivion and sleep. He saw in dream that he was a brahmana who was completely satisfied with his learning and holy conduct. He became a brahmana as a result of

mere imagination, like reaching one place from another.

11. Once, that brahmana, after the day's activities, slept deeply, like the tree in the form of seed. The brahmana saw himself as a great chieftain.

12. The chieftain, after food, slept deeply and saw himself in a dream as a great ruler with a vast kingdom.

13. As a king he slept deeply without any desire and saw himself as a celestial nymph.

14. The celestial nymph, tired of amorous sports, slept deeply and saw herself in dream as a deer.

15. The deer with fleeting looks fell asleep and because of intense thought saw herself as a creeper.

16. Even animals cognise dreams as a result of inherent nature. Mind has an indestructible tendency to remember things seen and heard.

17. The deer became a creeper, filled with flowers and fruits, in the bower, which a forest nymph frequented.

18. The creeper assuming the form of potential seed was self-cognisant and saw its own full form.

19. Spending some time in an inert form of sleep, the creeper saw itself as a bee.

20. The bee got attached to the lotus blossoms on the stalk. Even the mind of intelligent beings gets fascinated only by some object.

21. An elephant came to pluck the lotus. Stupid beings rise to power only for the destruction of the beautiful things.

22. The bee alongwith the lotus got crushed. She saw the elephant and as a result of contemplation of the

elephant while borne by its scented trunk, saw herself as elephant.

23. The bee became an elephant which fell into a huge pit.

24. The elephant became a king's favourite and was tamed suitably. It got killed in some battle.

25. The elephant by the contemplation of the bee over its neck became a bee again.

26. The bee got killed by an elephant again. By her cognition of the hamsa bird around, the bee became an ordinary hamsa bird.

27. The hamsa by uniting with other birds, became born as a hamsa bird in Brahmasaras lake. After being born in the Brahmasaras, it sported in the lake.

28. The bird saw once Rudra in his city. Then it had the firm understanding 'I am *Rudra*.'

29 & 30. It assumed the form of *Rudra* and happily went around. Because of the conduct as that of a devotee of Shiva, and because of association with persons of holy conduct, *Rudra* came to possess pure and complete knowledge about all past lives.

31. With a clear cognition of the past, the God Hara told him while in solitude, about the hundred dream manifestations of his.

32. "How wonderful is Maya? How does it delude the world! Though absolutely unreal like the waters of the mirage, they look real.

33. Thus in a variety of forms in the world of samsara, I have been wandering repeatedly in seemingly real environment.

34. In a creation I was a person called Jivata; in some

other a great brahmana and in another a king.

35 to 46. I was a hamsa in lotus pond, an elephant in Vindhya Hill. Having passed through such hundred lives, I have become a Rudra. Several yugas and thousands of years have been spent in these several lives. Let me see each such life and by imparting to each, the right vision make them all one with me.'

Deciding thus, *Rudra* went to the world where the hermit lived in a hermitage. He was there like a corpse. *Rudra* reminded the hermit of his real nature and the hermit too got over the illusion, recognised himself as Rudra. He also recognised how he became Jivata. Though there was nothing to be wondered at from the point of view of Reality, he still became wonderstruck.

Now *Rudra* and the hermit set out for the world of Jivata in some corner of Chit-akasa. They awakened him, reminded him and all the three were surprised.

Rudra, hermit and Jivata had one form and also three forms. Thereafter they passed other worlds and became united with their other forms in all previous lives. All of them had acquired divine knowledge, being aspects of Rudra. Permitted by Rudra, all of them in various forms returned to their own worlds. The hermit, Jivata, etc., seeing the nature of Maya and life, went back to their abodes and after spending their lives in the company of their spouses, they joined Rudra and along with him became one with the Supreme Reality.

47. Sri Vasishta said: "Whatever has been seen exists as it was seen in the chit-treasure. One attains from it whatever one wants because it is all-containing.

48. Whatever was seen in a dream, whatever was imagined exists in it for all time in the same manner.

49. The dream objects, the imagined objects, however are obtained only in the plane which can be attained by practice of supreme yoga.

50. Those who have attained this yogic vision and vision of wisdom see everything everywhere. Sankara and other Gods are among them.

51. All the aims of one are accomplished by one established in the single Consciousness. By walking southwards how can one reach a northern destination?

52. The desired object is attained only by him who pursues it in the appropriate plane. The object in front is obtained only by the one who seeks the object in the same plane.

53. When the object lodged in the mind is the one in front of him, and he pursues with effort to attain some other desired object, since he is not entirely attached to one, he loses both.

54. 'Let me be a Vidhyadhara now,' 'let me be a brahmana proficient in Vedic lore'-this kind of single-mindedness is the example in attainment of things.

55. Therefore through such single-minded absorption, the jiva as hermit became a Rudra and whatever Rudra willed became real.

56. Those jivas who seemingly came into existence as a result of the hermit's will began to see these distinct worlds, because being aspects of Rudra, their wishes materialised.

57 & 58. Thus, those who were born as jivas because of the hermit's will, went to their respective worlds as a result of Rudra's will. Afterwards they joined Rudra and

attained the plane of Supreme Rudra."

59. Sri Rama asked, "Then, as a result of the hermit's will, how could jivata, brahmana, etc., become real? How can an imagined object be real?"

60. Sri Vasishta said: "One becomes through sankalpa a thousand, like Janardhana assuming a hundred manifestations to keep the world in order.

61. Thus through the Will of the hermit comes into existence Jivata, brahmana, etc. Being aspects of Pure-Chit, they become real, as it were."

Chapter-7

The Story of a Vetala

Vasishta said:

1. "Becoming silent as if in sleep, discarding all mental fancies, and freed from all tainted desires, remain established in Supreme Consciousness."

2. Sri Rama asked, "O Divine Seer, Master of Silence, silence of speech, silence of senses, silence of body I know about. What is called silence of sleep?"

3. Sri Vasishta said: "O Rama, the muni, contemplative soul is considered to belong to two types by the knowledgeable seers. The one is physical penitent, the other is jivanmukta, the liberated soul.

4. The physical penitent is one who is not capable of contemplation of Self, who is attached to external rites and who forcefully restrains the sense through means like prana-control.

5. He is a liberated soul, who sees things as they are, who is absorbed in the contemplation of Self, who, though looks worldly, is fully satisfied within.

6. The decisive conviction manifesting at the mental plane in the case of these two types of ascetics is called by the word 'mounam,' 'silence.'

7. Restraint of speech is silence of mouth, forcible restraint of senses is silence of senses, abandoning all activities and remaining wood-like is silence of body.

8. All the three arise out of vasana-filled mind and the

person who observes these forced restraints is the physical penitent.

9. He who is established in Self-Consciousness, which is distinctionless, which is one's natural state, which is unborn and eternal, whether he keeps meditating or not, is practising the silence of sleep.

10. He who sees the manifold world as it really is and knows it as permeated by Brahman is practising what is called the silence of sleep.

11. The divergent perceptions are really the blissful Consciousness and abidance in infinite awareness is silence of sleep.

12. What is seen as space is not space really. The world exists and exists not. He who perceives thus is calm in spirit and is practising the silence of sleep.

13. This silence of sleep is attained by yogis of two types. Sankhya yogis are one group. Yoga-yogis are the other group.

14. They are called Sankhya yogis who through perfect wisdom alone pass into concentrated samadhi; those who through discrimination alone attain the supreme awareness.

15. They are called Yoga-yogis who by restraining prana, apana, etc., attain to the supreme state.

16. The plane of supreme beatitude that is natural is worthy of attainment by all. That which is attainable through Sankhya wisdom is attained as well by yoga.

17. That subtlest plane, in which the vasana ridden mind and prana, are not even cognised is indeed the supreme state.

18. Mind is non-existent. It manifests merely because of

lack of discrimination, like cognition of one's death in dream. When enquired, it ceases to exist.

19. Concentrated contemplation of single truth, control of prana, mental control-these represent all the means to Moksha, liberation.

20. Contemplation of single truth, restraint of prana, extinction of mind-if one of these is attained, the others are also attained.

21. The mind and prana of the creatures are inseparably connected with each other, like flower and fragrance, like the seed and oil.

22. They are mutually the support and the supported. If one is not there, the other also ceases to exist. By their extinction, they bring about supreme liberation.

23. Contemplate on the single truth, until the mind attains all-pervasiveness, as a result of continued practice.

24. As a result of long practice, when the mind rids itself of all fancies and contemplates on a single object, it becomes that instantly.

25. O Rama, do thou hear this dialogue, which comes to my mind in the present context, which was initiated by a vetala, so that the dream of worldly life may subside.

26. There is, in the Vindhya hill, a vetala of vast size. He came to a nearby kingdom with a view to kill people for food.

27. That vetala had lived before in a country of righteous people, duly fed by enormous offerings and so was happy and contented there.

28. Even when he was afflicted with hunger, he did not

kill one who had strayed into his sight, if he had not committed any fault. Wise persons always follow the righteous path.

29. In course of time, he walked into a neighbouring land. Propelled by hunger, he wanted to eat someone with a justifiable reason.

30. There he saw a king who had come out for nocturnal inspection. The vetala spoke to him in a loud and fierce voice.

31. Vetala said, 'O king, you have reached the hands of a frightful vetala, which I am. Where do you attempt to go? You are lost. Be my food today.'

32. King said, 'O the nocturnal wanderer! If without justification, you eat me, your head will break into a hundred pieces. Let there be no doubt about it.'

33. Vetala said, 'My eating you is not improper. I call it proper. Being a king, you have to fulfill all the desires of people who approach you for that purpose.

34. O king, it behoves you to give appropriate replies to my questions which I ask now.

35. Of the rays of which sun the brahmandas, universes are like particles floating in them?

What is the wind which tosses these about the vast sky like dust particles?

36. As one moves from one dream to another on numberless occasions, what does he discard and what is the pure luminous principle that he does not discard?

37. The plantain-trunk, uncovered veil after veil, is still the same stalk. What is the atom, which divided and divided further, is still the same?

38. Sun, Moon, etc., which pervade Brahmanda do not discard that atomic size and of what great atom, it is a part?

39. Of which partless atom or mountain, the three-world-complex is like a massive entity, like the inner substance of a stone?"

40. Sri Vasishta said: "When the vetala put these questions, the king spoke thus after a smile, in which the lustre of his teeth seemed to illumine his apparel and spear.

41. The king said, 'He is chit-Surya that illumines and heats all the universe. This effulgent sun of Consciousness, activating the minds of jivas, is a supreme sun.

42. All these worlds are particles of that supreme sun of wisdom; they are illuminated by it, created by it.

43. Time, Space, Movement, Jiva are all permeated by Chit, the pure Being.

44. In the presence of the wind of Paramatma, the Supreme Self, all the cosmic bodies keep revolving. The same supreme existence like the flower, itself manifesting as flower and fragrance, manifests in distinct forms which however are not real.

45. In the great dream of worldly life, a person moving from one dream-life to another does not abandon the basic nature of Brahman, that is peaceful.

46. Even as the plantain trunk, uncovered further and further, is only plantain stalk, the world also uncovered further and further is only an illusory modification of Brahman.

47. Since He is very subtle and also not attainable, He is

atom-like. Since He is infinite, He is the cause of even Meru.

48.   Even Meru appears like an atom in His presence.

49.   Since He is unattainable, He is sutble atom; since He is all-pervasive, He is vast like a mountain. Although He manifests with diverse limbs, He is partless.

50.   He is of the nature of mere Consciousness. He is the substrate of the universe. As such the world is the condensed essence of Consciousness. The world has, at its centre, the Consciousness, that being its substrate.'

51.   Thus hearing from the mouth of the king, vetala became silent, since he had pursued enquiry and contemplation of Self.

52.   Becoming very calm, he went to a lonely spot and forgetting the passing hunger, plunged into uninterrupted contemplation."

Chapter-8

The Story of Bhagiratha

1.   Sri Vasishta said: "Withdraw the mind from all objects and with a heart in which there is fullness, do attend to things of the moment and remain calm without desire.

2.   With an oneness of vision, make the mind, through the mind, expansive and remain the calm Self.

3.   Even the unattainable is attained by a person, if he is firm, intelligent and mindful of tasks that arise at the moment, as in the case of Bhagiratha."

4.   Sri Rama asked, "How, through mental sagacity, the descent of Ganga was achieved by Bhagiratha, the king, kindly explain, O Master!"

5.   Sri Vasishta said: "There was a virtuous ruler called Bhagiratha. His kingdom was like a shining mark on the forehead of the entire earth surrounded by waters.

6.   From him, who possessed moon-like countenance, people got whatever they desired, as from the gem Chintamani.

7.   Through the effort of him, who was the friend of the whole universe, Ganga was brought to the patala region and his ancestors there were united with Brahmaloka.

8 & 9. Though the king was young, he contemplated about the worldly life. He was plunged into deep enquiry by a mind that had become confounded, dispassionate and inquisitive, even in his youth. It was, as if, a

430

creeper had grown and spread in the desert.

10 & 11. The great ruler reflected in solitude thus: 'This worldly life so full of strife is meaningless. The day follows the night again. The same acts of charity again and again. The person engaged in ceaseless activity finds it a senseless repetition.

12. That is a good act by which nothing else is left to be attained and any other act is only a precursor to evil.

13. By doing repeatedly the same acts, a fool does not get ashamed. Should a wise man also do the same like the child?"

14. Disgruntled with worldly life thus and also frightened by it, Bhagiratha sought the preceptor Tritula and asked him.

15. "O Divine Seer, how are all the sorrows of life like old age, death, delusion and other fearful things brought to an end?"

16 & 17. Tritula said, "O blemishless one, through distinctionless perception of the knowable as a whole, through the practice of oneness of vision, and through fullness at heart, all sorrows perish, all fetters get loosened, all actions and doubts get destroyed.

18. The knowable is Atma, Self, of the nature of pure Consciousness. The Self is all-pervasive and eternal. He neither rises nor sets."

19 & 20. Bhagiratha asked, 'O great seer, the all-pervasive pure Consciousness alone exists and it is immutable. Other things like body do not exist. I know so much. But the understanding is not firm enough, O Master. How can I ever be mere Consciousness always?'

21. Tritula said, 'When mind, through wisdom, becomes one with the knowable, the Self shining within heart,

431

the jiva attains to all-pervasive nature and is not born again.

22 to 25. Non-attachment, non-identification with sons, wives, houses, etc., equanimity in attitude towards agreeable and disagreeable things, exclusive contemplation of Self without interruption, resort to solitude, disinterest in society, devout contemplation of Self, cognition of the Supreme Truth-all these are spoken of as jnanam, but are means to jnanam, wisdom. All things other than these pertain to ignorance.

O king, the extinction of ego brings about the extinction of desire and aversion, cures the malady of samsara. With such extinction of ego, wisdom dawns."

26. Bhagiratha said, "The ahambhava, ego, is well-entrenched in one's body as a deep-rooted tree in a mountain. O noble soul, tell me how this ego is abandoned?"

27. Tritula said, "Discard the desire for pleasures through spiritual discipline and where there is expanded awareness, the ego gets dissolved.

28. As long as the nest-like inner mind protected by modesty, etc., remains unpunctured and the state of utter non-possession is not attained, the ego will flourish.

29. If you renounce all these mentally and remain established in Consciousness, that leads to the extinction of ego. You have attained supreme beatitude.

30. With all thoughts got rid of, without any fear, without desires, if you give over the prosperous kingdom to the enemies and remain without any possession, and

if bereft of all pride, seek alms in the enemy's kingdom, and abandon the sense 'mine,' you have attained to a very lofty state."

31.   Sri Vasishta said: "Bhagiratha, after hearing these words of the preceptor, decided within himself what he should do and then pursued his routine tasks.

32.   After some days, he performed the Agnishtoma sacrifice so that he could make complete renunciation.

33.   He gifted away cows, horses, gold, wealth, completely to brahmanas, celestials, the needy, the relations, etc., in accordance with their merits.

34.   In a matter of three days, Bhagiratha gave away all that he had. He had only the clothes left on him.

35.   Then he gave away to his enemy, the king of neighbouring land, the kingdom which was full of wealth, but the people of which were distressed at heart.

36.   When the enemy had occupied his entire land and mansion, the new ascetic with his cloth alone as his possession, left his own kingdom.

37.   The courageous soul lived in that village, that forest, that city, where his name is not known and where he cannot be identified by his appearance.

38.   Within a short time, all his mental fancies and desires got extinguished. With supreme tranquility, he attained repose in the Self.

39.   He roamed all over the earth and by a coincidence, he happened to come to his own kingdom occupied by the enemy.

40.   He sought alms from all houses in the natural course, including from those of the nobles and ministers.

41.   The nobles and the ministers came to know that he was Bhagiratha and began to adore him in due manner, though with a heavy heart.

42.   "Master, take back the kingdom"-though he was thus requested by the enemy, the seer did not take anything. He accepted not even a straw excepting the food.

43.   After spending some days there, he went on to a different land. People were grief-stricken and lamented, 'This is Bhagiratha! What a misfortune!'

44.   Having attained perfect repose, he was happy and calm. Immersed in the bliss of Self, he once came across the preceptor Tritula.

45.   He received him properly, honoured him and lived with him for some time in the woods, village, city, etc.

46.   The Guru and disciple had attained perfect oneness of vision and were identical in conduct. Remaining contented, they considered the body a burden.

47.   'What does it matter whether the body remains or is abandoned? Let it carry on with its usual routines, usual conduct, usual disposition.'

48.   Deciding thus, they lived on and moved from one wood to another. They were not elated nor grief-stricken nor were distinctly conscious of either.

49.   Wealth, houses, prosperity, riches, eight-fold powers- all these were offered to them by the celestials who were delighted with them but they thought of them as mere straw.

50 to 57. Once, in the capital of the neighbouring kingdom, the king who had no progeny to succeed was snatched away by Yama, like meat by fish. The distressed

citizens were on the lookout for a king who was without a kingdom and who was endowed with noble qualities. They came across Bhagiratha seeking alms in the guise of a seer. They recognised him, brought him to the kingdom and made him the king. Bhagiratha was surrounded by an army instantly, like the lake getting filled with waters in the rainy season. He ascended the royal elephant. 'Hail Bhagiratha, the Lord of earth'-such shouts resounded everywhere-in caves and hills.

There, as he was ruling the kingdom duly honoured by people, the citizens of his previous kingdom came and told him, 'He who was made the king of our land before by you is dead. He has been swallowed by Mrityu, Death, as meat by the fish. Be pleased to rule over that kingdom as well. To abandon a thing which has come unsought is not proper."

58 to 61. Requested thus by citizens, the king approved their suggestion and became the sovereign of the land surrounded by the seven seas. He was calm even-minded in attitude, contemplative. Without desire and jealousy, he attended to the natural tasks without any deep interest.

He performed gruesome penance for several hundred years and brought down Ganga to the earth for the emancipation of his ancestors.

Ganga coursed through the earth a long distance singing all along the way the greatness of the ruler, Bhagiratha."

Chapter-9

The Story of Sikhidwaja

Sri Vasishta said:

1. "Renouncing, at the outset, this world and bringing the bird of mind under control, do thou get established in the peaceful Self, in an unwavering manner, like Sikhidwaja."

2. Sri Rama asked, "Who is Sikhidwaja? How did he attain to the supreme beatitude? Do thou explain to me, O Seer, so that my experience may get richer."

3. Sri Vasishta said: "In the Dwapara Yuga that is gone, during the period of seventh Manu, there was a prosperous king in the Malwa country called Sikhidwaja.

4. He was courageous, noble, compassionate, truthful, patient, and self-controlled. He was brave, proud, endowed with all virtues and of wise conduct.

5. That Sikhidwaja wedded the daughter of the king of Saurashtra land, called Chudala, who was virtuous and similar to him in all aspects.

6. Since they had given their hearts to each other, their mutual love was intense. They were engrossed in each other and they delighted each other by actions.

7. Both were proficient in the fine arts and they became so attached to each other, that they were as if one soul.

8. For several years, the young couple, full of love for each other, indulged in endless amorous sports.

436

9.   As years rolled by, as the same seasons came again and again, like water dripping out of the broken pot, their youthfulness began to decline.

10.   Like the fall of a ripe fruit, death is unavoidable, as old age, oppressive like the mist to the lotus, is about to set in like thunder.

11.   As life ebbs away constantly, like water from the palm of the hand, as desire alone keeps growing like the thumbi creeper in the rainy season;

12.   As youthfulness keeps declining like the banks washed by the rainy floods, as pleasures flee away like arrows discharged from the bow;

13.   As the worldly transactions become uninteresting like the insipid plantain trunk, supreme dispassion possessed them.

14.   'What in this world would be auspicious, abiding and extremely satisfying, by attaining which the mind would not get agitated by worldly ordeals?'

15.   Enquiring thus, the two set about to find remedy for the malady of samsara and studied deeply the scriptures concerning the Self.

16.   Resolving that the dreaded disease of samsara gets cured only by the mantra of the knowledge of Self, they devoted themselves to its pursuit.

17.   Becoming splendid in appearance, their minds dwelt deeply on that subject; their actions were oriented towards it; they remained absorbed in it. They sought the knowers of Self, worshipped them, and acted according to their instructions.

18.   They were delighted in it, practised disciplines for long towards it. Getting into intense practice, they mutually enlightened each other.

19 & 20. Then Rama, Chudala after hearing from the realised souls the scriptural teachings that were capable of taking one beyond the ocean of samsara continuously and in an appropriate manner, enquired into self, whether she was engaged in duties or otherwise, with a mind that is pure.

21. She reflected: 'Let me find out myself what I am. To whom does this delusion belong? How has it arisen and from where?

22. The body, being inert and un-intelligent, I am not the same is my conclusion. The senses of action, being non-different from the body are also inert.

23. The senses of knowledge also are seen to be inert, inasmuch as they are set in motion by mind, like the stone thrown with the help of a contrivance.

24. I think the mind, of the nature of thought, is also inert, as it is also acted upon by the intellect, like the stone thrown from a sling.

25. The intellect, possessing the delusive faculty is also inert and like the course of water getting affected by removal of earth, is acted upon by ahankara.

26. Even ahankara is without life and is like a corpse dead. It is given birth to by jiva, and, like the yaksha of the boy, is illusory in nature.

27. Jiva again, an imaginary entity, pervaded by Vayu abides in the heart. Some other inner principle imparts life to the jiva, subtle in form.

28. Ha! I have now known that the jiva's life is sustained by the Consciousness of Self, which is without beginning and which is tainted by objectifying tendency.

The sense of the above two verses is explained thus.

In respect of a pot, there can be said to exist the space conditioned by the pot and space unconditioned by it. Even so, in the heart of every creature, there are jiva and Ishvara, conditioned and unconditioned Consciousness respectively. Jiva is ruled by maya whereas Ishvara rules over maya. S.T.

29. The jiva, deluded by the object and identifying itself with it, is sustained by chit, as the fragrance by the wind, as the stream of water by the bed beneath it.

30. Because of intense identification with the world, inert, cognised matter, chit becomes inert by abandoning its own form like the fire on contact with vast waters.

31. This chit, which by virtue of externalisation has become, as it were, inert and void-like, gets illumined by pure Consciousness.

32. Let me know by what is chit made to act through mind, intellect, etc.

Ha, I have known the blemishless Reality after a long enquiry.

33. All entities, mind, intellect, senses, etc., are but manifestation of chit. They are really non-existent and have manifested because of lack of Self-awareness.

34. Maha Chit, great chit, alone exists and this is also known as Maha Satta, great existence. It is untainted, homogenous, pure and bereft of ahankara.

35. The ever-manifest pure Consciousness reveals itself totally and this is called by the names, Brahman, Paramatma, etc."

36. Sri Vasishta said: "Chudala, delighted in the pursuit of Self knowledge every day with inwardised mind, got absorbed in the Self always.

37. Attending to the affairs on hand, she was unenamoured, unattached, unconcerned with pairs of opposites, uninterested in enterprise; she neither rejected nor accepted anything.

38. Attaining the supreme gain and supreme fulfilment as a result of the realisation of Self, she reached an exalted and indescribable state.

39. As a result of Self-realisation through intense practice of spiritual discernment, she shone gloriously like the creeper with new blossoms.

40. Once, seeing beautiful Chudala shining with unusual lustre, Sikhidwaja, smilingly asked her,

41. "O beautiful lady, with youthfullness returning to you fully and with the new charm of the body, you shine gloriously.

42. O my beloved, you are exceedingly elegant, as if you have drunk the essence of elixir, as if you have attained the supreme beatitude, as if you are filled with the blissful nectar.

43. O my dear, I see thy mind free from craving, fully immersed in peace, evenly disposed, majestic and serene."

44. Chudala said, 'Abandoning the world which has no real form and attaining the supreme which is formless, I shine in a lustrous form.

45. Abandoning this all, which was different from me and attaining that which is all and supports the real and the unreal, I shine in a lustrous form.

46. I know That which is something, which is not anything, how it manifests and how it subsides and therefore, I shine in a lustrous form.

47.　I get delighted as much by things I experience as by things I do not experience. I get neither elated nor depressed. Therefore, I shine in a lustrous manner.

48.　I abide delightfully in the space-like heart and do not get fascinated by royal pleasures and, therefore, I shine in a lustrous manner.

49.　Being the Consciousness which is not any particular thing, I am the Lord of all and I am delighted in Self and therefore, I shine in a lustrous form.

50.　I delight, alongwith my friends, in the spiritual teachings of the scripture which wipe away desire and aversion and therefore, I shine in a lustrous form.

51.　My dear, that which I see with my eyes, other senses and mind are of no consequence. I see clearly something in the inner heart which is different from these and is formless and therefore, my Lord, I am joyous."

52.　Sri Vasishta said: "The king, without understanding the import of the words uttered by the beautiful woman, who had attained repose in the Self, smiled derisively and said:

53.　'O beautiful lady! You are immature and talk about false things. Even as I enjoy royal pleasures, O princess, you also happen to enjoy.

54.　You said that you have abandoned the unreal and attained the formless; how, by abandoning existent things directly perceived, you can shine in a lustrous form?

55.　How can one shine in lustrous form, if one, abandoning pleasures near at hand, is happy with things not experienced and is unfortunate and impoverished?

56.　How, indeed, he can shine in a lustrous form, if he

prattles that 'I see,' 'I see not,' and 'I see something else' which are false.

57. You are young, immature, unsteady and light-hearted. By speaking, incoherently, you seem to play, O beautiful lady; well, do play."

58. Sri Vasishta said: "After laughing boisterously at the beloved, Sikhidwaja left the damsel's abode for the mid-day bath.

59. With the distressed thought, 'how unfortunate! The king has not realised the Self nor has he understood my words!' Chudala turned her attention to tasks on hand.

60. O Rama, the two, with the same mental disposition, spent many days in a happy manner amidst royal delights.

61. Once, although she was fully desireless and thoroughly self-contented, Chudala developed a fancy for journey in space out of curiosity.

62 & 63. To become proficient in space-journey, the princess set aside all pleasures, went to a lonely spot and sitting in the same body posture and in solitary frame of mind concentrated on the practice of directing the prana upwards."

64. Sri Rama said, "What kind of control, practised for a long time, by the earnest practitioner, O Seer, this attainment of space-journey results from?"

65 & 66. Sri Vasishta said: "Discarding all the vasanas excepting the one that concerns the aim, through the constriction of the anus and other practices, and through the regulatory practices of prana, etc., what results are attained, do thou listen from me, in the midst of the story of the story of Sikhidwaja, as there

is warrant for it.

67 to 69. For the enlightened person, prana, apana, etc., simply obey like servants, as he is lord of them, in matters relating to abandonment, acceptance and restraint as a result of his adherence to purity of food, steadiness in the sitting posture, contemplation of the spiritual truths as taught by the scripture (virtuous conduct, company of the wise, complete renunciation and practice of Sukhasana), intense practice of pranayama, abandonment of anger, miserliness, and pleasures.

Abandonment, acceptance and restraint-refer to Rechaka, Puraka and Kumbhaka pranayamas according to S. T.

70. O Rama, all attainments from kingdom to liberation are got by regulation of the prana in the physical body.

71 to 79. Kundalini is in a circular nadi-complex and abides as the nerve-centre at nave. A hundred nerves join there alongwith the nerve antraveshtika.

She is similar to the top circular portion of the veena instrument and the circle forming in the stream and abides in all the creatures from the worm to Brahma.

She binds herself in circles like a sleeping serpent tormented by cold and remains ever activated by prana.

Within it is the cluster, soft like the trunk of the plantain and within it flows the supreme, sanctifying energy which quickens all other energies.

The energy, of the form of the breath of an angry serpent, remains always turned upwards and is cause of all movements.

It is connected to all nerves that meet at the junction

of the heart. Called as Kundalini, she is the cause of movement, sensation, knowledge and activity.

She is called, kala, aspect, because of limiting tendency, chit because of sentient faculty, jiva because of sustenance through prana and mind because of mentation.

She is 'thought' because of thinking trait, 'buddhi' because of intelligence. She herself becomes ahankara. She is also known as 'puryashtaka,' a city of eight constituents.

Kundalini is the excellent life-sustaining energy abiding within the body. Since it has two-fold forms of prana and apana, it moves upwards and downwards.

80.   When, she, who is known to comprise of prana, goes fully upwards or goes entirely downwards, the person meets with death.

81.   If prana remains in all circumstances within the body, abandoning all upward and downward movements, the diseases of the person perish, since prana is totally restricted within."

82.   Sri Rama asked, "How do mental and physical maladies arise and die in the body? O great seer, do thou explain as they are."

83.   Sri Vasishta said: "Bodily distress is physical malady and mental distress is of the nature of vasanas. Know that both owe origin to stupidity and when there is no knowledge of Truth.

The physical malady is termed as 'vyadhi' and the mental malady as 'adhi.'

84 & 85. By virtue of lack of knowledge of Truth, and absence of control over the senses, the mind, abandoning its

subtle nature, getting swayed by desire and aversion constantly manifesting as 'this is attained,' 'this is not attained,' becomes vastly inert and deluded and in such a state, mental afflictions keep growing up, like darkness in the rainy season.

86 to 89. As desires increase, stupidity gets expanded due to wrong conduct, visit to wrong places, activities at wrong time, wrong deeds, association with wrong people, wrong attitudes. When nerve channels carry too meagre or too much vayu, when at nerve centres prana is disproportionate, when the body gets into disorder as a consequence, because of these wrong conditions of the body, maladies arise in the body.

The changes in the nerve channels are akin to those of the rivers when they are dry in summer and full with waters in the rainy season.

90. The effort of the person, whether in the healthy direction or otherwise, is of two kinds-that of the past lives and that of the present one. Whatever is more effective leads the person in an appropriate manner.

91. Adhis, mental maladies, and vyadhis, physical maladies, arise in this manner in the body of five elements.

O Rama, do thou learn how do they get destroyed.

92. Mental maladies are of two types-ordinary and vital. The ordinary are incidental and the vital one is natal.

93. The incidental ones get destroyed by the attainment of desired objects. When such mental maladies perish, the bodily ones that arose from them also perish.

94. O Rama, the vital type of mental malady does not perish except through realisation of Self, even as illusory serpent does not perish except through the

knowledge of the rope.

95. Those bodily maladies, which do not arise from mental maladies, perish through resort to use of herbs, mantra, auspicious deeds and the remedies prescribed in Ayurveda, as you know."

96. Sri Rama asked, "How does mental malady transform into bodily malady and how does it perish?-O Divine Seer, explain to me in clear language."

97. When the mind gets unsettled, the body gets into a malfuctioning condition. The agitated person does not see the object in the right manner.

98. Leaving the right direction, he rushes in wrong direction, as the deer struck by arrows.

99. When the disease sets in, the nerve-channels abandon their normal balance while carrying the prana current. When the prana flow becomes abnormal, the nerve channels get paralysed.

100. When the king is not functioning with a sense of responsibility, the varna and the ashrama functions of the society get into disorder and even so, wrong digestion, indigestion and excessive digestion result from the paralysis of the nerve channels.

101. With the flow of prana in nerve channels getting paralysed, the food turns harmful.

102. Thus it is, bodily malady arises from the mental malady and perishes when the mental malady perishes.

How the bodily malady perish as a result of mantra, etc., do thou listen.

103. Even as the haritaki fruit has the property to cause loose motions, aksharas, letters, ya-ra-lav-va, etc., as

a result of contemplation can bring about the desired result.

104. As gold becomes pure by rubbing against touchstone, mind becomes pure as a result of pure holy deeds and service of the wise.

105. When the mind gets pure, bliss manifests in the body. When the full moon rises in the sky, effulgence spreads on the earth.

106. With the mind becoming pure, nerve channels carry the prana-current in the normal manner. The food gets digested and, as a result, the malady perishes.

107. The way the mental and bodily maladies arise and get cured has been described to you.

Now, do you hear about the present subject matter of Kundalini yoga.

108. Know the inner Kundalini to be life-giving force of the jiva, otherwise called as puryashtaka, as flower for the fragrance.

109. When the aspirant by practising puraka fills with prana the Kundalini and remains steady, he becomes as firm as Meru and his body becomes huge.

110 & 111. When, after filling with prana through puraka, the same is lengthened, then the kundalini is lifted upwards through contemplation as if to cool the system after it has become hot.

Kundalini, rising straight like stick, rushes upwards like serpent, trekking along all the creeper-like nadis bound up with the body.

112. At that, the entire body rises up and like the air-filled bladder in the waters, floats in space.

113. Through the practice of such yoga, the adepts achieve

this rare trait, like a poor person getting the status of Indra.

114 & 115. When the Kundalini power coursing through Brahma-nadi reaches the domain within twelve angulas above the skull and when through practice of rechaka accompanied by the restraint of flow of prana in the other nadi-channels, gets stabilised in that condition, one sees celestials passing through sky. (Angulas are shorter than inches).

116. O Rama, Siddhas, abiding in the sky are seen, as if in a dream, by the mental vision, inspired by Consciousness and such visions also fulfill one's wishes.

117. When through practice of rechaka, prana is retained outside the head, within the twelve angula domain, called dvadasanta, one is able to enter into a different body."

118. Sri Rama asked, "How is body rendered subtle or huge to pass through a small hole or expand into a vast size?"

119. *Sri Vasishta said: "There is only the Consciousness, which is pure, serene and unsullied. It is subtler than the subtlest. There is no world nor anything worldly.*

120. That Consciousness, becoming thought-oriented, restrict its own nature and at that state it is spoken of as Jiva, defiled in nature.

121. The jiva, out of delusion, perceives this body, as real, though unreal, as the stupid child sees yaksha. (a devil-like being).

122. Having perceived the body, in whatever manner he conceives intensely, in that very manner he perceives objectively.

123. Through intense contemplation, even ignorant men, O Rama, turn poison into elixir and elixir into poison.

124. Therefore, it is found to happen often, whatever is contemplated upon in whatever manner, with intense faith, that thing happens in the same manner.

125. When the body is cognised as real, it is real and when the body is considered non-existent, the body becomes so.

126. In regard to the attainments like anima, the method of contemplation is described. For those established in yogic consciousness, it is easily achieved.

127. Chudala, the wife of the king, given to intense practice, became proficient in the exercise of siddhis like anima.

128. She went through the sky, entered the nether world, roamed all over the earth, like Ganga of nectarine coolness.

129. When she is there with him, even for a brief while, for the act of embrace, she is eager to find out the means for enlightening her husband in Self-knowledge.

130. Like father teaching son, she took enormous effort to instruct the husband in the knowledge of Self in a variety of ways.

131. The king, her husband, had not yet attained repose in the Self, like the pearls strongly strung together cast in a heap.

Both the lines of this verse are not traceable in BYV. The question that arises for consideration is whether the text of BYV, as we have today, is a complete one.

132. Even after the long time that had passed, the king had not understood the attainments of Chudala, in

the way a child does not understand the esoteric wisdom.

133. As the man of fourth caste is not allowed to see the yaga, she too did not show to the unenlightened king her spiritual attainments."

134. Sri Rama asked, "O great master, if, in spite of the great effort of the spiritual adept, Chudala, Sikhidwaja did not attain realisation, how can anyone else attain?"

135. Sri Vasishta said: "The convention of instruction by the preceptor is for the sake of pursuing the tradition. For one's realisation of Truth, the disciple's clarified intelligence alone is the cause."

136. Sri Rama said, "O seer, if that be the case, how is it said in the world that Guru's instruction is the cause of Self-realisation?"

137. Sri Vasishta said: "There was a trader living in a hamlet adjoining the forest of Vindhya like a brahmana with wealth, grains and a family.

138. Once as he was walking along a bushy track, O Rama, a coin fell into a grass-thicket.

139. Out of miserliness, he searched with great effort for the coin among the grass and plants for three days.

140. After a three-day search, he obtained from that wretched heap a wish-fulfiling gem, lustrous like the full moon.

141 to 143. Even as a priceless gem is obtained by the trader, who was only searching for a coin, as a consequence of his tireless search for three days, through the received instruction, Self-knowledge is obtained. Something is sought from the Guru but something else is attained.

In regard to the valuable wisdom that is attained, the instruction by Guru, though not a cause, turns into a cause, as the coin is responsible for the attainment of the gem, in an indirect manner.

144. Thereupon, Sikhidwaja, bereft of knowledge of Truth, became a victim of great delusion, like people becoming blind during night.

145. With sorrow piercing his heart, he did not find happiness amongst royal pleasures and the things to which he was attached, like a person caught up in fire.

146. He made enormous gifts, went on pilgrimage, adhered to austere penance and roamed all around.

147. He could not by any means attain, even in a small measure, freedom from sorrow; becoming dejected, he began to see the kingdom, as if it were a prison.

148. Once, lying on the lap of Chudala, in a solitary place, Sikhidwaja spoke to her the following sweet words.

149. Sikhidwaja said: "The kingdom has been ruled by me for a long time. All pleasures have been experienced. I am now seized by dispassion. I shall go to the forest.

150. O fair lady, there are neither joys nor sorrows, neither disasters nor fortunes for the hermit in the woods.

151. There is no fear caused by country's defeat or soldier's death in the battle. I feel that the happiness of a hermit in the woods is greater than that of the king.

152. That happiness, which a serene mind enjoys in the solitude of the forest, is not to be seen either in the face of the moon or in the mansion of Brahma and Indra.

153. O fair lady, in this decision of mine, do not throw any

obstacle. Virtuous women do not set at naught the desires of their husbands, even in dream."

154. Chudala said, "O Lord, everything shines only when its time has come. In spring the flowers bloom and the fruits ripen in summer.

155. For the aged and diseased bodies, life in the forest is proper but not for the young like you. Hence the proposal does not please me.

156. Sikhidwaja said, 'Enough, fair-eyed woman, of this objection to my desire. Know that I am gone to a distant forest.

157. You are young, O flawless woman, you should not accompany me to the forest. The forests are inaccessible even for men.

158. You have to remain here ruling the kingdom. Maintaining the home is the responsibility of women, when husbands are gone."

159. Sri Vasishta said: "After speaking thus to the moon-faced beloved, the resolute king rose up to take bath and attend to the daily routines.

160. With people retiring from activity, the sun descended into the west. Night fall gained maturity. (Night-matured into a girl with lotus buds as breasts).

161. After doing Sandhya worship and other ablutions alongwith the dear Chudala, he slept well in the couch, like the Minaka mountain in the ocean.

162. When silence gripped the land, at the time of midnight, when all people were deeply lost in sleep, the king put aside from his lap the sleeping beloved and went out.

163. With an unperturbed mind, he told the gate-keepers,

'I am going on nocturnal inspection' and came out of the mansion and the city.

164. 'O Lakshmi, Goddess of prosperity, obeisance to thee'- with these words, he took leave of the country. He entered into a mighty forest and later reached a vast river.

165. Day and night followed again and again. Spending ten nights thus, he quickly went beyond several lands, mountains and rivers.

166. Then he reached the forest on the slope of the mandara mountain, not accessible for lay people and far from the city.

167. In that forest in which trees were surrounded by noisy torrents and lakes, dilapidated hermitages with remnants of altars once inhabited by learned brahmanas were seen, bowers haunted by siddhas only and not by ordinary species were found. The king chose a place and built a cottage and also collected things needed by one engaged in penance.

168 to 170. Tender bamboo stick, vessels for keeping food and fruits, water-pots, flower-basket, rosary, kamandalu, rugs for keeping off the cold, deer skin for seat-all these he collected and kept inside the hut in proper places.

171 & 172. In the first quarter of the day, he did Sandhya worship and japa, collected flowers in the second, performed bath and worship of the Gods in the third. The self-controlled person ate fruits, herbs available in the forest, practised japa thereafter and spent the night.

Thus Sikhidwaja lived in a hut in the wood.

173. Now, hear what Chudala did in the mansion.

174. When, at mignight, Sikhidwaja had left, like the deer kept in the village, she woke up in fear.

175. She saw the empty couch. The husband had gone away. With a painful heart and a faded face, she rose up.

176. Looking like a withering creeper that had lost the support, she sat for a while on the couch and thought, 'Alas! the Lord of the kingdom has left for the abode of the forest.

177. What is to be done by me? Let me go to him. By nature, husband is ordained to be the resort of a woman.'

178. Thinking thus, she rose up to follow the husband Chudala, emerging through the window, rose up into sky.

179. By her shining face, she caused a delusion to the siddhas that there was another moon. She saw her husband within a second going through the forest in the night.

180 & 181. Seeing the king in that condition from the sky, she thought of the future developments fully in respect of her husband. She thought of the inexorable happenings as she saw the king from the sky.

182 & 183. To achieve her aim, she returned from the space. 'Let my joining him wait. Only after a long time, I shoud go to him. Such is the cosmic will'-thinking thus, Chudala returned to her apartment and slept in the couch, like moon in the sky.

184. She told the nobles of the city, 'The king has gone out for some reasons' and pacified.

185. The even-minded princess ruled the kingdom as her husband did.

Time passed. Days, months and years rolled on.

186. Why speak much? Eighteen years passed. The woman Chudala lived in the mansion and Sikhidwaja in the forest.

187. 'The time to go near the husband has come'-thinking thus, she made up her mind to go to the mountain slope.

188. She left the abode in the night, swam through the sky, along the path of wind and reached the mountainous region.

189. In her own invisible form, she entered the forest through the sky.

She saw the king altogether in a different body as a consequence of his yogic practice.

190. The husband, (bereft as he was of garlands, bracelets, amulets and ear-ornaments) was emaciated, black in colour and fatigued.

191. Seeing him in that condition, the blemishless Chudala with large breasts, said to herself thus, with some sorrow in her heart, 'Alas, how obstinacy can harm much even the learned in the scripture? Such people, because of lack of discernment, fall into hardships.

193. I shall certainly and necessarily make my lord a knower of Truth and one who is fit for both enjoyment and liberation. Let there be no doubt.

194. Abandoning this form and taking another form, I go near him to impart to him supreme realisation.

195. 'My beloved is immature'-with such a thought, my advice would be set aside by him. Therefore, I shall enlighten my husband in the guise of an ascetic.

196. The impurities in the husband's mind have left and it

is pure. In such a pure mind, the truth will reveal itself."

197. Thinking thus, Chudala, contemplating for a while, assumed the form of a brahmana boy and descended before the husband.

198 & 199. Sikhidwaja saw before him a brahmana boy standing-he was white like molten gold, adorned with a garland of pearls, the white holy thread, covered with two white cloth pieces and standing above the ground.

200. Seeing the brahmana boy, Sikhidwaja stood up and taking him to be a celestial born, he removed his own sandals. (as a mark of reverence).

201. "O celestial boy, obeisance to thee. Here is seat, may you sit"-saying thus, he placed before him a seat.

202. "O kingly saint! Obeisance to thee." Saying thus, the brahmana sat. He also received the flowers that were offered to him.

203. Sikhidwaja said, "O celestial born! Blessed Soul! What has brought you here? This day is an auspicious day for me, for I have seen you today."

204. Saying thus, Sikhidwaja offered water for washing the holy feet, and to drink, flowers, garlands, etc., in order, as if he was offering to the chosen deity.

205. The brahmana said, "Because of your kind, appropriate and reverential conduct, I feel certain that you will live a long life.

206. By totally abandoning since long the imaginary fancy and with a calm mind, have you been able to pursue earnest penance for the sake of liberation.

207. The quiet austerity you pursue, O dear, is akin to a

walk on the razor's edge, because you have resorted to forest life after discarding a vast kingdom."

208. Sikhidwaja said, "O Divine Seer, you know all. You are a celestial born and what is there to wonder! The excellent radiant form is symbolic of your greatness.

209. Who are you? Whose son are you? What for you have come? O radiant soul, with a view to bless me, my curiosity may be dispelled."

210. The brahmana said, "O king, do thou listen. I tell everything you have asked for. Who indeed would be false to a sincere questioner?

211. There is in this world a pure soul called Narada Muni. The radiance of his face, by virtue of its holy serenity, is likened to a lump of camphor.

212. That ascetic was once absorbed in meditation in the cave, on the bank of Ganga of mighty flow.

213. At the end of the meditation on the bank of Ganga, Narada Muni heard sweet words in an endearing tone.

214. His curiosity was aroused and he asked, "What is this?." He casually looked in the direction of the river and saw a group of damsels.

215. They were akin to Ramba and Tilottama in beauty and with extreme joy, they sported in waters, discarding all clothes in the place where men could not be found.

216. With their features manifest, they were wholly visible. Their bodies, being mirror-like, reflected other bodies.

217. The mind of the seer, which had become infatuated at the sight of these, discarded the sense of discrimination and experienced inner relish.

218. When the mind gets excited by pleasure, the pranic

current gets agitated and as a result of his delight, the seminal flow followed."

219. 'The seer was so great and so learned and was also a liberated soul. How could such a person also become subject to passion?'

This is a question asked by Sikhidwaja.

220. The brahmana said, "When one's real and blemishless form of Consciousness is forgotten, even for a minute, the objective matter rises in a fascinating spectacle, like clouds in the rainy season.

221. The devil of objective mater does not becloud the Consciousness of Self, only if there is continuous awareness of it and there is no forgetfullness even for a minute.

222. Experiencing the states of pleasure and pain is bondage; the absence of such state is liberation. Thus, the condition of the jiva is two-fold.

223. By the pure realisation of the Truth, as non-different from the Self, one becomes a liberated soul, and one understands that happiness and sorrow do not exist.

224. When the conviction gets stabilised that all this is Consciousness, which is Brahman, jiva attains liberation, like the oil-less lamp.

225. From the Self, characterised by inherent nature has arisen the world and by virtue of association with vasanas, it gets established and is swayed by dharma, righteousness and adharma, unrighteousness.

226. When the vasana aspect has been eliminated from the mind, it is no longer susceptible to righteousness and unrighteousness and as a result, the jiva is not reborn-this is a main philosophical tenet.'

227. Sikhidwaja said, "O excellent speaker! You speak extremely noble and wonderful words, which are in harmony with experience and also the nature of the Supreme.

228. O beautiful friend, by hearing the words of yours, I feel as though I have drunk the elixir and my heart has become cool.

229. Now do thou tell the manner of your birth. Then I shall earnestly hear your exposition of spiritual wisdom.

230. Where was placed the semen, after the discharge, by Narada, the seer and son of Brahma? Do thou explain as it happened."

231 & 232. The brahmana said, "Restraining the riotous elephant of mind by the fetter of discrimination and the fetter of sharp intellect, the seer placed the semen in a crystal jug by his side and filled the vessel with milk that materialised by his mere wish.

233. The child grew up in a month's time like the moon and, withall limbs fully developed, he emerged from the pot.

234. After performing all samskaras, purifying ceremonies, the seer Narada transmitted to him all the wisdom, just like transferring things from one vessel to another.

235. Then he took the son with him to Brahma. The Creator God, conferred on his grandson the highest spiritual wisdom.

236. O wise man, I am the person called by the name Kumbha, since I was born from Kumbha, the pot.

237. The four Vedas are my well-wishers and friends; my mother is Sarasvati and her sister is Gayatri. I keep moving in the earth as I desire."

238. Sikhidwaja said, "O wise seer! I am standing much above all the blessed people of the earth, that I am able to hear thy nectarine words and also get your company.

239. The attainment of kingdom or even other great riches do not so much delight the heart as the company of the wise does."

240. Kumbha said, "Let my story stop here. I have told you everything. Do thou tell me, O wise man, who are you and what are you doing in this mountain?"

241. Sikhidwaja said, "O celestial born, you know spontaneously everything. If you still ask, let me tell. Listen. I am living in the woods because I am afraid of worldly life.

242. I am Sikhidwaja, the king who has come here after renouncing the kingdom. O Knower of Truth, as I am simply afraid of life leading to repeated births.

243. Despite my pursuit of all the rites in a proper way, I only pass on from one sorrow to another and even elixir has become poison to me."

244. Kumbha said, "It is wisdom that leads to great beatitude. One attains liberation completely through it. It is only for the sake of curiosity and spending away the time, kriya, activity has been advised.

245. O dear, for those who have not attained the perspective of wisdom, kriya, activity has been the refuge.

For the unenlightened, the actions are fruiful because they are manifestations of vasanas.

For the enlightened, the actions are fruitless, since their vasanas have been extinguished.

246. When the products of a season lose their form in another season, the fruits of actions also lose their significance when the particular vasanas get attenuated.

247. The creeper called Saralatha, in accordance with its own nature, does not yield fruit. Even so, actions characterised by absence of vasanas do not generate fruits.

The reading of the verse, as in BYV, 6, 88, 18, is more correct and the translation is based on the interpretation of the verse in BYV.

248. For an intelligent person whose ignorance has been destroyed by the contemplation 'all this is Brahman,' vasana, like the perception of mirage does not arise.

249. By total discarding of vasanas, the state bereft of old age, death and repeated birth is attained.

250. Truth associated with vasana is mind and mind disassociated from vasana is Truth. With the attainment of Truth through realisation, the jiva frees himself from rebirth.

251. It is wisdom that is the greatest beatitude-so Brahma and others have said. It is wisdom that takes one across the samsara. Why do you remain like an ignorant person?

252. 'Who am I? How has this world come into existence? How does it disappear?'-Why do not you enquire along these lines, O king? You remain like an ignorant person.

253. How does bondage arise and how is liberation attained?-asking such questions, why do you not take to the service at the feet of Knowers of the Supreme?

254. That understanding of Truth which leads to liberation

is attained by questioning and serving the wise knowers of Supreme, and by living in their company."

255. Sri Vasishta said: "When his beloved in the form of a celestial being enlightened him thus, Sikhidwaja with tear-filled eyes spoke thus.

256. Sikhidwaja said, "O Divine lad! After a long suffering, I stand enlightened by you. Owing to stupidity, I discarded the company of the wise and lived in the forest.

257. Ha! My sins, I believe, have been totally destroyed. You have come to the woods and have enlightened me.

258. Preceptor of mine you are, father and friend you are, O radiant soul! As a disciple I prostrate at thy feet.

259. Do thou instruct me the highest wisdom concerning Brahman, by attaining which one does not grieve and I will have mental repose."

260. Kumbha said, "If you are receptive to instruction, let me explain. Otherwise, a thing explained even in various ways is not understood.

261. The words become fruitless, like the vision in darkness, if one is not receptive and both the speaker and the listener are casual in approach.'

262. Sikhidwaja said, 'That which is instructed by you will be carried out by me, without any questioning, as if it is Vedic command. I speak only the truth."

263. Kumbha said, "As a child accepts the advice of the father without seeking to know the cause and justification, do thou receive my instruction.'

264. O king, do hear initially an interesting story. Later on I shall explain how it is connected to the subject matter.

265. There was a prosperous person endowed with all virtues. He was proficient in the teachings of the scripture but had not realised the plenary Reality.

266. Like the huge Vadava fire trying to extinguish the ocean at the time of deluge, he ventured to obtain chintamani, the wish-fulfilling gem, which can be got only through enormous effort.

267. With great effort, and resolution, he searched for it for a long time as he had large time at his disposal for the purpose.

268 to 276. The gem, shining like the moon over the crest of Meru appeared before him and was almost within hand's reach.

He laughed within himself and thought thus, 'Is chitamani attained or not attained by the enterprising people?

Is this the gem? Or is this not? Even if it is a jewel, it is not chintamani? Let me see it but not touch it, for it may fly away.

Is the precious jewel attained so soon? Only through life-long effort, is it attained-this is the teaching of the scripture.

A covetous man I am, through defective vision, perhaps I see the precious jewel, akin to the reddish creeper, out of delusion, as in the cognition of second moon.

How could I have attained such a huge fortune through the precious jewel, capable of giving all?

Rare are the great and fortunate souls, who can attain prosperity even during a short period.

I am an unfortunate miserable ordinary being. How can rare attainments be possible for one who is an abode of all misfortunes?'

Though the precious jewel was before him, he did not have the conviction, like the commoner who got the kingship unexpectedly.

277. Plagued by such doubts for a long time, the deluded man did not make effort to pick up the gem.

278. As he remained thus, the gem flew away. Powers leave the person who values them not, as the arrows leave the bow.

279. That individual again made effort to gain the gem. Enterprising persons do not get dejected with their endeavours.

280. He saw before a shining object, a piece of metal, before him, perhaps, kept by wicked people intending to deceive.

281. The stupid man took it in the thought that it was real gem. A deluded person sees even clay as gold.

282. Taking the metal-piece, he discarded his prior possessions. 'All things can be obtained from this gem itself. Where is the need for wealth?

283. This land is incongenial and unfavourable. It is occupied by unrighteous people. Let me go to a distant place and with the help of the new possession, let me live happily.'

284. With this intention, the fool took the metal piece and entered into a deserted forest. He underwent enormous hardship because of that metal piece.'

285. Kumbha said, 'O king, listen to another interesting story, which has relationship with the understanding of the Supreme.

286. There was an elephant-chief in the Vindhya hill whose tusks were long and strong like the bones constituting the vajra weapon.

287. He was chained by the mahout on all sides. Bound by sharp-edged fetters, he was in a helpless state.

288. By persistent and powerful effort in a period of two hours, he broke the chains.

289. Seeing that the elephant had freed himself and with a view to bind him again, the mahout, elephant's enemy, jumped on his head from the palmyra tree.

290. The fool, missed the head of the elephant and fell on the ground before the elephant. The great elephant seeing the fallen enemy was moved by pity.

291. Even among animals, some noble minded virtuous creatures do exist.

292. 'Is it valour to kill a fallen man?'-thinking thus, the elephant did not kill his enemy.

He simply left the place and went away to a different place.

293. When the elephant was gone, the unharmed mahout rose up. He began to search for the elephant again in the bushes-filled forest. After a long time, he spotted the elephant again in some forest.

294. He dug up pits around the forests and the wicked man covered them up with dry leaves and creepers.

295. The elephant, roaming freely in the forest, in a few days fell into the pit like the hill into the ocean.

296. Thus the elephant was again bound by the same mahout. Even now, the elephant remains a prisoner in his abode, as Bali is.

297. If the elephant had killed the enemy when he was at his feet, he would not have had to undergo the misery in the pit later.

298. Through stupidity, a person fails to ward off the future

danger by present caution and courts disaster like the elephant of the Vindhya hill.'

The Significance of the Story of Chintamani

299. Sikhidwaja asked, "O celestial born, what was indicated through the stories concerning chintamani and the elephant of Vindhya hill, do thou explain for my benefit again.

300. Kumbha said, "O king, that learned individual, who was proficient in the scripture but ignorant of Self-knowledge, and who obtained the gem is, you yourself.

301. You are acquainted with the scripture but are ignorant of Self-knowledge.

302. Know chitamani to be total renunciation resulting from perfect understanding. With the help of that renunciation, you intended to achieve the extinction of all sorrows.

303. The kingdom was renounced by you alongwith wife, wealth and relations.

You have come far away from home to the hermitage in forest.

304. In the renunciation of all, you have however not left the sense of ego.

Therefore, the renunciation of yours did not become total.

That being the case, the imperfect renunciation veiled your mind like clouds veiling the sky.

305. That which you have attained is not that total renunciation, which is supreme beatitude resulting from great effort but is something else.

306. When thoughts and obsessions took hold of your mind,

the renunciation flew away just like birds in the tree, tossed about by the mind.

307. O lotus-eyed king, when the gem of total renunciation had left you, the metal piece of penance was spotted by your desire-tainted eye.

308. He who, discarding the easy means that bring in supreme happiness, troubles himself to achieve a limited pleasure through difficulty has wronged the self and is known to be an ignorant man.

309. You were contented in the thought that you had obtained the chintamani, but in reality, O wise man, you did not get even a crystal piece.'

The Significance of the Story of Elephant-king

310. Kumbha continued, 'That which was said to be the elephant in the Vindhya hill is the king of this country, that is you. The two tusks of the elephant are viveka, discrimination, and vairagya, dispassion.

311. He who is intent on capturing the elephant is your ajnana, ignorance, that overpowers and gives sufferings.

312. O king, though very strong, you are led, like the elephant by the mahout from one sorrow to another, from one fear to another by ignorance.

313. Like the elephant getting entangled in the iron fetters, you have also bound yourself by desires and attachments.

314. Desire is stronger than the iron rope, more harmful, and firm. With the passing of time the metal loses the strength but the desire only increases in strength.

315. The act of the elephant in breaking the fetters forged

by his enemy, represents your renouncing the pleasures and the kingdom.

316. What was described as the accidental fall of the elephant's enemy from the palmyra tree is the decline of your ajnana as a consequence of the renunciation of the kingdom.

317. When, out of dispassion, an individual discards pleasures, ajnana, gets shaken, as it were, like the devil in the tree that is felled.

318. When the pleasure-objects are totally discarded by a wise seeker, the ajnana loses its hold.

319. When a tree is felled, the devil in it runs away. When you went away to the forest, the ajnana too was crippled. Though it got crippled, the ajnana was not killed by the sword of complete renunciation.

320 & 321. That was why, ajnana rose up again and remembering the past disgrace it suffered from, it pushed you into the deep pit of worldliness.

322. The deep pit dug by the enemy of the elephant for catching the elephant is all this activity that ajnana has foisted on you.

323. All the attendant facilities the enemy of the elephant had, O king, are the resting planes of mind of the king, ajnana.

324. The dry leaves and creepers that covered the pit are the penitential sufferings and the wise doings of yours.

325. Thus it is, in the sorrowful and frightful pit of penance, you remain trapped like Bali in bondage in the lower world."

326. Kumbha asked, "That wisdom which was imparted to you by the wise, virtuous Chudala, why was it not acted upon by you?

327. She is great even among knowers of Truth. Whatever she says or does is wise. Her words must be followed sincerely.

328. If you did not choose to accept the advice, why did you not make perfect, the renunciation which you had ventured upon?"

329. Sikhidwaja said, "The kingdom has been renounced, the home has been discarded, and so have been the land, wives and children. How is it not a perfect renunciation?'

330. Kumbha said, "Wealth, wives, house, kingdom, royal insignia, and relations are really not thine, O king, how is your renunciation total?

331. There is still unrenounced the most vital possession. By renouncing that alone, you will reach the state beyond sorrow.'

332. Sikhidwaja said, "If the kingdom etc., are not mine, if these possessions, the tree, the bower, etc., in the wood are mine, let me renounce them as well."

333. Vasishta said: "O Rama, prompted thus by the words of Kumbha, the self-controlled and courageous Sikhidwaja instantly wiped away from his heart the lingering desire, like the flood of the rainy season washing away from the bed the distinct sand stretches.

334. Sikhidwaja said, 'The desire in respect for the tree, wood, hut, also has been renounced by me. So my renunciation is total now.'

335 & 336. Kumbha said, "The mountain, wood, water, trees, abode-all these are not thine. How is thy renunciation total? There is still unrenounced the most important possessions.

337. Sikhidwaja said, "If these are not mine, let me surely renounce even vessel, hut, water, etc.'

338. Kumbha said, "This hermitage is not thine and by discarding it, renunciation does not become total. There still remains unrenounced the basic possession.

339. Sikhidwaja said, "If all these vessels, etc., are not mine, let me renounce even these deer skin, wooden plant, etc."

340. Sri Vasishta said: "Saying thus, he rose up, collected and brought together in one place things like the rosary and had them burnt as a mark of renunciation.

341. As the utensils etc., were getting burnt alongwith the dry fuel, the king stood completely alone, bereft of any attachment, and with a happy mind.

342 to 346. Sikhidwaja said to himself, 'Renouncing the desires towards all things, I am now a perfect renunciate. Ha! Realisation has come to me through the celestial lad. I have been easily made to see the pure Truth.

What is the attachment to the vessel, small things of utility, place, hut, etc., which are all of imaginary nature?

To the extent the various things fettering our mind are given up, to that extent mind perfect renunciation has been made.'

Sikhidwaja said, turning to Kumbha, 'I am now as unattached as space and equal to space I am. O celestial born, what is there left to be done apart from this great renunciation?'

347. Kumtha said: "O king Sikhidwaja! indeed everything has not been renounced by you. Do not assume that you experience the bliss of complete renunciation.

348. Sri Vasishta said: "As he said thus, O Rama, the lotus-eyed, the king thought for a while and spoke thus.

349. Sikhidwaja said, 'O celestial born! In this act of total renunciation, the body comprising of serpent-like senses, blood, etc., remains left behind.

350. Let me rise up and through fall from the mountain, I shall destroy the body and be a perfect renunciate."

351. Sri Vasishta said: "Saying thus, he went out to fall into the pit in front. As he rose up from the earth, Kumbha said to him these words."

353. "O lotus-eyed king, even by discarding the body, the renunciation made by you is not total. In fact, it is a wrong step.

354. That which imparts movement to the body, that which is the cause of rebirth and action is to be renounced and if you renounce it, you will have made great renunciation."

355. Sikhidwaja asked, 'By what is the body's movement caused? What is the cause of rebirth and action? O radiant youth! Renouncing what, renunciation becomes perfect?'

356. Kumbha said, "O wise man! There is an all-pervasive entity called 'jivanama.' It is neither sentient nor non-sentient. The mind, deluded as it is, is everything.

The translation is based on the BYV reading, 6, 93, 33.

357. Know the mind to be the cause of world-spectacle. Mind is also called bondage. O wise man, if that mind is renounced, there is total renunciation.

358. Mind is also the seed of rebirth and action. As a tree is tossed about by wind, the body is activated by the mind.

359. Those who have known the truth of renunciation call the renunciation of mind as total renunciation. When the mind is discarded, all categories, dual and non-dual, get extinguished.

360. There remains the residual, peaceful, pure, blissful Being. Total renunciation brings in supreme bliss and anything else is dreadful misery.

361. Accepting this suggestion and uttering 'Om,' do what you wish. Through perfect renunciation, you become tranquil, calm and akin to space. Abide in that state, O king.'

362. Sikhidwaja said, "O Divine Seer, initially do explain to me the nature of mind and thereafter its renunciation.'

363. Kumbha said, "O king, chitta, mind, is inherently of the nature of vasana, tendency. Chitta is known to be a synonym of vasana.

364. *The aham-artha, ego-spurt, is the cause of all sorrows, O wise man, and is the seed of the tree of chitta.*

365. From this first-born ahankara of the nature of experience, arises the sprout of buddhi which is the faculty of discrimination, and which is formless.

366. The sprout-like buddhi attains the grosser form, variously called as chitta, chetas and manas and manifests the trait of sankalpa, imagination.

367. Of this evil tree, as you keep felling the branches, make effort to destroy the roots. It is uprooting 'ahankara' that is called as perfect renunciation.

368. The branches called vasanas, bring forth various fruits and when, with the strength of discernment the vasanas are negated, the fruits become inwardly hollow.

369. He who is mentally detached, silent, uninvolved in discussions, alert in performing natural tasks, has creeper-like mind that is inwardly dry.

370. The tree of chitta is not destroyed by cutting off the branches which is seemingly effective, but by removal of roots; therefore, set about to remove its roots.

371. Chiefly, O noble soul, burn the roots completely of the thorny tree of chitta and there sets in the mindless-state."

372. Sikhidwaja said, "What is the fire, O sire, that can be used in the act of burning the root of 'ahambhava' of the tree of chitta?"

373. Kumbha said, "O king, in the act of burning the root of the tree of chitta, the enquiry into Self of the type, 'who am I,' is known to be the fire."

374 & 375. Sikhidwaja said, "O seer, I have enquired into the Self by my own intellect often enough.

I am not the body nor the world nor the aggregate of flesh, bones, etc., nor the group of senses of action nor the group of senses of knowledge. I am not also the mind, nor the intellect nor the ahankara. As bracelet-ness is false in gold, 'ahambhava' is false in chid-atma.'

376. Kumbha said, "If this group is not you, O ruler, because all these are inert, what are you really, that do thou tell."

377. Sikhidwaja said, "The eternal pure Consciousness is the intelligent Self, O seer. The objects become pleasurable because of it; their nature is determined by it.

378. Despite this nature of mine, it is tainted by the same impurity, without cause. That is the seed of ego lodged

in the heart of the tree of the chitta.

379. I do not know how to discard it. Discarded by me again and again, it sticks to me. I know not how to abandon it. Hence, O seer, I am terribly miserable."

380. Kumbha said, "From cause alone arises the effect. Do thou enquire into the cause of 'ahambhava' and let me know what it is."

381. Sikhidwaja said, "O seer, of the taint of 'aham,' awareness of 'aham' is the cause. How does that awareness of 'aham' subside, do tell me.

382. Kumbha said, "You are adept in finding the cause. Do thou tell me the cause of 'I-awareness.' Therefter I shall enlighten you about the causal and non-causal relationship.'

384. Sikhidwaja said, 'It is awareness that manifests as the existent body, in a false manner, like movement manifesting in breeze.

385. I am unable to realise the non-existence of the false thing, as a result of which the I-cognition, the seed of chitta tree, would subside.'

386. Kumbha said, "If the body, etc., have existence, the I-cognition might exist. Since the body, etc., do not have existence, where does the cognition originate?"

387. Sikhidwaja said, "This body comprising of hands, feet, etc., associated with activity and results, being constantly experienced by one, how can it be said to not exist?"

388. *Kumbha said, 'When the cause is not traceable for an effect, O king, that effect also does not exist and cognition of such effect is a delusion.*

389. *Know that you certainly do not exist. Such a cognition*

is false. That effect which has no cause is illusory, like the serpent on the rope."

390. Sikhidwaja asked, "This world was created originally by the Progenitor-God. O seer, why should he not be the cause?"

391. Kumbha said, "O ruler, prior to creation there is only the tranquil Brahman. Since there was not anything else, there is no cause for the Creator God.'

392. Sikhidwaja asked, 'Why is not Brahman the cause of the Creator God? O seer, I am unable to understand non-existence of cause in respect of the Creator.'

393. Kumbha said, "There is infinite, eternal, unmanifest, primeval intelligence. It is unquestionable, unknowable, immutable, blissful and imperishable. It is non-dual, beginningless and endless, auspicious and incorruptible.

394. How, at whose instance, through what and when, does It become a doer, enjoyer? Therefore, the world is not produced and the world does not exist.

395. The Creator, being the imagination of bare Consciousness is of the nature of Consciousness.

The creation born of bare Consciousness is nothing but Consciousness.

396. "I am not doer, nor enjoyer. All this is blissful Consciousness"-have this firm inner conviction that destroys ajnana, nescience.

397. Thus broken into pieces, ajnana ceases to exist, in the opinion of the wise. No change in prior condition can be brought about except through destruction of cause.

398. With ajnana vanishing, there is also change in the prior

condition and its extinction and the ahambhavana, I-cognition, ceases to manifest.

399. Therefore, O ruler, the Supreme Consciousness by virtue of Its own will manifest spontaneously as world. The Consciousness, remaining in the same nature calls Itself Padmaja, Creator God. Consciousness is the real nature and it is bliss.'

400. Sikhidwaja said, "O Divine Seer, I am enlightened. You have spoken what is in accord with reason. Since there is no creator, there is no creation. Therefore, there is no seer.

401. The fact being this, I am awakened, fully awakened and blissful. I salute myself. I have been taught there is no objective matter.

402. In the cognition of objects, only illusory objects manifests thus. Enough of such illusory cognitions. Let me remain at peace like the centre of akasa.

403. The cognition of the multiple forms of the worldly things, space, different directions, time, delights, action, etc., after a long time, becomes extinct. There is only immutable, blissful Brahman."

404. Sri Vasishta said: "Instructed by Kumbha in this manner, the king got enlightened and emerging from darkness of delusion, shone brilliantly.

405. Contemplating in the natural way on Kumbha's instruction, the king instantly became absorbed in Self-Consciousness.

406. With mind shutting itself in, eyes closed and tongue silent, he remained motionless like an idol sculpted out of a stone.

407. After an hour's time, when the king's eyes opened slowly, Chudala in the form of Kumbha spoke.

408. Kumbha said, "In that vast plane, pure, soft and taintless beautiful couch, did you experience the joy of transcendental minds?

409. Have you attained the inner vision? Have you discarded the delusion? Have you known the Knowable, seen the Supreme?"

410. Sikhidwaja said, "O Divine Seer! By thy grace I have attained the supreme plane and seen glorious states. I am on top of all existence.

411. The company of the wise, knowers of Truth, noble souls, has an unique ambrosial essence and is productive of great good.

412. That ambrosia which was not got by me since my birth has been obtained today, because of your contact.

413. O lotus-eyed seer! How did this infinite, nectarine plane of Self Consciousness remain unattained by me for so long?

414 to 416. Kumbha said, "When the desire for enjoyments dies, mind becomes extinct and all senses get purified, the words of the preceptor get impressed in the mind, like the colour-drops of flowers in the white cloth.

As ripened fruits fall from the tree, O lotus-eyed wise man, the impurities of the body fall away in course of time.

417. Perception of duality and non-duality is what is called ajnanam, and when these perceptions become extinct, there is wisdom and supreme attainment.

418. You are enlightened, you are liberated. O king, the mind stands discarded. Mind has attained supreme calmness. Do abide as pure Self."

419. Sikhidwaja said, 'For the realised knower of Truth,

477

chitta does not exist. How do the liberated souls keep moving in the world in a sportive manner?'

420. Kumbha said, 'That vasana which is capable of leading to rebirth, becomes intense and is called chitta and such chitta does not exist in the liberated soul.

421. That vasana, with the help of which liberated souls keep moving in the world, should be understood by you as sattva which does not cause rebirth.

422. The chitta of the ignorant is chitta proper and in the case of the enlightened it is known as sattva. Those who are activated by chitta are ignorant and those by sattva are exalted souls.

423. All pleasures, those of the heaven and liberation, are illusory and renouncing these, you are in supreme plane.

424. Without reacting to external pleasures, and with unexcited mind, abide within. The chitta immune to excitement does not undergo samsara.

425. O ruler, whatever sorrows are seen in the world have resulted from the chitta's cravings.

426. O Realised Soul! Going beyond the excited and unexcited conditions of chitta and getting established in oneness, remain in that imperishable state as long as you want."

427. Sikhidwaja said, "How do the excited and unexcited states of chitta get transcended into oneness, explain for me as this can set at rest all doubts.

428. Kumbha said, "There is only pure Consciousness and it appears as world, like waters of the ocean. The Consciousness is set in motion by the intellect, as the pure waters are by the waves.

429. O dear, that which is called Brahman, pure Consciousness, Reality, etc., is seen as world by the unwise.

430. The creation which is but the nature of spurt in pure Consciousness ceases to exist when there is total vision. It arises, when there is imperfect vision, like the cognition of serpent in rope.

431. Through study of scripture, association with the wise and practice of yoga, mind attains purity and shines like moon.

432. This is pure effulgence of the nature of Self-awareness; it spontaneously manifests in the heart of exalted souls.

433. O Sikhidwaja, thus has been explained to you everything-how the chitta rises and how it merges in Consciousness.

434. After imbibing these words, reflecting on them and understanding them, O seer, do thou abide in the manifest luminous state as you wish.

435. Let me go to the heaven. During this season, the seer Narada returns from the Brahmaloka, after attending the assembly of the celestials.

436. If he does not see me there, he will be angry. The elders should never be provoked by the disciplined youngsters.

437. Renouncing the last shred of desire and without wanting anything, you should abide, thus in the most holy state."

438. Sri Vasishta said: "After saying this, the Divine Seer Kumbha disappeared from view. When Kumbha was gone, the king was in a state of wonder.

439. Sikhidwaja said, 'Ha, this is a cool blissful state, caused, as it were, by alchemy and peace floods into heart."

440. Sri Vasishta said: "Thinking thus, the king, bereft of all vasanas remained immersed in silence, like an idol carved from stone.

441. In that undifferentiated awareness, he remained established and was majestic like the crest of the hill.

442. Sikhidwaja remained motionless like stone or wood. Now about Chudala.

443. In the form of Kumbha, after enlightening Sikhidwaja, she travelled through sky.

444. She discarded her charming celestial form and assumed the beautiful womanly form. She returned to the capital and entered into her mansion.

445. She became visible to others and performed the royal duties. After three days, she again took to the sky.

446. By her yogic powers, she became Kumbha and went to the forest of Sikhidwaja and found the king in the same spot.

447. She saw the king absorbed in superconscious state. She thought, 'Let me draw the king out from this supreme plane.'

448. Thinking thus, Chudala roared like a lion.She did it again and again in the king's presence causing fright to the animals.

449. In spite of the sound, the king remained unmoved like stones. After trying it again and again, she shook his body.

450. When, despite physical shaking, the king did not wake up, Chudala in the form of Kumbha reflected over the matter.

451 & 452. "Ha! This wise man, is totally absorbed in the divine state.

Let me examine his body to find out whether there is residual mind in him, the cause of sentience.

If it is there, let me live on to enable him to remain together as pair.

453. Otherwise, let me give up this womanly body and reach the state in which there is no rebirth. What is there on earth for me?"

454. Sri Vasishta said: "After thinking thus, Chudala touched the husband and saw subtle pulsation and said to herself.

455. "There is certainly still residual mind capable of conscious activity. "From the signs of Consciousness, she inferred the existence of the residual mind.

456. Sri Rama asked, "When a person's mind has merged in the cause, and the meditative individual is akin to wood or stone, O Divine Seer, how is the residual mind's existence known?"

457. Sri Vasishta said: "The residual mind, which is the cause of conscious activity exists in respect of the knower of Truth in an invisible minute form in the heart, as the essence of fruit and flower in the seed.

458. The body of him whose mind is bereft of movement and abides motionless in superconscious state, being non-responsive to stimuli, bears no indications of grief or happiness.

His mind rises not, sets not and remains still always.

459. I have told you what you have asked. Hear the story further.

460. Resolving, as aforesaid, Chudala discarded her body

and attained to the plane of eternal Chit.

461. From that plane, she activated the mind of Sikhidwaja, her Lord, and reentered into her body, like the bird from the sky into the nest.

462. Assuming the form of Kumbha, she sat in the appropriate seat and began to chant Sama Veda in a sound similar to that of bees.

463. Hearing the Sama chant, the residual mind associated with chit, woke up in the king's body, like the lotus blossoming in the spring.

464. The mind caused the eyes to open, like the sun the lotus.

Sikhidwaja saw before him Kumbha in a serene form.

465. 'We are indeed fortunate. The Divine Seer is here again'-Uttering these words, Sikhidwaja rose and offered a flower to Kumbha.

466. "By divine grace I have seen you. O Seer, you have come again to sanctify me."

467. Kumbha said, "Ever since I took leave of you quietly, my mind is dwelling on you only.

468. I do not delight in the celestial pleasures, but keep dwelling on you. I do not have in the world a relation, well-wisher, friend, reliable companion and disciple like you."

469. Sikhidwaja said, 'The holy tree of punya, religious merit, long tended by me has borne fruit. Though you are detached, you desire my company.

470. Because of your lofty and spiritual teaching, I myself have attained repose. So, wise seer, where is the need for heavenly pleasure for you?

471. Abiding in that luminous pure Consciousness, I want

to remain happy, in the earth itself as in heaven."

472. Kumbha said, "Are you established in the supreme felicitious state? Have you discarded the sorrow caused by perception of duality?

473. O king, having realised the Truth, has your mind been totally drawn away from the seeming plesures, desires and delights?

474. Is your mind serene enough, to be indifferent to both likes and dislikes, to be tranquil and even, and to remain unexcited in daily contacts.

475. Sikhidwaja said, "O Divine Seer! By thy grace has been attained the transcendental vision. I have gone beyond samsara, gained perfect understanding.

476. There is nothing to be instructed to me. I am exceedingly satisfied and I remain without fears.

477. I perfectly abide in akasa-like spacious plane, which is bereft of samsara, delusion, attachment, ever self-luminous and tranquil and which is all pervasive and rid of imagination."

478 & 479. Sri Vasishta said: "Thus speaking about the Self in a variety of ways, to each other, the two knowers of the knowable Truth, roamed about in the vast forest, various types of woods, river banks, lakes, bowers and caves.

480. Both had perfect friendship for each other. Both had equal intelligence, and equal energy and kept moving together.

481 to 483. They worshipped the manes and Gods and ate together, O Rama. Like the wind, their minds did not consider something desirable and something as not.

They roamed together in the forest, now with dust all

over their bodies, now with sandal paste, and with ashes at another time.

In a few days time, they became of one mind.

484. The king and Kumbha remained in an exalted state.

485. Chudala saw Sikhidwaja now shining in a new celestial lustre and the beautiful lady began to think on the following lines:

486 & 487. "A noble-minded husband, free from distress and youthful, abodes surrounded by flowers-a woman who would not desire to enjoy these is an unfortunate one.

What has the knower of Truth accomplished, if he were to be averse to happiness that spontaneously courts him, which is blemishless and vastly elevating?

488. With my intelligence, let me forge a new environment, in which my husband and king would delight in me."

489. Thinking thus, Chudala in the form of Kumbha, told the king somewhere in the wood, like the female cuckoo to the mate.

490. Kumbha said, "This is full-moon day of Chitra month and on the first day of the fortnight, there is a great festivals for Hari in heaven.

491. I have to be present there alongwith father. The established practice should not be given up anytime.

492. Without any sense of attachment, you keep spending the time in the wood by remaining in samadhi or sporting with flowers.

493. At the end of the day without doubt I return from the sky. Your company gives me greater happiness than life in the heaven."

494. Saying thus, Kumbha gave to his friend, nay, beloved,

a bunch of flowers of Mandara tree, as a token of pleasure.

495. "You should return speedily," said the king and she swam across the sky like the summer cloud.

496. Reaching beyond the range of Sikhidwaja's vision, she discarded her Kumbha form and assumed her natural form like the wavelet subsiding into the natural waters.

497. Assuming the form decorated with flowers, she entered the city, akin to the wish-fulfilling kalpavriksha. She entered into the inner apartment in an invisible form.

498. She attended to important royal duties quickly and descended before Sikhidwaja in the form of Kumbha.

499. The happy woman put on a sad face, which was like moon veiled by mist, lotus oppressed by night.

500. Seeing him in that condition, Sikhidwaja stood up, became sad and spoke in an affectionate manner thus.

501. "O celestial born! Obeisance to thee. You seem to be out of spirits. Discard this streak of sorrow. Be seated here.

502. The wise knowers of Truth do not become subject to pleasure and sorrow. They remain normal like the lotus leaves untainted by water."

503. Sri Vasishta said: "When she was told thus by the ruler of earth, Kumbha as he took the seat told, in grief-stricken words, which sounded like the cracking bamboo.

504. Kumbha said, "Those who do not conduct themselves with an even mind in various states, with senses of action functioning in appropriate ways are not knowers of Truth but wicked men.

505. O king, they are not knowers of Truth, who in a childish manner run away from situations that spontaneously confront one.

506. As long as sesame exists, there is oil-content; as long as there is body, there are mental states. He who does not remain in harmony with bodily state, surely tries to cut asunder the space.

507. The sorrows arising from bodily states, are truly abandoned only through the yoga of mind, that is, samadhi and not by the inactivity of the senses.

The BYV commentator comments thus: Through equanimity and absorption in samadhi, the sorrows arising out of bodily conditions are to be ignored and this is the kind of discarding that is meant and not the forcible control of senses.

508. O dear, as long as there is body, the discerning one should be acting with senses of action in appropriate ways, but not with senses of knowledge.

509. All exalted souls like the Progenitor conduct themselves in appropriate ways in various states and that is the cosmic rule.

510. All creatures of the earth are either knowers of Truth or otherwise. But all have to fall in line with cosmic necessity, as the river finds its way to the ocean.

511. The knowers of Truth keep the mind poised in Consciousness and set the senses of action in motion-thus they perfectly adhere to the cosmic necessity as long as the body is alive.

512. Those ignorant of Truth, agitated by the countless state of pleasure and sorrow, adhere imperfectly through sensual bodies to the cosmic necessity."

513. Sikhidwaja said, "O noble soul and master of speech

do thou explain how is it that you remain perturbed despite being celestial-born?"

514. Kumbha said, "I shall tell all that happened to me in the heaven today. When a sorrow is shared with a well-wisher, it torments less.

515. Leaving you here, after giving a bunch of flowers to you, I leapt across the sky and reached the heaven.

516. Alongwith father and Indra, I remained in the celestial assembly and when the time for departure came, father permitted me to leave.

517. I left the heaven and passed through sky to come here alongwith Sun's horses through the corridor of wind.

518. In one place, the sun chose a path and I another and came to the space, floating through it as if I were on ocean.

519. There, through rain-filled clouds, the seer Durvasa was coming in the opposite direction speeding and I saw him.

520. I offered obeisance to him and said, as I was borne away by the wind, that attired as he was in blue clothes, he looked like a woman on nocturnal visit to paramour.

521 to 523. Hearing this, the proud saint pronounced a curse on me, 'Go now. Because of your wicked remark, you will be, during night, a woman, with breasts, long hairs and the womanly traits.'

Hearing these unwelcome words of the old brahmana and before I could understand their meaning, he had disappeared.

Thus, indeed, O wise man, I have returned from the sky with a broken-heart.

524. How am I to pass on the period after day's end as a solitary woman who feels totally shy in the presence of preceptors, gods and brahmanas?

525. How I am to live alone as woman during night?"

526. Sikhidwaja said, "O celestial born! No purpose is served by grieving over the matter. Whatever happens to body, let it happen. The Self is untainted.

527. If you, an enlightened person, are also worried over matters that do not warrant it, how can others seek solution from one learned in the scripture like you."

528. Sri Vasishta said: "Consoling each other through such words, the two, attached to each other, remained sorrow-stricken.

529. The earthly lamp, sun also was, as it were, eager to transform Kumbha into a woman and it set like the lamp without oil.

530. The friendly pair rose up and after worshipping Sandhya, practised japa amidst different trees.

531. Then Kumbha slowly transformed the body into one with womanly features. In sobbing tone, he told Sikhidwaja sitting before him.

532. "My limbs throb and I feel, as it were, I change, and I flow like water. O king, it makes me shy that in the midst of a wood, I am changing into a woman.

533 & 534. See, O king, hairs growing in my head. See these rising breasts in the chest. The new apparel, outer and inner, cover my entire body. I feel inwardly the features changing in the lower part of the body."

535. Sri Vasishta said: "Saying thus, Kumbha became silent and sorrow-stricken, the king also seeing her, felt sad at heart.

536. Sikhidwaja said, "O wise man! You are knower of Truth. You understand the cosmic law. In matters which are certain to happen, do not succumb to grief."

537. Kumbha said, "Let it be so. O king, let me remain a woman. I am not perturbed. Who can ever disregard the cosmic law?"

538. Deciding thus and dismissing sorrow, they slept in the same couch and spent the night quietly.

539. When the dawn broke, the youthful womanly form with vessel-shaped breasts changed, and there was Kumbha.

540. Thus the princess Chudala remained as Kumbha and later as a woman in the company of her husband.

541. With Sikhidwaja as friend, Kumbha spent the day and during night, he assumed the womanly form.

542. As several days passed by in this manner, Chudala in the form of Kumbha, told her husband thus.

543. "O king, the lotus-eyed! Do thou listen to my words. Every night I thus become a woman.

544. I want to live the life of a woman perfectly. I shall give myself to an husband through marriage.

545. In all the worlds, you alone are acceptable to me as husband. Marry me and let me be your wife in the night.'

546. Sikhidwaja said, "In such deed, I do not see anything righteous or unrighteous. O great soul, do as you desire.'

547. Kumbha said, "If it is so, O king, today is an auspicious day. The full moon is in the Sravana Constellation. All the calculation has been done by me.

548. O valorous man, when the full moon rises in splendour

tonight, there shall be our wedding.

549. Do rise up, o lotus-eyed king, for the function of marriage, do collect sandal, flowers and jewels."

550. Sri Vasishta said: "Saying thus, Kumbha rose up alongwith the king and collected flowers and jewels.

551. After collecting all articles for marriage and arranging the nuptial couch, the affectionate two went to the river Mandakini for bath.

552. After bath, they worshipped the Gods, manes and seers. They were not enamoured of fruits of actions, nor were they interested in renouncing all activities.

553. After dressing themselves with the attire-like strips of the kalpa tree and after taking fruits, they came to the marriage bower.

554. By this time the sun set in the west. After the sandhya worship was over, Kumbha transformed himself into the bride.

555. She told, "My dear, do thou decorate me with jewels. Ignite the ceremonial fire and take my hand in the proper way.

556. O lotus-eyed, I am to be known by the name Madanika. I am your wife.' The king, did everything, as directed.

557. Thus, on the Mahendra slope, Kumbha and Sikhidwaja wedded on their own and became a very affectionate pair.

558. They rambled in the various attractive woods each day amidst fruit-bearing trees and flower-bearing creepers.

559. Every third day, when Sikhidwaja was asleep, Chudala went to the kingdom, attended to the royal

duties and returned again.

560. After some months passed thus, Chudala in the celestial form thought in the following manner.

561. Kumbha said, "Let me now test Sikhidwaja by exposing him to great pleasures to find out whether he delights himself in these pleasures."

562. Sri Vasishta said: After resolving thus, Chudala went into the wide forest. Sikhidwaja saw Indra arrive alongwith the celestials and nymphs.

563. Seeing that Indra had come with the retinue, Sikhidwaja, the forest-dweller worshipped him in an appropriate way.

564. Sikhidwaja asked, "O Celestial king, to confer what favour have you troubled yourself to come thus far? You may tell out of compassion."

565. Indra said, "We have been drawn to this place by your superior qualities, as a forest bird through a rope tied to it.

566. Rise up, come to the heaven. All the heavenly people await you. The celestial nymphs, having heard about you are struck by wonder.

567. Till the end of creation, you can enjoy the celestial pleasures in the heaven, as a liberated person. That is why I have come.

568. Sikhidwaja said, 'O Celestial Chief, I know all about the situation in the heaven. But I see heaven everywhere around me and not in any one place.

569. I am happy everywhere. I delight everywhere. Since I am not desirous of anything, I am blissful everywhere.

570. For some the heaven is abidance in one place. I do

491

not desire to go to heaven. O Indra, I am unable to keep thy command."

571. Sri Vasishta said: "As the king spoke thus, the entire celestial group, told, "Let happy things happen to you, O king,' and disappeared from view.

572 & 573. After withdrawing that illusory spectacle, Chudala reflected, 'Fortunately the king is not drawn towards pleasures. He was unexcited with the arrival of Indra. He conducted the affairs without agitation and with dignity.

574. Again, let me test him carefully through another ruse-by subjecting him to the experience of attachment and aversion that corrupts the mind.

575 to 577. Resolving thus, when the moon had just risen in the sky, when Sikhidwaja was engrossed in Sandhya worship and japa on the bank of the river, she contrived to have the entire abode covered with creepers and flowers like the home of the forest nymphs, and entered into it with a passionate heart, remained embracing with hands on the neck of a paramour created by her will in a couch bedecked with flowers.

578. After completing the japa, Sikhidwaja returned and searching for her amidst the bowers, found the pair with smiling faces within the abode.

Seeing them without a streak of sorrow in the heart, he was much happy.

579. 'Well the two lovers are very happy,' thought Sikhidwaja. 'Let the woman be happy. Let the paramour be happy.

580. Let there be no hindrance to them'-with that concern and speaking to himself, he came out of the abode.

581. In an hour's time, she approached the king in a form with features which revealed her previous amorous dalliance and saw the king on a stone block.

582. He was alone, absorbed in contemplation with eyes slightly opened.

583. Reaching that spot and overcome by shame, the damsel Madanika stood hanging her head down silently for a while with a sad face.

Sikhidwaja, in a second, woke up from meditation and told her words, pleasing and affectionate, with an unperturbed mind.

584 & 585. 'Beautiful lady! Why have you come away so soon putting an end to the pleasure? Do thou go again to please your paramour with lovely gestures. Mutual liking and friendship are hard to obtain in all the worlds.'

586. Madanika said, "O noble-soul. It is as you say. Woman's nature is unsteady. The passion of woman is eight-fold of man's. You should not get angry.

587. I am young and immature. I am wrong and foolish. O my husband, please forgive. Wise people possess much fortitude."

588. Sikhidwaja said, "O young woman, I can have no anger, as there can be no tree in space. But I do not wish to have you as consort because wise people would not approve of it."

589. Sri Vasishta said: "As Sikhidwaja remained tranquil prompted by his calmness, Chudala began to think over the matter.

590. "How fine! The noble soul has attained great equanimity. Neither desire for pleasure nor great fortune draws him its way.

493

591. Let me tell him all that I did. Let me also discard the form of Madanika and be Chudala."

592. Sri Vasishta said: "Thinking thus, Chudala assumed her natural form. Sikhidwaja saw before him the blemishless lady exuding loving affection.

593. Seeing his beloved and surprised, Sikhidwaja, with eyes expressing the sense of wonder, said these thoughtful words.'

594. "Who are you, the lotus-eyed lady? For what have you come: O fair woman, what do you desire? How long have you been here?

595. Your features, manner, smile, responsiveness-all indicate you to be my wife, Chudala."

596. Chudala said, "O Lord, it is so. I am Chudala without doubt. I have joined you in my natural form.

597. I contrived a hundred illusory spectacles in the wood like the creation of the body of Kumbha only to enlighten you.

598. You are now a knower of Truth. By your intelligence and contemplation, you can see everything. O knower of Truth, do thou see with the inner vision."

599. Sri Vasishta said: "As Chudala said this, the king assumed a firm sitting posture and through meditation saw everything that happened to him.

600. Beginning from the renunciation of kingdom and ending with the seeing of Chudala, the king saw everything and emerged from the state of samadhi.

601. Getting out from the samadhi and stretching his arms out at once, with tear-soaked eyes, embraced the beloved for long.

602. Experiencing for a second the intense delight,

Sikhidwaja, the king, saw her, who was silent and loving and resting her on his lap, said,

603. "With what can be compared your wisdom, by which, from this dreadful samsaric mire I have been pulled out?

604. Women, enterprising and virtuous, of good families, save fallen men from getting drowned in the gruesome ocean of delusion vastly deep and infinitely dangerous.

605. How can I adequately compensate thee for the great service in taking me across the ocean of samsara to the shore of desireless state?"

606. Chudala said, "O Lord, when you were engrossed in the meaningless rites, I became frequently sad on account of your condition.

607. Therefore, in the process of enlightening you, I was serving only my purpose. How can my lord be made to accord importance to me?

608. Those senseless desires and fancies, imagination and perversions are not to be seen in you now, O Lord, as mountains in the space.'

609. Sikhidwaja said, "I am desireless; I am without parts; I am as pure as space and without attachment. I am tranquil; I am self, established as I am in it for long.

610. I am nothing, I am mere pure Consciousness; I am neither delighted nor painful. I am neither this nor that.

611. I am equal to the effulgence that rises forth from the mass of light and falls on the wall-without any change in nature.

612. That which exists, that alone I am I cannot describe anymore; O woman with fleeting glances, you are my preceptor. Obeisance to thee.

613. Because of the grace of the wide-eyed woman, I am saved from the ocean of life. I am beyond all, I am all. I am, like space, all-pervasive."

614. Chudala said, 'O noble soul, my dear Lord, matters having come to such a stage, what is it that pleases you most? Tell me.'

615. Sikhidwaja said, "I reject nothing nor seek anything, O fair lady. As you decide, I act.

616. O fair woman, whatever is proper according to you, do that. I shall do the very thing, like the gem that merely reflects the image.

I praise not nor despise. Do as you desire, please."

617. Chudala said, "O valorous soul! If that is so, hear my view. A liberated soul you are. After hearing it, it would be proper to act accordingly.

618. By realising the supreme oneness everywhere, with ignorance and fear gone and with utter detachment, we are as lofty as the space.

619. Let us discard attachment to things that have a beginning, middle and end and attain to the Supreme.

620. Residing in the kingdom naturally associated with us and spending time governing it, O Lord, we shall attain to videha-mukti, disembodied liberation, at the proper time.

621. In your own city be the king again seated in your throne. I shall be thy queen, according, the most excellent of delights.

622. This is happiness, this is not-when such dual feelings become extinct, when there is abidance in the one supreme plane, continue to remain in it without any desire.'

623. Sikhidwaja said, 'O woman with large eyes! You have told what is reasonable. Where is there an object whether in kingdom or home or in the state of renunciation that can be compared to thy intellect?

624. Abandoning thoughts of pleasures and sorrows, and bereft of envy, we shall remain as we are, in a pure state."

625. Sri Vasishta said: "Then, Chudala, rising from the seat, so willed and the bejewelled vessel before her got filled with the waters of the seven oceans.

626. With the waters of that auspicious vessel, the wife ceremoniously bathed the husband, as he sat facing the east and established him as the ruler of the kingdom.

627. Thereafter seating the great lady in the throne, the king ceremoniously bathed her and told his beloved Chudala,

628. "O dear lotus-eyed woman! Do thou bring into existence a vast army by your will in a second."

629. Sri Vasishta said: "Hearing the words of her dear husband, the beautfiful Chudala thought of an army that would fill the entire woods.

630. The royal pair ascended the sweet-smelling chief elephant, duly adorned with royal seats and accompanied by the elated chief nobles.

631. Thereon, the king Sikhidwaja alongwith his beloved queen, leading the mighty army including the infantry and leaving the Mahendra Hill, reached in a short while his capital, attractive like the ocean.

632. The citizens, and the chieftains elated by the arrival of the royal couple hailed them with shouts of 'Jaya' and went about in great joy.

633 to 638. Welcomed by the sounds of trumpets and bugles and honoured by the nobles who went in front to receive, the king entered the city with added prestige.

He ruled over the earth for a ten thousand years alongwith Chudala, O Rama, before he became displeased with the embodied condition.

Leaving the body, the king, the noble soul, attained liberation, like the lamp without oil, not to be reborn.

After enjoying endless pleasures in the world, and remaining as the crest jewelled sovereign of all earth for a long time, he attained the ambrosial infinite state, leaving behind no residual karma.

Thus, Rama, by attending to the natural duties falling to one's lot without sorrow, they were self-established while experiencing the delights of sense pleasures and liberation-both manifestation of the Goddess Sri Lakshmi."

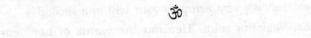

Chapter-10

The Story of Kacha

1. Sri Vasishta said: "I have thus told you the story of Sikhidwaja. By treading such a path, you do not court sorrow at any time.

2. As Birhaspati's son Kacha attained Realisation in the manner of Sikhidwaja, O Rama, you also realise the Truth."

3. Sri Rama asked, "O Divine Seer, how the all-knowing Kacha, son of the Divine Seer Brihaspati, became enlightened, please tell me in brief."

4. Sri Vasishta said: "Growing out of adolescent state and desirous of getting out from the ocean of samsara, Kacha, well-versed in the understanding of words and things asked Brihaspati.

5. Kacha said, "O Divine Seer, Knower of virtue, how does a creature, a sentient entity, get out of the cage of samsara? Please explain."

6. Brihaspati said, 'O son, one is easily emanicipated from this ocean of samsara filled with dreadful fishes, through total renunciation.'

7. Hearing the soul-purifying words of the father, Kacha renounced everything and went to the lonely forest.

8. His renunciation did not trouble Brihaspati. The noble souls do not get agitated because of union or separation of people.

9. O faultless man, after eight years had passed, Kacha came across father in some place of the forest.

10. The son adored the father and prostrated to him and as the father embraced the son, Kacha, asked Brihaspati in affectionate tone.

11. "It is eight years since I made total renunciation. In spite of it, father, I do not get mental repose."

12. Sri Vasishta said: "As Kacha spoke these agonising words in the wood, saying 'renounce completely all,' Brihaspati returned to the heaven.

13. As father returned, Kacha discarded even the bark worn around the body. He shone like the summer sky filled with white clouds, sun and stars.

14. Three years later, and in some other forest, in an afflicted frame of mind, he came across his father and preceptor again.

15. He worshipped the father and prostrated to him and the father embraced him. He again asked the father in grief-stricken words.

16. Kacha asked, "Father, everything has been renounced including the attire and the creeper-covered hut. In spite of it, there is no repose. What am I to do to obtain it?"

17. Brihaspati said, "Chitta is said to be everything and by renouncing it, O son, you will become serene. Renunciation of chitta is renunciation of everything, according to those well-versed in renunciation."

18. Sri Vasishta said: "After saying thus, Brihaspati flew through space. With undejected mind, Kacha tried to find out what chitta is, to renounce it.

19. Though he reflected on it in the woods, he did not know what it was. He did not lose heart and kept reflecting on.

20.   Kacha said, "The aggregate of body is not said to be Chitta. Why should I discard the blemishless body for no purpose?

21.   Let me go to father to know about the great enemy chitta. After knowing it, I shall renounce it and remain established without worry."

22.   Sri Vasishta said: "After thinking thus, Kacha left to meet his father and preceptor. With modesty, he asked, "Father, what is called chitta?"

23.   Brihaspati said, "Those who know about chitta say that it is 'ahankara.' The inner 'I-notion' of the Creator is called chitta.'

24.   Kacha said, "I think that it is difficult to discard the 'I-notion' and attain peace. O great yogi, how can this be discarded?"

25.   Brihaspati said, "It is easier than plucking the flower and opening the eyelid to renounce the 'I-notion' and there is certainly no hardship.

26.   There is pure Consciousness alone without beginning and end. It is purer than space and is all-knowing.

27.   Contemplating on that alone perfectly, remain steady without anxiety. The illusory notion becomes extinct on the contemplation of Reality.

28.   What is this 'I-notion' in chit and how has it arisen and what for? How could there exist a heap of dust in water, a sheet of water arise from fire?

29 & 30.   O son, give up the futile notion, 'I am this.' It is a limited entity, bound by space, time, etc., and truly non-existent.

31.   That which is not limited by time and space, that which is pure and self-luminous, which is non-dual

but manifests as manifold, that pure consciousness you are.'

32. Sri Vasishta said: "Brihaspati's son, receiving this supreme instruction and attaining to yoga became a liberated person, while alive.

33. Even as Kacha remained without the notions, 'I' and 'mine,' with the knot of ignornace cut asunder and with a tranquil mind, Rama, do thou also remain with a steady mind.

34. *Know that ahankara does not exist. Neither rely on it nor reject it. How can there be acceptance or rejection of the non-existent hare's horn."*

Chapter-11

The Story of an Illusory Person

Sri Vasishta said:

1. "Abandoning the conception of duality and non-duality, abide happily in the residual being. Do not needlessly be grief-stricken like the illusory individual."

2. Sri Rama asked, "I have attained to the supreme plane; I have obtained fulfillment through your elixir of wisdom. O Lord, though I am at peace, I again put questions to you.

3. O Seer, who is called as the illusory individual? The existent is made non-existent and the non-existent world existent. What is truth?"

4. Sri Vasishta said: "Rama, hear this interesting story of the illusory individual capable of generating laughter, I tell you for your enlightenment.

5. O valorous man, there is an individual-entirely of the illusory stuff of maya-who is immature like a boy, stupid and proud.

6. He was born in void and lived in it only. He was akin to the hallucinatory spectacle of the lump of effulgent hair in space and the illusory mirage in the desert.

7. There was nothing in the Chit apart from that illusory individual. Whatever was there, was only he. Whatever else was, was only a manifestation of himself. Being stupid, he was not also aware of self-existent Consciousness.

8.   As he developed a form, he entertained the desire, 'let me establish akasa, the object of my desire and protect it carefully.'

9.   After thinking thus, for the sake of protecting the akasa, he built a house. He developed attachment towards it, in the thought, 'the space is protected by the house now.'

10.   In course of time, the house met with destruction, like the lake in the summer and like the wave by the wind.

11.   'Alas! The space of the house is destroyed. Where have you gone in an instant? As the house is destroyed, the space is destroyed'-thus he bemoaned.

12.   Grieving over it in various ways, the stupid individual constructed a well for protecting the space and was engrossed in that protection.

13.   Even the well, in course of time, got destroyed. When the space of the well was gone, he again got immersed in sorrow.

14.   After bemoaning over the loss of the space of well, he made a pot. He was engrossed in the space of the pot and was peaceful.

15.   O Rama, even the pot broke at some time. Whatever the unfortunate individual contrived to build, that met with destruction.

16.   After bemoaning the loss of pot and other things, he built a small vessel for the protection of space and got absorbed in it.

17.   Even the small vessel got destroyed after some time, like darkness at the onset of light. He mourned over the loss of the vessel.

18.   At the death of the space of the vessel, he built a

large hall for the protection of space and was happily absorbed in it.

19. Time, the devourer of people, destroyed that as well, like the wind the dry leaf, and again he sank in sorrow.

20. After bemoaning the loss of the space of the hall, he built a warehouse for the protection of space and remained absorbed in it.

21. Like wind destroying the cloud, time destroyed it too and because of the destruction of the space of the container, he was engulfed in gloom.

22. Thus, through endless involvement in the space of house, well, pot, hall, container, etc., his entire time was spent in sorrow only.

23. Conducting himself in this way, the stupid individual cognising the space within and identifying himself with the house-space, moved from one intense sorrow to another because of stupid identification with things that are transitory."

24. Sri Rama asked, "In this story concerning the illusory individual, who is referred to as the illusory being what is meant by protection of space?"

25. Sri Vasishta said: "He who is referred to as the illusory individual, O Rama, is to be known as 'ahankara,' who rose up from the space-like Consciousness.

26. O wise man! That space-like Consciousness in which this world abides is infinite, really devoid of other things and remains as such, as it was prior to creation. From that arises, 'ahankara' like movement in wind.

27. The non-self ahankara, for the sake of the protection of the real Self, that is, Consciousness, creates various bodies, and when they get destroyed again and again, it becomes grief-stricken.

28. The ahankara creates bodies like the illusory individual creating well, vessel, hall, pot, etc., and deludes into thinking that the space-like Self has been protected.

29. Like the illusory individual who underwent hardship through the construction of pot, etc., in the hope of protecting the space, do not undergo misery.

30. Atma, Self, is subtler than space, more pervasive, pure, blissful and auspicious and how can such Atma be grasped or protected?

31. When the body, which is but the space of the heart, perishes, people grieve that the Atma has perished.

32. When pot, etc., get destroyed, the unconditioned space remains as before; in the same way, when the bodies die, the indwelling spirit remains unaffected.

33. The Self is pure Consciousness and it is subtler than the elemental akasa. It is merely of the nature of immediate awareness and like space, it does not perish.

34. Nothing is born, and nothing is dead, anywhere and anytime. Brahman alone manifests in the changed form of world.

35. All this is the non-dual blissful Being, bereft of beginning or end. It is beyond the existent and non-existent and knowing it to be so, be happy.

36. Ahankara is the abode of all hardships; it is impermanent and dependent; it is ignorant and on the verge of collapse. Through awareness, discard this ahankara principle and abide in the residual state of Supreme Consciousness.

Chapter-12

The Story of Bhringisa

Sri Vasishta said:

1. "O Rama, this world has come into existence only on account of the self-forgetfulness of the invisible reality and not from anything else, like snake in the rope.

2. O Rama, for him who sees the effulgence of sun as different from sun, it is so.

3. For him who sees the bracelet as different from gold, it is bracelet only.

4. For him who sees the effulgence as non-different from Sun, the effulgence is only sun and this is known as nirvikalpa, undifferentiated cognition.

5. For him who sees the bracelet as non-different from gold, it is only gold and this is known as nirvikalpa, undifferentiated cognition.

6. Abandoning all manifoldness, and releasing from externalising cognition, abide steadily in the principle of pure intelligence.

7. When Atma, Self, by its own power assuming the form of will creates, like wind the energy of movement; then mind, of the stuff of imagination, acquires a form of its own embracing the universe and manifests, as if it were separate.

8. This world of pleasure that is perceived is only an imagination. It is neither real, nor false. It is akin to the world of dream.

9.   As you see, hear, touch, smell, speak, sleep and interact, be convinced that all this is Consciousness only and nothing different manifests.

11.   Whatever you do, know that it is Consciousness only, Brahman in enlarged form. There is nothing apart from it.

12.   When all manifest things are seen to be the essence of intelligence, all this world is intelligence alone and there is no act of imagination.

13.   When the same intelligence can assume all forms (of seer and seen), the cognisable does not at all exist and so, how can there be bondage and liberation?

14.   'This leads to liberation,' 'This constitutes bondage'- such conception and misconception, do thou destroy and restrain the mind. Remain as a lofty soul, silent, self-controlled, bereft of pride and conceit and do your tasks without the 'I-notion.'

15.   O faultless man, summon great courage and discarding all doubts, be the supreme doer, supreme enjoyer and the supreme renunciate."

16.   Sri Rama asked, "Do thou explain clearly who is the supreme doer, the supreme enjoyer and the supreme renunciate?"

17.   Sri Vasishta said: "These three disciplines were taught, O Rama, by Lord Shiva to Bhringisa and as a result he became a liberated being.

18.   In the summit of Sumeru, Lord Shiva was seen in a fire-like radiant form alongwith his retinue.

19.   O Rama, the effulgent inquisitive seer Bhringisa, by offering obeisance to Him, asked him about the nature of Truth.

20. Bhringisa asked, "O Master, seeing the creator world, as fleeting as the wavelets, I get confounded, as I do not have the equanimity which the knowledge of Truth gives.

21. With what inner conviction, that is capable of leading to delightful repose, I can remain firm in this dilapidated house of world without worry?"

22. Ishvara said, "Discarding all doubts and summoning your strength, be the supreme doer, the supreme enjoyer and the supreme renunciate."

23. Bhringisa asked, "Who is to be known as the supreme doer? Who is the supreme enjoyer? And who is the supreme renunciate? O Lord, kindly explain to me?"

24. Ishvara said, "Regardless of its dualities of desire and hatred, joy and sorrow, virtue and vice, fruitful or otherwise, he who acts is the supreme doer:

25. He who acts without anxiety, while remaining silent, without 'I-notion,' pride and envy, is the supreme doer.

26. He who acts without any desire of his own, without any attachment and by remaining as a witness, is the supreme doer.

27. He is the supreme doer, who is without anxiety and elation, even-minded, pure and is without grief or joy.

28. He is the supreme doer whose mind remains in the same condition in all states of birth, existence, death, prosperity and decline.

29. He hates not anything nor covets anything. He enjoys all that is available-such a person is the supreme enjoyer.

30. He who is not perturbed by experience of pleasure and pain, activity, and inactivity, perceptions of illusory

and real things is the supreme enjoyer.

31. He who enjoys old age, death, kingdom, poverty-all as pleasure-is known as the supreme enjoyer.

32. Bitter, astringent, saltish, sour tastes, well-cooked, or not-he who treats all these inwardly equal is known as the supreme enjoyer.

33. Tasty or otherwise, pleasing or displeasing-he who is even-minded and accepts equally these all is the supreme enjoyer.

34. Saline water, sweet dish, auspicious and inauspicious things-are equal to him, who is known as the supreme enjoyer.

35. This is fit to be enjoyed and this is not-leaving aside such conceptions, as he who enjoys without any attachment is known to be the supreme enjoyer.

36. Fortune, disaster, grief, joy-he who experiences these intermittently with an even mind, is known to be the supreme enjoyer.

37. Virtue and vice, pleasure and sorrow, life and death-all these are completely renounced by whom as illusory, is the supreme renunciate.

38. All desires, all doubts, all cravings, all convictions, he by whom all these are renounced mentally is the supreme renunciate.

39. He who makes the inner renunciation of virtue and vice, contemplation and desire is known as the supreme renunciate.

40. The entire world, the entire range of perceived objects, he who renounces completely is the supreme renunciate.

41. Sri Vasishta said: "O faultless man, thus was told by Ishvara to Bhringisa. Do adhere to these disciplines, O Rama, and remain without care.

42. The ever manifest, pure, eternal Brahman alone exists and nothing else, real or illusory-do contemplate in this manner and attaining to blemishless state, enjoy the condition of liberation, with a mind bereft of modifications.

43. The Brahman, supreme in nature, is the single cause of all created things in all the aeons. It is huge like space and manifesting as all, exists and shines, as it were.

44. Nothing else anywhere and at anytime exists at all, whether it be real or unreal-with this firm conviction, O wise man, remain steady in the pure state, discarding all doubts.

45. With mind inwardised at all times, and doing externally everything demanded by the occasion, never do you become a victim of sorrow and you can remain established in the plane that transcends the I-notion."

Chapter-13

The Story of Ikshvaku

1. Sri Rama said, "O Divine Seer, Omniscient Saint, when chitta, also called as ahankara is renounced, what indications distinguish the subtle mind of such a person?"

2. Sri Vasishta said: "Miserliness, grief and such other faults, even if they manifest in a forcible manner, do not stick to the pure mind, as waters to the lotus-leaf.

3. When the evil ahankara gets discarded, joy and other traits like friendliness do not ever forsake the disposition of the person.

4. The knots formed by vasanas, as if cut into pieces, get completely destroyed, anger subsides and delusion becomes extinct.

5. Lust makes no appearance and covetousness flees from him. The senses do not dominate and pain torments not.

6. Sorrows do not accumulate nor pleasures entice. The vision of oneness that makes the heart cool arises towards all things.

7. If ever the indications of joy or sorrow manifest in the face of such a person, they are only appearances and do not taint the mind.

8. When the mind becomes extinct, even the celestials cease to attract, and oneness of vision, like the cool effulgence of moon, manifests.

9. The body becomes tranquil, lovable, worthy of respect,

unassailable, unchanging, confident, pure and blemishless.

10. The samsaric experiences of great souls-whether they are favourable or unfavourable, whether they are distinctive or not really produce neither joy nor sorrow.

11. He who would not strive for this state of liberation, in which no risk lurks and which is attainable by mere intellectual discernment is an unworthy person indeed.

12. For the seeker of liberation who wants to sever himself from the ocean of life filled with sorrows of attachment, the supreme means is the enquiry-Who am I? How has this world arisen? Who is the Supreme? What are pleasures?"

13. Sri Vasishta said: "The chief ancestor of your family, Ikshvaku, was the ruler of the whole earth. O scion of the Ikshvaku family, how he attained liberation, do thou listen.

14. The king Ikshvaku , while ruling over the kingdom, went into seclusion once and reflected thus.

15. Of his own accord, he tried to find out what is the cause of this perceived world characterised by miseries of birth and death and illusory pleasures and sorrows.

16. Though he thought over the matter, he could not find out the cause of the world.

So he asked the Divine Progenitor, Manu, who had come from the Brahmaloka and after receiving worship was sitting in his assembly.

17. Ikshvaku asked, 'O Divine Seer, it is only thy kindness that prompts me to ask you, an ocean of mercy, these questions.

18. Whence has this creation proceeded and what is its nature? What is its dimension? By whom, when and through what, was this made? Please enlighten.

19. Like the bird from the cage, how may I release myself from this miserable and intense delusion of samsara?

20. Manu said, 'Ha! After a long time, a profound question concerning luminous vision of the Absolute has been raised by you.

21. O king! All this, which is seen, does not at all exist, as the dream-castle, as the mirage on the desert.

22. That which is beyond the mind and the senses and which is not seen exists as imperishable Being and that is called Atma, Self.

23. O king, all this objective worldly creation is, as it were, a reflection in that great mirror of Atma.

24. The luminous potencies emerging from that effulgent Self assume the form of the Brahmanda somewhere and the form of the earth somewhere else.

25. *Bondage there is not; liberation there is not. Pure Brahman alone exists. There is neither oneness nor duality. Mere intelligence manifests as all.*

26. Even as waters manifesting as several waves, are one intrinsically, chit manifests as the manifold and the manifoldness is not real. Do thou cast away the conceptions of bondage and liberation and, being rid of the fear of samsara, abide as Self, which is essentially fearlessness.

27. The real conscious principle gets, as it were, externalised, like water assuming the form of wave, and thus passes into jiva-hood.

28. These jivas which had arisen earlier thus pass through

samsara. Joys, sorrows and grief exist only in the mind and not in Atma, Self.

29. The invisible Rahu becomes visible when it gets associated with moon; even so, Atma which is mere awareness, is cognised when associated with the adjuncts, body, etc.

30. Neither through scripture nor through Guru, the Supreme God is seen. He is seen by the Self as Self with one's pure intellect.

31. Those senses, have to be looked at without desire and without aversion, as the wayfarers look at things on the way.

32. One should not show any special interest in them nor should one despise them. Let them cognise objects and abide as such.

33. Renounce mentally objects like body and becoming cool at heart, remain as pervasive Self.

34. The notion 'I am the body' pushes one into samsaric experience; seekers of liberation should never entertain this attitude.

35. "I am nothing. I am mere chit. I am subtler than space." Such notion does not involve one in samsara.

36. Even as Sun's effulgence is to be seen both inside and outside the pure waters, Self characterises all the objects.

37. As the golden ornament through mere realignment of the gold particles appears as other than gold, Self appears in the form of world etc.

38 & 39. Do thou contemplate the Self as great Agastya who drinks away the waters of the ocean of Time, which remains unfilled completely even now, into

which rivers of worlds, carrying the waves of people exhaust themselves and which is ravaged by the Fire of Destruction.

40. Discard the notion of Self in the objective entities like body and remain mentally as inner blissful being.

41. The man who seeks to know the Self is like the mother who, oblivious of the fact of child lying in sleep on her breasts sobs for the loss of child.

42. Without realising the nature of Self as unborn and unaging the person identifying with the perishable body wails, 'Ha, I am lost. I have no saviour. I am destroyed.'

43. By virtue of the wind blowing over it, water appears as varied waves. By virtue of sankalpa, thought, chit appears as variegated Brahman.

44. Strip the mind, chitta of the stain of sankalpa, thought and unite it with Atma, Self. Even if there is activity in the chitta, be aware that in the all-capable Self, there is no activity and in a blissful state, do thou govern this kingdom.

Manu said:

45. The all-pervasive Self, like the child, plays on Its own, with sportive creation. Through the power of destruction, It withdraws into Itself everything and abides still.

46. Such power arises in It spontaneously by which It is bound. Such power arises in It spontaneously by which it becomes freed.

47 & 48. Even as the radiance emanating from iron, jewels moon etc., is non-different from them, even as leaves are non-different from the tree, even as the flying particles are non-different from the waters of the falls,

so are world etc., from Brahman and they are entirely imagined entities, which give sorrow to those who do not know their real nature.

49. Ha! My dear! Maya capable of deluding the whole universe is wonderful; Atma, though permeating all limbs, is not cognised as such.

50. The entire world is only space-like chit. Contemplating in this manner, he who remains withdrawn into himself, has Brahman as the protective armour and is blissful.

51. By releasing oneself from the 'I'-principle, through contemplation of it as non-existing, think that all this world is contentless and bare Consciousness.

52. The seed of successive sorrows is the conception, 'this is beautiful...this is not.' If that seed is burnt with the fire of equanimity, where is scope for sorrow?

53. O king, through the astra weapon of conviction that 'it does not exist,' strengthened by your own superior exertion, the notions beautiful and non-beautiful may be destroyed.

Astra is a missile charged with power through mantra.

54. My dear, through negation destroy the conception of the array of karma and attenuation of the vasana, abide as blissful Self.

55. Attaining to the distinctionless vast world of experience and acquiring the discriminative vision which wipes away mental fancies, abiding in the supreme bliss without taint, be the tranquil, even, effulgent, pure, fearless Principle of Consciousness.

56. Do thou initially develop intelligence through study of scripture, association with the wise, etc. For the

new entrants in the path of yoga, this is stated to be the first plane.

57. Enquiry is the second, and the third is contemplation of non-attachment. The fourth is of the nature of the destruction of vasanas.

58. At the fifth, one becomes the pure blissful Consciousness. He is a jivanmukta and remains half asleep and half awake.

59. The sixth is a plane where he does not cognise anything. As in sleep, he is a mass of blissful Consciousness.

60. The seventh plane represents the turiya, transcendental state of Consciousness, in which all other states completely get transcended, and which is liberation. He is even-minded, pure and serene.

61. The state of turiyatita is of the nature of the final liberation. This phase on the seventh plane is far too beyond the contemplation of the jiva.

62. The first three planes are regarded as jagrat, waking; the fourth is dream, wherein the world appears as dream.

63. The state of blissfulness relating to the fifth is sleep.
The state of non-awareness is the sixth and the turiya.

64. The seventh state called turiyatita is the self-luminous plane which is beyond the reach of mind and words.

65. With the mind interiorised, if the objective matter is not cognised, you are certainly liberated and have great equanimity, without doubt.

66. If a person wholly delighted within Self remains with a fullness of mind that does not get affected by experiences of pleasure and pain, is considered a liberated person.

67. Whether he is engaged in activity or withdrawn from it; is a house-holder or an ascetic; is associated with body or not, he should be endowed with such an attitude.

68. I am not dead nor alive, I am neither sat nor asat, I am not anything, I am chit alone-he who thinks thus does not grieve.

69. I am wholly unattached to anything, I do not grow old, I have no desire and am bereft of vasanas, I am partless and am but chid-akasa-thinking thus, a person does not grieve.

70. The 'I-notion' has been erased. There is only pure, enlightened, eternal, serene Being indifferent to the real and the unreal-thinking thus, he does not grieve.

71. At the tip of grass, in sky, in sun, in the human, in the serpent, in the celestial, That which is, is the Consciousness-thinking thus, one does not grieve.

72. There is only the glorious Consciousness on all sides, above and below and knowing that to be of infinite dimension, who would suffer?

73. Because of intense attachment, an object gives pleasure and what gives pleasure gives sorrow also on its disappearance.

74. Happiness and sorrow, it is well-known, do not exist without one another. When an object is experienced with a seeming attachment or no attachment, it does not give pleasure and so at the time of its destruction there is no sorrow.

75. When something is experienced with a mind stripped of vasanas, the experience is akin to condition of a burnt seed and it does not sprout again.

76. A deed is done through the organs and the body and

who among these is fit to be the doer or enjoyer?

77. Discarding all notions about objects, He who has a heart as cool as the moon shines with a lustre of the sun.

78. The deeds already done and being done by the body are driven away by wisdom like the tender growths of the salmal tree by the speedy wind.

79. *If there is no constant practice, all skills of the creatures perish. The fire-speck of wisdom, once risen, grows fast every day vigorously like seed sown in fertile soil.*

80. The all-inclusive non-dual Atma manifests in all objects, like water in the lakes and the oceans. With the extinction of the imagination of the manifoldness, know the entire world is bare existence.

81. The ultimate form of the Reality is Sanmatra, bare existentiality.

82. As long as the individual has desire for sense-enjoyment, he has jivahood and this has been brought about by non-discrimination; it is not natural.

83. When through discriminative vision, the desire is discarded, Atma, abandoning the jivahood becomes blemishless Brahman.

84. From up it goes down and from down it goes up in an unending manner the samsaric wheel and do not get bound by the rope to it.

85. Those who on account of excessive delusion, pursue notions, 'this is mine,' 'I belong to him,' etc., they go further and further to lower levels and are unworthy men.

86. Those who have cast away such delusion as 'I belong to him,' 'He is mine,' 'I am such and such'-through

discriminative vision go higher and higher.

87.   O king, see the Self as luminous and self-revealing and the worlds as pervasive Consciousness.

88.   When the nature of chit is completely understood as such, then the samsara is finally transcended and you have attained supreme lordship.

89.   Whatever Brahma, Indra, Vishnu and Varuna venture to do, I, of the nature of Consciousness, do-contemplate thus in this manner.

90.   O dear, whatever is taught in whatever scripture, all that is real and the chit manifests freely as all.

91.   He, who has attained to bare Consciousness and has crossed the ocean of samsara and is mind-less, experiences a delight which is beyond comparison.

92.   It is neither full nor void, neither insentient nor sentient, neither self nor non-self-contemplate the universe in this manner. On attaining this understanding prakriti, primordial matter, merges into Consciousness.

93.   What is stated to be liberation is not a particular place nor time nor any other state. What is called as prakriti is bhavana, imagination, and with ahankara ceasing to exist with the extinction of delusion, bhavana also merges in the cause, and that is liberation.

When ahankara caused by delusion becomes extinct, bhavana, also otherwise called as prakriti, merges in the cause and that is liberation. S. T.

94.   With the inquisitiveness to enquire into the teachings of the scripture disappearing, with the curiosity to experience the various rasas dispelled, with the various imaginations becoming extinct, one abides wholly in bliss permanently.

95. He covers himself with anything and eats anything, sleeps anywhere and yet he is as glorious as an emperor.

96. He emerges out, like the lion from the cage, from the web of worldly life, characterised by obligations pertaining to order, class, scripture, etc.

97. He is beyond the reach of words and he is bereft of desires for sense-objects. Like the summer sky, he shines with a rare charm.

98. Like the great lake amidst hills, he is majestic and serene and unagitated and he delights wholly in the Self.

99. He has renounced desires for fruits of all actions; he is ever contented and is not dependent on anything. He is not affected either by virtue or by vice or by anything else.

100. As the crystal does not develop attachment to the image reflecting in it, even so the knower of Truth does not develop attachment towards the fruit of karma.

    An object gets reflected in the crystal and when the object is taken away, the reflection disappears without leaving any trace. The mind of a knower of Truth is akin to the crystal. S. T.

101. Sporting among groups of people, the physical abuse or worship that he receives does not produce in him pain or joy, as though they pertain only to the reflected image.

102. He receives no praise, is unchanging; he neither worships nor is worshipped; he adheres to proper conduct and manners and disregards them also.

103. The world is not afraid of him nor is he afraid of the world. Desire, hatred, fear, and happiness-arise and arise not in him.

104. Lofty in thought, he is not accessible even to the big; devoid of small-mindedness, he is accessible even to the child.

105 & 106. Let him cast away the body in a holy place or in the cobbler's house; let him not pass away or let him pass away now. The moment realisation dawns, the noble soul has attained liberation.

The illusory, 'I-notion,' constitutes bondage and when through wisdom it becomes extinct, it is liberation.

107 & 108. If people are fortunate to come across him, he is worthy of worship always by people. He should be worshipped, adored and prostrated repeatedly. He should be seen respectfully, met and honoured with precious offerings.

109. That lofty holy plane is attained not by penance, sacrifice, holy pilgrimages but by devotion to the wise knowers of Self who are free from the maladies of worldly life."

110. Sri Vasishta said: "The Divine Seer, Manu, after speaking thus, returned to his abode. Ikshvaku also, adhering to that precept, remained stabilised in the Supreme."

Chapter-14

The Story of the Seer and the Hunter

1. Sri Rama asked, "O Divine Seer, this being the nature of the jivanmukta, the liberated soul, what is the unique distinction that characterises such wise knowers of Self?"

2. Sri Vasishta said: "O dear, the intellect of the knower of the Self acquires a new vision. He is totally satisfied within; He is tranquil and abides in the Self only.

3. Feats like going through sky are often accomplished through mantra, tapas, and ritualistic practices, etc., and what is the uniqueness about it?

4. By such means the powers like anima, etc., are attained frequently, through exclusive pursuit and these are not attained by Knowers of Self.

5. This is their uniqueness, that they are not similar to stupid men. Because they have discarded pleasures from all things, their mind is serene.

6. This alone is the indication of the people who otherwise have no external symbols and who have totally got rid of the illusion of worldly life. The enlightened soul, attaining to peace, effectively kills the emotions of lust, anger, grief, delusion and covetousness and avoids the dangers arising therefrom.

7. Just as the brahmana, by being indifferent to the wise conduct and by association with women of a low caste,

becomes a person of that caste, Ishvara also becomes jiva.

8 & 9. The things of the world belong to two categories and these alone manifest in every creation. The first arise on account of the initial spurt in Consciousness without any reason. Rising from Ishvara, others undergo several lives as a result of their own karma. Birth and karma are thus related to each other as cause and effect.

10. From the plane of Supreme Consciousness, all jivas have arisen without any reason. Later on their karmas become the cause of happiness and sorrow.

11. The sankalpa, thought, arising from the ignorance of Self is the cause of karma; the tendency to indulge in sankalpa, is the cause of bondage and therefore discard it.

12. Liberation is non-pursuit of sankalpa; practise it mentally.

13. Do thou remain as a witness when the seer-seen contact takes place and minimise slowly and surely the scope of sankalpa, desire.

14. Do not identify yourself with the seen object and do not identify yourself with the seer; renounce all imaginations and remain as the witness Consciousness.

15. When the senses forcefully take to an object, because of desire, he is bound by that object, and if he has no desire, he gets released from it.

16. If anything arouses relish in your heart, you get bound in life; if nothing causes such a relish, you remain free in life.

17. Therefore, O Rama, let not things of the moveable

and otherwise of the world from grass to Brahma-cause any relish in you.

18.   Whatever you eat, whatever you do, discard away without relish, you are not the doer of it, you are not enjoyer of it; you are a calm and liberated soul.

19.   Wise people grieve not over the past, nor anticipate the future; O faultless soul, they simply accept what comes to them in the present.

20.   Mind has been bound by fetters like desire, delusion, conceit, etc. Through mind only these fetters have to be cut off by the wise man.

21.   With the mind sharpened by discrimination and with mental strength, cut the mind, as iron through another iron, for quietening the delusion of worldly life.

22.   Those who know about cleansing, cleanse one kind of dirt by another; as one missile is countered by another, one poison is countered by another.

23.   Jiva has threefold forms-gross, subtle and transcendental. Retain that which is transcendental and discard the other two.

24.   The body comprising of hands and feet, which craves for pleasure, which is there for the jiva for the sake of pursuit of pleasure, may be known to be the gross form.

25.   The mind, which is merely of the nature of thought and imagination and which does not perish as long as samsara lasts, O Rama, is to be known as the ethereal form of jiva.

26.   That which is without beginning and end, which is bare Consciousness and undifferentiated, know that to be the third and transcendental form of the jiva.

27. This is turiya, transcendental state and remain stablised in it. Discard the other two forms and do not identify with them."

28. Sri Rama asked, "O Chief Seer, do thou explain to me distinctly turiya, the transcendental state which remains in an indistinguishable manner in waking, dreaming and sleeping states."

29. Sri Vasishta said: Discarding the states (of waking and dreaming) in which ahambhava manifests as also the state (of sleeping) in which ahambhava is not manifest, and discarding the manifest and unmanifest states (from the collective viewpoint), abide in the unattached, uniform, pure state; and that is turiya, the transcendental plane.

The translation of the verse is based on Anandabodhendra's commentary in BYV, 6, 125, 23.

30. The state of pure, even, calm awareness in which jivanmukta abides and which is the state of witness Consciousness during worldly conduct is called turiya.

31. This is neither waking nor dream state, inasmuch as thoughts do not arise; it is not also the sleeping state, as one is not in inert state.

32. When the world as it is, is non-existing, as it were; in the case of perfectly illumined souls, it is turiya state; in the case of the unenlightened, the world is thoroughly manifest.

33. When the luminous principle of 'ahamkara' is discarded and when equanimity manifests, and when chitta is destroyed, the turiya sets in.

34. O wise man! In this connection, hear the example I give. Though you are already enlightened, your understanding will become better.

35. In a big forest, seeing a seer wholly adhering to silence, and getting surprised at it, asked a hunter thus.

36. Chasing a deer that had been pierced by an arrow, he asked, 'O seer, did you see the deer that was struck by an arrow? Where has that deer gone?'

37. The seer replied: 'We hermits living in the forest are even-minded always. We do not have the ahankara, which manifests during worldly conduct.

38. The mind which activates all the senses is essentially ahankara, which has surely become extinct in me since long.

39. I always abide in turiya plane and am not aware of waking, dreaming and sleeping states. The objective world does not exist.'

40. O Rama, hearing the words of the great seer, the hunter did not understand what they meant and went his way.

41. O valorous man! That is why I tell that there are no states other than that of turiya. Chit unvitiated by any vikalpa, conception, is turiya and that alone exists and nothing else.

42. The mind has three states-waking, dreaming and sleeping. The chitta has also three characteristics-fierceness, tranquility, stupor.

43. The mind of the waking state is fierce; the mind of the dream state is tranquility; the mind of the sleeping state is the state of stupor. When the mind is stripped of all these three states, it becomes dead.

44. That mind which is dead, which is of the nature of mere existence and evenness-that is the state, which practioners of yoga try to attain through effort.

45. Do thou abide in blemishless turiya state which is totally free from all mental fancies, in which great seers and liberated souls, to whom all distinctions have completely disappeared, ever happily abide."

Chapter-15

The Seven Planes of Realisation

1. *Sri Vasishta said: "The final conclusion of all scripture pertaining to the self is the negation of all things. Avidya exists not, Maya exists not. The transcendental Brahman alone exists as blissful Being.*

    The last word of the verse is 'a-kramam,' as in BYV, 6, 125, 1, and not 'a-grimam' as in LYV. This is a very significant verse and the gist of the comment of Anandabodhendra on the verse is presented.

    The aim of the scriptures, which concern themselves with self, is to negate the three states caused by jiva's avidya as well as the world of five elements projected by Ishvara's Maya. It is not the aim of the scripture to enlighten about the Supreme Self. The self-existent, self-luminous principle of Consciousness does not need mind to reveal it. The transcendental, immediate, self-revealing Consciousness cannot be taught also by scriptural teaching.

2. The tranquil space-like chit abides as Self and endowed with all capacities, as it is, is also called Brahman.

3. Without understanding the Reality as described, and misled by their own wrong understanding, some scholars think of it as void, some think of it as mere intelligence and some as personal God and they mutually dispute amongst themselves.

4. *Rejecting all these false viewpoints, do thou get immersed in silence, O blemishless soul. Be without*

530

mentation, without thought. Be the tranquil liberated spirit.

5. Abiding in the peaceful Self completely and remaining like one who is dumb, blind and deaf, be immersed in Consciousness. Be the whole.

6. Remaining in waking state, as if you are asleep, do your duties, O Rama. Internally renounce everything and externally do everything.

7. The existence of mind is the cause of great pain and the annihilation of mind is the cause of great joy. Be aware of Self as mere Consciousness and annihilate chitta, mind, by not cognising it.

8. Remain like stone, whenever you see things pleasing or otherwise. Through one's own effort, samsara is vanquished.

9. One should cognise the pleasure or pain or the absence of both. By such an effort the infinite, which is bereft of all sorrows is attained.

10. The knower of Truth, like the full moon, is full of amrita, elixir and is inwardly blissful. He has known the essence of all things, of all the three worlds. Though he acts, he acts not and is established in the Supreme.

11. Sri Rama asked, "How does one practise the appropriate disciplines of the seven planes of yogic wisdom? What are the indications that characterise the yogi in each plane?"

12. Sri Vasishta said: "Man is generally inclined to act in two ways-he involves in activity that promotes worldly welfare or withdraws from such activity. They respectively lead to heavenly life and liberation. Hear their attributes.

13. 'What is liberation unless it is too ordinary? Worldly

life is preferable to me'-he who acts with such a conviction is said to be an 'active' person.

14. At the end of several lives, getting out of which is as difficult as it is for the tortoise to pass through between two consecutive whirlpools of water, a jiva is born as one possessed with discriminatory vision.

This is a difficult verse and the commentator of BYV offers more than one interpretation. The author of S. T. has adopted one of these interpretations.

15. The worldly life has no real happiness. I will have no more of it. Of what use are deeds which we keep repeating everyday. Is life only these deeds?

16. What is it that is beyond the existence brought about through karma and which would give repose to the mind?-the person who has the inquisitiveness is stated to be 'nivritta'-one who withdraws from activity.

17 to 23. 'How may I become dispassionate and cross beyond the ocean of samsara?-When a person is endowed with a good mind and has such enquiring disposition, the inner vasanas get destroyed through detachment everyday. He interests himself in noble deeds and delights in them daily. He is sceptical about the usefulness of meaningless activities of ordinary people. He does not discuss other people's sensitive affairs. He pursues holy deeds. He does only those things that are not provocative and are harmless. He is afraid of sinful actions always and does not seek pleasures. He speaks tenderly and affectionately in a pleasing manner, words that are appropriate in a particular place and time. When a person manifests these characteristics, he too attains to the first plane.

He who, through thought, word and deed serves wise

people, gets somehow scriptural works and studies them-he who has such an enquiring disposition for the sake of emancipation from sorrow is said to be the person who has ascended the first plane. Others who do not have similar attributes and enquiring spirit are called as self-centred.

24 to 27. Then the aspirant enters into the next plane called 'Vicharana.' He takes primarily refuge in learned scholars, who are proficient alike in Vedas, Smritis, wise conduct, meditation, etc., and who are capable of expounding truths.

He has distinct understanding of various things, knows what is proper conduct and what is otherwise, has learnt what should be learnt and knows the house as its master does. Though he may exhibit small desire, he discards, as the snake its slough, conceit, false identification, envy, pride, delusion, etc. Endowed with such traits, he betakes to the service of the preceptor and knows all truths as they are.

28 to 32. The aspirant now descends on the third yogic plane called 'asamsanga,' like the lover falling on a flower-decorated couch.

He obtains a clear understanding of the import of scripture; he takes to the ways of a hermit, talks about Self-knowledge, decries worldly life, develops vairagya, dispassion, spends time in wandering in woods, sitting and sleeping on rocks, and enjoys the happiness that arises from detached experience of things and that makes the mind composed. As he spends time in the study of scripture with wise persons and in the performance of virtuous acts he attains a true perception of things.

33 to 38. Reaching the third yogic plane thus, the awakened

soul experiences detachment at two levels. Know their distinction. This detachment, arising in this plane, is of two types, ordinary and distinctive.

'I am not the enjoyer or the doer, nor the wronged or the wrong-doer. The pleasures or sorrows are the results either of my past deeds or Ishvara's will, I am not their author. The great pleasures lead to serious ailments, fortunes turn into misfortunes. All union ends in separation and mental afflictions become diseases. Time, eager to devour all, destroys all things.'-He who, with such thoughts, keeps away from evil men and things, practises ordinary detachment.

39 to 44. Through such practices, association with the enlightened, avoidance of evil company, meditation on Self, intense effort, the Truth is known as clearly as a fruit on the palm. Contemplating 'I am not the doer, Ishvara is the doer,' keeping away all conceptions and things, attaining to the Supreme which is the cause of all world and abiding silently and peacefully in a steady posture is called distinctive detachment. He cognises not anything inner or outer, neither above or below, neither on earth nor in space, neither in things nor in ideas, neither in the sentient nor in the insentient. With the rise of thought, things manifest; with the extinction of thought, things cease to manifest. There is an eternal, unborn, lovable Reality and awareness of it is distinctive detachment.

45 & 46. The third yogic plane has this detachment as the fruit of the plant of which contentment is the sweet fragrance, virtuous deed is the tender shoots, mind is the stalk, impediments are the thorns, discrimination is the lotus, and inner vision is the sun that causes the lotus to blossom.

47 to 51. (To recapitulate) By the association with the wise, the accumulation of virtuous deeds, one, as if by chance, ascends to the first plane, what is akin to the sprouting of the seed through the waters of discriminative vision, the sprout has to be tended and protected carefully. Cultivate that habit appropriate to the plane, as the gardener cares for the plant everyday.

When this plane is properly nurtured through enquiry, it leads to manifestation of other planes, second, and third, after proper effort. In the third plane, he displays distinctive detachment and the person totally discards all desires and imaginations at this plane."

52. Sri Rama asked, "How can there be emancipation for one who is born in an uncultured family and who is stupid, ignoble and is uninitiated in yoga?

53. What is the future lot of one who has ascended to the first or second or third plane and who expires while pursuing yoga?"

54. Sri Vasishta said: "For one who is stupid and is a victim of vices, samsara is an unending travail, inasmuch as he does not find himself at the first plane, even after a number of births.

55. Or by a fortuitous occurence and by association with the wise, he ponders over the nature of samsaric life and develops dispassion.

56. When dispassion arises in the heart of the individual, one necessarily gets stablised in the first plane and thereafter samsara gets destroyed-this is the essential teaching of the scripture.

57. In respect of the individual who in the course of pursuit of yogic discipline passes away, the

individual's adverse karma of the previous lives gets destroyed according to the plane in which he remained, at the time of death.

58. Thereafter, he alongwith the beloved, sports in various celestial spheres and Meru mountains travelling in celestial planes.

59 & 60. When the enormous virtue and the sin he had committed earlier get destroyed as a result of experiences of pleasures and sorrows, the yogi is reborn on earth in the family, which is virtuous, wealthy, laudable and noble. They, prompted by their yogic tendencies, again pursue yoga.

61. Remembering the practice they had been pursuing in the respective plane, they get started on a higher plane than the ones which they had already reached.

62. O Rama, the first three planes are together called as jagrat, waking state, because in all the three, the knowledge of the manifold world persists as in the normal waking state.

63. For the practitioners of yoga, nobility manifests in this plane. Seeing the nobility of such yogis, even ignorant persons develop desire for liberation.

64. He is an arya, the noble-minded, who attends to what should be done and avoids what should not be done, and engages himself in performing the duties that are appropriate to him.

65. He is an arya, the noble-minded, who conducts himself as he should, thinks as he should, does as scripture stipulates and as per convention in the natural course of his duties.

66. That which sprouted in the first plane, blossomed in the second and bore the fruit of nobility in the third.

67.   He who dies as an arya, the noble-minded being endowed with pure sankalpa, thought, enjoys celestial pleasures for a long time and then is reborn as a yogi.

68 & 69. When through the practice of the first three planes, where ajnana is getting destroyed in phases, when perfect knowledge has arisen like full moon in the heart, when the yogi's mind abides in Consciousness, that is distinctionless and eternal he sees everywhere oneness, and has attained to the fourth plane.

70.   When he is stablised in non-dual awareness, when the manifoldness has totally disappeared, the person, established in the fourth plane, sees the world as a dream.

71.   The first three planes constitute the jagrat and the fourth constitutes the dream state. The chitta of the yogi in this plane disappears like summer cloud.

72.   The yogi who has reached the fifth plane is in the state of bare existence. Inasmuch as his chitta has merged in the Consciousness, world-experience does not manifest in him.

73.   Having attained to the fifth plane, which is called sushupti, his mind is totally devoid of perceptions and is absorbed in non-dual awareness.

74.   With perception of duality gone, he is delighted within himself and has become illumined. The yogi of this fifth plane remains, as it were, in deep sleep.

75.   He is inwardised mentally though he engages in external actions. Being totally calm, he appears as a sleepy person.

76 & 77. Pursuing the discipline appropriate to this plane without vasanas, one ascends in due course to the sixth plane, called turiya, in which there is no

cognition of the real or unreal, no manifestation of the 'I-notion' or the negation of it. Without any kind of mentation, and released from all notions of duality and non-duality, he is bare existence.

78. The knot of ignorance persists not; all doubts stand dispelled. He remains as a liberated soul without imagination. As there is no bondage, there is no state of liberation for him. He is steady as the picture of a shining lamp.

79. He is internally and externally empty as a pot in space. He is internally and externally full as a pot in water.

80. He appears to have attained something and appears also not to have attained anything. The yogi pracising in the sixth plane in course of time ascends to the seventh plane.

81. The seventh plane is said to be the disembodied state of liberation, which cannot be described in words and which is the highest plane of Consciousness in the domain of life.

82 & 83. It is called as Siva by some, as Brahma by some others, as Vishnu by some and as void by others. Some call it Matter, some as Time, some as Union of Prakriti and Purusha.

84. Though the Reality is unnameable, it is somehow called by various names by people who imagine it according to their inclinations.

85. O Rama, I have described to you thus the seven planes. By practising the disciplines of these planes, one does not have to experience sorrow.

86. There is a mighty proud elephant roaming with slow gait with two huge tusks, always eager for confrontation.

87. If that elephant, capable of doing immense harm, is not tamed, certainly there is no hope of a person victoriously establishing himself in any of these planes.

88. As long as the irate elephant is not vanquished by superior valour, which worthy warrior can gain victory in the battle-field?"

89. Sri Rama asked, "What is it that is called as the mighty elephant? What are the battle-fields? How is it killed? How can one abide blissfully for long?"

90. Sri Vasishta said: "O Rama, desire is the mighty elephant. Desire manifests in the form, 'may this be mine.' The elephant roams with pride and delight in the forest of one's body.

91. The sturdy senses are the fierce features, endearing speech is the tongue; its resting place is the deep mind and righteous and unrighteous deeds are the two tusks.

92. The wide ranging vasanas are the ichor exuding from its temples and this elephant of desire goes about killing helpless creatures.

93. Worldly experiences are the battle-fields and the individual repeatedly experiences victories and defeats in them.

94. The abode of desire is called by such names as vasana, craving, manas, chitta, sankalpa, bhavana, liking, etc.

95. The elephant of desire which is freely roaming about everywhere, do thou, at all cost vanquish through the special astra, weapon, of courage.

96. When there is the manifestation of thought, 'let this be mine,' this desire assumes an immense form in the heart and turns into a vicious virus of the dreadful samsara.

97. The thought, 'let this be mine,' is what is called samsara. Quietening this thought is called liberation- this is the essence of wisdom.

98. The illuminating and clear instruction of the preceptor spreads, in the desireless pure mind, and makes it more receptive like oil drop on the mirror.

99. If the harmful desire manifests even once, it should be cut to pieces, through the weapon of non-cognition, as it is akin to the sprout of poisonous plant.

100. He who is enslaved by desire is not able to discard helplessness. By practice of mere non-cognition, the desire, the seed of samsara, does not manifest.

101. That which is referred to as the weapon of non-cognition is the quietness of chitta. It is also known as pratyahara, withdrawal of mind from the desired object, and through that the desire is eliminated.

102. 'Let this be mine,' this thought is kalpana; non-contemplation of object is renunciation of kalpana.

103. To recollect a thing is to pursue kalpana and non-recollection is conducive to bliss.

104. *Raising both my hands, I cry out but no one listens to me. Not to have any sankalpa, thought is conducive to supreme good. Why is it not practised by any?*

105. *O Rama, by utterly keeping quiet one attains the supreme plane, in relation to which even sovereignty over an empire is a trifle.*

106. The legs of a person act disinterestedly when a person is on his way to a particular place and one's own activities should be likewise.

107. Where is the need to expatiate on it? This is the nutshell. To indulge in sankalpa, thought, is great

bondage; not to indulge in sankalpa is liberation.

108. See this entire world as the infinite tranquil, imperishable Consciousness; Abide peacefully in bliss.

109. Non-cognition is supreme yoga which leads to supreme bliss. Abiding in this yoga, perform or not the duties without any vasana.

The translation is based on the reading in BYV, 6-126-19.

111. Non-cognition is the yoga and this brings about the perfect extinction of chitta. Be totally immersed in that condition, O fortunate soul.

112. By the cognitions of 'I' and 'mine,' one does not get released from sorrow. Do what is desired by you.

113. *O Rama, exclusive contemplation of the blissful, all-pervasive, tranquil, eternal, auspicious Being of the nature of awareness is what is known as renunciation of karma."*

The translation of the verse is based on the reading in BYV, 6-126-24.

Chapter-16

The Result of Scriptural Study

This chapter, consisting of 34 verses is not traceable in BYV. The first 4 verses attributed to Vasishta are probably by the compiler of LYV Abhinanda Pandita. Among the remaining verses attributed to Valmiki some only, it appears, are by Valmiki.

Vasishta said:

1. Outshining even Brahma's creation, the poet aided by the grace of Brahma, verily a devotee and an orator has projected the fame of Rama.

2. Those who despise the ocean-like compassion of Harihara-arya, really despise the waters to which they have come for purifying themselves by beating them with hands.

3. The real waters do not purify the brahmana who dips into them every day, but the waters of compassion of Harihara-arya purify any number of brahmanas and wash them of the mist of ajnana.

4. To my mind, O great guru, only the ocean of thy nectarine speech is more laudable than the waters of the rivers which carry the honey flowing from the ripe fruits of the celestial trees.

Valmiki said:

5. As the seer spoke thus, the day came to a close. The audience, after offering obeisance to the seer, dispersed to do the evening ablutions. With the passing away of the night, the audience assembled

542

again in the next morning.

6. After spending 18 days in the lofty company of Vasishta, Ramachandra, discarding all the delusions of samsara, remained like the glorious ocean, waveless and full.

7. At that moment, the flowers of the celestial trees dropped by the devas, fell in a rain on the assembly.

8 to 11. Vishnu descended on the earth as a human-being bearing the name of Rama and was anguished because of samsara. He was enlightened by both yoga and jnana. Attaining realisation, Rama extolled the preceptor and offered prostrations to him alongwith father and mothers. He told, "The all-knowing jnani gets dispelled of all sorrows. You have destroyed all the inner darkness like the sun."

12. The seer called into Rama's presence all the seers who had assembled in the sky to hear the discourse.

13. The celestial seers of all groups were reverentially honoured by Rama and they told him.

14. "The wisdom which confers great beatitude was heard by us all.

We salute you two, who have dispelled the delusions and sorrows of all the three worlds.

15. The dialogue between you and your guru is full of sanctifying wisdom."

16. The siddhas who listened to the discourses in Ayodhya have caused it to spread in Kashmiri land out of compassion for people.

17. Now, Rama, the knower of Truth became free from all pain. He attended to all the duties like Janaka, without attachment and without the sense 'mine.'

18. Even as the lotus-leaf does not get wet by the waters, his mind did not get tainted by the royal pleasures.

19. This scripture must be taught only to those virtuous souls who are dispassionate and engaged in righteous deeds.

20. If persons are noble-minded, this scripture can be taught. For the Vidhya-dhanam gift of learning is vastly beneficial.

21. This secret scripture should not be revealed to persons who are possessed by evil spirits and who have evil traits and disregard for this scripture.

22. He who has not already been a worshipper of Shiva, Hari, Brahma, or Ravi would not be able to study this splendid scripture.

23. This wisdom is what was taught by Maheshwara, Divine Mother and seers like Narada.

24. *What is known as 'Maha-Ramayana' and 'Moksha upaya' is the nectarine essence of the ocean of milk.*

25. *A mere study destroys the sins of previous lives. Who would not, by perfect study of it attain supreme beatitude?*

26. Even a single study destroys the sins of persons and generates realisation of awareness.

27. If a dull person studies it with devotion, his mind becomes pure and there is no doubt.

28. By all persons, disciplined or otherwise, intelligent or otherwise, this supreme work should be studied. For realisation of Brahman is hard to attain.

29. For those who have got capacity for understanding, there is not another scripture like this which completely destroys ignorance.

30.   This is capable of giving both happiness of the world and liberation. For the yogis, the lovable chit comes within one's easy reach; only through previously earned merit, it is attained.

31.   Vasishta is known to be the repository of entire Agamic wisdom. This scripture is recognised everywhere as the very essence of liberating wisdom.

32.   Apart from this scripture, what other means is there for the elimination of sorrow caused to one by such occurrences like separation from the beloved.

33.   Arising from the space of chit, the full moon of the scripture filled with heavenly bliss and the elixir of literary delights and charms shines gloriously destroying all darkness around.

34.   He has indeed purified himself in all the sacred waters;

     He has given away all gifts including the earth;

     He has performed all the sacrifices and adored all the gods;

     He has also elevated the ancestors from the samsaric depth;

     He is indeed worthy of worship by all the worlds.

     He, who is capable of dwelling intently on Brahmic Truth even for a minute.

Chapter-17

Instructions to Bharadwaja

Valmiki said:

1. Hearing the essence of wisdom through the great sage, the scion of the Raghu family, Sri Rama, with mind rendered pure, did not ask any further question and with a calm, blissful mind remained fully established in the awareness of Truth.

2. He is indeed a supreme yogi, the chief of celestials and worthy of worship by the whole universe; he is devoid of birth and death and is of the nature of pure awareness. An abode of all wishes and the consort of Sita, he is capable of creating, protecting and emancipating all the three worlds.

3. As a result of the spiritual power transmitted by the preceptor, Rama became illumined and for a while remained as an ocean of bliss and pure Consciousness.

4. Without being distracted by question and reply, he remained as an ocean of nectarine bliss with tears gathering in the eyes, hairs standing on end and throat obstructed by emotion.

5 & 6. He remained as all-pervasive existential Consciousness and he, to whom the eight-fold siddhis, powers, were a straw-bit, spoke not anything and was fully soaked in spiritual bliss.

7. Bharadwaja said, "What a wonder! Sri Rama has attained to an exalted plane. O Chief of Seers, how can such a state be attained by us?

8.   Where are ignorant sinful people in pitiable condition like me? Where is the rare state of Rama, sought after even by Branma and other celestials?

9.   O, Seer and Preceptor! How is the difficult ocean of samsara crossed over by me and how may I remain established in peace, kindly tell me."

10.   Valmiki said, "The story of Rama and Vasishta's teachings have been described by me. Do thou reflect and contemplate on it. Let me now tell you what I have to tell.

11.   This world manifests on account of avidya, ignorance and even an atom of it is not real. Wise people understand it thus, while ignorant persons keep debating about its nature.

12.   There is nothing apart from Chit to condition it in anyway. Through repeated contemplation of Truth, enlarge your understanding.

13.   The cognition of the external world is called waking state, is identical with jiva's sleep. He only is awake in whose heart shines the lamp of chit.

14.   The root, the head and the middle of the world being only falsity, wise people do not place trust in it.

15.   As a result of the vasanas eternally operating, the non-existent world is being perceived. Like the cognition of the dream-city, the samsara is a feat of illusion.

16.   Without contemplating the immortal Principle of Consciousness that brings in joy, you imagine the poisonous tree of samsara through ignorance and get deluded by it.

17.   Those who have established themselves in pure intelligence, by holding on to the support of wisdom, have thrown down the worldly life and shine above

everything in the world.

18. The river of nectarine wisdom is full of fierce waves which keep one away from it only as long as one has not adopted the vision of Self.

19. This world has neither a beginning nor an end, my friend. It has no middle as well and is akin to dream.

20. *All distinctions arise from ignorance, like bubbles, and after manifesting for a while, get dissolved again into the waters of wisdom.*

21. Those who, out of delusion, have been roaming in the scorching heat of the external world may bathe in the cool river of realisation of Truth and be relieved of sorrow.

22 to 24. There is the vast ocean of ajnana which has even inundated the world. The waves rising in them on account of avidya boast themselves in the thought, 'I am great.' The distinctions caused by mental perception are like waves and the notion 'mine' is the great whirlpool. Desire and hatred are the two big crocodiles and getting caught by them, how can one escape being dragged to the lowest of worlds?

25. In the quiet ocean of nectarine wisdom, which is calm, do thou dip again and again. Of what use is the saltish ocean?

26. Who is yet here? Who has gone already? What has happened to whom? Would you fall into the delusion? Do not fall on account of negligence.

The translation is based on the reading in BYV, 6-127-26

27. There is only the Reality and the same is the world. That being so, where is another? Where is the need for you to grieve over anyone?

28. *It is only for the unenlightened young, the world is taught as the illusory projection. The enlightened are happy that the world is Brahmic bliss, without any change in form.*

29. The unenlightened man grieves for no reason and is elated for no reason. The realised soul is indifferent with a smile. His act of delusion is more an appearance.

30. The subtle truth remains veiled under ignorance, as in the case of earth surface under a sheet of water.

31. If the world is stated to be pervaded by atoms only, even then, there is no need to grieve for one who is dead.

32. The unreal has no existence and the real has no non-existence. Things simply manifest and subside in various forms in the Supreme.

33 & 34. The world of Maya produces sorrow because of the vasanas that have characterised past lives.

Be devoted to the Ishvara who manifests as half-woman and who is the preceptor of the world?

Even those past sins which remain unwiped get destroyed certainly.

It is the sins of people that have been described in the scripture as the 'pasas,' wielded by the God.

35. *Worship the Reality as endowed with form until mind becomes pure. Then you will find established in the realisation of the formless Supreme.*

36. After vanquishing the dark force of ignorance, pursue the discipline of sense-control, etc., and meditation with full conviction.

37. After stilling the mind for a second, see the Self in the Self. Like the darkness breaking into dawn, let the

ignorant mind get awakened.

38. Despite utmost personal effort and other deeds, that which is to be attained is attained by the individual only through Ishvara's Grace.

39. My dear, neither birth in a good family, nor conduct nor modesty nor boldness is strong. The past karmas are always stronger.

40. But why do you shrink from the practice of disciplines which can unquestionably, counter the past karma? Even Ishvara on his own does not erase the fate decreed in the form of writing in the forehead.

41. How could there be preceptor? Where is scholarship? How could there be the creeper of delusion? The cosmic process which has spread the dual snare is beyond comprehension indeed.

42. O Bharadwaja, through discriminative vision, conquer the ignorance. You would attain a singular spiritual union without doubt.

43. A great king endowed with great energy, even in distress, can function from distance. But an ordinary person gets depressed even when an ordinary difficulty strikes.

44. Realisation, attainable only by those who have accumulated merit, is got by one after several lives. In the case of jivanmukta, its existence is inferred by the attendant signs.

45. My son, the karma, pursued in a wrong way brought in this bondage and the same karma, rendered favourable, brings in liberation.

46. The virtuous deeds of the wise, destroy the sinful effects of past karmas and become the swelling flood which quenches the raging fire of sorrow of the people.

47. My dear, renouncing karma, be devoted to the contemplation of Brahman, if you do not wish to get dragged into the revolving samsaric cycle.

48. As long as there is manifold perception, the ocean of life is full of ferocious waves; when there is no external perception, the waters of the ocean are still without waves.

49. If your inner vision is veiled and you are caught up in sorrow, be thou led by the staff of discriminative vision and it will serve all the purpose.

50. Those who are easily carried away by joy and sorrow like the straw by stream waters, are not counted amongst worthy persons.

51. O friend, this world is tossed about like the cradle, day and night, by six kinds of maids and my dear, why do you give yourself to sorrow?

52. Time creates, withdraws, again re-creates and destroys the worlds repeatedly and with fervour.

53. With the Time Serpent swallowing all creatures, there is nothing which receives any special favour.

54. When even the celestials are within the reach of the evil Time, what to speak of mortal beings, who live only for a brief while?

55. Why do you dance when there is joy and are despondent when there is distress? Remain for a while without sorrow and as a spectator, watch the drama of life.

56. O Bharadwaja, the persons endowed with discrimination do not become gloomy even once in this world and are akin to an ocean full of waves, which die in a minute.

57. Discard the sorrow which is inauspicious. Visualise auspicious future, contemplate the Self as blissful, serene, pure, Consciousness.

58. Ishvara's Grace flows to one who is devoted to Gods, brahmanas, preceptors, scholars, celestials and wise people and who has faith in the authority of the Vedas."

Chapter-18

Dialogue between Rama and Vasishta

1. Sri Bharadwaja said, "All that has to be known has been known by me, by thy Grace. There is no greater beneficial possession like dispassion and there is no greater enemy than samsara.

2. I desire to know, in a few words, the essence of wisdom expounded by Vasishta in the whole discourse.

3. Valmiki said, "O Bharadwaja, hear this supreme wisdom which ushers in liberation. By merely listening to it, you will not get drowned in the ocean of life.

4. Obeisance to the non-dual Supreme which is the embodiment of existence, consciousness and bliss and which manifests in manifold forms of creation, sustenance and dissolution.

5. If the universe gets dissolved into the ultimate cause, the Truth shines and how this dissolution is done will be explained by me briefly on the lines taught by the Upanishad.

6 & 7. The seeker endowed with serenity, sense-control, who has withdrawn himself from the foolish and sinful deeds and sense-pleasures, possessed with earnestness may perfectly sit on a soft skin and with mind, senses and body controlled, may he utter 'Om' until his mind becomes calm.

8. Let him do thereafter pranayama, control of prana for

the purification of the mind. Let him withdraw all the senses from the respective sense-objects, step by step.

9.   Body, senses, mind, intellect, the knower-know from what all these emanate and later dissolve them all into It.

The verse as in LYV is totally wrong and and the reading in BYV is correct. 6-128-4.

10.   Initially contemplating oneself as abiding in the Virat plane, let him contemplate as Hiranyagarbha and thereafter abide in Avyakrita and finally in the final cause of pure Brahman.

The entire process of this contemplation, too briefly indicated in the verse, has been succinctly explained by the commentator of BYV, 6-128-4.

11.   Later let him mentaly integrate the earthly portion of the body, viz., flesh, etc., with the earth element, water portion like blood with the water element, fire portion with fire element, vayu portion with vayu and space portion with space.

12 & 13. The senses have to be integrated with their causes or sources like earth from which they came in order that the jiva may experience doership and enjoyership.

14 to 16. The ear may be integrated with direction, the sense of touch with lightning, eyes with sun, taste with waters, prana with vayu, speech with fire, hands with Indra, feet with Vishnu, anus with Mitra, the generative organ with Kashyapa, mind with moon, intellect with Brahman. The various senses and sense-organs really refer to the Divinities.

17.   This explanation has been given on the basis of the teachings in the Vedas and it is not a product of one's imagination. After thus disposing off the various

faculties, let the seeker contemplate 'I am Virat, the Cosmic Being.'

18. Let him also contemplate on ardha-nareesvara-half-male and half-female - who abides within the brahmanda and who are the progenitors of all beings and who, in the form of yajna, sacrifice, is protecting the earthly life.

19 & 20. Beyond the brahmanda, and twice its form is prithvi, the earth and twice the quantum of the earth is the water. Fire is twice the amount of water and twice the size of fire is wind and twice the quantum of wind is space.

21. The world has been knit together through a mighty process collectively and is an aggregate of parts.

21. After dissolving the earth in the water, dissolve water in the fire element. After dissolving the fire element in the vayu, dissolve vayu in space. Lastly dissolve space in the Supreme, the ultimate cause.

22. The yogi contemplating in this plane has only a subtle body, which comprises of the sense-organs, mind, intellect, vasanas, five subtle elements, karma and avidya.

23 to 25. Later abiding in the vayu beyond the brahmanda, let him contemplate 'I am Sutra-Atma, the subtle, cosmic Being,' Chaturmukha, the four-faced Lord, identifying himself with the aggregate form of the subtle-elements manifest in vayu.

Let the wise man merge the subtle-body in the Avyakrita, or Avyakta the unmanifest.

26 & 27. That principle into which stand dissolved names and forms and in which the world abides is called Prakriti by some, Maya by some others, Atoms by

some and Avidya by some others. All these persons are misled by their own false reasonings.

Into It have merged all things and remain in indistinct forms.

28. They remain without distinct cognition and awareness and rising from that form become distinct in form when creation takes place again.

The progressive sequence leads to creation and the opposite sequence leads to dissolution.

29. Let the yogi discard the three states and contemplate on the turiya state and for attaining it, dissolve the subtle body in the Supreme Consciousness.

30 & 31. When the sutble body has merged in the Avyakrita, with it have merged all-the five subtle elements, senses, mind, intellect, vasanas, karma, prana, and ajnana.

'Now I am released from the cage of subtle-body also by all means.

32. Since I am of the nature of Consciousness, I have entered into the ocean of Consciousness. Bereft of all adjuncts and being non-different from Consciousness, I am Paramatma, the Supreme Self.

33. I am immutable, solitary, all-pervasive, possessive of energy of both Consciousness and matter and pure like the space of the pot when the pot gets broken.

34 & 35. Vedas also propound the Reality as non-dual. The fire thrown into fire becomes identical with it. Originally of the same nature as fire, it becomes indistinguishable from the whole.

36 to 38. As grass thrown into salt lake becomes salt itself, the inert matter thrown into Consciousness becomes Consciousness.

A lump of salt thrown into ocean getting rid of name of form becomes the water itself.

When water is poured into water, milk into milk, the water and milk do not get lost but is not identifiable separately.

Even so, the yogi contemplating, 'I have entered into Consciousness has become wholly one with it.

39 & 40. That which is the eternal bliss, omniscient knowledge, the supreme cause, all-pervasive tranquil being, flawless and taintless, partless, actionless, pure Brahman, I am.

41. I am free from virtue and vice. I am the ultimate cause of the universe. I am the non-dual effulgent, blissful Brahman.'

42. Endowed with such attributes and really bereft of sattva and other gunas, let the fortunate yogi contemplate that he is one with the all-pervasive Brahman.

43. Through such practice, the mind becomes extinct and the Self reveals itself in luminous form spontaneously.

44. When Realisation takes place and the mind becomes serene, all sorrows cease and joy manifests in oneself. The Self experiences the bliss of Self through the Self.

45 & 46. Thus I have explained to you what Vasishta has taught.

Through the practice of wisdom and yoga, O wise Bharadwaja, you will know everything in a conclusive manner.

47. *Through the contemplation of the import of the scripture, understanding of the teaching of the preceptor and through repeated practice, the Truth is*

fully known-such is the enunciation of Vedanta.

Therefore, do thou discard all and cast your mind in practice, firmly."

48. Bharadwaja said, "Rama attained supreme oneness through the Self in the Self.   Seer, how was he rendered fit for external activity by the Seer Vasishta?

49. Knowing thus, I shall practise in such a manner that, on rising from samadhi, I will also act in a similar way."

50. Valmiki said, "When the wise soul got immersed in the natural being of Consciousness, Visvamitra spoke these words to the great seer Vasishta.

51. Visvamitra said, 'O great Vasishta, rich in penance, O Son of Brahma, you are indeed very great. You have proved, by instant transmission of spiritual power, your qualification to be Guru, the preceptor.

52. He who manifests in the body of the disciple spiritual power and bliss through look, touch, word, or thought is really the preceptor.

53. This Rama, a pure soul, already possessed dispassion. He needed only mental repose (arising out of Realisation of Truth) and has now attained it as a result of this discourse.

54. If enlightenment arises through Guru's word, only the intelligence of the disciple is the main cause. If the mind is not free from the three impurities (of Anava, Karma and Maya), how can he attain perfect Realisation?

55. The direct realisation of Truth is certainly proof of the fruitfulness of the association of Guru and Sishya. Both are knowers of Truth, as also all others, including myself.

56.   You may now draw Rama's mind out and make Rama cognisant of external world. He is fully absorbed in Consciousness. But we have to fulfill obligations.

57.   O Saint, remember the cause that has brought me here. I had with great difficulty secured the permission of Dasaratha for Rama's departure with me.

58.   O great seer, with all thy good will, ensure that the favourable development is not nullified. Do thou also remember the aim of the celestials that has to be accomplished, for which Rama is born.

59 & 60. Led by me, Rama will kill the rakshasas in the Siddhasramam. He will redeem Ahalya from the curse and by breaking the bow, marry the daughter of Janaka. Rama will thwart the ambition of Parasurama.

Rama's killing of the rakshasas in Visvamitra's hermitage, redemption of Ahalya from her husband's curse, wedding of Sita and defeat of Parasurama and also other events have been fully described in Valmiki's Purva-Ramayana.

61.   He will renounce the kingdom of his ancestors without a shred of desire and under the pretext of exile in the forest, will impart sanctity to the holy centres and relieve the hardships of the recluses in the forest.

62 to 64. As a result of abduction of Sita, he will reveal the plight and ordeal of those attached to women. He will kill Ravana, restore to life the vanaras killed in the battle and, like the people of the world, seek proof of purity of Sita.

65.   Although liberated and desireless, he will devote himself to the performance of karma to set an example to the world through the combined pursuit of jnana and karma.

559

66. He will bestow liberation-in-life on anyone who sees him or remembers him or hears about him or hears from him, whatever be his condition.

67. All these deeds, for the welfare of the three world, and for my sake as well, have to be accomplished by Ramachandra, the noble soul.

68. O seers in the assembly, do thou make obeisance to Rama. He who adores him becomes victorious. He who has the competence becomes liberated like him.

O Vasishta, out of compassion, do thou draw him out and divert his attention to the worldly affairs."

69. Valmiki said, "Saying thus, Visvamitra became silent. Vasishta told Rama of great effulgence thus:

Vasishta said: "O Rama, O Rama, valorous man, noble soul! You are Consciousness embodied. This is not the time for repose. Do thou delight the world.

70. As long as the understanding of the world has not become firm for the yogi, so long perfect and deep samadhi does not at all manifest.

71. Therefore, do thou attend to worldly affairs as also the obligations to the celestials, reflect upon them and renouncing them all, my son, be blissful."

72. Valmiki said, "Though addressed in this manner, Rama did not respond anything. His mind was totally absorbed in Consciousness. Vasishta's mind entered into Rama through the sushumna nadi and reached the heart slowly.

73. Opening his eyes slowly and with prana, mind, nadi-channels and other senses which were steadily getting energised and the soul awakened, Rama became delighted and enlightened like the chief seer Vasishta. Bereft of all desires and unconcerned with the

propriety or otherwise of things, Rama remained still, seeing all persons.

74. Sri Rama said, "By thy grace, I am no longer to be commanded to do this or avoid that. However thy words have to be obeyed by me always.

75. O great Seer, in all the Vedas, smritis and the puranas, Guru's word is a command to be carried out and Guru's prohibition is to be avoided."

76. Valmiki said, "Saying thus, the all-pervasive noble and compassionate soul reverentially took the feet of the great seer Vasishta and placing them on his head, addressed all,

77. 'May all know what is surely and decisively beneficial. There is nothing greater than the wisdom of Self and none greater than the teacher, the knower of Self.'

78. The seers said, 'O Rama, all of us think in the same manner. Through your grace, the dialogue has strengthened the conviction.

79. May you be happy, O king! Obeisance to thee, O Ramachandra. Permitted by Vasishta, we shall leave for our respective places.'

80. After saying these words, all the seers left extolling Rama.

There was a rain of flowers on the crest of Rama."

81. Valmiki said, "Thus have I told you all about the story of Rama. My son, follow the same path and be happy.

82. I have told you Rama's attainment through beautiful words, knit like an attractive garland of jewels, as it were. This composition is worthy of being studied by all great poets and yogis and this, through the Grace of God, will confer on them liberation.

83. He who listens to this conversation between Rama and Vasishta, gets into the path of liberation, whatever be his stage in life.

84. In this work on Vasishta's teaching are six sections. They are Dispassion, Aspirant's Conduct, Creation, Sustenance, Dissolution and Liberation."

Section-6
Liberation

Second Half

Synopsis

Nirvana Prakaranam is the last of the Prakaranas of Brihat Yoga Vasishta and the Prakaranam has nearly equally divided two portions. The Laghu Yoga Vasishta abridges the entire work upto the first half of the Nirvana Prakaranam. For reasons not disclosed by the author, Sri Ananda Pandita has left out the second half which consists of about 7000 slokas in 216 Sargas. The synopsis of the second half that follows is for the purpose of making this book Laghu Yoga Vasishta complete in its coverage. This final portion, according to traditional authority, contains the conclusive views of the author.

Sarga 1. With the total elimination of 'I-notion,' desires no longer trouble the seer.

Sarga 2 & 3. Karma is traced to the source of immutable Chit. Renunciation of karma is not non-performance of karma but the awareness of the Self as actionless Being.

Sarga 4. Real renunciation is not physical but spiritual.

Sarga 5 to 16. Busunda instructs a dull-minded Vidyadhara extensively on the means to be practised for Self-realisation. The I-notion and the world are inseperable. If the I-notion gets erased from Consciousness, world also ceases to exist.

564

37

samadhi in a place utterly free from worldly happenings. He searches for a quiet place in all the worlds. Not finding one, he enters into a big rock and choosing a corner in it, he sets up a cottage and practises samadhi. Rising up from meditation, after a long time, he hears a sweet voice, probably of a woman. Unable to find the source of the voice, Vasishta searched in all directions and yet failed. He entered into samadhi, and discarding all physical, and mental identifications, assumed the form of Chidakasa. He could hear the voice in a distinct manner and in due course perceive the maiden whose was the voice he had heard. She was by his very side in an ethereal form. Vasishta called her, "Who are you and for what have you come to me? Where is your abode?" The Vidyadhari replied, "There is the vast lokaloka mountain in the northern range of which, inside a rock I have been living for countless aeons alongwith my husband. My husband remains seated in samadhi for the past several yugas steadfastly adhering to it. He is so absorbed in penance that he does not feel the need for my company. With my youthful features and beauty thirsting for physical delight, he is averse to me and that is what makes me lose interest in life. In course of time, I became dispassionate. Now, I seek instruction from you so that I can attain liberation."

Vasishta was curious to know how she could live inside a rock. Vidyadhari invited the seer to visit her world. Vidyadhari herself could not see her own world as vividly as she had known it before. She saw it like an image within a mirror. Vasishta could not at all perceive to any degree. It is abhyasa, practice, that accounted for her experience of her world and because of the lack of it, Vasishta could not experience the new world. On Vidyadhari's advice, the seer practised samadhi and assumed the ethereal form again. He now entered alongwith Vidyadhari the world in which her husband was practising samadhi. Vidyadhari showed her husband to the seer. She also tried to arouse her husband from samadhi and told him, "Here is from another cosmos, the son of Brahma. Do offer appropriate worship to him."

The seer who practised samadhi was none other than Brahma of that cosmos. He welcomed Vasishta with appropriate words of praise and asked him to take the seat studded with jewels. A host of celestials welcomed Vasishta. Thereafter, Vasishta addressed the new Brahma, "O great Lord, what is the truth about the Vidyadhari's complaint against your indifference to her?" The new Brahma replied, "O Seer, to a wise person like you, I should say all. I am bare Consciousness and was never born at any time. Hence I am 'Swayambu.' Because of some vasana getting formed inside me, this woman emerged from me, as though she was different from me. Because of vasana, she got attached to her body and had the notion of 'I' in the body. She, on her own, considered me to be her husband. Really, I did not intend her to be my wife."

The new Brahma continued, "O Seer, I have to

568

discard my ethereal form and attain to the chidakasa state, the state of liberation. The cosmic deluge is to set in. The alloted span of Manu, Chandra and other divinities has come to an end. Since the whole creation is to get destroyed in the Final Deluge, she too has formed dispassion and seeks to merge in me. After all every being must come back to its creator. This rock is not really rock. It is chit. Innumerable worlds appear as the play of Maya. Maya, being the power of Brahma, has infinite delusive potency! O Vasishta, do thou return to thy world and to thy abode. Regain your poise. Let these worlds created by my fancy get merged in the primordial cause. Let me attain to Brahmic Consciousness.'

Saying thus, Brahma of that new cosmos intoned Pranava until his mind became extinct. The Vidyadhari too became contemplative and merged in his form. Vasishta beheld only the chit expanse. All the elements including plants, trees, seas, etc., started dissolving into each other. The vast process of dissolution of that cosmos passing through stages of Kala-ratri, the Dance of Bhairavi, the Dance of Shiva, the cosmic vision of Shiva, is graphically and extensively described.

Sarga 87 to 91. Vasishta describes how in a portion of his own cosmos he began to perceive the process creation and how he entered into all the five elements successively for long periods and underwent appropriate experiences.

Sarga 92 & 93. Having witnessed the dissolution of the cosmos of another Brahma, Vasishta returns to his world and his cottage. He finds his physical body in the meditative posture and by its side a siddha practising samadhi. Vasishta surmises that the siddha should have come in search of solitude to that cottage and not finding anyone but the body, he would have pursued samadhi. He now decides to leave the cottage finally so that siddha may remain continuously absorbed in samadhi. As he begins to leave and because his imagination has been terminated, the cottage disappears, and the siddha not having any support falls on the earth below. Out of solicitude for the siddha, Vasishta mentally descends to the earth to find him in the Padmasana posture absorbed in samadhi. By sending down rains on his head, Vasishta rouses him from the samadhi state. As the siddha gains consciousness of the external world, Vasishta enquired him about who he was.

The siddha pleads for sometime so that he can recollect the past events. He tells Vasishta, 'I have now recognised you, O Seer. I offer my salutations. After enjoying all the pleasures of life repeatedly and after becoming disgusted with them, I went in search of solitude and found that cottage in space. Now I understand that the cottage was yours. I had not properly applied my mind and had occupied it. This is what has happened. You may do now as you please.'

Vasishta tells the siddha, 'Not only you, O Seer, I have not also properly reflected over it. I could have allowed the cottage to remain as before. All right, rise up, let us dwell in the world of the siddhas for that world would be the right place.' Deciding thus, both rise up into the sky like stars. At some point they salute mutually and take leave of each other.

In some corner of the world, there was a city called 'Tatam, ruled by the king Vipaschit. He was valorous and exceptionally accomplished. Once his enemies surrounded his city from all sides and had easily vanquished his chieftains and generals. His ministers ran to him and pleaded for his direct intervention. The king despatched his generals and asked them to fight the enemies. He also told them that he would worship Agni and join them in the fight.

Vipaschit entered the sanctum and offered worship to Agni. He thought thus: "I have spent a lifetime fruitfully. The people have been living without fear in my kingdom. I have established my fame in all directions. I have seen all the worldly pleasures. My enemies have been crushed. Now old age has seized me. The enemies are having an upper hand. My victory is uncertain. Let me now make an offering of my head into the Agni." He told Agni, "O God, I offer oblation with my head. If this offering of mine pleases thee, let four persons effulgent like Narayana emerge from the pit. The enemies in all the four directions should face destruction. Let me have also vision of thee."

The king took the sword, cut off his head and as he was offering it into Agni, his body also fell into it. The Agni swallowed his body and from it arose four persons radiating lustre and adorned with ornaments and weapons. They were of equal age and of equal form. They strode out like Hari in excellent horses. Each went to a separate direction and fought the enemy in that side.

They met the enemies in all the four sides and by employing celestial missiles, decimated the enemy forces. The enemy from each side was defeated and the soldiers were made to flee. Chasing the enemies along each direction, the four Vipaschits reached the farthest portion of land. With enemies getting perished, they also gave up their fighting tendency. The people of the place showed to Vipaschits various interesting features of the landscape. Having reached the shores of the ocean, Vipaschits installed the boundary stones of their domain and prayed to Agni to confer on them the ability to continue to probe the extent of the objective universe either with physical body or ethereal one. "So be it," said Agni and disappeared from view. The next morning, despite the loud protestation of the followers, Vipaschits walked upon the ocean waters in pursuit of their mission of finding out the extent of avidya as manifesting in the objective form.

Setting out in different directions, Vipaschits, 1, 2, 3 and 4, took various births and met with destruction. At that time, their Consciousness, by virtue of its past identification appeared above in the space and cognised the entire cosmos before them. The four again decided to find out the nature of avidya and set out in different directions. Vipaschit 1 after undergoing some births attained supreme liberation. Vipaschits 2 and 3 has undergone repeated births again and again and are yet engaged in finding out the limit of the universe. Vipaschit 4, after a number of births, has now taken birth as a deer.

"Vipaschits 2 and 3 cannot be located, but Vipaschit 4 is seen to roam about as a deer," says Vasishta, when Rama asks to know specifically about the condition of Vipaschits. Rama wants to know the precise hill in which Vipaschit 4 is wandering as deer. Vasishta tells, "By chance, Vipaschit 4 is in this very cosmos of ours. O Rama, the king of Trigarta gifted you a deer for the sake of sporting with it. Know that deer to be Vipaschit 4."

Rama and other persons in the assembly get surprised. Servants are sent to fetch the deer from its zoo. The deer, strong and sturdy comes into the assembly and by its looks and jumps delights the people. Rama asks Vasishta whether the deer can be restored to its previous life. Vasishta replies that a person's future is shaped by the divinity that has been guiding its past. Vasishta sprinkles waters and raises Agni that is without fuel or smoke in the Assembly Hall. The deer, prompted by its devotion to Agni, enters into the Agni and discards its miserable body. In response to Vasishta's prayer, Agni restores the deer to its prior form as Vipaschit. There stands within Agni a calm person with rosary in hands and with beautiful apparel. He is so luminous, that the assembly addresses him as Bhasa, a shining one.

Bhasa, as the new born is now called, sits and contemplates about his past. He remembers the occurences in his previous lives. He opens his eyes, sees the assembly and then proceeds to Vasishta and offers salutations to him, "O sun of wisdom and giver of life! Obeisance to thee." Vasishta tells him, "O king, after this long travail, let avidya get extinguished." Bhasa hails Rama and salutes Dasaratha. Dasaratha tells Bhasa, "O king, welcome to thee. Be seated in this couch. May you rest from thy wanderings in countless lives." Bhasa salutes Visvamitra and other seers and occupies the seat.

Bhasa proceeds to tell his experiences in past lives-"I saw very many things and wandered over many places. I saw various kinds of worlds. Once I saw a huge dead body falling over the earth. It was so vast that I feared the whole earth would get destroyed by it. As the body pervading the vast sky was falling, I sought refuge in God Agni because of my earlier devotion to Agni. 'O God, protect me. Deluge is setting in perhaps.' Agni said, 'Rise up. Do not fear. Come with me to my world.' I went into sky alongwith Agni and saw the frightful body falling all over the earth. At my insistent request, Agni told me-

'In the vast space-like chit, there are innumerable worlds of the size of mere atoms. Because of the sankalpa of chit particles, the worlds come to be formed. There was a conceited being called Asura. Because Asura destroyed his hermitage, a seer cursed him to be reborn as masaka, mosquito. While he was a masaka, he got killed by a deer. Because his mind was absorbed in the thought of deer, he was reborn as deer. In a similar way he was born as a hunter.

As a hunter, he went about hunting and chanced to see the hermitage of a seer. The seer asked him why he was doing the cruel job. The hunter sought to know from the seer how could he lead a harmless life. The seer told the hunter, 'Do thou throw away the bow and arrow and lead life in silence in this abode.' The hunter changed his ways and started practising dhyana. The hunter sought to know from the seer the nature of phenomenal life. The seer extensively described his own experience in which discarding his body, he entered into another body to know more about dream-like worldly life. While he was tenanting another body and undergoing various experiences for years, a seer happened to visit him. The new seer was treated with all hospitality due to a revered soul. At this time, seer I wanted to visit his hermitage and find out the condition of his body and the other body he had started tenanting. He did not find any trace of the bodies or the hermitage. The seer I sought enlightenment from seer II. The seer II explained that each one's experiences were akin to dream experience and the individuals of waking life are like individuals seen in the dream world. During the conversation, the seer II addressed seer I as Vyadha Guru, one who was the preceptor of hunter. Surprised at this expression, seer I wanted to know the reason for such use. The seer II explained that a hunter would seek instruction from seer I in future and would attain enlightenment in course of time through his instruction.

The seer II told the seer I thus-'As both of us continue to do penance here, there will be famine and all-round destruction. We will continue to pursue penance. After some years, there will be again vegetation and forest growth. At that time, one hunter will approach you and out of compassion, you will enlighten him about the nature of life. Thus you will become a Guru, preceptor to him.'

Seer I told this conversation to the hunter who was surprised. The hunter took to practising dhyana seriously and after many years of practice, he asked the seer why he had not attained mental repose.

Seer I told the hunter-'I have instructed you in wisdom but for want of proper practice, you have not attained the result. Let me tell what is to happen in future. You are yet interested in knowing about the manifestation of avidya as the world. You will pursue intense penance with this end in view. Brahma will get pleased with your penance and appear before you. You will ask to be endowed with a very expansive form and death at your will. You will want to expand your form to the vast sky and thus measure the extent of avidya. Brahma will grant the boon. You will set out into the sky and expand your form to unimaginable size. But you will find that you have not gauged the extent of avidya. You will become disgusted with your body. By practising rechaka-dharana, you will discard the body and assume the form of a jiva and float in space. The discarded body of yours will fall on the earth crushing all things beneath it.

While your consciousness assumed a distinct form, you will think of yourself as the King Sindhu of a vast kingdom and be born as such. You will enjoy the pleasures of kingly life for several years and go to war with Viduratha (of Leela's story in 3rd section) another king. After defeating him in the battle, you will learn from your ministers how Viduratha had attained liberation as a result of the grace of Sarasvati whose staunch devotee Viduratha's wife Leela was. As Sindhu, you will feel remorse-stricken and seek to know from the ministers how you may attain liberation.

Ministers will enlighten you about the nature of Reality and also tell you how persistent and unrelenting effort on the part of one, will enable him to achieve the goal. After hearing this, you will renounce the kingdom, seek the company of illumined souls, pursue intense enquiry and attain liberation. O hunter, I have told you about the future course as if it is past. You may do what pleases you.'

Agni, who was narrating this entire story in reply to Vipaschit's question about the falling body from the sky, continued thus-'O Vipaschit, after the seer I spoke to the hunter, he became very curious. Both continued to be friendly and carried on penance. The seer discarded the body in course of time. The hunter got the boon from Brahma and attained vastly expansive form. But he did not succeed in the effort of understanding avidya. By exhaling prana, he discarded the weird form. He himself assumed the form of the king Sindhu, who was the enemy of Viduratha. It is his lifeless body that was falling on the earth and about which you were curious to know. O Vipaschit, you may go now as you please. I have now to go to attend to my official duty."

Bhasa, who was describing this story in the assembly of Dasaratha, continued, "The Divine Lord Agni, after narrating this sequence, disappeared. I again continued with my wanderings. Not being able to find the extent of avidya, I became disillusioned. I wanted to pratcise penance and attain liberation. Indra told me, 'You are again to be reborn as deer.' I pleaded with him to grant me liberation. He told me, 'The course of events is unalterable. You will be born as a deer. As deer, you will gain entry into Dasaratha's Hall. There you will come to know about your past events. God Agni will give you knowledge of your pure Self. You will attain liberation.' After Indra spoke thus, I thought of myself as deer and was born as one. I roamed in the woods in search of tender grass.

A chieftain saw me and I was finally captured by him. He had kept me with him for three days and brought me to you for delightful sport. I have told all about my past life. Avidya is really unsurmountable. It is vanquished only through knowledge of the Self."

175.   Scriptural knowledge serves to dispel the ignorance and once the ignorance is dispelled, liberation ensues.

176.   Not only the existing worlds, the past and future worlds also must be known to be mere illusion.

177.   The world-illusion does not admit of a cause.

178.   There is no material substance in the world; everything is only non-material chit.

179.   It is samvid, intelligence that manifests as seer, seen and sight.

180 to 185. Rama tells Vasishta, "While I was engaged in philosophical discussions in the school alongwith other learned persons, a brahmana came to me and on my request, he narrated to me these events-'I am a brahmana and was born in Vaideha land. I am called by the name Kunda-danta, because of the whiteness of my teeth. Having completed my learning, I had developed dispassion, I undertook a pilgrimage and practised penance to some extent there. I wandered in the forests around and was surprised to find one hanging in a tree with feet tied above. He was effulgent like sun and was practising penance. I waited patiently on him. When, after some days, he took note of my presence, I enquired of him about the aim of his penance. He replied, 'I belong to Mathura land. After completing my educaton, I had an urge to become the ruler of the land of seven islands. I came to this place and have been practising penance for the past twelve years. You may now leave me in my pursuit.' But I pleaded with him to permit me to stay on and serve him.

As months passed, the Sun-God appeared before the ascetic and told, 'Do cease thy penance. You will rule over the land of seven islands for 7000 years.' After the Sun-God disappeared, I requested the ascetic to resume the normal life of activity, as he had now got the expected boon. He took bath, practised japa and by taking delicious fruits of the tree, brought the fast to an end.

Thereafter, we set out towards Mathura. On the way, my companion wanted to visit the place known as Gauri-vanam. We went and searched all around but that hermitage was not found. My companion told me that he had stayed in that hermitage alongwith his seven brothers, all of whom had only the same aim. After some wandering, we saw a cool shady tree and a seer was deeply lost in meditation under it. We tried to awaken him from meditation but could not. I tried impatiently to draw him out and he finally opened his eyes and noticed us.

I told him, on his enquiry about the purpose of our visit, that being a seer, he could know all about us. He closed his eyes, remained in meditation and opening his eyes later, told us- 'In this forest dwelt for ten years Parvati and that is why it was known as Gauri-vanam. Thereafter, Gauri left the place and it became a deserted one. This tree alone because of her contact with it, has remained young and fresh. I was the king of Malawa. After leaving the kingdom, I came here to practise penance. While I was in this hermitage, the ascetic (companion of Kunda-danta) came alongwith seven brothers. While four of the eight later left for different places for penance, four remained here and pursued penance. All of them wanted to become the rulers of the land of the seven islands. The Goddess granted them the boon and disappeared. The brothers went back to their homes. All the hermits of the place left one after another. I alone have remained here like rock under this tree associated with Gauri. You may go back. The brothers will shortly be together and will have their wishes fulfilled.'

When I (Kunda-danta) asked the seer how all the eight brothers could independently rule over the land of seven islands, when there was only one such land, the seer of Kadamba wood replied thus-'This is not the only incongruity. There are incongruities galore. These eight brothers will become rulers of the land of seven islands within their house itself. Know from me what has transpired. When the eight brothers were away to practise penance, their wives observed rigorous vows and worshipped Parvati. Parvati appeared. They prayed to her, 'May our husbands love us in the way Shambu loves you and may they also be immortal.' Parvati asked them to desire something other than immortality. They prayed, 'If our husbands die, their souls should not go out of this abode of ours.' Gauri granted their wish and disappeared. At about the same time, the parents of the eight brothers alongwith their wives went to Kalagrama with a view to seek the blessings of the saints for the sake of their sons. As they were proceeding, they did not recognise an old person sitting on the path and walked past him, smearing him with a heap of dust. The old person became angry and told them, 'O stupid people, you disregard a Durvasa and go past him. Even if you secure boons for the sake of your sons, those boons will give only opposite results.' After saying thus, the old man disappeared. All the people including the old parents became disspirited.

I (Kunda-danta) asked the Kadamba seer again these questions. 'Firstly, how could all the brothers become sovereigns of the same land of seven islands? Secondly, how could the brothers become sovereigns of earth, if their lives could not go out of their house after death? How would the boons get fulfilled, when under the old man's curse, they have been nullified?

The seer of Kadamba wood explained, 'On the eighth day from this, the brothers will join together. They will enjoy life with relations and pass away from the world one after another. Their lives will remain distinctly in the Samvid-akasa. At that time the boons with their pleasing countenance, and curses with their dark countenance, will take their position in the houses. Boons will ask the curses to keep away as their time has come for fulfillment. Curses will ask the boons to keep away. After disputing among themselves, boons and curses will decide to seek the opinion of the Creator God, Brahma. Brahma will tell them, 'Whoever has superior inner strength is the stronger of the two. You may examine amongst yourselves and find out the position.' Curses deliberate and

584

decide that boons by virtue of their earlier origin are the stronger of the two and retire from the place.

At this time, conflict will arise between the boons that assume lordship over the land of the seven islands and the boons that prevent the lives of brothers from leaving the abode. How can both materialise? Brahma tells them that the boons can create separate lands in the Samvid-space and without going out of the house rule over different worlds.

Chit is subtle and infinite and so the eight brothers will simultaneously be lords of eight different lands. Since all these are dream-like manifestations, there will no absolute real world.

After describing thus, the seer of Kadamba wood resumes his meditation. We left him and reached Mathura within a few days. The brothers met together and after living happily they passed away one after another. My companion was the last to pass away. I was seized with sorrow and wanted to gain wisdom from the Kadamba-wood seer. I went to him and after I remained with him for about three months, he rose up from samadhi.

The Kadamba-wood seer told me thus-'I want to get immersed in samadhi and can scarcely be without it even for a while. Understanding of the supreme Truth is not possible except through repeated effort. There is a land called Ayodhya and Dasaratha is king of it. His son is Rama. Do thou go to him. Vasishta, the family preceptor will explain in the assembly the means to liberation. After hearing those excellent discourses, you will attain beatitude.'

After telling these words, the Kadamba-wood seer went into samadhi. I have come here to be with thee and have told you everything."

Rama, who describes to Vasishta this entire sequence, tells Vasishta, "The Kunda-danta who narrated to me these events is here by my side. He has listened to thy discourses on liberation. You may now enquire from him whether his doubts have been cleared."

Vasishta looked at Kunda-danta and asked him whether he had listened to the discourses.

Kunda-danta replied, "All glory to thee, O Preceptor, who can dispel all the doubts. I have known the Truth fully and have seen all that is to be seen. In the same house, there can be several sovereigns of the lands of the seven islands and yet there may be none. Whoever wills something, will experience it."

Sarga 186. Self is the objective world; Self is the seer of the world; Self is Consciousness; Self is inert matter and Self is Brahman.

Sarga 187. What is Niyati, Cosmic Necessity is explained.

Sarga 188. Jiva is Consciousness with external orientation.

Sarga 189. No cause-effect relationship really exists between pure Consciousness and the world.

Sarga 190. Consciousness undergoing objectification constitutes bondage and realisation consists in the awareness that Consciousness does not really undergo any change.

Sarga 191. Brahman alone appears as world.

586

of instructing one in wisdom; once the realisation takes place, duality ceases to exist.

213.   Vasishta tells Rama that, in an earlier life also, Rama had received instruction in wisdom from him.

214.   Visvamitra, Dasaratha, Rama, Lakshmana, Satrugna, etc., commend Vasishta's discourses.

The conclusion of the Discourses is celebrated in a befitting manner with feasts and festivities.

215.   Valmiki blesses Bharadwaja and asks him to follow the example of Rama.

216.   King Arishtanemi, Suruchi, Karunya and Sutikshana attain realisation.

All offer salutations to Sri Vasishta.